W9-BPQ-581

ACKNOWLEDGMENTS

A very special thanks to the presidents of
the clubs and councils for their cooperation in
obtaining recipes from their members.

Special thanks to Peggy Burdett,
Candace Akers, Sandra Cleveland,
Mary Boehm, Hazel Campbell,
Sandra Cooper, Georgia Glenn,
Lois Moman, Margie Harding,
Alice Walski, and Pauline Slusher.

This book is dedicated to the
never-ending spirit of the members
of the Alabama BellSouth
Pioneer Volunteers. You can't
live a perfect day without doing
something for someone who will
never be able to repay you.

Sandra Cleveland
Chapter President
1999–2000

COUNCIL/CLUB PRESIDENTS

CLUB PRESIDENTS

Betty Moon	*Birmingham Life Member Club*
John King	*Birmingham South Life Member Club*
Kathryn Pager	*Bon Secour Life Member Club*
Betty Darnell	*Gadsden Life Member Club*
Shirley Helms	*Montgomery Life Member Club*
Ed Martin	*Opelika Life Member Club*
Joe Small	*Selma Life Member Club*
Mary Ann Fulmer	*Shoals Life Member Club*

COUNCIL PRESIDENTS

Jim Miller	*Anniston Council*
Linda McGhee	*Birmingham Metro Council*
Donna Bowman	*Birmingham South Cahaba Council*
Judy Burrow	*Decatur Council*
Le Nora Focht	*Huntsville Council*
Barbara Berry	*Jasper Club*
Cathy Midgette	*Mobile Council*
Debbie Speaks	*Montgomery Council*
Deborah Scalisi	*Riverchase Council*
Dick Johnson	*Tuscaloosa Council*

Mary Boehm	*Chapter Liaison*
Sara Cooley and Helen Shirley	*Chapter Cookbook Chairmen*

CELEBRATIONS

RECIPES FROM
THE FOLKS WHO BROUGHT YOU
Calling All Cooks

CELEBRATIONS

RECIPES FROM
THE FOLKS WHO BROUGHT YOU
Calling All Cooks

This is a collection of favorite recipes,
which are not necessarily original recipes.

Published by: Telephone Pioneers of America
Alabama Chapter #34

Copyright© Telephone Pioneers of America
Alabama Chapter #34
3196 Highway 280 South, Room 301N
Birmingham, Alabama 35243

Library of Congress Number: 99-075758
ISBN: 0-87197-481-9

Designed, Edited, and Manufactured by
Favorite Recipes® Press
an imprint of

FRP

P.O. Box 305142
Nashville, Tennessee 37230
1-800-358-0560

Manufactured in the United States of America
First Printing 1999 25,000 copies

CONTENTS

PREFACE

Recipes for *Celebrations* were collected from
the Telepone Company's active and retired employees and
their families. The huge success of *Calling All Cooks, Calling
All Cooks two,* and *Calling All Cooks three* prompted us to
produce this special holiday cookbook.

When we think of a holiday cookbook, we usually think of
Christmas and Thanksgiving, but this book is for "all" the
holidays throughout every season of the year, including Easter,
the Fourth of July, Labor Day, birthdays, and many others.
We hope you enjoy your *Celebrations.*

Happy Holidays to you.

Sara Cooley   Helen Shirley
Cookbook Chairmen

Celebrate

WINTER

Dill Dip

2 cups mayonnaise
2 cups sour cream
3 tablespoons parsley flakes
3 tablespoons grated onion

1 tablespoon Beau Monde
   seasoning
1 tablespoon dillweed

Combine the mayonnaise and sour cream in a bowl and blend well. Add the parsley flakes, onion, Beau Monde and dillweed and mix well. Chill until serving time. Serve with assorted bite-size fresh vegetables for dipping. Yield: 4 cups.

Sharon Coffield, Birmingham South Cahaba Council

Festive Pumpkin Dip

12 ounces cream cheese,
   softened
3/4 cup canned or mashed
   cooked pumpkin
2 tablespoons taco
   seasoning mix
1/8 to 1/4 teaspoon garlic powder

1/3 cup chopped dried beef
1/3 cup chopped green bell
   pepper
1/3 cup chopped red bell pepper
1 (2-ounce) can sliced black
   olives, drained

Combine the cream cheese, pumpkin, seasoning mix and garlic powder in a mixer bowl and beat until smooth. Stir in the dried beef, bell pepper and black olives. Chill, covered, until serving time. Serve with assorted party crackers or corn chips. Yield: 3 cups.

Frankie (A.T.) Vaughn, Selma Life Member Club

Layered Nacho Dip

2 (16-ounce) cans refried
    beans
1 (4-ounce) can chopped
    green chiles
1 envelope taco seasoning mix
1 (8-ounce) package Mexican
    cheese blend

1 cup avocado dip
1 cup sour cream
3 green onions, thinly sliced
2 (2-ounce) cans sliced black
    olives, drained
1 large tomato, chopped

Combine the refried beans, green chiles and seasoning mix in a bowl and mix well. Spread the mixture evenly in a 7x11-inch baking dish or a 9-inch deep-dish pie plate. Bake at 350 degrees for 25 minutes or until heated through. Sprinkle evenly with the cheese. Bake for 5 minutes longer or until the cheese melts. Spread with the avocado dip and sour cream in the order listed. Sprinkle the green onions, black olives and tomato over the top. Serve immediately with tortilla chips or other corn chips.
Yield: 8 to 10 servings.

Donna Daniel, Montgomery Council

Spinach Dip

1 (10-ounce) package frozen
    spinach, thawed, drained
2 cups sour cream
1 cup mayonnaise

1 envelope vegetable soup mix
1 (8-ounce) can water
    chestnuts, drained, chopped
3 green onions, chopped

Squeeze the excess moisture from the spinach. Mix the spinach, sour cream, mayonnaise, soup mix, water chestnuts and green onions in a bowl. Chill, covered, for 2 hours. Stir just before serving. Serve with tortilla chips. Yield: 4 cups.

Marla Appling, Alabama Telco Credit Union

Blue Moon Cheese Sandwiches

2 cups finely shredded sharp
  Cheddar cheese
1/3 cup chili sauce
3/4 cup mayonnaise
1 teaspoon Worcestershire
  sauce

1/2 cup chopped pimento-
  stuffed green olives
1/2 cup chopped pecans
32 slices white or whole
  wheat bread, crusts
  trimmed

Combine the cheese, chili sauce, mayonnaise and Worcestershire
sauce in a bowl and mix well. Add the olives and pecans and mix
well. Chill, covered, in the refrigerator. Spread half the bread slices
with the cheese mixture. Top with the remaining bread slices. Cut
each sandwich into 3 strips. May shape the cheese mixture into a
ball and serve with assorted party crackers.
Yield: 48 finger sandwiches.

Sue Small, Selma Life Member Club

Cayenne Cheese Wafers

1 cup (2 sticks) margarine,
  softened
4 cups finely shredded sharp
  Cheddar cheese

2 cups flour
2 teaspoons salt
1 teaspoon cayenne pepper
2 cups chopped pecans

Combine the margarine and cheese in a mixer bowl and beat until
well blended. Add the flour, salt and cayenne pepper and mix well.
Mix in the pecans. Shape the mixture into a log and wrap in plastic
wrap. Chill for several hours. Cut the log into thin slices. Arrange
on a lightly greased baking sheet. Bake at 325 degrees for 15
minutes or until the edges are light brown. Cool slightly on the
baking sheet. Remove to a wire rack to cool completely. The log
may be frozen and baked for later use. Yield: 5 dozen.

Jan Williams, Riverchase Council

Lucky Surprise Pots

1 (3-ounce) package lime
  gelatin
1/2 cup boiling water
1 1/2 cups reduced-fat vanilla
  yogurt
2 tablespoons margarine

2 cups miniature
  marshmallows
1/2 cup finely crushed
  chocolate cookies
6 gummy worms

Dissolve the gelatin in the boiling water in a bowl. Whisk in the yogurt until well blended. Chill in the refrigerator until partially set. Spray a small microwave-safe bowl with nonstick cooking spray. Combine the margarine and marshmallows in the prepared bowl. Microwave on High for 1 to 2 minutes or until the margarine and marshmallows are melted. Stir until completely blended. Add the marshmallow mixture to the gelatin mixture and whisk until blended. Sprinkle about a teaspoonful of the cookie crumbs into each of six 5-ounce cold drink cups. Place a gummy worm in the bottom of each cup. Spoon about 1/2 cup of the gelatin mixture into each of the prepared cups and sprinkle with the remaining cookie crumbs. Freeze the cups for 15 to 20 minutes or chill for 1 hour or just until set. Yield: 6 servings.

Brenda Reeves, Birmingham South Cahaba Council

Puppy Chow

1 large package Golden
  Grahams cereal

1 large can cocktail peanuts
White chocolate bark

Mix the cereal and peanuts in a large bowl. Melt the chocolate in a microwave-safe bowl using package directions. Pour the melted chocolate over the cereal mixture and toss to coat. Pour onto a waxed paper-lined surface. Let stand until cool and dry to the touch. Break into pieces. Store in an airtight container.
Yield: 16 to 18 servings.

Melba Jean Campbell, Tuscaloosa Council

Sittin' on the Ritz

1 (14-ounce) can sweetened
  condensed milk
8 ounces dates, chopped
1/2 cup chopped nuts
Butter crackers
3 ounces cream cheese,
  softened

1/4 cup (1/2 stick) margarine,
  softened
3 cups (about) confectioners'
  sugar
1 tablespoon (about) milk

Combine the condensed milk and dates in a saucepan and mix well. Cook over low heat until thickened, stirring frequently. Stir in the nuts. Spread the date mixture on the crackers. Arrange on a baking sheet. Bake at 350 degrees for 8 minutes. Remove to a wire rack to cool. Blend the cream cheese and margarine in a bowl until smooth and creamy. Add enough confectioners' sugar and milk to make a mixture of spreading consistency. Spread over the date mixture. Yield: 2 to 3 dozen.

Ila M. Skidmore, Shoals Life Member Club

Bambinos

1 (6-ounce) can tomato paste
1 teaspoon garlic salt
1/4 teaspoon oregano
Butter crackers or melba
  rounds

4 ounces Cheddar or
  mozzarella cheese, cubed
4 ounces salami or pepperoni,
  cubed

Combine the tomato paste, garlic salt and oregano in a bowl and mix well. Spoon a small amount of the tomato mixture onto each cracker. Top with the cheese and salami cubes and sprinkle with additional oregano. Arrange the crackers on a baking sheet. Bake at 400 degrees for 3 to 5 minutes or until the cheese melts. Serve hot. Yield: 5 to 6 dozen.

Dottie Drennon, Birmingham Metro Council

Garlic Buffalo Wings

10 pounds chicken wings
Vegetable oil for deep-frying
1/2 cup (1 stick) butter
3/4 cup olive oil
1 small bottle Crystal hot
  sauce

1 large bottle Crystal wing
  sauce
1 whole garlic bulb
1/2 onion
Salt to taste

Remove and discard the small wing tip from the chicken wings and cut the wings apart at the joint. Rinse the wings and pat completely dry. Deep-fry the wings in several batches in the hot oil; do not overcook the wings. Drain the wings and place in a large baking pan. Heat the butter and 3/4 cup olive oil in a large saucepan over low heat. Heat until the butter melts. Add the desired amount of the hot sauce and about 3/4 of the wing sauce. Simmer for several minutes. Cut the garlic cloves and onion into pieces small enough to fit into a garlic press. Press the garlic and onion through the press over the simmering sauce to allow the juices and pulp to fall into the sauce. Season with salt. Simmer for several minutes longer. Adjust the seasonings. Pour the sauce over the fried chicken wings and mix until the wings are coated. Pour the remaining wing sauce over the chicken and mix well. Bake at 325 degrees until very hot, stirring 2 or 3 times. Broil for several minutes until sizzling and slightly crisp if desired. Serve with celery sticks and a mixture of crumbled bleu cheese, sour cream and olive oil, stirring until of the desired consistency. Prepare the bleu cheese mixture several hours before serving for improved flavor. Yield: 100 to 120 chicken wings.

Jennifer McAllister, Birmingham South Cahaba Council

Champagne Punch

2 (16-ounce) cans frozen
  lemonade concentrate,
  thawed
2 (12-ounce) cans orange
  juice concentrate, thawed

2 ounces grenadine
2 (24-ounce) bottles ginger
  ale, chilled
2 fifths pink Champagne,
  chilled

Combine the lemonade and orange juice concentrates in a punch bowl. Blend in the grenadine. Add the ginger ale and Champagne just before serving. Ladle into punch cups. Yield: 30 servings.

Pat Ramsey, sister of Cathy Kelley, Birmingham South Cahaba Council

Cranberry Punch

46 ounces pineapple juice
1½ cups sugar

5 cups cranberry juice
2 liters ginger ale

Combine the pineapple juice and sugar in a saucepan. Cook until the sugar dissolves, stirring occasionally. Remove from heat and pour into a large freezer container. Add the cranberry juice and ginger ale. Freeze until slushy. Yield: 40 servings.

Celia Stephens, Montgomery Council

Hot Cider Punch

1 (6-ounce) can frozen
  lemonade concentrate,
  thawed
½ (6-ounce) can frozen orange
  juice concentrate, thawed

3 (6-ounce) cans water
1 gallon apple cider
½ cup sugar
Red hot cinnamon candies

Combine the lemonade and orange juice concentrates, water, cider and sugar in a large saucepan. Heat to serving temperature, stirring until the sugar dissolves; do not boil. Place 1 teaspoon candies in each mug. Fill the mug with the hot punch. Yield: 25 servings.

Sharon Coffield, Birmingham South Cahaba Council

Sweet-and-Sour Chicken

1 each small carrot and onion
1/4 green bell pepper
1/4 red bell pepper
1 rib celery
Margarine
1 pound boneless skinless
   chicken breasts

Salt and pepper to taste
1/2 (8-ounce) can water
   chestnuts, drained, chopped
1 (8-ounce) can juice-pack
   pineapple chunks
1 (24-ounce) jar sweet-and-
   sour sauce

Chop the carrot, onion, bell peppers and celery into pieces of a similar size. Stir-fry the vegetables in a small amount of margarine in a skillet until tender-crisp and set aside. Cut the chicken into bite-size pieces. Sprinkle with salt and pepper. Stir-fry the chicken in a small amount of margarine just until the chicken is cooked through; do not brown. Mix the vegetables, chicken, water chestnuts, pineapple chunks and sweet-and-sour sauce with a small amount of water in a bowl. Pour into a greased 9x13-inch baking dish. Bake at 350 degrees for 30 minutes or until bubbly. Serve plain or over hot cooked rice. Yield: 4 to 6 servings.

Francis M. Tucker, Selma Life Member Club

Crab Meat Mornay

1 small bunch green onions,
   chopped
1/2 cup minced fresh parsley
1/2 cup (1 stick) butter
2 tablespoons flour

2 cups heavy cream
2 cups shredded Swiss cheese
2 tablespoons sherry
Salt and red pepper to taste
1 pound white crab meat

Cook the green onions and parsley in butter in a heavy saucepan, stirring constantly. Mix in the flour. Stir in the heavy cream gradually. Cook until thickened, stirring constantly. Stir in the cheese. Cook until the cheese melts, stirring constantly. Stir in the sherry, salt and red pepper. Fold in the crab meat. Serve over rice or in puff pastry shells as a main dish or from a chafing dish with melba toast or crackers as an appetizer. Yield: 15 servings.

Ken Wilson, Birmingham South Cahaba Council

Good Luck Black-Eyed Peas

1 pound ham or meaty ham
  bone from a baked ham
1 piece hog jowl
2 pounds dried black-eyed
  peas
2 large onions, chopped

1 large green bell pepper,
  chopped
1 teaspoon salt
1 teaspoon pepper
2 teaspoons dry mustard
Hot pepper sauce to taste

Combine the ham and hog jowl in a large saucepan. Add enough water to cover generously. Boil until tender. Drain, reserving the cooking liquid. Discard any fat and bone and chop the meat. Chill the meat and cooking liquid for 8 to 10 hours. Skim the congealed fat from the cooking liquid and add enough water to measure 4 quarts. Place in a large saucepan. Sort and rinse the black-eyed peas. Add to the cooking liquid. Soak the peas for 8 to 10 hours in the refrigerator. Place the peas and cooking liquid on the stove. Add the onions, green pepper, salt, pepper, dry mustard, hot pepper sauce and chopped meat. Bring to a full rolling boil; reduce heat. Simmer, covered, for 2½ to 3 hours or until the peas are tender, stirring occasionally. Yield: 8 servings.

Sue (Joe) Small, Selma Life Member Club

Turnip Greens

3 pounds turnip greens
2 ounces fatback
1 can chicken broth

1 teaspoon salt
White pepper to taste

Rinse the greens well. Score or slice the fatback. Place the fatback in a large heavy saucepan. Add water to a depth of 1 inch. Boil for 30 minutes. Add the greens, broth, salt and pepper and enough additional water to cover. Bring to a boil; reduce heat. Simmer for 1 to 2 hours or until tender, adding small amounts of additional water as necessary to prevent the greens from boiling dry. Yield: 6 to 8 servings.

Betty Darnell, Gadsden Life Member Club

Zucchini Bake

6 zucchini
1 large onion
1 cup grated Parmesan cheese

Salt, pepper and garlic powder
to taste
2 tomatoes, sliced

Slice the zucchini as desired. Cut the onion into large chunks. Combine the zucchini, onion, half the Parmesan cheese, salt, pepper and garlic powder in a large bowl and toss to mix. Spoon into a shallow baking dish. Arrange the tomatoes over the top. Sprinkle with the remaining Parmesan cheese. Do not add water. Bake, covered, at 325 degrees for 1 hour. Yield: 6 servings.

Candy Bird, Birmingham South Cahaba Council

Cheese Grits

1 cup grits
5 cups water
6 ounces Cheddar cheese,
   cubed
1 cup (2 sticks) butter

2 eggs
Milk
Grated Parmesan cheese
   to taste
Paprika to taste

Combine the grits and water in a saucepan. Cook using package directions. Add the cubed cheese and butter and stir until melted. Break the eggs into a 1-cup measure and beat well. Add enough milk to measure 1 cup. Stir the egg mixture into the cooked grits. Pour the mixture into a buttered baking dish. Bake at 300 degrees for 45 minutes. Sprinkle with Parmesan cheese and paprika. Bake for 10 minutes longer. Yield: 8 to 10 servings.

Judy Howard, Riverchase Council

Macaroni and Cheese

8 ounces elbow or shell
  macaroni
1 pound Velveeta cheese,
  cubed
8 ounces sharp Cheddar
  cheese, shredded
8 ounces Monterey Jack or
  Swiss cheese, shredded

1 tablespoon flour
1 cup milk
2 eggs, beaten
1½ cups bread crumbs
¼ cup (½ stick) butter or
  margarine, melted

Cook the macaroni using package directions; drain. Combine the
cheeses in a large saucepan. Sprinkle with the flour and add the
milk. Cook over low heat until the cheeses melt and the mixture is
smooth, stirring constantly. Stir a small amount of the hot mixture
into the beaten eggs; stir the eggs into the hot mixture. Remove
from heat. Add the macaroni and mix gently. Spoon into a greased
baking dish. Sprinkle the bread crumbs over the top and drizzle
with the melted butter. Bake at 375 degrees for 10 to 15 minutes or
until the crumbs are brown. Yield: 8 servings.

Donna Jean Bowman, Birmingham South Cahaba Council

Angel Biscuits

2½ cups flour
1½ tablespoons sugar
1½ tablespoons baking powder
½ teaspoon baking soda

1 teaspoon salt
1 envelope dry yeast
½ cup shortening
1 cup buttermilk

Sift the flour, sugar, baking powder, baking soda and salt into a
bowl. Add the dry yeast. Cut in the shortening until crumbly. Add
the buttermilk and mix well. Knead several times on a lightly
floured surface. Pat into a rectangle and cut with a floured biscuit
cutter. Arrange on a greased baking sheet. Let stand until risen.
Bake at 350 degrees until brown. May refrigerate the dough in a
covered bowl for several hours to several days before shaping and
baking. Yield: 8 to 12 biscuits.

Judy Howard, Riverchase Council

Broccoli Corn Bread

4 eggs
1 teaspoon salt
¾ cup cottage cheese
1 (7-ounce) package
   corn muffin mix

1 (10-ounce) package frozen
   chopped broccoli, thawed
1 large onion, chopped
½ cup (1 stick) margarine,
   melted

Beat the eggs in a medium bowl. Add the salt, cottage cheese and muffin mix and mix well. Add the broccoli, onion and margarine and mix well. Pour into a greased 9x13-inch baking pan. Bake at 400 degrees for 30 minutes. Yield: 8 to 12 servings.

Fay Clark, Riverchase Council

Cheesy Broccoli Corn Bread

15 to 16 ounces broccoli,
   chopped
1 (7-ounce) package
   corn muffin mix

½ cup (1 stick) reduced-fat
   margarine
1 cup shredded mild cheese

Blanch the broccoli in boiling water in a saucepan for 2 minutes; drain. Combine the corn bread mix, margarine and cheese in a bowl and mix well. Mix in the broccoli. Pour into a greased cast-iron skillet. Bake at 350 degrees for 30 minutes or until brown. Serve with black-eyed peas and barbecued ribs or pork chops. Yield: 6 servings.

Betty Hyte, Montgomery Council

Jalapeño Corn Bread

1 pound ground beef
2 cups self-rising cornmeal
1 (16-ounce) can cream-style
   corn
1 large onion, chopped

1 pound Cheddar cheese,
   shredded
3 or 4 jalapeño chiles,
   chopped

Brown the ground beef in a skillet, stirring until crumbly; drain. Combine the cornmeal and cream-style corn in a bowl and mix well. Pour half the mixture into a greased 9x13-inch baking pan. Add layers of ground beef, onion and cheese. Top with the remaining batter. Bake at 400 degrees for 1 hour or until golden brown. Flavor improves if prepared and baked two hours before serving. Serve with your favorite chili. Yield: 6 to 10 servings.

Earline Weaver, Shoals Life Member Club

Reduced-Fat Rolls

6 cups flour
1 tablespoon salt
5½ tablespoons sugar
¼ cup dry yeast

¼ cup dry milk powder
⅓ cup applesauce
¼ cup vegetable oil
1 cup (or more) warm water

Combine the flour, salt, sugar, yeast and milk powder in a large bowl and mix well. Add the applesauce, oil and enough warm water to make a medium dough, mixing well. Turn the dough onto a lightly floured surface and knead until smooth and elastic. Place in a greased bowl, turning to coat the surface. Let rise, covered, in a warm place until doubled in bulk. Shape the rolls as desired and arrange on a greased baking sheet. Let rise until doubled in bulk. Bake at 350 degrees for 15 to 20 minutes or until golden brown. May add an additional cup sugar to make cinnamon rolls or add shredded ham and cheese to the dough to make ham and cheese rolls. Yield: 2 to 3 dozen rolls.

Mary Gillis, Mobile Council

Amish Friendship Loaves

2 cups flour
1 cup sugar
1 (6-ounce) package vanilla
   instant pudding mix
1 1/4 teaspoons baking powder
1/2 teaspoon salt
1/2 teaspoon baking soda

1 teaspoon cinnamon
2 cups Amish Friendship
   Starter
3/4 cup vegetable oil
3 eggs
1 teaspoon vanilla extract
1/2 to 1 cup chopped nuts

Combine the flour, sugar, pudding mix, baking powder, salt, baking soda and cinnamon in a large bowl and mix well. Add the Starter, oil, eggs and vanilla and mix until well blended. Stir in the nuts. Pour into 2 greased and sugared loaf pans. Sprinkle lightly with additional sugar if desired. Bake at 350 degrees for 50 minutes or until the loaves test done. Yield: 2 loaves.

Amish Friendship Starter

1/2 teaspoon dry yeast
2 tablespoons warm water

1 cup each sugar and flour
1 cup milk

Mix the yeast, water and a pinch of the sugar in a small container. Let stand until the mixture begins to foam. Combine the remaining sugar, flour and milk in a large bowl and mix well. Stir in the yeast mixture with a wooden or plastic spoon. Pour into a nonmetallic container and cover loosely. On day 1, do nothing. (This day is baking day for the Starter you have or the tenth day if you have just received your Starter from a friend.) On days 2 through 4, let the mixture stand at room temperature, stirring daily with a nonmetallic spoon. On day 5, feed the starter by adding 1 cup sugar, 1 cup flour and 1 cup milk and mix well. Let stand for 4 days, stirring daily. On day 10, feed the starter by adding 1 cup sugar, 1 cup flour and 1 cup milk. Divide the Starter into 1 cup portions: Keep 1 portion to use for your next batch; use 2 portions to make the loaves and give the remaining portions to friends with the instructions for making the loaves and feeding the Starter.

Susan Poe, Riverchase Council

Butter Pecan Cake

2⅔ cups chopped pecans
¼ cup (½ stick) butter
2 cups sugar
1 cup (2 sticks) butter,
   softened
4 eggs

3 cups flour
2 teaspoons baking powder
½ teaspoon salt
1 cup milk
2 teaspoons vanilla extract
Butter Pecan Frosting

Toast the pecans in ¼ cup butter in a large baking pan at 350 degrees for 20 to 25 minutes, stirring frequently. Cream the sugar and 1 cup softened butter in a mixer bowl until light and fluffy. Add the eggs 1 at a time, beating well after each addition. Combine the flour, baking powder and salt. Add to the creamed mixture alternately with the milk, mixing well after each addition. Stir in the vanilla and 1⅓ cups of the toasted pecans. Spoon into 3 greased and floured 9-inch round cake pans. Bake at 350 degrees for 25 to 30 minutes or until the layers test done. Cool in the pans on a wire rack for 10 minutes. Remove to wire racks to cool completely. Spread Butter Pecan Frosting between layers and over the top and side of the cake. Yield: 12 servings.

Butter Pecan Frosting

1 cup (2 sticks) butter,
   softened
8 to 8½ cups confectioners'
   sugar

1 (5-ounce) can evaporated
   milk
2 teaspoons vanilla extract
1⅓ cups toasted pecans

Cream the butter and confectioners' sugar in a mixer bowl until light and fluffy. Add the evaporated milk and vanilla and beat until of spreading consistency. Stir in the toasted pecans.

Betty Foshee, Decatur Council

Chocolate Pound Cake

3 cups sugar
1 cup (2 sticks) margarine,
    softened
5 eggs
1/2 cup vegetable oil
1 teaspoon vanilla extract

3 cups flour
1/4 cup baking cocoa
1/2 teaspoon salt
1 cup milk
1/2 teaspoon baking powder

Cream the sugar and margarine in a large mixer bowl until light and fluffy. Add the eggs, oil and vanilla and beat until smooth. Mix the flour, cocoa and salt together. Add the flour mixture to the creamed mixture alternately with the milk, beating well after each addition. Add the baking powder and mix until smooth. Spoon the batter into a greased and floured tube pan. Bake at 300 degrees for 1 hour and 20 minutes or until the cake tests done. Cool in the pan on a wire rack for 10 to 15 minutes. Invert onto a wire rack to cool completely. Yield: 16 servings.

Bernice Moore, Birmingham South Cahaba Council

Chocolate Chip Pound Cake

1 (2-layer) package yellow
    cake mix with pudding
1 (6-ounce) package chocolate
    instant pudding mix
1/2 cup sugar
3/4 cup vegetable oil

3/4 cup water
4 eggs
1 tablespoon vanilla extract
1 cup sour cream
1 cup semisweet chocolate
    chips

Combine the cake mix, pudding mix and sugar in a large bowl and mix with a wire whisk until no lumps remain. Add the oil, water, eggs, vanilla and sour cream and mix until smooth. Stir in the chocolate chips. Pour into a greased and floured 12-cup bundt pan. Bake at 350 degrees for 1 hour or until the cake tests done. Cool in the pan on a wire rack for 10 minutes. Invert onto the wire rack to cool completely. Garnish with a sprinkle of confectioners' sugar. Yield: 16 servings.

Ila M. Skidmore, Shoals Life Member Club

Saucy Gingerbread

1 package gingerbread mix   1 cup milk
½ cup sugar   ¼ cup (½ stick) butter
¼ cup flour   2 teaspoons vanilla extract

Prepare and bake the gingerbread mix using package directions.
Combine the sugar, flour and milk in a saucepan and mix well.
Cook until thickened, stirring constantly. Add the butter and
vanilla and blend well. Serve the warm sauce over the gingerbread.
Yield: 8 servings.

Sharon Coffield, Birmingham South Cahaba Council

Chocolate Pizza

2 cups semisweet chocolate   1 (6-ounce) jar red
  chips   maraschino cherries,
1 pound white almond   drained, cut into halves
  bark   3 tablespoons drained
2 cups miniature   quartered green maraschino
  marshmallows   cherries
1 cup crisp rice cereal   ⅓ cup shredded coconut
1 cup peanuts or pecans   1 teaspoon vegetable oil

Combine the chocolate chips and 14 ounces of the almond bark in
a large microwave-safe bowl. Microwave for 2 minutes and stir until
smooth. Microwave for additional 1 minute increments if necessary
to completely melt. Stir in the marshmallows, cereal and peanuts.
Spread evenly in a 12-inch greased pizza pan. Sprinkle the cherries
and coconut over the cereal layer. Combine the remaining 2
ounces almond bark and oil in a small microwave-safe bowl.
Microwave for 1 minute and blend until smooth. Drizzle over the
top. Chill until firm. Yield: 12 to 15 servings.

Catherine M. Martin, Birmingham Metro Council

Beef Dip

1 pound ground beef
1 cup chopped onion
1 (10-ounce) can tomato soup
1 cup salsa

½ cup milk
1 small can chopped olives
1 cup shredded Cheddar
  cheese

Brown the ground beef with the onion in a large skillet, stirring until the ground beef is crumbly; drain. Add the soup, salsa, milk and olives and mix well. Stir in the cheese. Pour into a 2-quart baking dish. Bake at 400 degrees for 20 to 30 minutes. Serve as a dip with your favorite dippers or use as a filling for tacos. Yield: 4 to 6 servings.

Sherry A. Liles, Huntsville Council

Dog Dip

8 ounces ground beef
8 ounces bulk sausage
½ onion, chopped
½ green bell pepper, chopped
1 pound Velveeta cheese,
  cubed

1 (10-ounce) can tomatoes
  with green chiles and green
  peppers

Brown the ground beef and sausage with the onion and green pepper in a large skillet, stirring until the ground beef and sausage are crumbly; drain. Combine the cheese and tomatoes with green chiles in a slow-cooker. Heat until the cheese melts, stirring occasionally. Stir in the ground beef mixture. Heat the mixture to serving temperature. Serve with corn chips. Yield: 6 to 10 servings.

Susan Poe, Riverchase Council

Mexican Dip

2 pounds ground beef
1 pound bulk pork sausage
1 small onion, chopped
1 small green bell pepper,
  chopped
2 garlic cloves, minced
1 pound Velveeta cheese,
  cubed

1 pound Mexican Velveeta
  cheese, cubed
2 (10-ounce) cans tomatoes
  with green chiles
1 envelope taco seasoning mix

Brown the ground beef and sausage with the onion, green pepper and garlic in a large skillet, stirring until the ground beef and sausage are crumbly; drain. Place the mixture in a slow cooker. Add the cheeses, tomatoes and seasoning mix and mix well. Heat until the cheeses melt, stirring occasionally. Serve as a dip with tortilla chips or as a topping on baked potatoes. Yield: 12 to 15 servings.

Sue Johnston, Birmingham South Cahaba Council

Reuben Dip

3 ounces cream cheese,
  softened
1/4 cup sour cream
1 tablespoon spicy brown
  mustard
1 teaspoon catsup

4 ounces corned beef, finely
  chopped
1/4 cup chopped sauerkraut,
  drained
1/2 cup shredded Swiss cheese

Combine the cream cheese and sour cream in a bowl and blend until smooth. Stir in the mustard and catsup. Add the corned beef, sauerkraut and Swiss cheese and mix well. Spoon into a small baking dish. Bake at 350 degrees just until the mixture is bubbly. Serve with wheat crackers or slices of party rye bread.
Yield: 4 servings.

Mrs. Bob H. Henson, Birmingham South Life Member Club

Sausage Dip

1 pound hot bulk sausage
2 pounds Velveeta cheese,
  cubed

¼ cup milk
1 (2-ounce) jar pimento,
  drained, finely chopped

Brown the sausage in a large skillet, stirring until crumbly; drain. Heat the cheese in a saucepan over low heat until melted and smooth, stirring frequently. Add the milk and blend well. Stir in the sausage and pimento. Heat to serving temperature and keep warm. Serve with corn chips. Yield: 8 to 10 servings.

Mrs. Bob H. Henson, Birmingham South Life Member Club

Cheese Ball

16 ounces cream cheese,
  softened
1 tablespoon grated onion
2 teaspoons Worcestershire
  sauce

Cayenne pepper to taste
2 cups chopped pecans

Combine the cream cheese, onion, Worcestershire sauce and cayenne pepper in a bowl and mix well. Chill until firm enough to be shaped. Shape the mixture into a ball and roll in the pecans. Chill, wrapped in plastic wrap, until serving time. Unwrap the cheese ball, place on a serving plate and garnish with a maraschino on top. Yield: 32 servings.

Rebecca J. Stancil, Decatur Council

Shrimp Butter

8 ounces cream cheese,
  softened
½ teaspoon MSG
½ cup (1 stick) butter (do not
  substitute), softened

2 tablespoons lemon juice
¼ cup mayonnaise
1 tablespoon minced onion
¼ teaspoon horseradish
1 (4-ounce) can tiny shrimp

Combine the cream cheese and MSG in a small mixer bowl and beat until smooth. Add the butter, lemon juice and mayonnaise and beat until well blended. Mix in the onion and horseradish. Drain the shrimp and mash with a fork. Stir the shrimp into the cream cheese mixture. Chill, covered, for 8 to 10 hours to enhance the flavor. Let stand at room temperature to soften before serving. Serve with assorted party crackers, chips or other favorites. Yield: 1½ to 2 cups.

Donna McNulty, Riverchase Council

Bacon-Wrapped Pineapple Chunks

1 cup catsup
¼ cup dark corn syrup
1 tablespoon Worcestershire
  sauce
⅛ teaspoon hot sauce

1 (15-ounce) can pineapple
  chunks, drained
1 pound sliced bacon
1 (11-ounce) can mandarin
  oranges, drained (optional)

Mix the catsup, corn syrup, Worcestershire sauce and hot sauce in a saucepan. Stir in the pineapple chunks. Bring the mixture to a boil; reduce heat. Simmer for 10 minutes, stirring frequently. Cut the bacon slices crosswise into halves. Drain the pineapple, reserving the sauce. Wrap each pineapple chunk with a bacon slice and secure with a wooden pick. Arrange on a rack in a shallow roasting pan. Bake at 400 degrees for 15 minutes. Baste with the reserved sauce. Bake for 15 minutes longer or until the bacon is crisp. Skewer a mandarin orange slice to the bottom of each pineapple chunk. Serve with the remaining sauce. Yield: 35 servings.

Susan Friday, Montgomery Council

Barbecue Smokies

1 (32-ounce) bottle catsup
1 (1-pound) package light
　brown sugar

2 packages little smokies

Combine the catsup and brown sugar in a saucepan and mix well.
Bring to a boil and add the little smokies, stirring until coated.
Reduce the heat to low and simmer until heated through. Pour into
a slow-cooker on Low to keep warm for several hours.
Yield: 8 or more servings.

Sherrie Poynor, Montgomery Council

Sweet-and-Sour Cocktail Bites

2 (15-ounce) cans juice-pack
　pineapple chunks
1 cup packed brown sugar
3 tablespoons flour
2 teaspoons dry mustard

½ cup vinegar
2 tablespoons vegetable oil
2 teaspoons soy sauce
Smoked sausage links or
　cocktail sausages

Drain the pineapple, reserving 1 cup of the juice. Set the pineapple
chunks aside. Combine the brown sugar, flour and dry mustard in a
saucepan and mix well. Stir in the reserved pineapple juice,
vinegar, oil and soy sauce. Cook over medium heat until thickened,
stirring constantly. Cut the sausage links into bite-size pieces. Cook
the sausage in a skillet until light browned or steam. Drain well and
add to the sauce. Bring the mixture to a boil. Add the pineapple
chunks and heat to serving temperature. Pour into a chafing dish to
keep warm. Serve with wooden picks. Yield: 12 servings.

Berniece Peterson, Birmingham South Life Member Club

Sesame Chicken Wings

½ cup soy sauce
⅓ cup water
¼ cup sugar
2 tablespoons sesame or
  olive oil
Sliced bulbs and tops of
  4 green onions

½ medium onion, sliced
2 garlic cloves, minced
1 to 2 tablespoons sesame
  seeds
Red or black pepper to taste
2½ pounds chicken wings

Combine the soy sauce, water, sugar, sesame oil, green onions, onion, garlic, sesame seeds and pepper in a large plastic bag and mix well. Add the chicken wings, squeezing most of the air from the bag; seal tightly. Knead until the wings are well coated with the marinade. Marinate in the refrigerator for 3 to 10 hours, turning occasionally. Drain the chicken wings and discard the marinade. Arrange the wings in a shallow baking pan. Bake at 350 degrees for 30 minutes. Turn the wings over and bake for 20 minutes longer. Yield: 6 to 8 servings.

Iris Rowe, Birmingham South Life Member Club

Marinated Crab Claws

1 cup chopped green onions
  with tops
1 cup chopped celery with
  leaves
4 garlic cloves, chopped
1 cup chopped fresh parsley
2 cups olive oil

2 cups tarragon vinegar
Juice of 6 lemons
2 tablespoons salt
1 tablespoon pepper
8 to 10 cups cooked crab
  claws or boiled shrimp

Combine the green onions, celery, garlic and parsley on a chopping block and chop as fine as possible. Add to a mixture of olive oil, tarragon vinegar, lemon juice, salt and pepper in a bowl and mix well. Let the mixture stand, covered, at room temperature for 48 hours. Add the crab and mix until well coated. Let stand for 30 minutes before serving. Yield: 15 to 20 servings.

Ken Wilson, Birmingham South Cahaba Council

Garlic Pretzels

1 (10- to 14-ounce) package
  mini pretzel twists
¾ cup vegetable oil
1½ teaspoons dillweed

1 teaspoon garlic powder
½ teaspoon cayenne pepper
1 envelope ranch salad
  dressing mix

Spread the pretzels in a 9x13-inch baking pan. Combine the oil, dillweed, garlic powder, cayenne pepper and dressing mix in a blender container. Process until well mixed. Pour the mixture over the pretzels and stir gently until coated. Bake at 225 degrees for 30 minutes, stirring twice. Let stand until cool, stirring gently occasionally to allow the coating to cling to the pretzels. Store in an airtight container. Yield: 6 to 12 servings.

Frankie (A.T.) Vaughn, Selma Life Member Club

Spiced Nut and Pretzel Mix

1 egg white
2 tablespoons sugar
2 teaspoons ground cumin
1½ teaspoons salt
¾ teaspoon cayenne pepper

1 pound unsalted almonds
8 ounces unsalted cashews
1 (9- or 10-ounce) package
  pretzel sticks

Beat the egg white in a large bowl with a wire whisk or fork. Add the sugar, cumin, salt and cayenne pepper and beat well. Add the almonds and cashews and mix until coated. Spray a 10x15-inch baking pan with nonstick cooking spray. Spread the nuts in a single layer in the prepared pan. Bake at 350 degrees for 30 minutes, turning the nuts with a spatula every 5 minutes. Spread the hot nuts on a large baking sheet on a wire rack to cool completely. Toss the nuts with the pretzels and store in an airtight container. Yield: 9 cups.

Brenda Reeves, Birmingham South Cahaba Council

Cheese Soup

3 slices bacon
½ cup chopped onion
2 tablespoons flour
1 (10-ounce) can cream of
    celery soup

2 cups shredded Cheddar
    cheese
2½ cups milk

Fry the bacon in a skillet until crisp. Drain, reserving the pan drippings. Crumble the bacon. Add the onion to the reserved pan drippings and cook until tender, stirring frequently. Remove the skillet from the heat and stir in the flour. Stir the onion mixture into the soup in a saucepan. Bring to a simmer over medium-low heat, stirring constantly. Add the cheese and cook until melted, stirring frequently. Add the milk gradually, stirring constantly until well mixed. Heat to serving temperature. Ladle into soup bowls. Top with a sprinkle of the bacon. Yield: 6 servings.

Vauline Terry, Tuscaloosa Council

Hearty Soup

6 large green onions
2 green bell peppers
1 bunch celery
1 large head cabbage
1 envelope onion soup mix

1 or 2 (28-ounce) cans diced
    tomatoes
Salt, pepper, curry powder
    and chopped fresh parsley
    to taste

Cut the green onions, green peppers, celery and cabbage into medium pieces and combine in a large soup pot. Add enough water to cover. Add the soup mix, undrained tomatoes and seasonings. Bring to a boil. Boil for 10 minutes, stirring occasionally; reduce heat. Simmer, covered, until the vegetables are tender, stirring occasionally. Adjust the seasonings. Ladle into soup bowls. Yield: 8 to 10 servings.

Mickey Deal, Birmingham South Cahaba Council

Red Pepper Bisque

8 red bell peppers
2 yellow onions, chopped
1/4 cup (1/2 stick) butter
2 teaspoons minced garlic

1/2 cup minced basil leaves
6 cups rich chicken stock
2 cups heavy cream
Salt and pepper to taste

Seed the red peppers and cut into 1-inch pieces. Cook the red peppers and onions in butter in a large skillet or saucepan over medium heat until the onions are translucent, stirring frequently. Add the garlic, basil and 2 cups of the chicken stock. Simmer for about 10 minutes or until the red peppers are tender, stirring occasionally. Process the mixture in batches in a blender or food processor until smooth. Strain into a soup pot and blend in the remaining 4 cups chicken stock. Simmer for 10 to 15 minutes or until slightly thickened, stirring occasionally. Blend in the heavy cream gradually. Add the salt and pepper. Heat to serving temperature; do not boil. Ladle into soup bowls. Yield: 2 1/2 quarts.

Jennifer McAllister, Birmingham South Cahaba Council

Hamburger Soup

1 pound ground beef
1 cup chopped onion
1 1/2 cups chopped carrots
2 cups chopped potatoes
2 cups tomato juice

2 cups water
1 1/2 teaspoons seasoned salt
1/2 teaspoon pepper
4 cups milk
Flour

Brown the ground beef in a large saucepan, stirring until crumbly; drain. Add the onion and cook until onion is transparent, stirring frequently. Add the next 6 ingredients and mix well. Cook, covered, over low heat until all the vegetables are tender, stirring occasionally. Blend a small amount of milk with the amount of flour necessary to make the soup of the desired consistency. Stir the mixture into the soup. Cook until thickened, stirring constantly. Stir in the remaining milk. Heat to serving temperature, stirring frequently; do not boil. Ladle into soup bowls. Yield: 10 servings.

Rebecca Stancil, Decatur Council

Taco Stew

1 pound lean ground beef
1 medium onion, chopped
1 (15-ounce) can whole kernel
  corn
1 (15-ounce) can pinto beans
1 (10-ounce) can tomatoes
  with green chiles

1 (10-ounce) can tomato soup
1 cup water
1 envelope taco seasoning mix
Shredded Monterey Jack
  cheese

Brown the ground beef with the onion in a large saucepan, stirring until the ground beef is crumbly; drain. Add the undrained corn, pinto beans, tomatoes with green chiles and tomato soup. Stir in the water and taco seasoning mix. Simmer for 20 to 30 minutes. Ladle into soup bowls and sprinkle with cheese. Serve with tortilla chips or other corn chips. Yield: 6 servings.

Betty Yancy, Birmingham Life Member Club

Easy Reduced-Fat Turkey Stew

5 pounds potatoes, peeled,
  chopped
1 large onion, chopped
8 cups canned tomatoes

3 (16-ounce) cans cream-style
  or whole kernel corn
1½ pounds cooked turkey,
  chopped

Combine the potatoes and onion in a large saucepan. Add water to cover. Cook, covered, until the potatoes are tender. Add the tomatoes and corn. Bring to a simmer and add the turkey. Heat to serving temperature. Ladle into soup bowls. Serve with hot corn bread. Yield: 8 to 10 servings.

Jan Holmes, Decatur Council

Ground Beef Casserole

1 pound lean ground beef
1 large green bell pepper,
  chopped
1 large onion, chopped
2 tablespoons vegetable oil
1 (10-ounce) can cream of
  mushroom soup
1 (16-ounce) can tomatoes
1 beef bouillon cube

1 cup water
1 tablespoon sugar
2 teaspoons salt
1/2 teaspoon pepper
1 (8-ounce) package medium
  noodles, cooked, drained
6 slices American cheese
Butter to taste
Paprika to taste

Brown the ground beef with the green pepper and onion in the oil in a large skillet, stirring until the ground beef is crumbly. Add the soup and tomatoes. Simmer for 10 minutes, stirring occasionally. Dissolve the bouillon cube in the water. Stir the bouillon, sugar, salt and pepper into the ground beef mixture. Cook for 5 minutes. Alternate layers of the noodles and ground beef mixture in a baking pan until all the ingredients are used. Bake at 350 degrees for 30 minutes. Arrange the cheese slices on top. Dot with butter and sprinkle with paprika. Bake until the cheese melts. Yield: 8 servings.

Mary Jo Payne, Gadsden Life Member Club

Hogs in a Quilt

1 (11-ounce) package
  refrigerator French bread
  dough

2 tablespoons prepared mustard
1 (16-ounce) can sauerkraut
1 pound kielbasa

Roll the bread dough into a 4x18-inch rectangle on a lightly floured surface. Spread the mustard on the dough, leaving a 1/2-inch border. Drain the sauerkraut and spoon over the mustard. Cut the rectangle in half crosswise. Cut the kielbasa in half and place a piece on each rectangle. Wrap the dough around the kielbasa and seal tightly. Place seam side down on a baking sheet. Bake at 350 degrees for 30 to 35 minutes or until golden brown. Cut into 1/2-inch slices. Yield: 12 servings.

Mary Gillis, Mobile Council

Hawaiian Banana Nut Bread

3 cups flour
2 cups sugar
1 teaspoon baking soda
1 teaspoon salt
1 teaspoon cinnamon
1 cup chopped nuts

3 eggs, beaten
2 cups mashed bananas
1½ cups vegetable oil
2 teaspoons vanilla extract
1 (8-ounce) can crushed
   pineapple, drained

Combine the flour, sugar, baking soda, salt, cinnamon and nuts in a large bowl and mix well. Combine the eggs, bananas, oil, vanilla and pineapple in a medium bowl and mix well. Add the egg mixture to the flour mixture and mix just until moistened. Spoon the batter into 2 greased and floured 5x9-inch loaf pans. Bake at 350 degrees for 65 minutes or until the loaves test done. Cool in the pans on a wire rack for 10 minutes. Remove to a wire rack to cool completely. Yield: 2 loaves.

Angie Bolton, Montgomery Council

Simple Pecan Rolls

½ cup (1 stick) butter,
   softened
½ cup packed brown sugar
½ teaspoon cinnamon

¾ cup pecan halves
1 (12-count) package brown
   and serve rolls

Combine the butter, brown sugar and cinnamon in a bowl and beat until well blended. Spread in a 9-inch round baking pan. Arrange the pecan halves in the pan. Arrange the rolls upside down in the pan. Bake at 450 degrees for 8 to 10 minutes or until golden brown. Invert onto a serving plate. Serve warm. Yield: 4 to 6 servings.

Brenda Reeves, Birmingham South Cahaba Council

Champagne Cake

1 (2-layer) package white
  cake mix
1 (3-ounce) package
  pistachio instant
  pudding mix
1 cup club soda
4 eggs
½ cup vegetable oil

1 (4-ounce) jar red
  maraschino cherries,
  drained
1 (20-ounce) can crushed
  pineapple, drained
½ cup chopped pecans
Coconut Pecan Cream Cheese
  Frosting

Combine the cake mix, pudding mix, club soda, eggs and oil in a large mixer bowl and beat until well blended. Stir in the cherries, pineapple and pecans. Pour into 3 greased and floured layer cake pans. Bake at 350 degrees for 20 minutes or until the layers test done. Cool in the pans on wire racks for 10 minutes. Remove to wire racks to cool completely. Spread Coconut Pecan Cream Cheese Frosting between layers and over top and side of cake. Yield: 12 servings.

Coconut Pecan Cream Cheese Frosting

8 ounces cream cheese,
  softened
6 tablespoons margarine,
  melted
1 (1-pound) package
  confectioners' sugar

2 tablespoons vanilla extract
1 cup chopped pecans
1 (6-ounce) package frozen
  shredded coconut

Beat the cream cheese in a mixer bowl until creamy. Add the margarine, confectioners' sugar and vanilla and beat until smooth. Stir in the pecans and coconut.

Frankie (A.T.) Vaughn, Selma Life Member Club

German Chocolate Upside-Down Cake

1 cup shredded coconut
1 cup chopped pecans
1 (2-layer) package German
  chocolate cake mix

8 ounces cream cheese
½ cup (1 stick) margarine
1 (1-pound) package
  confectioners' sugar

Sprinkle the coconut and pecans in the bottom of a 9x13-inch cake pan. Prepare the cake mix using the package directions and pour into the prepared pan. Heat the cream cheese and margarine in a saucepan over medium heat until blended, stirring constantly. Remove from the heat and blend in the confectioners' sugar. Spoon over the cake batter. Bake at 350 degrees for 35 to 40 minutes. Cool on a wire rack. Cut into serving portions. Invert each portion onto a dessert plate. Yield: 15 servings.

Elizabeth Aldridge, Alabama Telco Credit Union

Quick Toffee Cake

2 cups whipped topping
½ cup caramel topping
½ teaspoon vanilla extract

1 (16-ounce) angel food cake
6 Heath candy bars, crushed
  (optional)

Blend the whipped topping, caramel topping and vanilla in a large bowl. Cut the cake horizontally into 3 layers. Spread the topping mixture between the cake layers, sprinkling crushed candy as desired. Spread remaining topping over top and side of cake, adding any remaining candy as desired. Store in the refrigerator.
Yield: 12 servings.

Mary Ann Sparks Fulmer, Shoals Life Member Club

No-Bake Chocolate Oatmeal Cookies

2 cups sugar
1/4 cup baking cocoa
1/2 cup milk
1/2 cup (1 stick) butter

1 tablespoon vanilla extract
1/4 cup peanut butter
3 cups rolled oats

Combine the sugar, baking cocoa, milk and butter in a large saucepan. Bring to a boil, stirring constantly. Boil for 2 minutes. Remove from heat and stir in the vanilla and peanut butter. Add the oats and mix well. Drop by spoonfuls onto waxed paper. Yield: 20 cookies.

Rebecca Stancil, Decatur Council

Chocolate Pie

1 cup sugar
1/4 cup baking cocoa
1/2 cup flour
Pinch of salt
2 egg yolks
2 cups milk

1 teaspoon vanilla extract
2 tablespoons butter
1 baked (9-inch) pie shell
2 egg whites
Sugar

Combine the 1 cup sugar, baking cocoa, flour and salt in the top of a double boiler. Beat the egg yolks and blend in the milk. Add about 1/3 of the milk mixture to the cocoa mixture and mix until a smooth paste forms. Blend in the remaining milk mixture. Place the top of the double boiler over boiling water over medium heat. Cook until thickened, stirring constantly. Stir in the vanilla and butter. Pour into the pie shell. Beat the egg whites with the desired amount of sugar in a mixer bowl until stiff peaks form. Spread over the filling, sealing to the edge. Bake at 350 degrees until the meringue browns. Turn off the oven. Let stand in the oven with the door ajar until cool. Yield: 6 servings.

Sue Johnston, Birmingham South Cahaba Council

Cheese Dip

1 pound ground beef
1 (26-ounce) can cream of
   mushroom soup
1 onion, chopped

1 (16-ounce) can tomatoes
1 (32-ounce) package Velveeta
   cheese, sliced

Brown the ground beef in a skillet, stirring until crumbly; drain. Combine with the soup and onion in a large saucepan. Add the undrained tomatoes, mashing the tomatoes. Cook over medium heat, stirring constantly. Add the cheese 1 slice at a time, stirring until melted after each addition. Cook, covered, for 15 to 20 minutes or until hot and bubbly, stirring frequently. Serve warm with tortilla chips. Yield: 12 servings.

Ramona Davis, Alabama Telco Credit Union

Dill Dip

2 cups sour cream
2 cups mayonnaise
2 tablespoons minced parsley

2 tablespoons each Beau
   Monde seasoning, dillweed
   and dillseed

Combine the ingredients in a bowl and mix well. Chill, covered, for 8 to 10 hours. Serve with rye or onion rye bread. Yield: 4 cups.

Susan Poe, Riverchase Council

Gentlemen's Morsels

8 thin slices whole wheat
   bread
Apricot jam

4 ounces very thinly sliced
   smoked ham
Dijon mustard

Spread half the bread slices with jam. Add ham. Spread the remaining bread slices with mustard and place mustard side down on the ham. Trim the crusts and cut the sandwiches into squares, fingers or triangles. Yield: 16 small sandwiches.

Brenda Reeves, Birmingham South Cahaba Council

Homemade Salsa

1 gallon chopped tomatoes
2 cups chopped onions
1/2 to 1 cup chopped jalapeño
chiles
2 cups chopped green bell
peppers

1/2 cup sugar
1 cup vinegar
2 teaspoons black pepper
1 1/2 tablespoons chili pepper
1 tablespoon garlic powder
2 tablespoons cumin

Combine the tomatoes, onions, chiles, green peppers, sugar, vinegar and seasonings in a stockpot and mix well. Bring to a boil. Cook for 30 minutes, stirring frequently. Drain enough liquid to make of the desired consistency if you prefer chunky salsa. Process in batches in a food processor for a smoother salsa. Ladle into hot sterilized jars; seal with 2-piece lids. Process in a boiling water bath for 10 minutes. Yield: about 10 pints.

Pam Dyer, Riverchase Council

Boursin Spread

16 ounces cream cheese,
softened
1 garlic clove, minced
1 teaspoon oregano
1/4 teaspoon basil

1/4 teaspoon thyme
1/4 teaspoon pepper
1/4 teaspoon marjoram
1/4 teaspoon dillweed

Combine the cream cheese, garlic, oregano, basil, thyme, pepper, marjoram and dillweed in a blender container or food processor and process until smooth. Store, covered, in the refrigerator. Serve with assorted party crackers or warm bread. Yield: 2 cups.

Susan Poe, Riverchase Council

Cheese Ball

16 ounces cream cheese
1 envelope ranch salad
   dressing mix

Seasoned pepper

Let the cream cheese stand until softened. Mix with the dressing mix in a bowl. Chill until firm. Shape into a ball. Coat with seasoned pepper. Chill, wrapped in plastic wrap, until serving time. Serve with assorted party crackers. Yield: 15 to 20 servings.

Gail Davis, Montgomery Council

Cheese Ring

1 pound Cheddar cheese,
   shredded
3/4 cup mayonnaise
1 onion, finely chopped
1/2 teaspoon Tabasco sauce

1/2 teaspoon garlic powder
1 cup chopped pecans
Raspberry or strawberry
   preserves

Mix the first 6 ingredients in a bowl. Press into a ring mold. Chill for 8 to 10 hours. Invert onto a serving platter. Fill the center with preserves. Serve with assorted party crackers. Yield: 20 to 25 servings.

Catherine M. Martin, Birmingham Metro Council

Cheese Straws

1 pound New York sharp
   Cheddar cheese, shredded
2 cups self-rising flour

1/4 teaspoon cayenne pepper
3/4 cup (1 1/2 sticks) butter,
   softened

Let the cheese stand until softened. Mix in the flour and cayenne pepper. Add the butter and mix well. Place the mixture in a cookie press. Press straws of the desired length onto a baking sheet. Bake at 300 degrees until light brown. Remove to a wire rack to cool. Store in an airtight container. Yield: 7 to 8 dozen.

Polly (Ed) Martin, Opelika Life Member Club

White Trash

1 (10-ounce) package mini
   pretzels
5 cups Cheerios cereal
5 cups corn Chex cereal
2 cups peanuts

1 pound "M & M's" chocolate
   candies
4 cups white chocolate chips
3 tablespoons vegetable oil

Combine the pretzels, cereals, peanuts and candies in a large bowl and mix gently. Combine the white chocolate chips and oil in a microwave-safe bowl. Microwave on Medium for 2 minutes, stirring once. Microwave on High for 10 seconds and stir until smooth. Pour over the pretzel mixture and mix until coated. Pour onto waxed paper and let stand until cool. Break into pieces and store in an airtight container. Yield: about 20 cups.

Susan Poe, Riverchase Council

Banana Punch

1½ cups sugar
6 cups water
1 (46-ounce) can pineapple
   juice
1 (6-ounce) can frozen orange
   juice concentrate, thawed

6 very ripe bananas, mashed
Juice of 2 lemons
2 quarts lemon-lime soda or
   ginger ale, chilled

Combine the sugar and water in a saucepan. Bring to a boil, stirring until the sugar dissolves. Boil for 3 minutes. Cool to room temperature. Combine with the pineapple juice, orange juice concentrate, bananas and lemon juice in a large freezer container and mix well. Freeze until a few hours before ready to serve. Let stand at room temperature for several hours. Pour into a punch bowl. Add the soda just before serving and stir until the mixture is slushy. Ladle into punch cups. Yield: 25 servings.

Pat Ramsey, sister of Cathy Kelley,
Birmingham South Cahaba Council

Fruit Crush

2 cups sugar
3 cups water
1 (46-ounce) can pineapple
  juice

1/4 cup lemon juice
1 1/2 cups orange juice
3 very ripe bananas, mashed
3 quarts ginger ale, chilled

Combine the sugar and water in a large saucepan. Bring to a boil, stirring until the sugar dissolves. Remove from heat. Stir in the pineapple juice, lemon juice, orange juice and bananas. Pour into ice cube trays and freeze until firm. Fill tall glasses with the frozen cubes and add the ginger ale just before serving.
Yield: 24 to 30 servings.

Judy Howard, Riverchase Council

Quick Fruit Punch

1 cup red Hawaiian punch
1/2 cup orange instant
  breakfast drink mix
1 envelope unsweetened
  strawberry drink mix

1 cup sugar
2 to 2 1/2 quarts water

Combine the punch, drink mixes and sugar in a large pitcher. Stir until the sugar dissolves. Chill until serving time or pour over ice in glasses. Yield: 8 to 10 servings.

Judy Howard, Riverchase Council

Homemade Fruit Slush

1 cup fresh strawberries or blueberries	1/4 cup water
1 1/2 cups juice-pack crushed pineapple	1 very ripe banana
	Ice cubes

Combine the berries, pineapple, water and banana in a blender container. Add enough ice cubes to fill to the 40-ounce mark on the container. Process until smooth. Yield: 10 servings.

Bill and Barbara Dalton, Riverchase Council

Strawberry Party Punch

4 (10-ounce) packages frozen sliced strawberries, partially thawed	1 (6-ounce) can frozen pink lemonade concentrate, thawed
1 cup sugar	2 quarts club soda, chilled
2 quarts strawberry soda	

Combine the strawberries and sugar in a large container and mix well. Stir in half the strawberry soda. Let stand at room temperature for 1 hour. Add the lemonade concentrate and mix well. Chill until ready to serve. Pour into a punch bowl and stir in the remaining strawberry soda and club soda. Add an ice ring if desired. Ladle into punch cups. Yield: 50 servings.

Brenda Reeves, Birmingham South Cahaba Council

Rainbow Salad

6 (3-ounce) packages gelatin   2 cups sour cream
6 cups boiling water   2¼ cups cold water

Select 6 flavors and colors of gelatin. Dissolve 1 of the gelatins in 1
cup boiling water and let stand until cool. Blend half the dissolved
gelatin with ⅓ cup sour cream and pour into a 9x13-inch dish.
Chill until set. Add 3 tablespoons cold water to the remaining
dissolved gelatin; pour over the congealed layer. Chill until set.
Continue preparing each color of gelatin in the above manner,
adding to the dish to produce a pleasing progression of colors. Chill
until serving time. Cut into squares. Remove from the dish
carefully to retain the color layers. Yield: 15 to 18 servings.

Mary Gillis, Mobile Council

Fruit Salad

1 (16-ounce) package   1 (16-ounce) can pineapple
  frozen strawberries,   tidbits, drained
  thawed   1 (11-ounce) can mandarin
1 (21-ounce) can peach   oranges, drained
  pie filling   3 bananas, sliced

Combine the strawberries, pie filling, pineapple and oranges in a
bowl and mix gently. Chill, covered, until serving time. Add the
bananas just before serving and mix gently. Yield: 8 to 10 servings.

Sue Woodruff, sister of Cathy Kelley,
Birmingham South Cahaba Council

Broccoli Salad

2 bunches broccoli, chopped
1/2 cup shredded Cheddar
  cheese
1/4 cup chopped red onion
1/2 cup raisins

1/2 cup chopped pecans
1/2 cup mayonnaise
2 tablespoons cider vinegar
1/4 cup sugar

Combine the broccoli, cheese, onion, raisins and pecans in a salad bowl. Blend the mayonnaise with the vinegar and sugar in a bowl. Add to the broccoli mixture and toss until well mixed. Chill, covered, until serving time. Yield: 8 to 10 servings.

Sue Woodruff, sister of Cathy Kelley,
Birmingham South Cahaba Council

Sausage Ring

2 pounds hot bulk sausage
1 green bell pepper, chopped
1 onion, chopped
2 (10-count) cans biscuits

Shredded Cheddar cheese
  to taste
Dillweed to taste

Brown the sausage with the green pepper and onion in a large skillet, stirring until the sausage is crumbly; drain. Cut the biscuits into quarters. Combine the biscuits, sausage mixture and cheese in a large bowl and mix well. Press into a large ring mold and sprinkle with dillweed. Bake at 375 degrees for 15 minutes or until the biscuits are baked through. Let stand for 10 to 15 minutes before inverting onto a serving plate. Yield: 8 to 10 servings.

Dabney Morris, Riverchase Council

Heavenly Cherry Dessert

2 cups flour
1 cup chopped nuts
1 cup (2 sticks) margarine,
  melted
8 ounces cream cheese,
  softened

1 (1-pound) package
  confectioners' sugar
16 ounces whipped topping
1 (21-ounce) can cherry pie
  filling

Combine the flour, nuts and margarine in a bowl and mix well. Pat into a 9x13-inch baking pan. Bake at 350 degrees for 30 minutes. Let stand until completely cooled. Beat the cream cheese and confectioners' sugar in a mixer bowl until smooth. Fold in the whipped topping. Spread over the cooled crust. Top with the pie filling. Chill for several hours. Yield: 8 servings.

Joann Ford, Gadsden Life Member Club

Fruit Cobbler

2 cups fruit of choice
1 cup milk
1 cup sugar
¼ cup (½ stick) margarine

Salt to taste
4 slices white bread
Butter to taste
Sugar to taste

Combine the fruit, milk, 1 cup sugar, margarine and salt in a saucepan. Add enough water to cover and mix well. Cook over medium heat until the fruit is tender, stirring frequently. Set aside. Spread the bread with butter and sprinkle lightly with sugar. Place in a toaster oven or on a baking sheet and toast until golden brown. Cut 2 of the slices into small pieces and stir into the fruit mixture. Pour the mixture into a baking dish. Place the remaining toasted bread slices on top to form a crust. Bake at 350 degrees for 15 minutes. Yield: 4 to 6 servings.

Lillian Weaver, Huntsville Council

Eclair Dessert

2 small packages sugar-free
   vanilla instant pudding mix
3 cups skim milk
12 ounces reduced-fat
   whipped topping

1 (16-ounce) package graham
   crackers
1 can reduced-fat chocolate
   frosting

Prepare the pudding mix with the skim milk using package directions. Blend in the whipped topping. Arrange a layer of the graham crackers in a 9x13-inch dish. Add alternate layers of pudding mixture and graham crackers until all the ingredients are used, ending with graham crackers. Spread with a layer of frosting. Chill, covered, for 3 days before serving. Yield: 12 to 15 servings.

Catherine M. Martin, Birmingham Metro Council

Raspberry Swirl

¾ cup graham cracker crumbs
3 tablespoons butter, melted
2 tablespoons sugar
3 egg yolks
8 ounces cream cheese,
   softened
1 cup sugar

⅛ teaspoon salt
3 egg whites
1 cup whipping cream,
   whipped
1 (10-ounce) package frozen
   raspberries, partially
   thawed

Mix the first 3 ingredients in a bowl. Press evenly into a 7x11-inch baking dish. Bake at 350 degrees for 8 minutes. Cool. Beat the egg yolks in a mixer bowl until thick and pale yellow. Beat in the cream cheese, 1 cup sugar and salt until smooth. Beat the egg whites in a mixer bowl until soft peaks form. Fold in the whipped cream. Fold the egg white mixture into the cream cheese mixture. Process the raspberries in a blender until puréed. Swirl half the raspberries into the cream cheese mixture and spread over the cooled crust. Spoon the remaining raspberries over the top and swirl with a knife to marbleize. Freeze until firm. Store, covered, in the freezer until serving time. Yield: 12 servings.

Sue (Joe) Small, Selma Life Member Club

Strawberry Pizza

1½ cups flour
½ cup packed brown sugar
1 cup (2 sticks) butter, melted
1 cup chopped pecans
8 ounces cream cheese,
  softened
2 cups confectioners' sugar

16 ounces whipped topping
1 (3-ounce) package
  strawberry gelatin
1 cup sugar
1 cup water
¼ cup cornstarch
4 cups sliced strawberries

Press a mixture of the first 4 ingredients over the bottom of a pizza pan. Bake at 400 degrees for 15 minutes. Cool. Cream the cream cheese and confectioners' sugar in a mixer bowl. Fold in the whipped topping. Spread over the prepared crust. Mix the gelatin, sugar, water and cornstarch in a saucepan over high heat. Bring to a boil, stirring constantly. Remove from the heat. Cool. Fold in the strawberries. Chill, covered, for 1 hour. Spread over the cream cheese mixture. Serve immediately. Yield: 12 servings.

Narice Sutton, Birmingham Life Member Club

My Sister's Famous Coconut Cake

1 (2-layer) package yellow
  cake mix
1 egg yolk
2 cups sugar

1 cup water
1 large package frozen
  shredded coconut

Prepare the cake mix using package directions with the following modifications: Separate the number of eggs called for, add the extra egg yolk and reserve all the egg whites. Pour the batter into a greased and floured 9x13-inch cake pan. Bake using package directions. Cool in pan on a wire rack. Combine the sugar and water in a saucepan. Bring to a boil, stirring until the sugar dissolves completely. Cook until the mixture forms a syrup. Beat the reserved egg whites in a mixer bowl until stiff peaks form. Add the hot syrup, beating constantly. Pour over the top of the cake. Sprinkle with the coconut. Store, covered, in the refrigerator. Yield: 15 servings.

Billie Harrison, Shoals Life Member Club

Lemon Cake

1 cup (2 sticks) butter,
  softened
½ cup (1 stick) margarine,
  softened
3 cups sugar
5 eggs

3 cups sifted flour
1 teaspoon vanilla extract
1 teaspoon lemon extract
¾ cup lemon-lime soda
Cream Cheese Frosting

Cream the butter, margarine and sugar in a large mixer bowl until light and fluffy. Add the eggs 1 at a time, beating well after each addition. Add the flour and flavorings and beat until smooth. Blend in the lemon-lime soda. Pour the batter into 3 greased and floured 9-inch layer cake pans. Place the pans in a cold oven. Bake at 325 degrees for 50 minutes or until a toothpick inserted in the center comes out clean. Cool in the pans on a wire rack for 10 minutes. Remove to wire rack to cool completely. Spread Cream Cheese Frosting between the layers and over the top and side of the cake. May bake in a greased and floured tube pan for 1½ hours. Yield: 12 servings.

Cream Cheese Frosting

8 ounces cream cheese,
  softened
¼ cup (½ stick) margarine,
  softened

1 teaspoon vanilla extract
1 (1-pound) package
  confectioners' sugar
1 cup chopped nuts (optional)

Beat the cream cheese and margarine in a mixer bowl until well blended. Add the vanilla and confectioners' sugar and beat until of spreading consistency. Stir in the nuts.

Phillis Cooks, Birmingham South Cahaba Council

Orange Date Cake

1 cup (2 sticks) butter,
  softened
2 cups sugar
4 eggs
1⅓ cups buttermilk
1 teaspoon baking soda
1 pound dates, chopped
1 cup chopped nuts

2 tablespoons grated orange
  zest
4 cups flour
Pinch of salt
2 cups sugar
2 tablespoons grated orange
  zest
1 cup orange juice

Cream the butter and 2 cups sugar in a large mixer bowl until light and fluffy. Add the eggs 1 at a time, beating well after each addition. Combine the buttermilk and baking soda and stir until dissolved. Combine the dates, nuts and 2 tablespoons orange zest in a bowl. Add enough of the flour to coat the dates and nuts and mix well. Add a mixture of the remaining flour and salt to the creamed mixture alternately with the buttermilk mixture, mixing well after each addition. Stir in the date mixture. Pour into a greased and floured tube pan. Bake at 350 degrees for 1½ hours. Cool in the pan for 10 minutes. Invert onto a serving plate. Combine 2 cups sugar, 2 tablespoons orange zest and orange juice in a bowl and mix until the sugar dissolves completely. Drizzle the mixture over the hot cake. Let stand until cool. Yield: 16 servings.

Judy Howard, Riverchase Council

If you have a problem opening jars, try using latex dishwashing gloves. They give a non-slip grip that makes opening easy.

Red Velvet Cake

1½ cups sugar
1⅓ cups vegetable oil
2 eggs
1 teaspoon vanilla extract
1½ cups flour
1 teaspoon baking powder or
    baking soda

1 teaspoon salt
1 cup buttermilk
1 teaspoon baking cocoa
1 teaspoon vinegar
1 (1-ounce) bottle red food
    coloring
Cream Cheese Frosting

Combine the sugar, oil, eggs and vanilla in a mixer bowl and beat until blended. Add a mixture of the flour, baking powder and salt alternately with the buttermilk, mixing well after each addition. Blend the baking cocoa, vinegar and food coloring in a small bowl. Add to the batter and beat until well blended. Pour into greased and floured layer cake pans. Bake at 350 degrees for 35 minutes or until the layers test done. Cool in the pans on wire racks for 10 minutes. Remove to wire racks to cool completely. Spread Cream Cheese Frosting between layers and over top and side of cake. Yield: 12 servings.

Cream Cheese Frosting

8 ounces cream cheese,
    softened
½ cup (1 stick) margarine,
    softened

1 (1-pound) package
    confectioners' sugar
1 cup chopped nuts (optional)

Beat the cream cheese and margarine in a bowl until well blended. Add the confectioners' sugar and beat until of spreading consistency. Stir in the nuts.

Rosa Stodghill, Riverchase Council

Red Velvet Pound Cake

1½ cups (3 sticks) butter,
   softened
3 cups sugar
6 eggs
1 teaspoon vanilla extract
1 (1-ounce) bottle red food
   coloring

3 cups flour
1 teaspoon baking soda
1 teaspoon salt
1 cup buttermilk
Cream Cheese Frosting

Cream the butter and sugar in a mixer bowl until light and fluffy. Add the eggs 1 at a time, beating well after each addition. Beat in the vanilla and food coloring. Mix the flour, baking soda and salt together. Add to the creamed mixture alternately with the buttermilk, beating well after each addition. Pour into a greased and floured tube pan. Bake at 325 degrees for 1 hour and 20 minutes or until the cake tests done. Cool in the pan on a wire rack for 10 to 15 minutes. Invert onto the wire rack to cool completely. Frost with Cream Cheese Frosting. Yield: 16 servings.

Cream Cheese Frosting

6 ounces cream cheese,
   softened
½ cup (1 stick) butter,
   softened

1 teaspoon vanilla extract
1 (1-pound) package
   confectioners' sugar
1 tablespoon milk

Beat the cream cheese and butter in a bowl until well blended. Add the vanilla and confectioners' sugar and beat until smooth. Add enough of the milk to make the frosting of spreading consistency.

Bernice Moore, Birmingham South Cahaba Council

Top-Hat Divinity

2½ cups sugar
½ cup light corn syrup
½ cup water
2 egg whites
1 teaspoon vanilla extract

½ cup chopped nuts (optional)
½ cup chopped candied
  cherries (optional)
1 cup chocolate chips
  (optional)

Combine the sugar, corn syrup and water in a saucepan and mix well. Cover the saucepan and bring to a boil. Uncover and boil to 235 degrees on a candy thermometer, fine thread stage; do not stir. Remove from heat. Beat the egg whites in a mixer bowl until stiff peaks form. Add half the syrup to the egg whites gradually, beating constantly. Cook the remaining syrup to 250 degrees on a candy thermometer, hard-ball stage. Add to the egg white mixture, beating constantly until the mixture loses its gloss. Beat in the vanilla. Stir in the nuts and cherries. Drop by teaspoonfuls onto waxed paper. Let stand until firm and cool. Melt the chocolate chips over hot water. Dip each candy piece halfway into the chocolate and replace on the waxed paper to cool.
Yield: 1¾ pounds.

Sue (Joe) Small, Selma Life Member Club

Chocolate-Covered Peanuts

2 cups (or more) chocolate
  chips
2 cups (or more) butterscotch
  chips

1 tablespoon (rounded)
  creamy peanut butter
1 (15-ounce) jar dry roasted
  peanuts

Combine the chocolate chips and butterscotch chips in a microwave-safe bowl. Microwave for 4 minutes or until the chips are melted. Stir until blended and blend in the peanut butter. Add the peanuts and stir until coated. Drop by spoonfuls onto a waxed paper-covered tray. Freeze until the coating hardens. Store in plastic bags in the freezer. Yield: 60 pieces.

Charlotte Flach, aunt of Cathy Kelley,
Birmingham South Cahaba Council

Chocolate-Covered Cherries

2 (10-ounce) jars maraschino
   cherries with stems
½ cup (1 stick) butter,
   softened
1 tablespoon evaporated milk

2 tablespoons vanilla extract
1 (1-pound) package
   confectioners' sugar
Milk chocolate bark

Drain the cherries well and pat dry. Combine the butter, evaporated milk and vanilla in a mixer bowl and beat until blended. Add the confectioners' sugar and mix until smooth. Divide the mixture into small portions and press around each cherry, enclosing completely. Place on waxed paper-covered trays and chill or freeze until firm. Melt the chocolate over hot water. Dip each covered cherry in the chocolate to cover completely while holding the stem. Place on waxed paper. Let stand until chocolate is firm. Store in an airtight container.
Yield: 20 to 25 cherries.

Melba Jean Campbell, Tuscaloosa Council

Milky Way Bars

6 Milky Way candy bars,
   chopped
¾ cup (1½ sticks) butter,
   chopped

6 cups crisp rice cereal
1 cup chopped pecans
6 ounces chocolate bark

Combine the candy bars and butter in a large microwave-safe bowl. Microwave for 5 minutes or until melted and stir until well blended. Stir in the cereal and pecans. Press the mixture into a 9x13-inch pan. Microwave the chocolate bark in a small microwave-safe bowl and pour over the cereal layer. Chill until firm. Cut into bars. Yield: 2 to 3 dozen bars.

Ann Sellers, Tuscaloosa Council

Boiled Cookies

2 cups sugar
1/2 cup (1 stick) margarine
1/3 cup baking cocoa
1/2 cup milk

1/2 teaspoon salt
1 teaspoon vanilla extract
   (optional)
3 cups quick-cooking oats

Combine the sugar, margarine, baking cocoa, milk and salt in a saucepan. Heat until the margarine melts and the mixture is well blended, stirring constantly. Boil for 2 minutes. Remove from heat. Add the vanilla and oats and mix until slightly cooled. Drop by spoonfuls onto waxed paper. May substitute 1 cup of nuts or shredded coconut for 1 cup of the oats. Yield: 2 to 3 dozen cookies.

Judy Howard, Riverchase Council

Rich Chocolate Brownies

1 cup (2 sticks) butter
4 ounces unsweetened
   chocolate
2 cups sugar
4 eggs, lightly beaten

1 teaspoon vanilla extract
1 cup flour
1/8 teaspoon salt
2 cups chocolate chips

Melt the butter and unsweetened chocolate in a saucepan or microwave. Blend in the sugar. Add the eggs, vanilla, flour and salt and mix well. Stir in the chocolate chips. Spread in a lightly greased 9x13-inch baking pan. Bake at 350 degrees for 30 minutes or until the brownies pull from the side of the pan. Cool and cut into squares. Yield: 2 to 3 dozen brownies.

Judy Howard, Riverchase Council

No-Bake Chocolate Oatmeal Cookies

2 cups sugar
½ cup baking cocoa
½ cup milk

½ cup (1 stick) margarine
½ cup peanut butter
2½ cups rolled oats

Combine the sugar, baking cocoa, milk and margarine in a large saucepan. Bring to a boil, stirring constantly. Boil for 2 minutes. Add the peanut butter and mix well. Add the oats 1 cup at a time, mixing well after each addition. Drop by spoonfuls onto waxed paper. Yield: 2 to 3 dozen cookies.

Becky Diggs, Riverchase Council

Boogie Woogies

1 ounce semisweet chocolate,
  chopped
⅓ cup strong coffee
1 cup (2 sticks) butter
1 cup sugar
1 cup packed brown sugar
2 teaspoons vanilla extract
2 eggs
2 cups flour

⅓ cup baking cocoa
1 teaspoon baking soda
1 teaspoon salt
1 cup chopped pecans
1 cup semisweet chocolate
  chips
1 cup "M & M's" baking
  pieces
2 cups rolled oats

Combine the chopped semisweet chocolate and coffee in a microwave-safe dish. Microwave on High for a minute or less or until the chocolate melts; stir. Cream the softened butter, sugar and brown sugar in a large mixer bowl. Add the vanilla and coffee mixture and beat until creamy. Beat in the eggs 1 at a time. Mix the flour, baking cocoa, baking soda and salt together. Add to the creamed mixture and beat at low speed until well mixed. Add the pecans, chocolate chips, M & M's and oats and mix well. Drop by heaping tablespoonfuls onto a lightly greased cookie sheet. Bake at 350 degrees for 10 to 12 minutes or until set. Cool on the cookie sheet for 2 to 3 minutes. Remove to a wire rack to cool completely. Yield: 4 to 5 dozen cookies.

Brenda Reeves, Birmingham South Cahaba Council

Rocky Road Fudge Cookie Bars

1 ounce unsweetened
  chocolate
1/2 cup (1 stick) butter
1 cup sugar
2 eggs
1 teaspoon vanilla extract
1 cup flour
1 teaspoon baking powder
1/2 to 1 cup chopped nuts
6 ounces cream cheese,
  softened
1/2 cup sugar
2 tablespoons flour
1/4 cup (1/2 stick) butter,
  softened

1 egg
1/2 teaspoon vanilla extract
1/4 cup chopped nuts
1 cup semisweet chocolate
  chips
2 cups miniature
  marshmallows
1/4 cup (1/2 stick) butter
1 ounce unsweetened
  chocolate
2 ounces cream cheese
1/4 cup milk
1 (1-pound) package
  confectioners' sugar
1 teaspoon vanilla extract

Melt 1 ounce chocolate and 1/2 cup butter in a saucepan over low heat, stirring until blended. Remove from the heat. Add 1 cup sugar and mix well. Add 2 eggs and 1 teaspoon vanilla and mix well. Add a mixture of 1 cup flour and baking powder and mix well. Stir in 1/2 to 1 cup nuts. Spread in a greased and floured 9x13-inch baking pan. Combine 6 ounces cream cheese, 1/2 cup sugar, 2 tablespoons flour, 1/4 cup butter, 1 egg and 1 teaspoon vanilla in a mixer bowl and beat until smooth. Stir in 1/4 cup nuts. Spread over the chocolate layer. Sprinkle with the chocolate chips. Bake at 350 degrees for 25 to 35 minutes or until a wooden pick inserted in the center comes out clean. Sprinkle the marshmallows over the top. Bake for 2 minutes longer. Combine 1/4 cup butter, 1 ounce chocolate, 2 ounces cream cheese and milk in a saucepan. Heat over low heat until well blended, stirring constantly. Remove from heat and add the confectioners' sugar and 1 teaspoon vanilla and mix until smooth. Pour over the marshmallows and swirl together. Let stand until cool. Cut into bars. Yield: 3 dozen bars.

J. Jordan, Riverchase Council

Chocolate Caramel Squares

1 (14-ounce) package
  caramels
1/3 cup evaporated milk
1 (2-layer) package German
  chocolate cake mix
1/3 cup evaporated milk

3/4 cup (1 1/2 sticks) butter,
  softened
1 cup chopped pecans
1 cup semisweet chocolate
  chips

Combine the caramels and 1/3 cup evaporated milk in a double
boiler over boiling water. Cook until the caramels melt and the
mixture is well blended, stirring frequently. Remove from heat.
Combine the cake mix, 1/3 cup evaporated milk and butter in a
mixer bowl and beat until the mixture holds together. Stir in the
pecans. Press half the mixture into a greased 9x13-inch baking pan.
Bake at 350 degrees for 6 minutes. Sprinkle the chocolate chips
over the baked layer. Spread with the caramel mixture. Top with
the remaining cake mixture and pat lightly. Bake for 18 minutes
longer. Let stand until cool. Chill for 30 minutes and cut into small
squares. Yield: 2 to 3 dozen squares.

Cindy (Tom) Somerville, Montgomery Council

Simple Sesames

2 cups (4 sticks) butter,
  softened
1 1/2 cups sugar
3 cups flour

1 cup sesame seeds
2 cups shredded coconut
1/2 cup finely chopped almonds

Cream the butter in a large bowl. Add the sugar gradually, beating
until light and fluffy. Add the flour and stir just until mixed. Stir in
the sesame seeds, coconut and almonds. Divide the dough into 3
equal portions. Shape each portion into a log about 2 inches in
diameter. Wrap in waxed paper. Chill until firm. Cut the logs into
1/4-inch slices and arrange on an ungreased cookie sheet. Bake at
300 degrees for 30 minutes. Cool on the cookie sheet for 1 to 2
minutes. Remove to a wire rack to cool completely. Yield: 4 dozen.

Susan Poe, Riverchase Council

Snickerdoodles

1 cup shortening	1 teaspoon baking soda
1½ cups sugar	2 teaspoons cream of tartar
2 eggs	½ teaspoon salt
2¾ cups flour	Cinnamon-sugar

Cream the shortening and sugar in a mixer bowl. Add the eggs and mix well. Combine the flour, baking soda, cream of tartar and salt. Add to the creamed mixture and mix well. Chill the dough until easy to handle. Shape the dough into walnut-size balls, roll in cinnamon-sugar and arrange on a cookie sheet. Bake at 400 degrees for 8 to 10 minutes or until light brown. Cool on cookie sheet for 1 to 2 minutes. Remove to a wire rack to cool completely. Yield: 2 to 3 dozen cookies.

Pat Ramsey, sister of Cathy Kelley,
Birmingham South Cahaba Council

Snowdrop Cookies

1 cup (2 sticks) butter, softened	2 cups self-rising flour
⅓ cup sugar	2 cups chopped nuts
½ teaspoon vanilla extract	Confectioners' sugar

Cream the butter, sugar and vanilla in a bowl. Add the flour and nuts and mix well by hand. Shape by tablespoonfuls into balls and arrange on a cookie sheet. Bake at 300 degrees for 30 minutes. Roll the hot cookies in confectioners' sugar and place on a wire rack to cool. Yield: 2 to 3 dozen cookies.

Betty Darnell, Gadsden Life Member Club

Painted Sugar Cookies

Evaporated milk
Food coloring

1 recipe favorite sugar
cookie dough

Pour desired amounts of evaporated milk into small containers and tint as desired with food coloring. Prepare the cookie dough, roll and cut as desired and arrange on a cookie sheet. Paint outlines and designs on the cookies using paint brushes of assorted sizes. Do not allow the lines to cross. Bake at 350 degrees until light brown. Paint accent colors on the cookies after baking. Cool the cookies on a wire rack. Yield: variable.

Jane (Jim) Hetherington, Huntsville Council

Cookie Pizza

1 roll refrigerator cookie dough
½ cup sugar
½ cup orange juice
1 tablespoon cornstarch
4½ ounces whipped topping
8 ounces cream cheese,
   softened

1 cup confectioners' sugar
1 pint fresh strawberries
1 (15-ounce) can pineapple
   tidbits, drained
2 bananas, sliced
2 kiwifruit, sliced

Slice the cookie dough and arrange with edges touching on a pizza pan. Flute the edge to form a slight ridge. Bake at 350 degrees until golden brown. Let stand until cool. Combine the sugar, orange juice and cornstarch in a saucepan and mix well. Cook over low heat until thickened, stirring constantly. Let stand until cool. Blend the whipped topping, cream cheese and confectioners' sugar in a bowl. Spread over the cooled crust. Arrange the fruit in a decorative pattern on the cookie crust and drizzle the orange juice glaze over the top. Chill until serving time. Cut into wedges. Yield: 10 to 12 servings.

Sue Woodruff, sister of Cathy Kelley,
Birmingham South Cahaba Council

Cherry Cream Pie with Almond Crust

1 stick pie crust mix
1/2 cup slivered almonds,
   finely chopped
1 (14-ounce) can
   sweetened condensed
   milk
1/3 cup lemon juice
1 teaspoon vanilla extract
1/2 teaspoon almond extract

1/2 cup whipping cream,
   whipped
2/3 cup cherry juice
1/4 cup sugar
1 tablespoon cornstarch
2 or 3 drops of red food
   coloring (optional)
2 cups pitted sour cherries,
   drained

Prepare the pie crust mix using package directions, adding the almonds. Roll and fit the pastry into a pie plate, flute the edge and prick the side of the pastry only. Bake using package directions. Let stand until completely cooled. Combine the condensed milk, lemon juice and flavorings in a bowl and mix until the mixture thickens. Fold in the whipped cream. Spoon into the cooled pie shell. Combine the cherry juice, sugar and cornstarch in a saucepan. Cook until thickened and clear, stirring constantly. Add the food coloring and the cherries. Spoon over the filling. Chill until serving time. Yield: 6 servings.

Mrs. Bob H. Henson, Birmingham South Life Member Club

Chocolate Pie

1 cup chocolate chips
3 tablespoons milk
1/4 cup sugar
4 egg yolks

1 teaspoon vanilla extract
4 egg whites
1 baked (9-inch) pie shell
Whipped topping

Mix the chocolate chips, milk and sugar in a double boiler. Heat over boiling water until well blended, stirring frequently. Cool. Beat in the egg yolks 1 at a time. Add the vanilla. Beat the egg whites in a mixer bowl until stiff peaks form. Fold into the chocolate mixture. Pour into the pie shell. Chill until firm. Spread whipped topping over the filling, sealing to the edge. Yield: 6 servings.

Janet Williams, Bon Secour Life Member Club

Fudge Pie

½ cup (1 stick) margarine,
  melted
½ cup flour
1 cup sugar

3 tablespoons baking cocoa
2 eggs
1 teaspoon vanilla extract

Combine the margarine, flour, sugar, baking cocoa, eggs and vanilla
in a bowl and mix well. Pour into a lightly greased 9-inch pie plate.
Bake at 350 degrees for 25 minutes. Serve warm with whipped
cream or ice cream. Yield: 6 servings.

Fran Coleman, Huntsville Life Member Club

Citrus Cheesecake Pudding Pie

¼ cup raspberry spread
1 (9-inch) graham cracker
  pie shell
1 cup fresh or frozen
  raspberries
2 (4-ounce) packages
  cheesecake instant
  pudding mix

1½ cups cold milk
1 teaspoon grated lime or
  lemon zest
8 ounces frozen whipped
  topping, thawed

Spread the raspberry spread over the bottom of the pie shell.
Arrange the raspberries evenly over the raspberry spread. Combine
the pudding mixes, milk and lime zest in a large bowl. Whisk for 2
minutes or until thickened and smooth. Fold in the whipped
topping. Spoon over the raspberries. Chill, covered, for 3 hours or
until set. Yield: 8 servings.

Eula Mae Watson, Gadsden Life Member Club

Million Dollar Pies

½ cup flaked coconut
1 (14-ounce) can sweetened
  condensed milk
¼ cup fresh lemon juice
1 (20-ounce) can crushed
  pineapple, drained
1 (11-ounce) can mandarin
  oranges, drained, cut into
  halves

1 cup coarsely chopped pecans
8 ounces whipped topping
½ cup flaked coconut
2 baked (9-inch) pie shells or
  graham cracker pie shells

Sprinkle ½ cup coconut in a small baking pan. Bake at 350 degrees for 4 minutes or until light brown. Blend the condensed milk and lemon juice in a large bowl. Mix in the pineapple, oranges and pecans. Fold in the whipped topping and ½ cup coconut. Spoon into the pie shells. Sprinkle with the toasted coconut. Chill for 4 hours or longer. Yield: 12 servings.

Mary Crittenden, Huntsville Council

Easy Strawberry Pie

12 ounces whipped topping
1 pint fresh strawberries,
  sliced
1 (14-ounce) can sweetened
  condensed milk

⅓ cup lemon juice
1 (9-inch) graham cracker
  pie shell

Combine the whipped topping, strawberries, condensed milk and lemon juice in a large bowl and mix well. Pour into the pie shell. Chill for 1 hour or longer. Yield: 6 servings.

Brenda Reeves, Birmingham South Cahaba Council

Artichoke Dip

1 (12-ounce) can artichoke
   hearts, drained, chopped
1 cup mayonnaise
1 cup shredded mozzarella
   cheese

1 cup grated Parmesan cheese
¼ cup minced scallions or
   green onions

Combine the artichokes, mayonnaise, mozzarella cheese, Parmesan cheese and scallions in a bowl and mix well. Spoon into an ungreased baking dish. Bake at 350 degrees for 20 to 25 minutes or until light brown. Serve with chips, fresh vegetable chunks and/or crackers. Yield: 20 to 25 servings.

Deborah Lawrence, Bon Secour Life Member Club

Old El Paso Bean Dip

1 (16-ounce) can refried
   beans
¼ envelope taco seasoning mix

½ onion, finely chopped
1 cup shredded Cheddar
   cheese

Spread the beans in an 8- or 9-inch round microwave-safe dish. Sprinkle with the seasoning mix, onion and cheese. Microwave on Medium until the cheese melts. Serve with tortilla chips. Yield: 6 to 8 servings.

Chuck Harman, Riverchase Council

Nacho Dip

1 pound hot sausage
1 pound ground beef
2 pounds Velveeta cheese, cubed
1 (10-ounce) can tomatoes with green chiles
1 (10-ounce) can cream of mushroom soup
1 (4-ounce) can chopped green chiles
1 tablespoon chili powder
Garlic powder to taste

Brown the sausage and ground beef in a skillet, stirring until crumbly; drain. Combine the cheese, undrained tomatoes, soup, chiles, chili powder and garlic powder in a large nonstick saucepan or slow cooker and mix well. Cook over low heat until the cheese melts, stirring constantly. Add the sausage mixture and mix well. Spoon into a slow cooker to keep warm. Serve with corn chips. Yield: 25 servings.

Carole Varden, Riverchase Council

Cheese Ball

10 to 16 ounces Cheddar cheese, shredded, softened
10 ounces cream cheese, softened
Minced garlic to taste
Finely chopped pecans to taste
Chili powder to taste

Beat the Cheddar cheese and cream cheese in a mixer bowl until blended. Stir in the garlic and pecans. Shape the cheese mixture into a ball. Sprinkle with chili powder. Chill, wrapped in plastic wrap, until serving time. Serve with assorted party crackers. Yield: 10 to 12 servings.

Flo Watters, Selma Life Member Club

Quick and Easy Cheese Ball

16 ounces cream cheese,   Finely chopped pecans or
   softened   paprika
1 envelope ranch salad
   dressing mix

Beat the cream cheese and dressing mix in a mixer bowl until
blended. Shape the cheese mixture into a ball. Roll in pecans or
sprinkle with paprika. Chill, covered in plastic wrap, until serving
time. Serve with assorted party crackers. Yield: 8 servings.

Ann Sellers, Tuscaloosa Council

Shrimp Mold

1 envelope unflavored gelatin   1 cup finely chopped celery
1 (10-ounce) can cream of   1 (4-ounce) can shrimp,
   shrimp soup   drained, chopped
8 ounces cream cheese,   1 cup mayonnaise
   softened

Soften the gelatin in a small amount of cold water. Heat the soup
in a saucepan until warm. Stir in the gelatin mixture. Cook until
the gelatin dissolves, stirring constantly. Add the celery and mix
well. Stir in the shrimp and mayonnaise. Spoon into a mold coated
with additional mayonnaise. Chill, covered, for 2 to 10 hours or
until set. Invert onto a serving platter. Serve with saltine crackers.
Yield: 10 to 12 servings.

Melba Jean Campbell, Tuscaloosa Council

Tuna Log

8 ounces cream cheese,
  softened
1 (6-ounce) can oil-pack tuna

¾ cup chopped pecans
Minced onion (optional)

Combine the cream cheese and undrained tuna in a mixer bowl. Beat at low speed until mixed. Stir in the pecans and onion. Shape the tuna mixture into a log or ball. Chill, covered in waxed paper or plastic wrap, until firm. Serve with butter crackers.
Yield: 10 to 12 servings.

Sharon Coffield, Birmingham South Cahaba Council

No-Cabbage Egg Rolls

1 pound sausage
1 pound ground beef
3 large carrots, grated
6 to 7 green onions, chopped
6 to 8 garlic cloves, minced
1 (14-ounce) can bean
  sprouts, drained, chopped
1 (8-ounce) can water
  chestnuts, drained, chopped

1 (8-ounce) can bamboo
  shoots, drained, chopped
1 (3-ounce) can mushrooms,
  drained, chopped
Salt and pepper to taste
¼ cup soy sauce
2 packages egg roll wraps
1 egg, beaten
Vegetable oil for deep-frying

Brown the sausage and ground beef with the carrots, green onions and garlic in a skillet, stirring until the sausage and ground beef are crumbly and the carrots are tender; drain. Stir in the bean sprouts, water chestnuts, bamboo shoots, mushrooms, salt and pepper. Add the soy sauce and mix well. Cook for 10 minutes, stirring frequently. Let stand until cool. Spoon a small amount of the sausage mixture in the center of each egg roll wrap. Fold as desired to enclose the filling. Brush the edges with the egg and seal tightly; do not stack uncooked egg rolls as they will stick together. Add enough oil to a skillet to measure 2 inches. Deep-fry the egg rolls in the hot oil until golden brown on both sides; drain.
Yield: 16 to 20 servings.

Celia Bell Hay, Riverchase Council

Sausage Pinwheels

2 (8-count) cans crescent rolls   8 ounces cream cheese,
1 pound mild sausage   softened

Separate each can of roll dough into 2 rectangles, pressing the
perforations to seal. Brown the sausage in a skillet, stirring until
crumbly; drain. Add the cream cheese and mix well. Spread the
sausage mixture on the rectangles. Roll to enclose the filling. Chill,
covered, until firm. Cut each roll into slices. Arrange the slices on
a baking sheet. Bake at 400 degrees for 10 minutes or until brown.
Yield: 16 to 20 servings.

Ann Sellers, Tuscaloosa Council

Fresh-Squeezed Lemonade

6 cups water   ½ cup fresh lemon juice
¾ cup sugar   1 tablespoon grated lemon zest

Combine the water and sugar in a 2-quart pitcher, stirring until the
sugar dissolves. Add the lemon juice and lemon zest and mix well.
Chill until serving time. Pour over ice in glasses. Garnish with
sprigs of fresh mint and lemon slices. Yield: 7 servings.

Brenda Reeves, Birmingham South Cahaba Council

*To easily remove burnt-on food from your skillet, simply
add a drop or two of dish washing soap and enough water to
cover the bottom of the skillet, and bring to a boil on the
stovetop—the skillet will be much easier to clean.*

White Chili

2 pounds boneless skinless
chicken breasts, chopped
Margarine
½ cup each chopped onion
and green bell pepper
3 (16-ounce) cans great
Northern beans, drained
2 (14-ounce) cans chicken
broth

1 (16-ounce) can light kidney
beans, drained
1 hot green chile, chopped
3 tablespoons chili powder
1 teaspoon chopped garlic
1 cup (or more) nonfat sour
cream
1 cup shredded Monterey Jack
cheese

Brown the chicken in margarine in a skillet, turning occasionally.
Transfer the chicken to a slow cooker. Sauté the onion and green
pepper in a nonstick skillet until tender. Transfer to the slow
cooker. Add the great Northern beans, broth, kidney beans, chile,
chili powder and garlic to the chicken mixture and mix well. Cook,
covered, for 4 hours or until of the desired consistency, adding the
sour cream and cheese 1 hour before the end of the cooking
process. Ladle into chili bowls. Yield: 6 to 8 servings.

Becky Diggs, Riverchase Council

Stuffed Pepper Soup

2 pounds ground beef
1 (28-ounce) can diced
tomatoes
1 (28-ounce) can tomato
sauce
2 cups cooked rice

2 cups chopped green bell
peppers
¼ cup packed brown sugar
2 beef bouillon cubes
2 teaspoons salt
1 teaspoon pepper

Brown the ground beef in a large saucepan or stockpot, stirring
until crumbly; drain. Stir in the undrained tomatoes, tomato sauce,
rice, green peppers, brown sugar, bouillon cubes, salt and pepper.
Bring to a boil; reduce heat. Simmer, covered, for 30 to 40 minutes
or until the green peppers are tender, stirring occasionally. Ladle
into soup bowls. Yield: 10 servings.

Frankie (A.T.) Vaughn, Selma Life Member Club

Spicy Potato Soup

1 pound ground chuck
4 cups chopped potatoes
1 onion, chopped
3 (8-ounce) cans tomato sauce

4 cups water
1 tablespoon hot sauce
Salt and pepper to taste

Brown the ground chuck in a large saucepan, stirring until crumbly; drain. Add the potatoes, onion and tomato sauce and mix well. Stir in the water, hot sauce, salt and pepper. Bring to a boil; reduce heat. Simmer for 1 hour or until the potatoes are tender and the soup has thickened, stirring occasionally. Yield: 6 to 8 servings.

Donna Jean Bowman, Birmingham South Cahaba Council

Pretzel Strawberry Salad

2²/₃ cups crushed pretzels
³/₄ cup (1¹/₂ sticks) margarine,
  melted
3 tablespoons sugar
8 ounces cream cheese,
  softened
1 cup sugar

8 ounces whipped topping
1 (6-ounce) package
  strawberry gelatin
2 cups boiling water
2 (10-ounce) packages frozen
  strawberries

Combine the pretzels, margarine and 3 tablespoons sugar in a bowl and mix well. Press the pretzel mixture over the bottom of a 9x13-inch baking dish. Bake at 350 degrees for 8 minutes. Let stand until cool. Beat the cream cheese and 1 cup sugar in a mixer bowl until creamy. Fold in the whipped topping. Spread over the baked layer. Chill in the refrigerator. Dissolve the gelatin in the boiling water in a heatproof bowl. Stir in the frozen strawberries. Chill until partially set. Spoon over the prepared layers. Chill until set. Top with additional whipped topping if desired. Yield: 15 servings.

Emily Coburn, Selma Life Member Club

Spring Salad

6 to 8 ounces cream cheese,
  cubed
2 tablespoons vinegar
1 (20-ounce) can crushed
  pineapple, drained
1 cup chopped nuts

2½ cups miniature
  marshmallows
1 (6-ounce) package lime
  gelatin
3 cups boiling water

Soften the cream cheese in the vinegar in a bowl. Stir in the pineapple and nuts. Chill, covered, in the refrigerator. Combine the marshmallows, gelatin and boiling water in a heatproof bowl and stir until the gelatin dissolves and the marshmallows melt. Chill until partially set. Fold in the cream cheese mixture. Spoon into a shallow dish. Chill, covered, until set. Yield: 6 servings.

Mary Smith and Carleen White, Birmingham South Cahaba Council

Cracker Salad

1 sleeve saltines, crushed
1 cup chopped drained sweet
  pickles
1 cup chopped onion
1 cup chopped green bell
  pepper

1 (2-ounce) jar pimento,
  drained
1½ cups mayonnaise
5 hard-cooked eggs, chopped

Combine the crackers, pickles, onion, green pepper and pimento in a bowl and mix well. Stir in the mayonnaise. Fold in the eggs. Chill, covered, until serving time. Yield: 4 to 6 servings.

Vauline Terry, Tuscaloosa Council

Green Wonder Salad

1 (16-ounce) can French-style
    green beans, drained
1 (14-ounce) can Chinese
    vegetables, drained
2 (8-ounce) cans sliced water
    chestnuts, drained
1 (8-ounce) can green peas,
    drained

3 medium red onions, sliced
1 cup chopped celery
1 cup sugar
3/4 cup cider vinegar
1 teaspoon salt
1/4 teaspoon pepper

Combine the green beans, Chinese vegetables, water chestnuts,
peas, onions and celery in a bowl and mix gently. Whisk the sugar,
vinegar, salt and pepper in a bowl. Pour over the vegetable mixture
and toss to coat. Chill, covered, until serving time.
Yield: 6 to 8 servings.

Sharon Coffield, Birmingham South Cahaba Council

Oriental Slaw

2 (3-ounce) packages beef
    ramen noodles with
    seasoning packets
1 to 2 pounds Chinese
    cabbage, shredded
1 cup thinly sliced purple
    onion

1 cup slivered almonds,
    toasted
1 cup sunflower seed kernels
1/2 cup salad oil
1/2 cup sugar
1/3 cup white vinegar

Crush the noodles, reserving the seasoning packets. Toss the
noodles, cabbage, onion, almonds and sunflower seed kernels in a
bowl. Whisk the reserved seasoning packets, salad oil, sugar and
vinegar in a bowl until the sugar dissolves. Pour over the noodle
mixture and toss gently to coat. Yield: 10 to 12 servings.

Debra Thompson, Birmingham South Cahaba Council

Beef and Mushroom Casserole

1 to 2 pounds beef tips
1 (10-ounce) can cream of
  mushroom soup

1 (10-ounce) can French
  onion soup

Brown the beef in a skillet; drain. Stir in the soups. Simmer until the beef is of the desired degree of tenderness and the sauce is of the desired consistency, stirring occasionally. Serve over hot cooked rice. The longer the simmering time the more tender the beef. Yield: 4 or 5 servings.

Jana Harmon, Alabama Telco Credit Union

Swedish Meat Rolls

1 head cabbage
1 pound beef steak, ground
1 cup cooked rice
2 tablespoons chopped green
  bell pepper

2 tablespoons chopped onion
Salt and pepper to taste
2 cups sauerkraut

Separate the cabbage into leaves. Dip the leaves in hot water just until wilted; drain. Combine the ground steak, rice, green pepper, onion, salt and pepper in a bowl and mix well. Shape the steak mixture into small logs. Wrap each log in a cabbage leaf. Arrange the rolls touching in a skillet. Add just enough hot water to almost cover the rolls. Top with the sauerkraut. Cook, covered, over low heat for 1 hour. Yield: 6 to 8 servings.

Lillian Jones, Riverchase Council

Cabbage Rolls

1 large head cabbage
1 pound ground chuck
1 small onion, finely chopped
1 rib celery, finely chopped
1/4 cup instant rice, cooked
1 teaspoon salt
1/2 teaspoon MSG

1/4 teaspoon pepper
1/4 teaspoon soy sauce
Vegetable oil for frying
1 (10-ounce) can cream of
  mushroom soup
1 (10-ounce) can onion soup
Flour

Boil the cabbage in enough water to cover in a large saucepan until tender-crisp; drain. Separate the leaves. Combine the ground chuck, onion, celery, rice, salt, MSG, pepper and soy sauce in a bowl and mix well. Spoon about 2 tablespoons of the ground chuck mixture in the center of each cabbage leaf. Roll up, folding in the sides to enclose the filling; secure with kitchen twine. Fry in oil in a skillet until brown on all sides. Transfer to a Dutch oven using a slotted spoon, reserving the pan drippings. Pour a mixture of the soups over the rolls. Add enough flour and water to the reserved drippings to make gravy, scraping the brown bits off the bottom of the skillet. Add to the Dutch oven and mix well. Cook over low heat for 3 hours, stirring occasionally or bake in a 325-degree oven for several hours. Yield: 6 to 8 servings.

Mrs. Bob H. Henson, Birmingham South Life Member Club

Idaho Tacos

1 pound ground beef
1 envelope taco seasoning mix
4 baking potatoes, baked

1 cup shredded sharp Cheddar
  cheese
1 cup chopped green onions

Brown the ground beef in a skillet, stirring until crumbly; drain. Stir in the seasoning mix. Cook using package directions. Cut an x in the top of each potato. Fluff the pulp with a fork. Spoon the ground beef mixture over the potatoes. Sprinkle with the cheese and green onions. Serve with salsa. Yield: 4 servings.

Vauline Terry, Tuscaloosa Council

Colcannon

1 pound kale
Salt to taste
⅔ cup milk or half-and-half
2 green onions, chopped
1 pound unpeeled potatoes,
  cooked, drained

¼ cup (½ stick) butter,
  softened
Pepper to taste

Remove the stalks from the kale and finely chop the leaves, discarding the stalks. Combine the kale and salt with enough water to cover in a saucepan. Cook until tender; drain. Simmer the milk and green onions in a saucepan for 5 minutes. Peel the potatoes and mash in a bowl. Stir in the kale, milk mixture and butter. Season with salt and pepper. Stir until fluffy, adding additional butter and milk if needed. Serve with a dollop of additional butter on top. Yield: 4 to 6 servings.

John Kemp, Birmingham South Life Member Club

Tomato Pie

1½ cups drained chopped
  tomatoes
1 baked (9-inch) pie shell,
  cooled

1 cup mayonnaise
1 cup shredded cheese
3 tablespoons chopped green
  onions with tops

Spread the tomatoes over the bottom of the pie shell. Combine the mayonnaise, cheese and green onions in a bowl and mix well. Spoon over the tomatoes. Bake at 350 degrees for 30 minutes. Yield: 6 servings.

Johnnie Brown, Montgomery Life Member Club

Daddy Huff Corn Bread

1 cup self-rising cornmeal   1½ cups buttermilk
1 cup self-rising flour   ½ cup water
2 teaspoons sugar   2 eggs
1 teaspoon baking powder   1 tablespoon mayonnaise

Sift the cornmeal, flour, sugar and baking powder into a bowl and
mix well. Combine the buttermilk, water, eggs and mayonnaise in
a bowl and stir until blended. Add the cornmeal mixture and mix
well. Spoon the batter into a greased cast-iron skillet. Bake at 400
degrees until brown. Yield: 6 servings.

Judy Howard, Riverchase Council

Broccoli Corn Bread

½ cup (1 stick) margarine   1 cup cottage cheese
1 (9-ounce) package corn   1 onion, chopped
   muffin mix   4 eggs, lightly beaten
1 (10-ounce) package frozen   ¼ cup vegetable oil
   broccoli, chopped, drained

Heat the margarine in a skillet in a 400-degree oven until melted.
Combine the muffin mix, broccoli, cottage cheese, onion, eggs and
oil in a bowl and mix well. Spoon into the prepared skillet. Bake
for 30 minutes. Yield: 6 servings.

Rebecca Stancil, in memory of her mother, Betty Jones,
Decatur Council

Corn Muffins

1½ cups self-rising cornmeal
½ cup self-rising flour
1 cup buttermilk
½ cup egg substitute
¼ cup soft spread, melted

½ cup drained whole kernel
corn
½ cup cubed Cheddar cheese
⅓ cup chopped red bell pepper
¼ cup chopped green onions

Combine the cornmeal and flour in a bowl and mix well. Stir in the buttermilk, egg substitute and soft spread. Add the corn, cheese, red pepper and green onions and mix well. Spoon the batter into 12 greased muffin cups. Bake at 350 degrees for 20 to 25 minutes or until brown. Serve warm. Yield: 12 muffins.

Della Pearl Dukes, Bon Secour Life Member Club

Brownie Delight

1 (22-ounce) package
brownie mix
1 cup chopped pecans

2 (4-ounce) packages
chocolate instant
pudding mix
8 ounces whipped topping

Prepare and bake the brownies using package directions, adding 1 cup pecans. Let stand until cool. Crumble the brownies into a 9x13-inch dish. Prepare the pudding mixes using package directions. Spread over the prepared layer. Top with the whipped topping. Garnish with additional chopped pecans and/or chocolate chips. Yield: 15 servings.

Faye Harper, Tuscaloosa Council

Six-Flavor Pound Cake

3 cups sifted flour
1/2 teaspoon baking powder
3 cups sugar
1 cup (2 sticks) butter,
　softened
1/2 cup shortening
5 eggs
1 teaspoon vanilla extract

1 teaspoon coconut extract
1 teaspoon almond extract
1 teaspoon lemon extract
1 teaspoon vanilla butter and
　nut extract
1 teaspoon rum extract
1 cup evaporated milk
Six-Flavor Glaze

Combine the flour and baking powder in a bowl and mix well. Beat the sugar, butter and shortening in a mixer bowl at medium speed until creamy. Add the eggs 1 at a time, beating well after each addition. Add the flavorings 1 at a time, mixing well after each addition. Add the flour mixture alternately with the evaporated milk, mixing at low speed until blended. Spoon the batter into a greased and floured 10-inch tube pan. Bake at 300 degrees for 1 3/4 hours. Pierce the top of the warm cake with a wooden pick. Drizzle with the cooled Six-Flavor Glaze. Let stand for 15 to 20 minutes. Remove to a cake platter to cool completely. Yield: 16 servings.

Six-Flavor Glaze

1 cup sugar
1/4 cup water
1/2 teaspoon vanilla extract
1/2 teaspoon coconut extract
1/2 teaspoon almond extract

1/2 teaspoon lemon extract
1/2 teaspoon vanilla butter and
　nut extract
1/2 teaspoon rum extract

Combine the sugar, water and flavorings in a saucepan and mix well. Cook over low heat until the sugar dissolves, stirring constantly. Let stand until cool.

Mauntez Mayer, Anniston Council

Old-Fashioned Rice Pudding

2 cups cooked rice   *2 eggs, lightly beaten*
2 cups milk   *½ teaspoon vanilla extract*
⅓ cup sugar

Combine the rice, milk, sugar, eggs and vanilla in a bowl and mix well. Spoon into a greased 1½-quart baking dish. Place in a shallow baking pan. Add enough water to reach halfway up the sides of the baking dish. Bake at 350 degrees for 1 hour or until set.
Yield: 6 servings.

Vauline Terry, Tuscaloosa Council

Peanut Brittle

2 cups raw peanuts   *1 cup light corn syrup*
2 cups sugar   *1 teaspoon baking soda*
1 cup water

Combine the peanuts, sugar, water and corn syrup in a saucepan and mix well. Bring to a boil. Boil until golden brown or until the peanuts start popping. Remove from heat. Stir in the baking soda quickly. Spread on a buttered baking sheet. Let stand until cool. Break into pieces. Yield: 2 pounds.

Susan Poe, Riverchase Council

Stuff a miniature marshmallow in the bottom of a sugar cone to prevent ice cream drips.

Oatmeal Nut Cookies

1½ cups sifted flour
1 teaspoon baking soda
½ teaspoon salt
2 cups quick-cooking oats
1 cup chopped nuts

1 cup shortening
¾ cup sugar
¾ cup packed brown sugar
2 eggs
1 teaspoon vanilla extract

Sift the flour, baking soda and salt into a bowl and mix well. Stir in the oats and nuts. Beat the shortening, sugar, brown sugar, eggs and vanilla in a mixer bowl until creamy. Stir in the flour mixture. Drop by teaspoonfuls 2 inches apart onto a lightly greased cookie sheet. Bake at 375 degrees for 10 minutes. Cool on cookie sheet for 2 minutes. Remove to a wire rack to cool completely.
Yield: 6 dozen cookies.

Pat Ramsey, sister of Cathy Kelley,
Birmingham South Cahaba Council

Redwood Room Apple Pie

½ cup sugar
1 tablespoon cornstarch
¼ cup heavy cream
3 tablespoons butter
1 tablespoon lemon juice
1 (16-ounce) can sliced
   apples, drained

1 baked (9-inch) pie shell
8 ounces cream cheese,
   softened
½ cup sugar
1 egg
½ cup shredded coconut
½ cup chopped pecans

Combine ½ cup sugar and cornstarch in a saucepan and mix well. Stir in the cream. Bring to a boil over medium heat, stirring frequently. Stir in the butter and lemon juice. Add the apples and mix well. Simmer for 10 minutes, stirring occasionally. Let stand until cool. Spoon the apple mixture into the pie shell. Beat the cream cheese and ½ cup sugar in a mixer bowl until fluffy. Add the egg and beat until blended. Spread over the filling, sealing to the edge. Sprinkle with the coconut and pecans. Bake at 350 degrees for 15 to 20 minutes or until golden brown. Yield: 6 to 8 servings.

Sadie Williams Bryars, Mobile Council

Caramel Pie

2 (14-ounce) cans sweetened
    condensed milk
1 (9-inch) graham cracker pie
    shell

8 ounces frozen whipped
    topping, thawed
1 (1-ounce) English toffee
    candy bar, coarsely chopped

Pour the condensed milk into a 1-quart slow cooker. Cook, covered, on Low for 6 to 7 hours or until caramel in color, whisking every 30 minutes. Pour into the pie shell. Let stand until cool. Spread the whipped topping over the filling, sealing to the edge. Sprinkle with the candy. Chill, covered, until serving time. Yield: 6 to 8 servings.

Susan Poe, Riverchase Council

Coconut Pie

2 cups milk
1 cup shredded coconut
4 eggs, lightly beaten

½ cup baking mix
¼ cup (½ stick) margarine,
    melted

Combine all the ingredients in a bowl and mix for 3 minutes. Pour into a greased pie plate. Let stand for 5 minutes. Bake at 350 degrees for 40 to 45 minutes or until set. Yield: 6 servings.

Susan Poe, Riverchase Council

Impossible Coconut Pies

1¾ cups sugar
4 eggs
¼ cup (½ stick) margarine,
    melted

2 cups milk
1 can flaked coconut
½ cup flour
1 teaspoon vanilla extract

Combine the sugar, eggs and margarine in a mixer bowl. Beat until blended. Add the milk, coconut, flour and vanilla and beat until mixed. Pour into 2 buttered pie plates. Bake at 350 degrees for 30 minutes. Yield: 12 servings.

Bernice Moore, Birmingham South Cahaba Council

Egg Custard Pie

1 cup sugar
5 tablespoons flour
1/8 teaspoon salt
1 cup milk
4 eggs, beaten

1 (5-ounce) can evaporated
  milk
2 teaspoons margarine, melted
1 teaspoon vanilla extract

Combine the sugar, flour and salt in a bowl and mix well. Stir in the milk, eggs, evaporated milk, margarine and vanilla. Pour into a buttered pie plate. Bake at 375 degrees for 30 to 35 minutes or until set. May add 1 cup shredded coconut for a coconut custard pie. Yield: 6 servings.

Eloise Simmons, Anniston Council

Pecan Tarts

1/2 cup (1 stick) margarine,
  softened
3 ounces cream cheese,
  softened
1 cup flour
1 3/4 cups pecan halves
3/4 cup sugar

3/4 cup corn syrup
1/2 cup (1 stick) margarine
1/4 cup packed light brown
  sugar
3 eggs, beaten
1 teaspoon vanilla extract
1/8 teaspoon salt

Beat 1/2 cup margarine, cream cheese and flour in a mixer bowl until blended. Press the cream cheese mixture over the bottom and up the sides of 24 miniature muffin cups. Place approximately 4 pecan halves in each muffin cup. Combine the sugar, corn syrup, 1/2 cup margarine and brown sugar in a saucepan. Bring the mixture to a boil over medium heat, stirring constantly. Stir a small amount of the hot mixture into the eggs. Stir the eggs into the hot mixture. Add the vanilla and salt and mix well. Pour into the prepared muffin cups, filling 3/4 full. Bake at 375 degrees for 30 minutes. Yield: 2 dozen tarts.

Judy Boozer, Birmingham South Cahaba Council

SPRING

Buttermilk Salad

1 (15-ounce) can crushed
    pineapple
1 (6-ounce) package apricot
    gelatin

2 cups buttermilk
8 ounces whipped topping
1 cup chopped pecans

Drain the pineapple, reserving the juice. Bring the reserved juice
and gelatin to a boil in a small saucepan, stirring frequently. Let
stand until cool. Combine the gelatin mixture, buttermilk and
pineapple in a bowl and stir until blended. Fold in the whipped
topping. Stir in the pecans. Spoon into a 9x13-inch serving dish.
Chill, covered, for 8 hours or until set. May substitute your favorite
flavored gelatin. Yield: 8 to 10 servings.

Mrs. Bob H. Henson, Birmingham South Life Member Club

Fruit Salad

2 to 3 bananas, sliced
Lemon juice
1 (21-ounce) can peach
    pie filling
1 (20-ounce) can pineapple
    chunks, drained

1 (10-ounce) package frozen
    strawberries, thawed,
    drained

Sprinkle the bananas with lemon juice. Combine the bananas, pie
filling, pineapple and strawberries in a bowl and mix well. Chill,
covered, until ready to serve. Yield: 6 servings.

Faye King, Huntsville Council

Orange Salad

1 (3-ounce) package orange
  gelatin
1 (3-ounce) package lemon
  gelatin
1 cup boiling water
1 (20-ounce) can crushed
  pineapple, partially drained
3 (11-ounce) cans mandarin
  oranges, partially drained

1 (10-ounce) package
  miniature marshmallows
8 ounces whipped topping
1 cup mayonnaise
2 cups shredded sharp
  Cheddar cheese

Dissolve the gelatin in the boiling water in a heatproof bowl. Stir in the pineapple and mandarin oranges. Pour the gelatin mixture into a 9x13-inch serving dish. Let stand until partially set. Sprinkle the marshmallows over the top. Chill, covered, until set. Combine the whipped topping and mayonnaise in a small bowl and stir until blended. Spread the mayonnaise mixture over the marshmallows. Sprinkle with the Cheddar cheese. Chill, covered, until ready to serve. Yield: 8 to 10 servings.

Berniece Peterson, Birmingham South Life Member Club

Orange Carrot Salad

3 cups shredded carrots
2 oranges, sectioned
3 tablespoons lemon juice

1 tablespoon sugar
1 teaspoon cinnamon
Dash of salt

Combine the carrots and oranges in a bowl and mix well. Add the lemon juice, sugar, cinnamon and salt and mix well. Chill, covered, until ready to serve. Yield: 4 to 6 servings.

Iris Rowe, Birmingham South Life Member Club

Pineapple Cream Cheese Molded Salad

1 (20-ounce) can juice-pack   1 (2-ounce) jar pimento,
  crushed pineapple   drained
1 (3-ounce) package lemon   ½ cup chopped celery
  gelatin   1 cup whipped cream
3 ounces cream cheese,   ⅛ teaspoon salt
  softened

Drain the pineapple, reserving the juice. Combine the reserved juice and gelatin in a small saucepan and mix well. Cook over low heat until gelatin is dissolved, stirring constantly. Combine the cream cheese and pimento in a bowl and mix well. Stir in the gelatin mixture. Add the pineapple, celery, whipped cream and salt and mix well. Pour into a gelatin mold. Chill, covered, for 3 to 8 hours. May substitute sugar-free gelatin and low-calorie whipping cream. Yield: 6 servings.

Mrs. Bob H. Henson, Birmingham South Life Member Club

Yum-Yum Salad

1 (20-ounce) can crushed   16 ounces cottage cheese
  pineapple   1 cup chopped pecans or
1 envelope unflavored gelatin   walnuts
2 tablespoons cold water   Maraschino cherries
1 cup sugar   (optional)
2 tablespoons lemon juice
1 cup whipping cream,
  whipped

Drain the pineapple, reserving the juice. Soften the gelatin in the cold water in a saucepan. Stir in the sugar, reserved juice and lemon juice. Bring to a boil, stirring constantly. Remove from the heat. Let stand until cool. Fold in the whipped cream. Stir in the cottage cheese, pineapple, pecans and cherries. Spoon into a gelatin mold or serving dish. Chill, covered, until set. Yield: 8 servings.

Betty Hyte, Montgomery Council

Coleslaw

1 head cabbage, shredded
2 carrots, shredded
1 onion, chopped
½ cup mayonnaise

½ cup sugar
2 tablespoons tarragon vinegar
2 tablespoons vegetable oil
1 teaspoon salt

Combine the cabbage, carrots and onion in a large bowl and mix well. Combine the mayonnaise, sugar, vinegar, oil and salt in a bowl and stir until blended. Pour over the cabbage mixture, tossing to coat. Chill, covered, until ready to serve. Yield: 6 to 8 servings.

Betty Foshee, Decatur Council

Rice Salad

3 cups cooked rice
1 cup chopped cucumber
1 cup chopped seeded tomato
1 cup chopped purple onion

1 (6-ounce) jar marinated
   artichoke hearts
Salt to taste

Combine the rice, cucumber, tomato, onion, artichoke hearts and salt in a bowl and mix well. Chill, covered, until ready to serve. Serve over your favorite salad greens. Yield: 6 to 8 servings.

Marcelle Kelley, mother-in-law of Cathy Kelley,
Birmingham South Cahaba Council

Shrimp and Artichoke Pasta

3 tablespoons olive oil
2 garlic cloves, minced
1 onion, cut into eighths
1 pound shrimp, cooked
2 (6-ounce) jars marinated
    artichoke hearts
1 (7-ounce) jar pimentos

½ cup black olives
Salt to taste
Pepper to taste
¾ pound angel hair pasta,
    cooked, drained
Parmesan cheese

Heat the oil in a large skillet over medium heat. Add the garlic and onion and cook for 10 minutes or until translucent, stirring occasionally. Stir in the shrimp and heat through. Stir in the artichoke hearts, pimentos and olives and heat through. Sprinkle with salt and pepper. Spoon over the pasta on a serving platter. Sprinkle with the Parmesan cheese. Yield: 4 servings.

Patricia Newton, Huntsville Council

Chicken Pie

1 (3½-pound) chicken
1 (10-ounce) can cream of
    chicken soup

½ cup (1 stick) margarine
1½ cups self-rising flour
1 cup milk

Boil the chicken in water to cover in a stockpot until cooked through. Remove the chicken to a cutting board, reserving 2 cups of the broth. Chop the chicken, discarding the skin and bones. Combine the reserved broth and soup in a bowl and stir until blended. Add the chicken and mix well. Spoon the mixture into a 9x13-inch baking dish. Cut the margarine into the flour in a small bowl until crumbly. Stir in the milk gradually until blended. Drop the flour mixture by spoonfuls over the chicken mixture. Bake at 375 degrees for 45 minutes. Yield: 8 servings.

Janice Bass, Riverchase Council

Herbed Chicken

3 whole chicken breasts
1 (6-ounce) package long
  grain and wild rice
3/4 cup sauterne
1 (10-ounce) can cream of
  chicken soup

1/4 cup (1/2 stick) margarine
1/2 cup sliced celery
1 (3-ounce) can sliced
  mushrooms, drained
2 tablespoons chopped pimento

Boil the chicken in water to cover in a stockpot until cooked through. Remove the chicken to a cutting board. Let stand until cool. Chop the chicken, discarding the skin and bones. Prepare the rice using package directions. Spoon the rice into a 1½-quart baking dish. Arrange the chicken over the top of the rice. Add the sauterne to the soup in a skillet over medium heat, stirring until blended. Add the margarine, celery, mushrooms and pimento. Cook until the margarine is melted, stirring constantly. Bring to a boil, stirring frequently. Pour the soup mixture over the chicken. Bake, covered, at 350 degrees for 25 minutes. Bake, uncovered, for 15 to 20 minutes longer or until cooked through. Yield: 6 servings.

Kathy R. Pager, Bon Secour Life Member Club

Chicken Potpie

3/4 cup sliced carrots
1/2 cup chopped onion
1/2 cup chopped celery
2½ cups chicken broth
2½ cups chopped cooked
  chicken

1 (10-ounce) can cream of
  chicken soup
3/4 cup frozen green peas
2 hard-cooked eggs, chopped
1 recipe (2-crust) pie pastry

Cook the carrots, onion and celery in the broth in a large skillet until tender-crisp. Remove from the heat. Add the chicken, soup, peas and eggs and mix well. Spoon the chicken mixture into a pastry-lined baking dish. Top with the remaining pastry, sealing the edge and cutting vents. Bake at 400 degrees for 45 minutes. Yield: 8 servings.

Faith Kirby Richardson, Gadsden Life Member Club

Chicketti

2 cups bite-size spaghetti
   pieces, cooked, drained
2 cups chopped cooked
   chicken
1 cup chicken broth
1 (10-ounce) can cream of
   mushroom soup
½ cup shredded Cheddar
   cheese

½ onion, chopped
¼ cup pimentos, drained
¼ cup chopped green bell
   pepper
½ teaspoon salt
¼ teaspoon pepper
½ cup shredded Cheddar
   cheese

Combine the pasta, chicken, broth, soup, ½ cup Cheddar cheese, onion, pimentos, green pepper, salt and pepper in a large bowl and mix well. Spoon into a greased 3-quart baking dish. Sprinkle with ½ cup Cheddar cheese. Bake at 325 degrees for 45 to 60 minutes or until cooked through. Yield: 8 servings.

Maureen W. Sewell, Birmingham Life Member Club

Chicken that is pierced with a fork while cooking loses its flavorful juices, so always turn chicken with tongs.

Chicken Casserole

1 quart water
4 ounces elbow macaroni
1 tablespoon olive oil
3 cups chopped cooked
  chicken
1 cup sour cream
2 (3-ounce) cans sliced
  mushrooms, drained
1 (8-ounce) can sliced water
  chestnuts, drained
1 (10-ounce) can cream of
  mushroom soup

1 (10-ounce) can cream of
  celery soup
1 tablespoon poppy seeds
1/4 teaspoon salt
1/4 teaspoon pepper
1 cup shredded sharp Cheddar
  cheese
1 sleeve butter crackers,
  crushed
1/2 cup (1 stick) margarine,
  melted (optional)

Bring the water to a boil in a large saucepan over high heat. Add the macaroni and olive oil. Cook using package directions; drain. Combine the macaroni, chicken, sour cream, mushrooms, water chestnuts, soups, poppy seeds, salt and pepper in a large bowl and mix well. Spoon the chicken mixture into a 9x13-inch baking dish. Top with the cheese. Sprinkle the crackers over the cheese. Pour the margarine over the top. Bake at 350 degrees for 35 to 45 minutes or until cooked through. Yield: 8 to 10 servings.

Barbara and Bill Dalton, Riverchase Council

Chicken Pleaser Casserole

8 ounces medium noodles,
cooked, drained
2 cups chopped cooked
chicken
1 (10-ounce) can cream of
chicken soup
¼ cup (½ stick) butter, melted
1½ cups sour cream

1½ cups shredded Cheddar
cheese
3 green onions, chopped
½ teaspoon salt
¼ teaspoon pepper
½ cup shredded Cheddar
cheese
½ cup cornflakes

Mix the noodles and chicken in a large bowl. Combine the soup and butter in a bowl and mix well. Stir in the sour cream, 1½ cups Cheddar cheese, green onions, salt and pepper. Pour the soup mixture over the chicken mixture and stir until blended. Spoon into a greased 2½-quart baking dish. Bake at 350 degrees for 30 minutes. Mix ½ cup Cheddar cheese and cornflakes in a small bowl. Sprinkle over the chicken mixture. Bake for 10 to 15 minutes longer or until the cheese is melted. Yield: 6 to 8 servings.

Faye S. King, Huntsville Council

Boston Butt Roast

1 (4- to 6-pound) Boston
butt roast
½ (10-ounce) bottle Dale's
steak seasoning
Salt and pepper to taste
1 onion, chopped

½ green bell pepper, chopped
½ red bell pepper, chopped
½ yellow bell pepper, chopped
Meat tenderizer to taste
Cajun seasoning to taste
Bacon bits

Place the roast on 2 large sheets of heavy-duty foil. Pour the Dale's seasoning over the top. Sprinkle with salt and pepper. Arrange the onion and bell peppers over the top. Sprinkle with the meat tenderizer and Cajun seasoning. Sprinkle the bacon bits over the top. Fold the foil to enclose and seal the edges. Grill over hot coals for 4 to 5 hours or until the roast is cooked through and the vegetables are tender. Yield: 10 servings.

Bernice Adams, Huntsville Council

Ham Steak

1 (14-ounce) jar spiced apple
   rings
1 cup packed brown sugar

1 teaspoon dry mustard
1 (1½-inch-thick) ham steak
Cumberland Sauce (optional)

Drain the apples, reserving the juice. Combine the reserved juice, brown sugar and mustard in a shallow dish and mix well. Marinate the ham steak in the brown sugar mixture for 2 hours. Grill over hot coals for 20 minutes, turning once. Place the ham steak on a serving platter. Arrange the apple rings around the ham steak. Serve with the Cumberland Sauce. Garnish with julienned lemon and orange peel. Yield: 4 servings.

Cumberland Sauce

1 cup red currant jelly
1 cup orange juice
½ cup chopped onion
½ cup lemon juice
½ cup port

1 tablespoon dry mustard
¼ teaspoon ground ginger
Tabasco sauce to taste
1½ tablespoons arrowroot

Combine the jelly, orange juice, onion, lemon juice, port, mustard, ginger and Tabasco sauce in a saucepan and mix well. Bring to a boil over medium heat, stirring frequently. Strain the mixture, discarding the onion. Return the juice mixture to the saucepan. Stir in the arrowroot. Cook over medium heat until thickened, stirring constantly.

Betty B. Bush, Montgomery Council

Greek-Grilled Grouper

2 (1-pound) grouper fillets   2 tablespoons lemon juice
½ cup olive oil   1 teaspoon oregano

Cut the fillets into halves. Rinse and pat dry. Arrange the fillets in
a shallow dish. Whisk the olive oil, lemon juice and oregano in a
bowl. Pour ⅓ cup of the marinade over the fillets, turning to coat.
Marinate, covered, in the refrigerator for 2 hours. Place the fillets
in a grilling basket. Grill over hot coals until the fish flakes easily.
Serve with the remaining marinade. Yield: 4 servings.

Mickey Deal, Birmingham South Cahaba Council

Broccoli Casserole

½ cup chopped celery   1 (8-ounce) roll garlic cheese
  (optional)   2 (10-ounce) packages frozen
½ cup chopped onion   broccoli, cooked, drained
  (optional)   ½ cup cracker crumbs
½ cup (1 stick) margarine   ½ cup sliced almonds
  (optional)
1 (10-ounce) can cream of
  mushroom soup

Sauté the celery and onion in the margarine in a small skillet over
medium heat until brown. Combine the soup and garlic cheese in
a saucepan. Cook over medium heat until blended, stirring
frequently. Combine the celery mixture, soup mixture and broccoli
in a bowl and mix well. Spoon into a 2-quart baking dish. Combine
the cracker crumbs and almonds in a small bowl, tossing to mix.
Sprinkle over the broccoli mixture. Bake at 350 degrees for 15
minutes or until brown. Yield: 6 to 8 servings.

Ann Sellers, Tuscaloosa Council

Broccoli Cheese Casserole

2 (10-ounce) packages frozen
    broccoli
1 onion, chopped
¼ cup (½ stick) margarine
1 (10-ounce) can cream of
    mushroom soup
1 (3-ounce) can mushrooms,
    chopped

¼ cup Cheez Whiz
¼ cup slivered almonds
Parsley to taste
¼ cup (½ stick) margarine,
    melted
2 cups herb-seasoned
    stuffing mix

Cook the broccoli in a saucepan until tender-crisp using package directions; drain. Sauté the onion in ¼ cup margarine in a small skillet over medium heat until tender. Combine the broccoli, onion, soup, mushrooms, Cheez Whiz, almonds and parsley in a bowl and mix well. Spoon into a greased 2-quart baking dish. Combine ¼ cup melted margarine and stuffing mix in a bowl and mix well. Spread over the broccoli mixture. Bake at 350 degrees for 30 minutes. Yield: 6 to 8 servings.

Linda Cunningham, Birmingham Metro Council

*To keep potatoes from budding, place an apple
in the bag with the potatoes.*

Carrot Coin Casserole

12 carrots, sliced
1 onion, cut into ¼-inch
  pieces
2 cups frozen green peas
1 tablespoon butter or
  margarine
2 tablespoons flour
1 teaspoon salt

¼ teaspoon pepper
¼ teaspoon nutmeg
2½ cups milk
1½ cups shredded Cheddar
  cheese
3 tablespoons butter or
  margarine
1 cup crushed butter crackers

Cook the carrots in a small amount of water in a saucepan over
medium heat for 6 minutes or until tender-crisp. Stir in the onion.
Bring to a boil. Reduce the heat and simmer, covered, for 4 to 6
minutes or until the onion is tender-crisp; drain. Add the peas and
toss to mix. Melt 1 tablespoon butter in a small saucepan over
medium heat. Add the flour, salt, pepper and nutmeg, stirring until
blended. Add the milk gradually, stirring constantly. Bring to a boil.
Boil for 2 minutes, stirring constantly. Spoon 4 cups of the carrot
mixture into a shallow greased 3-quart baking dish. Sprinkle with
the cheese. Spoon the remaining carrot mixture over the cheese.
Pour the milk mixture over the top. Melt 3 tablespoons butter in a
small saucepan over medium heat. Stir in the crackers. Cook until
crackers are toasted, stirring frequently. Sprinkle over the prepared
dish. Bake at 350 degrees for 30 to 40 minutes or until bubbly.
Yield: 10 to 12 servings.

Donna Jean Bowman, Birmingham South Cahaba Council

Green Bean and Corn Casserole

2 (16-ounce) cans French-
style green beans, drained
1 (11-ounce) can Shoe Peg
corn, drained
1½ cups shredded Cheddar
cheese

1 cup sour cream
1 (10-ounce) can cream of
celery soup
1 sleeve butter crackers,
crushed
½ cup (1 stick) butter, melted

Arrange the green beans in a 9x13-inch baking dish. Pour the corn over the green beans. Combine the Cheddar cheese, sour cream and soup in a bowl and mix well. Spread the cheese mixture over the corn. Sprinkle with the cracker crumbs. Pour the butter over the top. Bake at 350 degrees for 35 to 45 minutes or until hot and bubbly. Yield: 8 to 10 servings.

Lori Ann Avant, Alabama Telco Credit Union

Zucchini Casserole

2 zucchini, sliced
2 carrots, sliced
1 onion, chopped
2 tablespoons margarine
1 cup shredded Cheddar
cheese

1 cup sour cream
½ teaspoon salt
½ teaspoon pepper
2 tablespoons Italian-style
bread crumbs

Sauté the zucchini, carrots and onion in the margarine in a skillet over medium heat for 8 to 10 minutes or until tender-crisp. Remove from the heat. Stir in the cheese, sour cream, salt and pepper and mix well. Spoon into a greased 1-quart baking dish. Sprinkle with the bread crumbs. Bake at 350 degrees for 25 minutes. Yield: 6 servings.

Mary Ann Sparks Fulmer, Shoals Life Member Club

Easy Cheese Apples

2 (20-ounce) cans sliced
  apples, drained
1/2 cup (1 stick) butter,
  softened

1 cup sugar
3/4 cup self-rising flour
2 cups shredded Velveeta
  cheese

Arrange the apples in a 9x13-inch baking dish. Beat the butter and sugar in a mixer bowl until light and fluffy. Stir in the flour until mixture is crumbly. Add the Velveeta cheese and mix well. Sprinkle the cheese mixture over the apples. Bake at 325 to 350 degrees for 20 to 30 minutes or until light brown.
Yield: 8 to 10 servings.

Jan Holmes, Decatur Council

Easy Macaroni and Cheese

2 cups milk
1 1/2 cups shredded sharp
  Cheddar cheese
1/4 cup (1/2 stick) butter,
  melted

1 cup elbow macaroni
1 teaspoon salt
Dash of pepper
Dash of paprika

Pour the milk into a microwave-safe bowl. Microwave on High for 3 minutes. Combine the milk, Cheddar cheese, butter, macaroni, salt, pepper and paprika in a bowl and mix well. Spoon into a 1 1/2-quart baking dish. Bake, covered, at 350 degrees for 45 to 60 minutes or until cooked through. Yield: 6 servings.

Betty Darnell, Gadsden Life Member Club

Pineapple Casserole

2 (20-ounce) cans pineapple
  chunks
1/2 cup sugar
5 tablespoons flour
1 1/2 cups shredded Cheddar
  cheese

1 1/2 cups shredded mozzarella
  cheese
3/4 cup crushed butter crackers
1/2 cup (1 stick) butter, melted

Drain the pineapple, reserving 1/4 cup of the juice. Arrange the pineapple in a 2-quart baking dish. Combine the sugar and flour and mix well. Sprinkle over the pineapple. Combine the Cheddar cheese and mozzarella cheese and mix well. Sprinkle over the sugar mixture. Sprinkle with the cracker crumbs. Drizzle with the butter. Bake at 350 degrees for 30 minutes. Pour the reserved juice over the top. Serve immediately. Yield: 8 servings.

Donna McNulty, Riverchase Council

Broccoli Bread

1 (10-ounce) package frozen
  chopped broccoli, thawed,
  drained
1 (8-ounce) can Mexican
  corn, drained
4 eggs, beaten
1 onion, chopped

3/4 cup cottage cheese
1/2 cup (1 stick) margarine,
  melted
3/4 teaspoon salt
1 (9-ounce) package corn
  muffin mix

Combine the broccoli, corn, eggs, onion, cottage cheese, margarine and salt in a bowl and mix well. Add the corn muffin mix and stir just until moistened. Pour into a 9x13-inch baking pan. Bake at 375 degrees for 25 minutes. Yield: 12 to 15 servings.

Debbie Speaks, Montgomery Council

Sausage and Cheese Muffins

½ pound ground pork sausage
1 egg, beaten
1 cup milk
¼ cup (½ stick) butter,
  melted
2 cups flour

2 tablespoons sugar
1 tablespoon baking powder
¼ teaspoon salt
½ cup shredded Cheddar
  cheese

Brown the sausage in a skillet, stirring until crumbly; drain. Combine the egg, milk and butter in a bowl and mix well. Mix the flour, sugar, baking powder and salt in a mixer bowl. Make a well in the center. Pour in the milk mixture and stir just until moistened. Stir in the sausage and cheese. Spoon into paper-lined muffin cups, filling the cups. Bake at 375 degrees for 20 minutes or until golden brown. Yield: 12 servings.

Ann Sellers, Tuscaloosa Council

Cinnamon Squares

2 cups sifted flour
1½ tablespoons cinnamon
1 teaspoon salt
1 cup sugar
½ cup (1 stick) butter,
  softened

½ cup (1 stick) margarine,
  softened
1 egg, separated
1½ cups chopped pecans

Sift the flour, cinnamon and salt together. Cream the sugar, butter and margarine in a mixer bowl until light and fluffy. Stir in the egg yolk and flour mixture and mix well. Press the mixture into a greased and floured 10x15-inch baking pan. Beat the egg white in a mixer bowl until foamy. Spread over the prepared mixture in the pan. Press the pecans over the top. Bake at 325 degrees for 30 minutes. Cut into squares. Yield: 18 servings.

E.B. Thornton, Tuscaloosa Council

Graham Cracker Eclair Dessert

1 (6-ounce) package
   butterscotch instant
   pudding mix
1 (3-ounce) package chocolate
   instant pudding mix

1 cup confectioners' sugar
8 ounces whipped topping
1 (16-ounce) package graham
   crackers

Prepare the pudding mixes using package directions. Combine the butterscotch pudding and confectioners' sugar in a bowl and mix well. Fold in the whipped topping. Arrange a single layer of graham crackers in a 9x13-inch dish. Layer with half the butterscotch pudding mixture, graham crackers, remaining butterscotch pudding mixture and graham crackers. Top with the chocolate pudding. Chill, covered, until ready to serve. Yield: 18 servings.

Vicki Weyerbacher, Birmingham South Cahaba Council

Peach Delight

1 cup flour
1 cup chopped pecans
½ cup (1 stick) butter, melted
1 (6-ounce) package vanilla
   instant pudding mix
8 ounces cream cheese,
   softened

1 cup confectioners' sugar
1 cup whipped topping
1 (21-ounce) can peach pie
   filling

Combine the flour, pecans and butter in a bowl and mix well. Spread in a 9x13-inch baking dish. Bake at 375 degrees for 10 minutes. Let stand until cool. Prepare the vanilla pudding using package directions. Combine the cream cheese, confectioners' sugar and whipped topping in a bowl and stir until blended. Spread over the baked crust. Layer the vanilla pudding and peach pie filling over the top. Chill, covered, until ready to serve. Yield: 10 to 12 servings.

Polly Martin, Opelika Life Member Club

Strawberry Angel Food Cake Mold

1 (12-ounce) package frozen
  sliced strawberries, thawed
Hot water
1 (3-ounce) package
  strawberry gelatin

1 cup whipping cream,
  whipped
1 angel food cake, torn into
  pieces

Drain the strawberries, reserving the juice. Add enough hot water to the reserved juice to measure 2 cups. Dissolve the gelatin in the juice mixture in a mixer bowl. Chill, covered, until the mixture is slightly thickened. Beat the gelatin mixture until light and foamy. Fold the whipped cream into the gelatin mixture. Stir in the strawberries and angel food cake. Spoon into a 2-quart gelatin mold. Chill, covered, until set. Serve with whipped cream. Yield: 6 to 8 servings.

Mrs. Bob H. Henson, Birmingham South Life Member Club

Chocolate Chip Cheesecake

8 ounces cream cheese,
  softened
1 (14-ounce) can sweetened
  condensed milk
1 egg
1 teaspoon flour

1 teaspoon vanilla extract
1 cup semisweet chocolate
  chips
1/4 cup heavy cream
1/2 cup semisweet chocolate
  chips

Beat the cream cheese, condensed milk, egg, flour and vanilla in a mixer bowl until blended. Stir in 1 cup chocolate chips. Pour into a 9-inch springform pan. Bake at 350 degrees for 35 minutes or until set. Let stand until cool. Heat the cream and 1/2 cup chocolate chips in a small saucepan over low heat until blended, stirring constantly. Pour over the cheesecake. Chill, covered, until ready to serve. Yield: 6 to 8 servings.

April Sims, Birmingham South Cahaba Council

Best Banana Pudding

½ cup sugar
3 tablespoons flour
3 eggs, separated
1¾ cups milk
1 (14-ounce) can sweetened
   condensed milk

1 teaspoon vanilla extract
6 bananas, sliced
1 (12-ounce) package vanilla
   wafers
Pinch of cream of tartar
¼ cup sugar

Combine ½ cup sugar and flour in a double boiler and mix well. Stir in the egg yolks and milk. Cook over boiling water until the mixture begins to thicken, stirring constantly. Add the condensed milk. Heat until mixture thickens, stirring constantly. Remove from the heat. Stir in the vanilla. Alternate layers of the bananas, vanilla wafers and milk mixture in a 2-quart baking dish. Beat the egg whites and cream of tartar in a mixer bowl until stiff peaks form. Beat in ¼ cup sugar. Spread over the layers. Bake at 375 degrees for 10 to 12 minutes or until the top is browned. Yield: 8 servings.

Donna Jean Bowman, Birmingham South Cahaba Council

Banana Split Dessert

2 to 3 cups crushed vanilla
   wafers
½ cup (1 stick) margarine,
   melted
5 bananas, sliced
2 (14-ounce) cans sweetened
   condensed milk
½ cup lemon juice

1 (20-ounce) can crushed
   pineapple, drained
2 (10-ounce) packages frozen
   strawberries, thawed,
   drained
16 ounces whipped topping
½ cup chopped pecans

Mix the vanilla wafer crumbs and margarine in a bowl. Press over the bottom of a 9x13-inch dish. Arrange the bananas over the crust. Combine the condensed milk and lemon juice in a bowl and stir until blended. Spread over the top of the bananas. Layer the pineapple, strawberries and whipped topping over the top. Sprinkle with the pecans. Chill, covered, for 4 to 6 hours. Yield: 10 servings.

Kathryn Morgan, Gadsden Life Member Club

Angel Food Cake

2 packages angel food cake   1 teaspoon almond extract
  mix   1 teaspoon vanilla extract
1 cup water   4 to 5 egg whites

Combine 1 package angel food cake mix and water in a mixer bowl
and beat at low speed until blended. Beat at high speed for 5
minutes. Add the flavorings and mix well. Add the egg whites and
beat at high speed for 5 minutes. Add the remaining package of
angel food cake mix gradually, beating at low speed until blended.
Pour into a tube pan. Place in a cold oven. Bake at 350 degrees for
40 minutes. Invert on a funnel to cool completely. Loosen the cake
from the side of the pan. Invert onto a cake plate.
Yield: 16 servings.

Charlotte Flach, aunt of Cathy Kelley,
Birmingham South Cahaba Council

German Chocolate Upside-Down Cake

1 cup shredded coconut   ½ cup (1 stick) margarine
1 cup chopped pecans   8 ounces cream cheese
1 package German chocolate   1 (1-pound) package
  cake mix   confectioners' sugar

Combine the coconut and pecans in a bowl and mix well. Spread
over the bottom of a greased 9x13-inch cake pan. Prepare the cake
mix using package directions. Pour over the coconut mixture. Heat
the margarine and cream cheese in a saucepan over medium heat
until blended, stirring frequently. Stir in the confectioners' sugar.
Spoon over the top of the cake mixture. Bake at 350 degrees for 35
to 40 minutes or until cake tests done. Yield: 15 servings.

Judy Howard, Riverchase Council
Flo Watters, Selma Life Member Club

Coconut Cake

1½ cups sugar
¾ cup shortening
2 eggs
2 cups flour
1 cup milk
1 teaspoon vanilla extract

1 cup sugar
1 egg yolk
1 cup milk
1 (7-ounce) package frozen
    flaked coconut
Seven-Minute Frosting

Cream 1½ cups sugar and shortening in a mixer bowl until light and fluffy. Add the eggs 1 at a time, mixing well after each addition. Add the flour, 1 cup milk and vanilla and beat until blended. Pour into 3 greased and floured 9-inch round cake pans. Bake at 350 degrees for 30 minutes or until layers test done. Cool in the pans for 10 minutes. Remove to a wire rack to cool completely. Combine 1 cup sugar and egg yolk in a saucepan and stir until blended. Stir in 1 cup milk and coconut. Cook over low heat until the mixture is thickened, stirring constantly. Spread the coconut mixture between the layers of the cooled cake. Frost with Seven-Minute Frosting. May sprinkle additional coconut over the top.
Yield: 12 to 16 servings.

Seven-Minute Frosting

¾ cup sugar
⅓ cup light corn syrup
2 egg whites

2 tablespoons water
¼ teaspoon salt
¼ teaspoon cream of tartar

Beat the sugar, corn syrup, egg whites, water, salt and cream of tartar in a double boiler over high heat for 7 minutes or until stiff peaks form. Remove from heat. Beat until thickened.

Betty Foshee, Decatur Council

Easy Delicious Coconut Cake

1 (2-layer) package white
   cake mix
1½ cups milk
1 cup flaked coconut

½ cup sugar
3½ cups whipped topping
1 cup flaked coconut

Prepare and bake the cake using package directions for a 9x13-inch cake pan. Combine the milk, 1 cup coconut and sugar in a saucepan and mix well. Bring to a boil. Reduce the heat and simmer for 1 minute, stirring frequently. Punch holes in the top of the warm cake. Pour the coconut mixture over the cake. Let cake stand until cool. Combine the whipped topping and ½ cup of the coconut in a bowl and mix well. Spread cake with the whipped topping mixture and sprinkle with the remaining ½ cup coconut. Chill, covered, until ready to serve. Yield: 15 servings.

Sharon Coffield, Birmingham South Cahaba Council

Lemon Custard Cake

1 angel food cake, torn into
   1-inch pieces
1 (4-ounce) package lemon
   instant pudding mix

1½ cups milk
1 cup sour cream
1 (21-ounce) can cherry or
   strawberry pie filling

Arrange the angel food cake pieces in a 9x13-inch cake pan. Combine the pudding mix, milk and sour cream in a mixer bowl and beat for 2 minutes or until thickened. Spread over the angel food cake. Spoon the pie filling over the top. Chill, covered, until ready to serve. Yield: 10 servings.

Vauline Terry, Tuscaloosa Council

Orange Mound Cake

1 cup (2 sticks) butter,
  softened
2 cups sugar
4 eggs
1 teaspoon salt
1½ cups buttermilk
1 teaspoon baking soda

4 cups flour
1 pound dates, chopped
2 cups chopped pecans
2 tablespoons grated orange
  zest
2 cups sugar
1 cup orange juice

Cream the butter, 2 cups sugar, eggs and salt in a mixer bowl until light and fluffy. Combine the buttermilk and baking soda in a small bowl and mix well. Stir the buttermilk mixture into the creamed mixture. Add the flour and mix well. Stir in the dates, pecans and orange zest. Pour into a greased tube pan. Bake at 350 degrees for 1½ hours. Combine 2 cups sugar and orange juice in a saucepan and mix well. Bring the mixture to a boil. Boil for 5 minutes, stirring constantly. Pour over the warm cake. Let cake cool in the pan for 1½ hours. Yield: 16 servings.

Frankie (A.T.) Vaughn, Selma Life Member Club

Pea-Picking Cake

1 (2-layer) package yellow
  cake mix
1 (4-ounce) package
  vanilla instant
  pudding mix
4 eggs
1½ cups vegetable oil

1 (11-ounce) can mandarin
  oranges
2 (4-ounce) packages vanilla
  instant pudding mix
13 ounces whipped topping
1 (20-ounce) can crushed
  pineapple, drained

Mix the cake mix and 1 package pudding mix in a bowl. Add the eggs and oil and beat until blended. Stir in the mandarin oranges. Pour into a 9x13-inch cake pan. Bake at 350 degrees for 40 to 60 minutes or until cake tests done. Cool in the pan. Mix 2 packages pudding mix, whipped topping and pineapple in a bowl. Spread over the top of the cooled cake. Yield: 15 servings.

Julie Collier, Birmingham South Cahaba Council

Chocolate Pound Cake with Cream Cheese Icing

1 cup (2 sticks) butter or
  margarine, softened
3 cups sugar
5 eggs
½ cup vegetable oil or
  applesauce
¼ cup baking cocoa
½ teaspoon salt
½ teaspoon baking powder
1 teaspoon vanilla extract

3 cups cake flour
1 cup milk
½ cup (1 stick) butter or
  margarine, softened
8 ounces cream cheese,
  softened
1 teaspoon vanilla extract
1 pound confectioners' sugar
½ cup chopped pecans
  (optional)

Cream 1 cup butter in a mixer bowl. Add the sugar gradually, beating until light and fluffy. Add the eggs 1 at a time, beating well after each addition. Beat in the oil, baking cocoa, salt, baking powder and 1 teaspoon vanilla. Add the flour alternately with the milk, beating well after each addition. Pour into 3 greased 9-inch round cake pans. Bake at 350 degrees for 40 minutes. Cool in the pans for 10 minutes. Remove to a wire rack to cool completely. Cream ½ cup butter and cream cheese in a mixer bowl. Stir in 1 teaspoon vanilla. Add the confectioners' sugar gradually, beating until blended. Stir in the pecans. Spread between the layers and over the top and side of the cooled cake. Yield: 12 to 16 servings.

Gloria Wadsworth, Birmingham South Cahaba Council

Double-Rich Pound Cake

2 cups flour
1 teaspoon baking
  powder
¾ cup (1½ sticks) butter,
  softened

8 ounces cream cheese,
  softened
2 cups sugar
2 teaspoons vanilla extract
6 eggs, at room temperature

Combine the flour and baking powder in a bowl and mix well. Beat the butter and cream cheese in a mixer bowl until creamy. Add the sugar gradually, beating for 6 minutes or until light and fluffy. Beat in the vanilla. Add the eggs 1 at a time, beating well after each addition. Add the flour mixture and beat at low to medium speed until blended. Pour into a greased and floured tube pan, bundt pan or two 8-inch loaf pans. Bake at 325 degrees for 60 to 65 minutes for a tube or bundt pan or for 60 to 70 minutes for loaf pans or until cake tests done. Cool in the pan for 10 minutes. Remove to a wire rack to cool completely. Yield: 16 servings.

Judy Boozer, Birmingham South Cahaba Council

Sweet Potato Pound Cake

3 cups flour
2 teaspoons baking powder
1 teaspoon baking soda
1 teaspoon cinnamon
1 teaspoon vanilla extract
½ teaspoon nutmeg
¼ teaspoon salt

1 cup (2 sticks) butter
2 cups sugar
4 eggs
2½ cups mashed cooked sweet
  potatoes
½ cup flaked coconut
½ cup chopped pecans

Mix the first 7 ingredients in a bowl. Cream the butter and sugar in a mixer bowl until light and fluffy. Add the eggs 1 at a time, beating well after each addition. Beat in the sweet potatoes. Add the flour mixture gradually, beating until blended. Stir in the coconut and pecans. Pour into a well-greased tube pan. Bake at 350 degrees for 1¼ hours. Yield: 16 servings.

Frankie (A.T.) Vaughn, Selma Life Member Club

Chocolate Chip Treasure Cookies

1½ cups graham cracker
  crumbs
½ cup flour
2 teaspoons baking powder
1 cup chopped candied red or
  green cherries (optional)
1 (14-ounce) can sweetened
  condensed milk

½ cup (1 stick) butter or
  margarine, softened
2 cups milk chocolate chips
1½ cups flaked coconut
1 cup chopped pecans

Combine the graham cracker crumbs, flour and baking powder in a bowl and mix well. Add the cherries and toss to coat. Beat the condensed milk and butter in a mixer bowl until blended. Add the graham cracker mixture and mix well. Stir in the chocolate chips, coconut and pecans. Drop by rounded teaspoonfuls 2 inches apart onto a cookie sheet. Bake at 375 degrees for 8 to 9 minutes or until light brown. Cool on the cookie sheet for 2 minutes. Remove to a wire rack to cool completely. Yield: 3 dozen cookies.

Judy Howard, Riverchase Council

Chocolate Chip Cookies

½ cup shortening
6 tablespoons sugar
1 egg, beaten
1 cup plus 1 tablespoon
  self-rising flour
½ teaspoon salt

½ teaspoon baking soda
1 teaspoon vanilla extract
1 cup semisweet chocolate
  chips
½ cup chopped pecans

Cream the shortening in a mixer bowl. Add the sugar and beat until light and fluffy. Add the egg, flour, salt and baking soda and beat until blended. Stir in the vanilla. Stir in the chocolate chips and pecans. Drop by rounded teaspoonfuls 2 inches apart onto a greased cookie sheet. Bake at 325 degrees for 10 minutes. Cool on the cookie sheet for 2 minutes. Remove to a wire rack to cool completely. Yield: 2 dozen cookies.

Judy Howard, Riverchase Council

Perfect Apple Pie

6 cups thinly sliced apples
¾ cup sugar
2 tablespoons flour
1 tablespoon lemon juice
¾ tablespoon cinnamon

¼ teaspoon salt
⅛ teaspoon nutmeg
1 recipe (2-crust) pie pastry
1 tablespoon sugar

Combine the apples, ¾ cup sugar, flour, lemon juice, cinnamon, salt and nutmeg in a bowl and mix well. Spoon the apple mixture into a pastry-lined pie plate. Top with the remaining pastry, sealing edge and cutting vents. Brush lightly with water. Sprinkle with 1 tablespoon sugar. Bake at 425 degrees for 40 to 50 minutes or until golden brown. Yield: 8 servings.

Shirley Cummings, Decatur Council

Cocoa Cream Pie

1½ cups sugar
½ cup baking cocoa
¼ cup cornstarch
¼ teaspoon salt
2 cups milk

3 eggs, separated
1 teaspoon vanilla extract
1 baked (9-inch) pie shell
1 teaspoon cream of tartar
3 tablespoons sugar

Combine 1½ cups sugar, baking cocoa, cornstarch and salt in a bowl and mix well. Beat the milk and egg yolks in a double boiler until blended. Stir in the sugar mixture. Cook until thickened, beating constantly. Remove from heat. Stir in the vanilla. Pour into the pie shell. Beat the egg whites with the cream of tartar in a mixer bowl until soft peaks form. Add 3 tablespoons sugar gradually, beating until stiff peaks form. Spoon over the filling. Bake at 325 degrees until light brown. Yield: 8 servings.

Sue (Joe) Small, Selma Life Member Club

Coconut Pies

5 eggs, beaten
½ cup (1 stick) margarine,
   melted
¾ cup buttermilk

2 cups sugar
1 (7-ounce) can flaked
   coconut
2 unbaked (9-inch) pie shells

Beat the eggs and margarine in a mixer bowl until blended. Stir in the buttermilk, sugar and coconut. Pour into the pie shells. Bake at 400 degrees for 5 minutes. Reduce the temperature to 325 degrees and bake for 30 minutes. Yield: 16 servings.

Sue Woodruff, sister of Cathy Kelley,
Birmingham South Cahaba Council

Coconut Pie

4 eggs, beaten
2 cups milk
1⅓ cups sugar
1⅓ cups flaked coconut

½ cup self-rising flour
¼ cup (½ stick) butter,
   melted
2 teaspoons vanilla extract

Combine the eggs, milk sugar, coconut, flour, butter and vanilla in a bowl and mix well. Pour into a 9-inch pie pan. Bake at 325 degrees for 30 minutes or until golden brown. Yield: 8 servings.

Betty Darnell, Gadsden Life Member Club

For a beautiful glossy finish on a top pie pastry,
brush with beaten egg white before baking.

Lemon Pie

1 (14-ounce) can sweetened
  condensed milk
1 (6-ounce) can frozen
  lemonade concentrate,
  thawed

8 ounces whipped topping
1 (9-inch) graham cracker
  pie shell

Combine the condensed milk, lemonade concentrate and whipped topping in a bowl and mix well. Spoon into the pie shell. Chill, covered, until ready to serve. Yield: 8 servings.

Susan Smalley, Alabama Telco Credit Union

Pineapple Pie

3 cups chopped pineapple
2 eggs, beaten
1 tablespoon lemon juice
1 tablespoon grated
  lemon zest

1 recipe (2-crust) pie pastry
1 1/2 cups sugar
2 tablespoons flour

Combine the pineapple, eggs, lemon juice and lemon zest in a bowl and mix well. Spoon into a pastry-lined pie plate. Combine the sugar and flour in a bowl and mix well. Sprinkle over the pineapple mixture. Top with the remaining pastry, sealing the edge. Bake at 425 degrees for 40 minutes. Yield: 8 servings.

Mauntez Mayer, Anniston Council

Basic Dip

8 ounces cream cheese,
  softened
¼ cup mayonnaise
1 small onion, finely chopped
Louisiana Hot Sauce to taste

2 to 3 dashes of
  Worcestershire sauce
3 to 4 tablespoons dill pickle
  relish
Salt and pepper to taste

Beat the cream cheese in a bowl until light and fluffy. Add the
mayonnaise and mix well. Add the onion, hot sauce and
Worcestershire sauce and mix well. Add the relish and mix well.
Season with salt and pepper. Chill to allow the flavors to blend.
May use to stuff celery. May substitute one 7-ounce can drained
minced clams or one 4-ounce can drained crab meat for the dill
pickle relish. Yield: 8 servings.

Mrs. Jack E. Gentle, Sr., Opelika Life Member Club

Fruit Dip

1 (8-ounce) can juice-pack
  crushed pineapple
¾ cup skim milk

½ cup sour cream
1 (4-ounce) package coconut
  cream instant pudding mix

Combine the undrained pineapple, milk, sour cream and pudding
mix in a blender container. Process until smooth. Serve with fresh
grapes, pineapple, strawberries and/or kiwifruit. Yield: 2 cups.

Vauline Terry, Tuscaloosa Council

Pizza Dip

8 ounces cream cheese,
    softened
1 jar pizza sauce
Shredded mozzarella cheese

Pepperoni slices
Mushrooms, sliced
Pizza toppings of choice

Spread the cream cheese over the bottom of a small baking dish.
Pour the pizza sauce over the cream cheese. Sprinkle the mozzarella
cheese, pepperoni, mushrooms and pizza toppings over the sauce.
Bake at 325 degrees for 15 to 20 minutes. Serve with corn chips.
May be doubled. Yield: 6 servings.

Nancy D. Murray, Birmingham South Cahaba Council

Chicken and Cream Cheese Ball

16 ounces cream cheese,
    softened
1 envelope ranch salad
    dressing mix
1 tablespoon mayonnaise

1 (10-ounce) can white
    chicken, drained
1 bunch green onions,
    chopped (optional)
Chopped pecans to taste

Combine the cream cheese, salad dressing mix and mayonnaise in
a bowl and mix well. Add the chicken and green onions and mix
well. Shape into a ball. Chill, covered, until firm. Roll in pecans to
coat. May substitute three 4-ounce cans chicken for the 10-ounce
can. Yield: 16 to 20 servings.

Sue (Joe) Small, Selma Life Member Club

Tuna Spread

8 ounces reduced-fat cream
  cheese, softened
1/4 cup mustard
1/3 cup mayonnaise
3 (5-ounce) cans tuna,
  drained

1/2 cup chopped pecans
1/3 cup finely chopped green
  onions, or 2 teaspoons onion
  powder

Combine the cream cheese, mustard and mayonnaise in a bowl and
mix well. Add the tuna, pecans and green onions and mix well.
Spoon into a mold or serving bowl. Cover and chill completely.
Serve with crackers or bread. Yield: 8 to 10 servings.

Barbara Dunaway, Riverchase Council

Creamy Bacon Bites

3 ounces cream cheese,
  softened
4 slices bacon, crisp-cooked,
  crumbled

2 teaspoons chopped onion
1/8 teaspoon pepper
1 (8-count) can crescent rolls

Combine the cream cheese, bacon, onion and pepper in a bowl and
mix well. Separate the crescent dough into 2 rectangles. Press the
seams and perforations together to seal. Spread half the cream
cheese mixture over each rectangle. Roll to enclose the filling,
starting with the long edge. Seal the edges and ends. Cut each roll
into 16 slices. Place cut side down on a greased baking sheet. Bake
at 350 degrees for 12 to 15 minutes or until golden brown. Serve
warm. Yield: 32 servings.

Brenda B. Reeves, Birmingham South Cahaba Council

"Never Can" Cucumber Pickles

1 gallon cucumbers, cut into strips	Vinegar
1 gallon water	1 to 2 tablespoons pickling spice
1 cup salt	12 cups sugar
1 tablespoon lump alum	½ teaspoon turmeric

Place the cucumbers in a large container. Combine the water and salt in a large container. Pour over the cucumbers. Let stand for 3 days. Drain the cucumbers, leaving them in the container. Rinse and drain 3 times. Add enough water to the cucumbers to cover. Add the alum. Let stand for 24 hours. Drain the cucumbers, leaving them in the container. Rinse and drain 3 times. Add enough vinegar to cover. Let stand for 7 days. Drain the cucumbers, leaving them in the container. Tie the pickling spice up in cheesecloth, making a 1-inch ball. Add the pickling spice, 3 cups of the sugar and turmeric to the cucumbers and stir to coat. Add 3 cups of sugar each day for the next 3 days. Store in a 1-gallon glass wide-mouth jar. Yield: 1 gallon pickles.

Martha L. Bryan and Jewell Lancaster, Huntsville Council

Nonalcoholic Frozen Piña Coladas

2½ cups pineapple juice	Maraschino cherries
½ cup flaked coconut	(optional)
3 cups vanilla ice cream	

Combine the pineapple juice, coconut and ice cream in a blender container. Process until smooth. Serve in stemmed glasses topped with cherries. May add 8 to 10 ice cubes before processing for a frostier drink. May add ½ cup light or dark rum before processing for an alcoholic drink. Yield: 6 servings.

Angie Bolton, Montgomery Council

Frozen Fruit Cups

2 (20-ounce) cans crushed
    pineapple
2 (10-ounce) packages frozen
    sweetened strawberries,
    thawed
2 (20-ounce) cans fruit
    cocktail
1 (11-ounce) can mandarin
    oranges, drained

6 medium bananas, cubed
1 (12-ounce) can frozen
    orange juice concentrate,
    thawed
1 (12-ounce) can frozen
    lemonade concentrate,
    thawed

Combine the undrained pineapple, strawberries, undrained fruit cocktail, mandarin oranges, bananas, orange juice concentrate and lemonade concentrate in a large bowl and mix well. Spoon into plastic 9-ounce beverage glasses or into foil-lined muffin cups. Freeze until solid. Thaw for 30 minutes before serving.
Yield: 12 to 14 servings.

Frankie (A.T.) Vaughn, Selma Life Member Club

Pudding and Fruit Salad

4 bananas, cut into slices
Lemon juice
1 (15-ounce) can fruit cocktail
1 (15-ounce) can crushed
    pineapple
1 (6-ounce) package vanilla
    instant pudding mix

1 (16-ounce) can sliced
    peaches, drained, chopped
1 (20-ounce) can pineapple
    chunks, drained
2 (11-ounce) cans mandarin
    oranges, drained

Combine the bananas with a small amount of lemon juice in a bowl and toss to coat. Combine the undrained fruit cocktail, undrained crushed pineapple and pudding mix in a large bowl and mix well. Stir in the peaches, pineapple chunks, mandarin oranges and banana slices. Chill, covered, for up to 24 hours. May be spooned into 9-ounce beverage glasses and frozen. Thaw for 30 minutes before serving. Yield: 12 servings.

Frankie (A.T.) Vaughn, Selma Life Member Club

Slaw

1 head cabbage, shredded
½ cup sugar
½ cup vinegar
¼ cup vegetable oil

½ teaspoon salt
2 tablespoons dried onion
1 tablespoon dried green bell
   pepper (optional)

Place the cabbage in a large bowl. Combine the sugar, vinegar, oil, salt, onion and green pepper in a small bowl and mix well. Pour over the cabbage and mix well. Chill in the refrigerator. Yield: 8 servings.

Betty Darnell, Gadsden Life Member Club

Layered Salad

½ medium head lettuce, torn
   into bite-size pieces
1 bunch green onions with
   tops, chopped
1 (8-ounce) can sliced water
   chestnuts, drained
1½ cups chopped celery
1 (8-ounce) can green peas,
   drained

2 cups mayonnaise
2 tablespoons sugar
1½ cups shredded Cheddar
   cheese
3 or 4 hard-cooked eggs,
   chopped
6 to 8 slices bacon, crisp-
   cooked, crumbled

Layer the lettuce, green onions, water chestnuts, celery and green peas in the order listed in a serving bowl. Mix the mayonnaise and sugar in a bowl. Spread over the green peas. Sprinkle with the cheese. Chill, covered, until serving time. Top with the eggs and bacon. Yield: 6 to 8 servings.

Dale Sanders, Birmingham Metro Council

"Wow" Potato Salad

4 cups chopped cooked
 potatoes, chilled
1 small onion, chopped
2 tablespoons chopped parsley
1 tablespoon chopped green
 bell pepper

1 cup chopped celery
1 teaspoon salt, or to taste
Mustard Salad Dressing
Crisp lettuce

Combine the potatoes, onion, parsley, green pepper, celery, salt
and Mustard Salad Dressing in a large bowl and toss gently. Chill,
covered, for 1 hour. Line a serving bowl with lettuce leaves. Spoon
the potato salad into the prepared bowl. Yield: 5 servings.

Mustard Salad Dressing

1/4 cup mustard
3 tablespoons heavy cream
2 tablespoons sugar

2 tablespoons vinegar
4 teaspoons salt
Dash of cayenne pepper

Combine all ingredients in a mixer bowl. Beat at low to medium
speed until light and fluffy.

Vicki Weyerbacher, Birmingham South Cahaba Council

Shrimp Salad

1 tablespoon grated onion
2 tablespoons chopped sweet
 pickles
1/2 teaspoon salt
Pepper to taste

1/4 cup mayonnaise
12 ounces cooked deveined
 shrimp
1 cup chopped celery
Lettuce leaves

Combine the onion, pickles, salt, pepper and mayonnaise in a bowl
and mix well. Stir in the shrimp and celery. Chill, covered, until
serving time. Line 4 salad plates with lettuce leaves. Divide the
shrimp salad among the plates. Yield: 4 servings.

Vauline Terry, Tuscaloosa Council

Pasta and Shrimp Salad

1 (16-ounce) package rainbow
  pasta
1 (4-ounce) can chopped black
  olives
2 (14-ounce) cans artichoke
  hearts, chopped
1 (10-ounce) can corn niblets
1 (4-ounce) can button
  mushrooms, chopped

1 pound boiled shrimp, peeled
1 (16-ounce) bottle zesty
  Italian salad dressing
White pepper to taste
Parmesan cheese to taste

Cook the pasta using the package directions; drain. Let stand until cooled. Combine the cooked pasta, olives, artichoke hearts, corn, mushrooms, shrimp, salad dressing, pepper and Parmesan cheese in a large bowl and mix well. Chill, covered, for 8 to 12 hours. Serve with crackers. Yield: 6 to 8 servings.

Betty (Bob) Passet, Mobile Council

Stir-Fry

1 (7-ounce) package fried rice
3 green onions, chopped
1 cup sliced mushrooms
1/4 cup chopped bell pepper
1 (10-ounce) package frozen
  peas and carrots

1/4 cup black olives
2 chicken breasts, cooked,
  chopped
2 to 3 tablespoons olive or
  vegetable oil

Prepare the rice using the package directions. Sauté the green onions, mushrooms, bell pepper, peas and carrots, olives and chicken in the hot oil in a wok or nonstick skillet over medium heat for 15 to 20 minutes or until vegetables are tender-crisp. Remove to a serving bowl. Spoon the rice over the chicken mixture. Serve with soy sauce. Yield: 4 or 5 servings.

Stephanie R. Hurst, Riverchase Council

Cinnamon Apples

1 (4-ounce) package red hot   2 cups quartered peeled apples
  cinnamon candies   ¼ cup water

Place the candies over the bottom of a 2-quart saucepan. Add the apples and water. Cook over low heat until the candies are dissolved; do not stir. Cook until the apples are a red-pink color. Serve hot or cold. May substitute one 20-ounce can apple pie filling for the apples and water. Yield: 4 to 6 servings.

Betty M. Jones-Moon, Birmingham Life Member Club

Spinach Pizzazz

2 eggs   4 ounces grated Land O'Lakes
¼ teaspoon salt   Chedarella Cheese
¼ teaspoon pepper   ½ cup shredded Sargento
1 teaspoon garlic salt with   Fancy 3-Cheese Variety
  parsley   ½ cup cooked rice (optional)
1 (8-ounce) package frozen   1 (4-ounce) can mushroom
  spinach, thawed, drained   bits and pieces, drained
1 large onion, grated   (optional)
3 or 4 slices baby Swiss   1 (8-ounce) can water
  cheese, torn into small   chestnut slices, drained
  pieces   (optional)

Beat the eggs, salt, pepper and garlic salt in a mixer bowl. Combine the spinach, onion, Swiss cheese, Cheddar cheese and 3-Cheese Variety in a separate bowl and mix well. Add the egg mixture and mix well. Add the rice, mushrooms and water chestnuts and mix well. Spoon into a pie plate or baking dish. Bake at 350 degrees for 45 minutes or microwave for 20 to 25 minutes or until cheeses bubble and are brown. Yield: 6 to 8 servings.

Annette E. Turner, Birmingham Life Member Club

Buttermilk Pancakes

3 cups flour
1½ teaspoons baking soda
1 teaspoon cream of tartar
1 teaspoon salt

3 eggs, lightly beaten
1 cup sugar
1 quart buttermilk

Combine the flour, baking soda, cream of tartar and salt in a bowl and mix well. Add the eggs and mix well. Add the sugar and mix well. Pour in the buttermilk and mix until smooth. Pour ¼ cup at a time onto a lightly greased hot griddle. Cook until bubbles appear on surface and underside is golden brown. Turn pancake over. Cook until golden brown. Yield: 12 to 16 servings.

Eileen Smaha, Birmingham South Cahaba Council

Apple Dumplings

2 Granny Smith apples,
   peeled, cut into quarters
1 (8-count) can crescent rolls,
   separated into sections

½ cup (1 stick) margarine,
   melted
1 cup sugar
1 cup orange juice

Place 1 apple quarter on 1 section of dough. Fold the dough over to enclose the apple, sealing the edges. Place in a 6x10-inch baking dish. Repeat the process for each apple quarter. Combine the margarine, sugar and orange juice in a bowl and mix well. Pour over the dumplings. Bake at 350 degrees until brown. Yield: 8 servings.

Hazel E. Campbell, Birmingham Life Member Club

Pizza Lafret

1 envelope dry yeast   Pinch of salt
½ cup lukewarm water   Vegetable oil for frying
2 cups flour   Confectioners' sugar

Combine the yeast and water in a large bowl. Let stand for 3 to
4 minutes. Add the flour and salt and mix until smooth; dough
will be thick. Let stand, covered, for 5 minutes. Heat oil in a
skillet until hot. Shape the dough into circles thin enough to see
through. Cook in the hot oil. Remove and drain. Sprinkle with
confectioners' sugar. Yield: 4 to 6 servings.

Di Riccio, Riverchase Council

Bachelor's Pie

½ cup (1 stick) margarine   1 to 2 cups drained canned
1 cup whole milk   fruit, such as strawberries,
1 cup sugar   blackberries or peaches
1 cup self-rising flour

Heat the margarine in a large ovenproof skillet until melted.
Remove from heat. Combine the milk, sugar and flour in a bowl
and mix well. Pour over the margarine; do not stir. Spoon the fruit
over the flour mixture. Bake at 325 degrees until a golden crust rises
and forms over the fruit. Yield: 6 to 8 servings.

Tommy J. Waldrop, Birmingham South Cahaba Council

Basic Banana Pudding

6 egg yolks
3 cups milk
1½ cups sugar
2 tablespoons flour
1 pound vanilla wafers

6 medium bananas, sliced
6 egg whites
2 tablespoons sugar
Vanilla extract to taste

Combine the egg yolks, milk, 1½ cups sugar and flour in the top of a double boiler and mix well. Cook until the mixture thickens. Remove from the heat. Let stand until cooled. Layer the vanilla wafers and banana slices alternately in a large glass baking dish. Pour the milk mixture over the layers. Beat the egg whites in a mixer bowl until stiff peaks form. Beat in 2 tablespoons sugar and vanilla. Spread over the top, sealing to the edge. Bake at 350 degrees until golden brown. Yield: 10 servings.

Cathy Kelley, Birmingham South Cahaba Council

Banana Pudding

1 (6-ounce) package vanilla
  instant pudding mix
3 cups milk
1 (14-ounce) can sweetened
  condensed milk

12 ounces whipped topping
1 (12-ounce) package vanilla
  wafers
5 to 7 bananas, thinly sliced

Beat the pudding mix and milk in a bowl until smooth. Add the condensed milk and mix well. Add the whipped topping and mix well. Arrange the vanilla wafers over the bottom of a glass dish. Arrange the banana slices over the wafers. Spoon the pudding mixture over the bananas. Chill for 2 to 3 hours. Yield: 6 to 8 servings.

Susan Poe, Riverchase Council

Fruity Delight

1 (15-ounce) can light fruit
  cocktail
1 (15-ounce) can pineapple
  tidbits
1 (15-ounce) can sliced
  peaches
2 apples, chopped

2 bananas, sliced
1/2 cup crushed pecans
  (optional)
1/2 cup flaked coconut
  (optional)
1 large package sugar-free
  vanilla instant pudding mix

Combine the undrained fruit cocktail, undrained pineapple, undrained peaches, apples, bananas, pecans and coconut in a bowl and mix well. Add the pudding mix and mix well. Chill in the refrigerator. Yield: 10 to 12 servings.

Trudy B. McCann, Huntsville Council

Mississippi Mud Dessert

1/2 cup (1 stick) margarine,
  softened
1 cup flour
2 tablespoons sugar
1/2 cup crushed walnuts
1 cup whipped topping
8 ounces cream cheese,
  softened

1 cup confectioners' sugar
1 teaspoon vanilla extract
1 (6-ounce) package chocolate
  instant pudding mix
2 1/2 cups milk
16 ounces whipped topping
1/2 cup chopped walnuts

Combine the margarine, flour, sugar and crushed walnuts in a bowl and mix well. Press over the bottom of a 9x13-inch baking pan. Bake at 350 degrees for 10 to 15 minutes or until light brown. Let stand until cool. Combine 1 cup whipped topping, cream cheese, confectioners' sugar and vanilla in a bowl and mix well. Spread over the cooled crust. Beat the pudding mix with the milk in a mixer bowl until smooth. Spread over the cream cheese layer. Combine the 16 ounces whipped topping and the chopped walnuts in a bowl and mix well. Spread over the layers. Yield: 15 servings.

Susan Currie, Birmingham South Cahaba Council

Four-Layer Chocolate Dessert

1 cup self-rising
  flour
½ cup (1 stick) margarine,
  melted
1½ cups chopped nuts
2 tablespoons sugar
1 cup sugar
1 cup whipped topping

8 ounces cream cheese,
  softened
2 (4-ounce) packages chocolate
  instant pudding mix
3 cups milk
Whipped topping
Chopped nuts (optional)
Toasted coconut (optional)

Combine the flour, margarine, 1½ cups nuts and 2 tablespoons sugar in a bowl and mix well. Press over the bottom of a 9x13-inch baking dish. Bake at 350 degrees for 20 minutes or until light brown. Let stand until cool. Beat 1 cup sugar, 1 cup whipped topping and cream cheese in a mixer bowl until smooth. Spread over the crust. Beat the pudding mixes and milk in a mixer bowl until smooth. Spread over the cream cheese layer. Spread whipped topping over the layers. Sprinkle additional nuts and coconut over the top. Chill in the refrigerator. Yield: 15 servings.

Edith Harrison, Montgomery Council

Truffle Dessert

1 (2-layer) package chocolate
  cake mix
1 cup Kahlúa
2 packages chocolate instant
  pudding mix

16 ounces whipped topping
5 Heath candy bars,
  crumbled

Prepare and bake the cake using the package directions. Let stand until cool. Crumble into a large bowl. Pour the Kahlúa over the crumbled cake and mix well. Prepare the pudding mix using the package directions. Spread over the cake mixture. Spread the whipped topping over the pudding layer. Sprinkle the crumbled candy bars over the whipped topping. Chill in the refrigerator. Yield: 15 to 20 servings.

Diane Sullivan, Riverchase Council

Chocolate Nut Torte

7 eggs
1/4 teaspoon salt
1 cup sugar
1 teaspoon vanilla extract
1 1/4 cups ground hazelnuts
1 1/4 cups ground pecans
1/4 cup dry bread crumbs
1 teaspoon baking powder
1/2 teaspoon salt
1 cup whipping cream, chilled

1/2 cup confectioners' sugar
1 teaspoon vanilla extract
4 ounces unsweetened
   chocolate
1/4 cup butter or margarine
3 cups sifted confectioners'
   sugar
1/2 cup hot water or coffee
1 1/2 teaspoons vanilla extract

Line the bottoms of three 8-inch round cake pans with waxed paper. Separate the eggs, placing the whites in a large mixer bowl and the yolks in a small mixer bowl. Bring the egg whites to room temperature. Beat with 1/4 teaspoon salt until soft peaks form. Beat in 1/2 cup of the sugar gradually until stiff peaks form. Beat the egg yolks until pale yellow and thick. Beat in remaining 1/2 cup sugar gradually, beating for 3 minutes. Beat in 1 teaspoon vanilla. Mix the next 5 ingredients in a bowl. Stir into the egg yolk mixture. Fold the egg yolk mixture into the egg white mixture. Spoon into the prepared pans, smoothing the surfaces. Bake at 375 degrees for 25 minutes or until surface springs back when pressed gently. Cool upside down, placing each pan upside down between 2 other pans for 1 hour. Beat the cream, 1/2 cup confectioners' sugar and 1 teaspoon vanilla in a mixer bowl until stiff. Chill. Melt the chocolate and butter in a double boiler over hot water. Remove from the water. Add 3 cups confectioners' sugar, hot water and 1 1/2 teaspoons vanilla and mix until smooth. Loosen the sides of the layers from the pans. Place 1 layer on a cake plate. Spoon half the cream mixture over the layer. Place another layer over the cream mixture. Spoon the remaining cream mixture over the layer. Place the remaining layer over the cream mixture. Place 1 cup of the chocolate mixture in a pastry bag with a number 2 star tip. Chill. Frost the torte with the remaining chocolate frosting. Decorate using the frosting in the pastry bag. Garnish with hazelnuts and pecan halves. Chill in the refrigerator for 1 hour. Yield: 12 servings.

Judy Howard, Riverchase Council

Fancy Chocolate Dessert

1¾ cups flour
¾ cup (1½ sticks) reduced-fat
  margarine
¾ cup packed brown sugar
1 cup chopped nuts
8 ounces reduced-fat cream
  cheese, softened
1 cup reduced-fat whipped
  topping

1¼ cups confectioners' sugar
1 small package sugar-free
  vanilla instant pudding mix
1 small package sugar-free
  chocolate instant pudding
  mix
3 cups skim milk
Whipped topping

Combine the flour, margarine, brown sugar and nuts in a bowl and mix well. Press over the bottom of a 9x13-inch baking pan sprayed with nonstick cooking spray. Bake at 350 degrees for 15 minutes. Let stand until completely cool. Combine the cream cheese, 1 cup whipped topping and confectioners' sugar in a bowl and mix well. Spread evenly over the cooled crust. Combine the pudding mixes and milk in a bowl and beat until smooth. Spread evenly over the cream cheese layer. Spread additional whipped topping over the pudding layer. Garnish with chocolate shavings or chopped nuts. Yield: 15 servings.

Judy Howard, Riverchase Council

*When a cake recipe calls for flouring the baking
pan, use some of the dry cake mix instead—there will be no
white mess on the outside of the cake.*

Hot Fudge Pudding Cake

3/4 cup sugar
1 cup flour
1/4 cup baking cocoa
2 teaspoons baking powder
1/4 teaspoon salt
1/2 cup milk
1 1/2 teaspoons vanilla extract

1/3 cup butter or margarine,
  melted
1/2 cup sugar
1/2 cup packed brown sugar
1/4 cup baking cocoa
1 1/4 cups hot water

Combine 3/4 cup sugar, flour, 1/4 cup baking cocoa, baking powder and salt in a bowl and mix well. Add the milk, vanilla and butter and mix until smooth. Pour into a 9x9-inch baking dish. Combine 1/2 cup sugar, brown sugar and 1/4 cup baking cocoa and mix well. Sprinkle over the batter. Pour the hot water over the top; do not stir. Bake at 350 degrees for 30 to 40 minutes or until the center is almost set. Let stand for 15 minutes. Spoon into dessert dishes. Spoon the sauce from the bottom of the baking dish over the cake. Serve with ice cream. Yield: 9 servings.

Faye S. King, Huntsville Council

Fruit Cocktail Cake

2 cups flour
1 1/2 cups sugar
2 teaspoons baking soda
2 cups fruit cocktail
2 eggs
1 cup chopped pecans

1/2 cup packed brown sugar
1 cup flaked coconut
1 cup evaporated milk
1/2 cup (1 stick) margarine
1 1/2 cups sugar

Mix the flour, sugar, baking soda, undrained fruit cocktail and eggs in a bowl. Spoon into a greased 9x13-inch baking pan. Combine the pecans, brown sugar and coconut in a bowl and mix well. Sprinkle over the batter. Bake at 350 degrees for 45 minutes. Combine the evaporated milk, margarine and sugar in a saucepan. Bring to a boil, stirring constantly. Boil for 2 minutes. Pour over the hot cake. Serve with whipped topping. Yield: 15 servings.

Judy Howard, Riverchase Council

Chocolate Brownie Cake

2 cups sugar
2 cups self-rising flour
½ cup (1 stick) margarine
½ cup vegetable oil
3 tablespoons baking cocoa

1 cup water
1 teaspoon vanilla extract
2 eggs
½ cup buttermilk
Chocolate Icing

Combine the sugar and flour in a bowl and mix well. Combine the margarine, oil, baking cocoa and water in a saucepan. Bring to a boil, stirring frequently. Pour over the sugar mixture and mix well. Add the vanilla, eggs and buttermilk and mix well. Pour into a 9x13-inch baking pan sprayed with nonstick cooking spray. Bake at 300 degrees for 45 to 60 minutes or until a wooden pick inserted in the center comes out clean. Spread the Chocolate Icing over the hot cake. Yield: 12 servings.

Chocolate Icing

1 (1-pound) box confectioners'
   sugar
½ cup (1 stick) margarine
3 tablespoons baking cocoa

6 tablespoons buttermilk
1 teaspoon vanilla extract
1 cup chopped nuts (optional)

Place the confectioners' sugar in a large bowl. Combine the margarine, cocoa, buttermilk and vanilla in a saucepan. Bring to a boil, stirring frequently. Pour over the confectioners' sugar. Beat until smooth. Stir in the nuts.

Sherron Sanders, Riverchase Council

Four-Layer Cake

2 cups sugar
1 cup shortening
4 eggs
1 teaspoon vanilla extract
2 cups all-purpose flour

1 cup self-rising flour
1 cup milk
Caramel Frosting (below) or
    Coconut Icing (page 145)

Cream the sugar and shortening in a mixer bowl until light and fluffy. Add the eggs 1 at a time, mixing well after each addition. Beat in the vanilla. Add the all-purpose flour and self-rising flour alternately with the milk, mixing well after each addition. Pour into 4 greased and floured round cake pans. Bake at 325 degrees until a wooden pick inserted in the center comes out clean. Cool in the pan for 10 minutes. Remove to a wire rack to cool completely. Spread the Caramel Frosting or Coconut Icing between the layers and over the top and side of the cooled cake.
Yield: 16 servings.

Caramel Frosting

½ cup sugar
1 tablespoon flour
3 cups sugar
1 tablespoon corn syrup

1 cup milk
½ cup (1 stick) margarine
1 teaspoon vanilla extract

Brown ½ cup sugar in a small skillet. Remove from heat. Combine the flour, 3 cups sugar, corn syrup, milk and margarine in a saucepan. Bring to a boil, stirring constantly. Add the browned sugar. Cook over medium heat to soft-ball stage. Remove from heat. Stir in the vanilla. Beat until of a spreading consistency.

Coconut Icing

2 cups sugar
1 cup milk
1 egg yolk
⅛ teaspoon salt

3 tablespoons butter
½ teaspoon vanilla extract
6 ounces frozen flaked
  coconut, thawed

Combine the sugar, milk, egg yolk and salt in a saucepan. Bring to a boil, stirring constantly. Boil for 1 minute. Remove from heat. Add the butter, stirring until the butter melts. Stir in the vanilla and coconut. Poke holes in the cake with a fork. Pour the icing over the cake, spreading to cover.

Polly (Ed) Martin, Opelika Life Member Club

Lemon Supreme Cake

1 (2-layer) package lemon
  supreme cake mix
1 cup apricot nectar
¾ cup vegetable oil

½ cup sugar
4 eggs
Lemon Icing

Combine the cake mix, nectar, oil and sugar in a bowl and beat until smooth. Add the eggs 1 at a time, mixing well after each addition. Pour into a greased and floured tube pan. Bake at 325 degrees for 1¼ hours or until a wooden pick inserted in the center comes out clean. Cool in the pan for 10 minutes. Invert onto a serving plate. Pour Lemon Icing over the warm cake.
Yield: 16 servings.

Lemon Icing

1 cup confectioners' sugar   Juice of 1 lemon

Combine the confectioners' sugar and enough lemon juice to make of the desired consistency in a bowl and mix until smooth.

Janice Bass, Riverchase Council

Oatmeal Cake

1 1/4 cups boiling water
1 cup quick-cooking oats
1 cup packed brown sugar
1 cup sugar
1/2 cup (1 stick) margarine,
    softened
1/2 to 1 teaspoon cinnamon

2 eggs
1 1/3 cups flour
3/4 cup packed brown sugar
6 tablespoons margarine
1 tablespoon evaporated milk
1 cup chopped nuts
1 cup flaked coconut

Pour the boiling water over the oats in a bowl and set aside. Beat 1 cup brown sugar, sugar, 1/2 cup margarine, cinnamon, eggs and flour in a mixer bowl until smooth. Stir in the oat mixture. Pour into a 9x13-inch baking pan. Bake at 350 degrees for 35 minutes. Combine 3/4 cup brown sugar, 6 tablespoons margarine and evaporated milk in a saucepan and mix well. Cook for 1 minute, stirring constantly. Stir in the nuts and coconut. Spread over the warm cake. Bake for an additional 3 minutes. May bake cake in layer pans and spread coconut mixture between the layers.
Yield: 15 servings.

Susan Poe, Riverchase Council

Coconut-Topped Oatmeal Cake

1¼ cups boiling water
1 cup quick-cooking or old-
  fashioned oats
1½ cups sifted flour
1 teaspoon baking powder
1 teaspoon salt
1 teaspoon cinnamon
½ teaspoon baking soda
½ cup (1 stick) margarine
1 cup sugar
1 cup packed brown sugar
2 eggs
1 cup raisins (optional)
Coconut Topping

Pour the boiling water over the oats in a bowl and set aside. Sift the flour, baking powder, salt, cinnamon and baking soda together. Cream the margarine, sugar and brown sugar in a mixer bowl until light and fluffy. Add the eggs 1 at a time, beating well after each addition. Stir in the oat mixture and raisins. Add the sifted dry ingredients and mix well. Pour into a greased and floured 9x9-inch baking pan. Bake at 350 degrees for 40 minutes or until a wooden pick inserted in the center comes out clean. Cool in the pan. Spread Coconut Topping over the cake. Yield: 9 to 12 servings.

Coconut Topping

1⅜ cups flaked coconut
1 cup chopped pecans
  (optional)
½ cup packed brown sugar
¼ cup (½ stick) margarine,
  softened
1 (5-ounce) can evaporated
  milk
1 teaspoon vanilla extract

Combine the coconut, pecans, brown sugar, margarine, evaporated milk and vanilla in a bowl and mix well.

Annette E. Turner, Birmingham Life Member Club

Peanut Butter Fudge Cake

2 cups sugar
2 cups flour
1 teaspoon baking soda
2 eggs, well beaten
1 cup water
1/4 cup baking cocoa

1 cup (2 sticks) margarine
1/2 cup buttermilk
1 teaspoon vanilla extract
1 1/2 cups peanut butter
Chocolate Frosting

Combine the sugar, flour and baking soda in a bowl and mix well. Combine the eggs, water, cocoa, margarine and buttermilk in a saucepan. Cook over medium heat until bubbly, stirring occasionally. Remove from heat. Add the sugar mixture and beat until smooth. Stir in the vanilla. Pour into a greased and floured 9x13-inch baking pan. Bake at 350 degrees for 25 minutes. Cool in the pan. Spread the peanut butter over the cake. Spread the Chocolate Frosting over the peanut butter. Yield: 15 servings.

Chocolate Frosting

1/4 cup baking cocoa
7 tablespoons buttermilk
1/2 cup (1 stick) margarine

1 (1-pound) package
    confectioners' sugar
1 teaspoon vanilla extract

Combine the cocoa, buttermilk and margarine in a saucepan. Cook until bubbly, stirring constantly. Remove from heat. Add the confectioners' sugar and beat until smooth. Stir in the vanilla.

Barbara Dunaway, Riverchase Council

Chocolate Pound Cake

3 cups flour
2 teaspoons baking powder
½ cup baking cocoa
½ teaspoon salt
1 cup (2 sticks) butter,
 softened

½ cup shortening
3 cups sugar
5 eggs
1¼ cups milk
1 tablespoon vanilla extract
Good Chocolate Frosting

Sift the flour, baking powder, cocoa and salt together 3 times. Cream the butter and shortening in a bowl. Add the sugar gradually, beating until light and fluffy. Add the eggs 1 at a time, beating well after each addition. Add the sifted dry ingredients and milk alternately, mixing well after each addition. Stir in the vanilla. Pour the batter into a large greased and floured tube pan. Bake at 325 degrees for 1½ hours. Cool in the pan for 10 minutes. Invert onto a serving plate. Frost with the Good Chocolate Frosting. Yield: 16 servings.

Good Chocolate Frosting

1 cup sugar
5 tablespoons butter

⅓ cup milk
1 cup chocolate chips

Combine the sugar, butter and milk in a saucepan. Bring to a boil, stirring constantly. Boil for 1 minute. Remove from heat. Add the chocolate chips and beat until smooth.

Mabel Craig, Birmingham Life Member Club

Coconut Pound Cake

3 cups sifted cake flour
1/4 teaspoon salt
1 1/2 cups shortening
2 1/4 cups sugar

5 eggs
1 cup milk
1 (7-ounce) can flaked
   coconut

Combine the flour and salt in a bowl and mix well. Cream the shortening and sugar in a mixer bowl until light and fluffy. Add the eggs 1 at a time, beating well after each addition. Add the flour mixture alternately with the milk, beginning and ending with the flour mixture and mixing well after each addition. Stir in the coconut. Pour into a greased and floured 10-inch tube pan. Bake at 325 degrees for 1 hour and 25 minutes or until a wooden pick inserted in the center comes out clean. Cool in the pan for 15 minutes. Remove to a wire rack to cool completely.
Yield: 16 servings.

Susan Poe, Riverchase Council

Snowdrift Cake

½ cup finely chopped pecans
2¼ cups sifted cake flour
2 teaspoons baking powder
1 cup (2 sticks) butter,
  softened
1½ cups sugar
8 ounces cream cheese,
  softened

1½ teaspoons vanilla extract
4 eggs
¼ cup sifted cake flour
2 cups chopped candied fruit
½ cup coarsely chopped
  pecans
Sifted confectioners' sugar

Grease a 10-inch tube or bundt pan. Sprinkle with the finely chopped pecans. Sift 2¼ cups cake flour and baking powder together. Beat the butter, sugar, cream cheese and vanilla in a mixer bowl until light and fluffy. Add the eggs 1 at a time, beating well after each addition. Add the sifted dry ingredients and mix well. Combine ¼ cup cake flour and candied fruit in a bowl, tossing to coat. Stir into the batter. Stir in the coarsely chopped pecans. Pour into the prepared pan. Bake at 325 degrees for 1 hour and 10 minutes to 1 hour and 20 minutes or until a wooden pick inserted in the center comes out clean. Cool in the pan for 5 minutes. Invert onto a serving plate. Sprinkle with confectioners' sugar. Garnish with candied cherries and pineapple. Yield: 16 servings.

Francis M. Tucker, Selma Life Member Club

Peanut Brittle

2 cups sugar
½ cup light corn syrup
¼ cup boiling water
2 cups dry-roasted peanuts

1 tablespoon butter or
  margarine
1 teaspoon baking soda

Combine the sugar, corn syrup and boiling water in a saucepan. Cook over low heat until the sugar dissolves, stirring constantly. Cook, covered, for 2 to 3 minutes or until the steam washes the sugar crystals from the side of the pan. Stir in the peanuts. Cook, uncovered, to 300 degrees on a candy thermometer, hard-crack stage, stirring occasionally. Remove from heat. Add the butter and baking soda, stirring until butter melts. Pour into a buttered 10x15-inch baking pan, spreading thinly. Let stand until cooled. Break into pieces. May substitute 1 cup pecan pieces and 1 cup dry-roasted peanuts for the 2 cups dry-roasted peanuts. Yield: 1 pound.

Betty Foshee, Decatur Council

Microwave Peanut Brittle

1 cup sugar
1 cup peanuts
½ cup light corn syrup
⅛ teaspoon salt

1 tablespoon margarine
1 teaspoon vanilla extract
1 teaspoon baking soda

Combine the sugar, peanuts, corn syrup and salt in a 4-cup microwave-safe bowl and mix well. Microwave on High for 4 minutes; stir. Microwave on High for 3½ to 4 minutes; stir. Add the margarine and vanilla and mix well. Microwave on High for 30 seconds to 1 minute. Stir in the baking soda; mixture will be foamy. Pour onto a greased baking sheet immediately. Let stand until cooled. Break into pieces. Yield: ½ pound.

Susan Currie, Birmingham South Cahaba Council

Brown Sugar Cookies

2 cups packed brown sugar
1 cup shortening, melted
3 eggs
¼ cup milk

1 teaspoon vanilla extract
2 teaspoons baking powder
Flour
Brown sugar

Beat 2 cups brown sugar and shortening in a mixer bowl until light and fluffy. Add the eggs and mix well. Add the milk, vanilla and baking powder and mix well. Add enough flour to make a stiff dough. Roll ⅛ inch thick on a floured surface. Cut with a cookie cutter. Place on a cookie sheet. Sprinkle with additional brown sugar. Bake at 350 degrees for 10 to 12 minutes. Remove to a wire rack to cool. Yield: 8 dozen cookies.

Beveley Vaughn, Alabama Telco Credit Union

Date Cream Cheese Roll-Ups

1 cup (2 sticks) butter,
  softened
8 ounces cream cheese,
  softened

2 cups sifted flour
¼ teaspoon salt
Confectioners' sugar
Pitted dates

Beat the butter and cream cheese in a mixer bowl until light and fluffy. Add the flour and salt and mix well. Chill, covered, for 6 to 8 hours. Roll into a ⅛-inch-thick rectangle on a surface sprinkled with confectioners' sugar. Cut the rectangle into 1x3-inch strips. Place a date in the center of each strip and roll the strip up. Place seam side down on a cookie sheet. Bake at 375 degrees for 15 minutes. Remove to a wire rack to cool. Sprinkle with confectioners' sugar. Yield: 2 dozen cookies.

Judy Howard, Riverchase Council

Forgotten Cookies

2 egg whites   1 cup semisweet chocolate
Pinch of salt   chips
Pinch of cream of tartar   1 cup pecans
½ cup sugar

Beat the egg whites, salt and cream of tartar in a mixer bowl until stiff peaks form. Beat in the sugar gradually. Fold in the chocolate chips and pecans. Drop by teaspoonfuls onto a cookie sheet. Place in a preheated 350-degree oven. Turn off the oven. Leave in the oven for 4 hours or longer. Yield: 2 dozen cookies.

Susan Poe, Riverchase Council

Honey Snaps

2 cups sifted flour   ¾ cup shortening
1½ teaspoons baking soda   1 cup packed brown sugar
1 teaspoon salt   1 egg
½ teaspoon cinnamon   ⅓ cup honey
½ teaspoon ginger   1 teaspoon lemon zest
¼ teaspoon ground cloves   1 cup finely chopped walnuts

Sift the flour, baking soda, salt, cinnamon, ginger and cloves together. Beat the shortening and brown sugar in a mixer bowl until light and fluffy. Beat in the egg, honey and lemon zest. Add the sifted dry ingredients and mix well. Stir in ½ cup of the walnuts. Chill for 30 minutes. Shape by teaspoonfuls into balls. Dip the top of each ball in the remaining ½ cup walnuts. Place 2 inches apart on a lightly greased cookie sheet. Bake at 350 degrees for 12 minutes or until the edges are light brown. Cool on the cookie sheet for 3 to 4 minutes. Remove to a wire rack to cool completely. Yield: 2 dozen cookies.

Susan Poe, Riverchase Council

Oatmeal Butterscotch Cookies

1 ¾ cups sifted flour
1 teaspoon baking soda
1 teaspoon baking powder
1 teaspoon salt
1 teaspoon cinnamon
1 teaspoon nutmeg
1 cup shortening

1 ½ cups packed brown sugar
2 eggs
½ cup buttermilk or sour milk
3 cups quick-cooking oats
1 cup butterscotch chips
½ cup chopped nuts

Sift the flour, baking soda, baking powder, salt, cinnamon and nutmeg together. Beat the shortening and brown sugar in a mixer bowl until light and fluffy. Beat in the eggs. Add the buttermilk and mix well. Add the sifted dry ingredients and mix well. Stir in the oats, chips and nuts. Drop by tablespoonfuls 2 inches apart onto a lightly greased cookie sheet. Bake at 400 degrees for 8 minutes. Cool on the cookie sheet for 2 minutes. Remove to a wire rack to cool completely. May substitute sweet milk for the buttermilk, reducing the baking soda to ¼ teaspoon and increasing the baking powder to 2 teaspoons. Yield: 5 dozen cookies.

Catherine M. Martin, Birmingham Metro Council

Place a slice of apple in a package of hardened brown sugar for a few days to make the brown sugar soft again.

Orange Slice Cookies

1 (1-layer) package yellow
  cake mix
1 egg
3 tablespoons vegetable oil
1 cup chopped pecans

10 orange slice candies,
  chopped
½ cup chopped dates
  (optional)

Combine the cake mix, egg and oil in a bowl and mix well. Stir in the pecans, candies and dates. Drop by spoonfuls 2 inches apart onto an ungreased cookie sheet. Bake at 350 degrees for 8 to 10 minutes or until the edges begin to brown. Remove to a wire rack to cool. Yield: 2½ dozen cookies.

Emily Coburn, Selma Life Member Club

Tea Cakes

2¼ cups sugar
1 cup (2 sticks) butter or
  margarine, softened
1 cup shortening
2 eggs

1 tablespoon vanilla extract
1 tablespoon lemon extract
5 cups flour
¼ teaspoon salt
2 teaspoons baking soda

Beat the sugar, butter and shortening in a mixer bowl until light and fluffy. Beat in the eggs. Add the vanilla and lemon extract and mix well. Add the flour, salt and baking soda and mix well. Chill, covered, until firm. Roll ⅛ inch thick on a floured surface. Cut with a biscuit cutter. Place on an ungreased cookie sheet. Bake at 325 degrees until brown. Remove to a wire rack to cool. Yield: 5 dozen.

Ila M. Skidmore, Shoals Life Member Club

Ambrosia Pie

1 (20-ounce) can crushed
    pineapple
1 (11-ounce) can mandarin
    oranges, drained
1 (14-ounce) can sweetened
    condensed milk

8 ounces cream cheese,
    softened
2 cups whipped topping
1 (4-ounce) can flaked
    coconut, toasted
1 baked (9-inch) pie shell

Drain the pineapple, reserving 2 tablespoons of the juice. Pat the oranges and pineapple dry with paper towels. Combine the condensed milk and cream cheese in a bowl and mix well. Add the whipped topping and reserved pineapple juice and mix well. Stir in the oranges, pineapple and coconut. Spoon into the pie shell. Freeze for 6 hours. Let stand at room temperature for 20 minutes before serving. Yield: 6 to 8 servings.

Sue Johnston, Birmingham South Cahaba Council

Buttermilk Pie

3 eggs
2 cups sugar
2 cups buttermilk
1 tablespoon flour

½ cup (1 stick) butter, melted
1½ teaspoons vanilla extract
Pinch of salt
1 unbaked (10-inch) pie shell

Beat the eggs and sugar in a mixer bowl. Beat in the buttermilk. Add the flour, butter, vanilla and salt and mix well. Pour into the pie shell. Bake at 350 degrees until the top is set. Reduce the oven temperature to 300 degrees. Bake for 45 to 50 minutes or until piecrust is golden brown. Yield: 6 servings.

Brenda Smith, Birmingham South Cahaba Council

Frozen Lemonade Pie

1 (6-ounce) can frozen
lemonade concentrate,
thawed
8 ounces cream cheese,
softened

1 (14-ounce) can sweetened
condensed milk
8 ounces whipped topping
1 (9-inch) graham cracker
pie shell

Combine the lemonade concentrate, cream cheese and condensed milk in a blender container. Process until smooth. Pour into a bowl. Fold in the whipped topping. Pour into the pie shell. Chill, covered, for 2 to 3 hours. Yield: 6 servings.

Susan Poe, Riverchase Council

Pecan Pie

1 cup sugar
½ cup (1 stick) butter, melted
3 eggs, lightly beaten
¾ cup dark corn syrup

¼ teaspoon salt
1 teaspoon vanilla extract
1 cup chopped pecans
1 unbaked deep-dish pie shell

Combine the sugar and butter in a bowl and mix well. Add the eggs and mix well. Add the corn syrup, salt and vanilla and mix well. Stir in the pecans. Spoon into the pie shell. Bake at 350 degrees for 40 to 45 minutes or until set. Yield: 6 servings.

Mary D. Palmer for Louise Palmer, Birmingham Life Member Club

Mexican Bean Dip

8 ounces cream cheese,
  softened
1 cup sour cream
1 envelope taco seasoning mix
2 tablespoons chili powder
  (optional)
1 (9-ounce) can bean dip

1 cup shredded sharp Cheddar
  cheese
1 cup shredded mozzarella
  cheese
1/4 cup chopped green onions
  (optional)
Salt and pepper to taste

Combine the cream cheese, sour cream, seasoning mix and chili powder in a bowl and mix well. Add the bean dip and mix well. Set aside a small amount of the Cheddar cheese and mozzarella cheese. Add the remaining Cheddar and mozzarella cheeses, green onions, salt and pepper and mix well. Spoon into a baking dish coated with nonstick cooking spray. Bake at 350 degrees for 28 minutes. Sprinkle the reserved Cheddar and mozzarella cheeses over the top. Turn off the oven. Let stand in the oven for 2 minutes or until the cheeses melt. Serve with tortilla chips. Yield: 16 servings.

Holly Thompson, Riverchase Council

Layered Mexican Dip

1 large can refried beans
2 envelopes taco seasoning mix
1 cup sour cream
1 large container guacamole
  dip
1 small jar picante sauce

1 bunch green onions,
  chopped
2 medium tomatoes, chopped
1 can black olives, chopped
1 package shredded Mexican
  cheese

Combine the refried beans and seasoning mix in a bowl and mix well. Spread evenly in a 9x13-inch dish. Spread the sour cream, guacamole dip and picante sauce in layers over the bean mixture. Sprinkle the green onions, tomatoes and black olives over the layers. Sprinkle the cheese over the top. Serve with corn chips. Yield: 16 servings.

Barbara McGee, Birmingham South Cahaba Council

Tex-Mex Bean Dip

3 medium avocados
2 tablespoons lemon juice
½ teaspoon salt
¼ teaspoon pepper
1 cup sour cream
½ cup mayonnaise
1 envelope taco seasoning mix
2 (10-ounce) cans plain or
  jalapeño bean dip
1 bunch green onions with
  tops, chopped

3 medium tomatoes, chopped
2 (3-ounce) cans pitted black
  olives, drained, chopped
Jalapeño chiles to taste,
  chopped (optional)
1 (8-ounce) package shredded
  sharp Cheddar cheese
1 (20-ounce) package tortilla
  chips

Peel and pit the avocados. Mash with the lemon juice, salt and
pepper in a bowl. Combine the sour cream, mayonnaise and
seasoning mix in a bowl and mix well. Spread the bean dip evenly
over a large shallow serving platter. Spread the avocado mixture
over the bean dip. Spread the sour cream mixture over the layers.
Sprinkle the green onions, tomatoes, olives and jalapeño chiles
over the layers. Sprinkle the cheese over the top. Serve with the
tortilla chips. Yield: 16 to 18 servings.

Pat White, Montgomery Council

Salsa

2 (14-ounce) cans crushed
  tomatoes
2 (4-ounce) cans chopped
  green chiles
1 medium onion, finely
  chopped

1 (24-ounce) can tomatoes
  with green chiles
Salt and pepper to taste

Combine the crushed tomatoes, green chiles, onion, tomatoes with green chiles, salt and pepper in a bowl and mix well. Chill, covered, until serving time. Serve with tortilla chips. Yield: 10 servings.

Kay B. (Tom) Mingus, Opelika Life Member Club

Montana Salsa

2 to 6 jalapeño chiles, seeded
Garlic to taste
6 tomatoes, chopped
1 onion, finely chopped
1 green bell pepper, chopped
2 tablespoons coarsely chopped
  parsley

2 tablespoons coarsely chopped
  cilantro
Juice of 1 lime
½ teaspoon salt
Pinch of cumin (optional)

Chop the jalapeño chiles and garlic in a food processor. Add the tomatoes and process to chop. Add the onion, green pepper, parsley, cilantro, lime juice, salt and cumin. Process to mix. Chill in the refrigerator. Serve with chips or as a relish with any meat or poultry dish. Yield: 4 to 6 servings.

Donna Jean Bowman, Birmingham South Cahaba Council

Mexican Roll-Ups

1 cup sour cream
8 ounces cream cheese,
  softened
1 (4-ounce) can chopped
  green chiles, drained
1 (4-ounce) can chopped black
  olives
½ cup chopped green olives

1 cup shredded Cheddar
  cheese
¼ cup minced onion
1 teaspoon garlic salt
Chopped jalapeño chiles to
  taste (optional)
12 flour tortillas

Combine the sour cream and cream cheese in a bowl and mix until
well blended and smooth. Add the green chiles, black olives, green
olives, cheese, onion, garlic salt and jalapeño chiles and mix well.
Spread evenly over the tortillas. Roll up the tortillas and place
seam side down in a dish. Chill for 8 hours or until firm. Cut into
½-inch slices. Place on a serving platter. Tortillas may be wrapped
in foil and warmed in a 350-degree oven for 5 minutes to soften
before spreading with the cream cheese mixture. Yield: 12 servings.

Brenda Reeves, Birmingham South Cahaba Council

Make-Ahead Cottage Cheese and Corn Salad

1 (12-ounce) can Mexican
  corn
1 large container cottage
  cheese
1 (4-ounce) can mushrooms,
  drained (optional)

2 or 3 green onions, chopped
1 red, green or yellow bell
  pepper, chopped
½ cup sour cream
½ cup prepared mustard
1½ cups corn chips, crushed

Combine the corn, cottage cheese, mushrooms, green onions and
bell pepper in a bowl and mix well. Combine the sour cream and
mustard in a small bowl and mix well. Add to the corn mixture and
mix well. Chill in the refrigerator. Sprinkle the crushed corn chips
over the salad before serving. Yield: 6 to 8 servings.

Mary Smith and Donna Frederick, Birmingham South Cahaba Council

Mexican Casserole

1 pound ground beef
1 (11-ounce) can tomatoes
  with green chiles
1 (10-ounce) can cream of
  mushroom soup
1 (10-ounce) can cream of
  chicken soup
1 cup shredded Cheddar cheese
1 (9-ounce) package nacho
  cheese tortilla chips

Brown the ground beef in a skillet, stirring until crumbly; drain. Stir in the tomatoes, mushroom soup, chicken soup and cheese. Arrange part of the chips in a thin layer over the bottom of a 9x13-inch baking dish. Spoon the ground beef mixture evenly over the chips. Arrange the remaining chips over the top. Bake at 350 degrees for 20 minutes. Yield: 6 servings.

Mauntez Mayer, Anniston Council

Chicken Enchiladas

¼ cup chopped onion
3 tablespoons butter
16 ounces Monterey Jack
  cheese, shredded
1 (5-ounce) can white chicken
Vegetable oil
12 corn tortillas
2 tablespoons flour
1 (10-ounce) can chicken broth
1 or 2 (7-ounce) cans diced
  green chiles
1 cup sour cream

Sauté the onion in 1 tablespoon of the butter in a skillet until tender. Mix with the cheese and chicken in a bowl. Heat oil in a skillet. Dip each tortilla quickly in the hot oil; do not fry; drain. Spoon 2 tablespoons of the chicken mixture down the center of each tortilla and roll up. Place seam side down in a 9x13-inch baking dish. Heat the remaining butter in a saucepan until melted. Stir in the flour. Add the broth, whisking constantly. Cook until slightly thickened, stirring constantly. Stir in the chiles. Simmer for 2 to 3 minutes. Remove from the heat. Stir in the sour cream. Pour over the enchiladas. Sprinkle with additional cheese. Bake at 350 degrees for 20 to 30 minutes or until hot and bubbly. Let stand for 20 minutes before serving. Yield: 6 servings.

Pat White, Montgomery Council

Fruit Dip

8 ounces cream cheese,
  softened
1 (8-ounce) can cream of
  coconut

1 cup confectioners' sugar

Combine the cream cheese, cream of coconut and confectioners' sugar in a large mixer bowl. Beat until smooth. Chill, covered, until serving time. Serve with assorted fresh fruit. Yield: 2½ cups.

Paula Sorrow, Riverchase Council

Vegetable Dip

2 cups sour cream

1 envelope vegetable soup mix

Combine the sour cream and soup mix in a bowl and mix well. Chill, covered, for at least 2 hours before serving. Stir gently immediately before serving. Serve with crackers or assorted fresh vegetables. Yield: 2 cups.

Eileen Smaha, Birmingham South Cahaba Council

Slush Punch

3 cups boiling water
2 cups sugar
1 (3-ounce) package any
  flavor gelatin

46 ounces pineapple juice
1 (6-ounce) can frozen
  lemonade concentrate
5 cups cold water

Combine the boiling water, sugar and gelatin in a large bowl and mix well. Add the pineapple juice, lemonade concentrate and cold water and stir until well blended. Pour the punch into a 1-gallon plastic milk jug. Freeze for 3 to 4 days. Remove from the freezer 6 hours before serving time. Cut the top off the plastic jug and stir until slushy. Pour into a punch bowl. Yield: 1 gallon.

Susan Friday, for Betty C. Gray, Montgomery Council

Yellow Punch

4 cups water
2 cups sugar
2 (46-ounce) cans orange
   juice
2 (46-ounce) cans pineapple
   juice

4 (6-ounce) cans frozen
   lemonade concentrate
4 (28-ounce) bottles ginger ale
Ice Ring

Combine the water and sugar in a saucepan. Bring to a boil over medium heat, stirring constantly until sugar is dissolved and mixture is a syrup consistency. Remove from heat and chill. Combine the syrup, orange juice, pineapple juice and lemonade concentrate and mix well. Store punch mixture in the refrigerator until serving time. May be stored in the refrigerator for up to 2 weeks. Add the ginger ale and Ice Ring immediately before serving. Yield: 100 servings.

Ice Ring

Orange juice
Maraschino cherries

Pineapple slices
Orange slices

Fill ring mold half full with orange juice and freeze. Top the frozen layer with cherries, pineapple and oranges. Fill the ring mold with orange juice and freeze.

Marjorie S. (Francis) Tucker, Selma Life Club Member

Bow Tie Chicken Salad

4 cups chopped cooked
  chicken
3 cups cooked bow tie pasta
¾ cup sliced almonds
¼ cup chopped celery
¼ cup chopped onion

1 teaspoon salt
1 (11-ounce) can mandarin
  oranges
1½ cups green or red grapes
Mayonnaise

Combine the chicken, pasta, almonds, celery, onion and salt in a large bowl and mix well. Fold in the mandarin oranges and grapes. Stir in enough mayonnaise to make of the desired consistency. Store, covered, until serving time. Yield: 8 servings.

Marilyn King, Tuscaloosa Council

Fruity Chicken Salad

4 boneless skinless chicken
  breasts, cooked
2 ribs celery, chopped
1 medium apple, chopped

½ cup chopped pecans
12 red grapes, sliced
Mayonnaise

Chop the chicken into bite-size pieces. Combine the chicken, celery, apple, pecans and grapes in a large bowl. Stir in enough mayonnaise until of the desired consistency. Serve on a bed of lettuce with crackers or crescent rolls. May substitute almonds or walnuts for the pecans. Yield: 4 to 6 servings.

Dee Ann H. Weaver, Birmingham Life Member Club

Shrimp and Rice Salad

2 cups cooked rice, chilled
1 cup chopped nectarines
4 ounces cooked shrimp,
  peeled, deveined, chilled

2 tablespoons honey
2 tablespoons lime juice
2 teaspoons olive oil

Combine the rice, nectarines and shrimp in a large bowl and mix well. Mix the honey, lime juice and olive oil in a bowl. Pour over the rice mixture and toss lightly just before serving. Serve on a bed of lettuce and garnish with chopped fresh cilantro or parsley. Yield: 3 servings.

Mary Smith and Donna Frederick,
Birmingham South Cahaba Council

Husband's Delight

1 pound ground beef
Garlic salt to taste
Pepper to taste
1 tablespoon sugar
2 (8-ounce) cans tomato sauce
1 cup sour cream
3 ounces cream cheese,
  softened

1/3 cup chopped onion
1 (8-ounce) package egg
  noodles
1/2 cup shredded Cheddar
  cheese

Brown the ground beef in a skillet, stirring until crumbly; drain. Add the garlic salt, pepper, sugar and tomato sauce; mix well. Cover and simmer for 15 minutes. Combine the sour cream, cream cheese and onion in a bowl and mix well. Cook the noodles according to the package directions. Drain and keep warm. Grease a 9x13-inch baking dish with butter. Arrange a single layer of noodles over the bottom of the baking dish. Alternate layers of meat sauce, cheese, sour cream mixture and remaining noodles. Top with cheese. Bake, uncovered, at 350 degrees for 20 minutes. Yield: 8 servings.

Betty Darnell, Gadsden Life Member Club

Chicken Potpie

1 chicken, cooked
3 (16-ounce) cans mixed
   vegetables
2 to 3 cups chicken broth

2 (10-ounce) cans cream of
   chicken soup
Lemon pepper (optional)
2-crust pie pastry

Skin, debone and chop chicken into bite-size pieces. Combine the vegetables and chicken broth in a large saucepan and cook over medium heat for 10 minutes. Drain, reserving 1 cup of the chicken broth. Combine the cream of chicken soup and the reserved chicken broth in a bowl and mix well. Add the lemon pepper. Spray a 9x13-inch baking dish with nonstick cooking spray. Layer the vegetables, chicken and soup mixture in the bottom of the dish in the order listed. Top with the pie pastries, trimming edges to fit the dish. Bake at 350 degrees until bubbly and the crust is golden brown. Yield: 8 to 10 servings.

Stephanie Hurst, Riverchase Council

Rice Casserole

2 cups cooked rice
1 (10-ounce) can cream of
   chicken soup
1/2 cup mayonnaise
1/4 cup vegetable oil
1 cup finely chopped celery

1/4 cup sliced almonds
2 tablespoons finely chopped
   onion
4 ounces sliced water
   chestnuts
2 cups cornflakes, crushed

Combine the rice, soup, mayonnaise and oil in a large bowl and mix well. Stir in the celery, almonds, onion and water chestnuts. Spoon into a lightly greased baking dish. Bake at 350 degrees for 25 minutes. Remove from the oven and top with the crushed cornflakes. Return to the oven and bake for 10 more minutes or until golden brown. Yield: 8 servings.

Johnnie Brown, Montgomery Life Club Member

Vegetable Medley

1 (16-ounce) can French-style
  green beans
1 (10-ounce) package frozen
  lima beans
1(10-ounce) package frozen
  green peas
2 cups mayonnaise
4 hard-cooked eggs, chopped

1 medium onion, chopped
1/4 cup vegetable or olive oil
1 tablespoon prepared mustard
1 tablespoon Worcestershire
  sauce
1/8 teaspoon Tabasco sauce
Paprika to taste

Cook the green beans, lima beans and peas according to the package directions. Keep warm. Combine the mayonnaise, eggs, onion, oil, mustard, Worcestershire sauce and Tabasco sauce in a bowl and mix until well blended. Pour the mixture over the vegetables and stir until well coated. Sprinkle the top with paprika before serving. May prepare a day in advance. May serve hot or cold. Yield: 10 to 12 servings.

Faye S. King, Huntsville Council

Biscuits

2 cups flour
2½ teaspoons baking powder
1 teaspoon salt

1/4 teaspoon baking soda
6 tablespoons shortening
3/4 to 1 cup buttermilk

Sift the flour, baking powder, salt and baking soda in a bowl. Cut in the shortening until crumbly. Stir in the buttermilk gradually until a soft dough forms. Pat the dough out ½ inch thick on a heavily floured surface. Cut with a biscuit cutter and place on a greased baking sheet. Bake at 450 degrees for 12 to 15 minutes. Yield: 2 dozen biscuits.

Sue Walton, Birmingham Life Member Club

New York Cheesecake

4 (8-ounce) containers
  whipped cream cheese
2 cups sour cream
½ cup (1 stick) butter
5 eggs

1¼ cups sugar
2 tablespoons cornstarch
1¼ teaspoons vanilla extract
1 teaspoon lemon juice

Let the cream cheese, sour cream, butter and eggs stand at room temperature for approximately 1 hour. Combine the cream cheese, sour cream and butter in a large mixer bowl. Beat at high speed until well blended. Add the sugar, cornstarch, vanilla and lemon juice and beat well. Add the eggs 1 at a time, beating well after each addition. Continue beating until the mixture is very smooth. Pour the mixture into a greased 9-inch springform pan. Place in a large pan filled with enough warm water to come halfway up the side of the springform pan. Bake at 375 degrees for 1 hour or until the top is golden brown. Turn off the oven and let the cheesecake cool in the oven with the door open for 1 hour. Remove from the oven and let stand for 2 hours. Chill, covered, for at least 6 hours before serving. Yield: 12 to 16 servings.

Judy Howard, Riverchase Council

Try whipped cream, flavored with a little honey and cinnamon, as a topping in hot chocolate or coffee.

Peanut Butter Ice Cream

12 ounces crunchy peanut
  butter
2 cups half-and-half
2 cups sugar
2 tablespoons flour
½ teaspoon salt

6 eggs, lightly beaten
1 (12-ounce) can evaporated
  milk
4 cups half-and-half
1 tablespoon vanilla extract
Milk

Combine the peanut butter and 2 cups half-and-half in a saucepan. Cook over low heat until the peanut butter is melted, stirring constantly. Do not bring to a boil. Remove from the heat and set aside. Combine the sugar, flour and salt in a large bowl. Add the eggs and evaporated milk and stir until well blended, adding a small amount of the peanut butter mixture while stirring. Add the remaining peanut butter mixture, 4 cups half-and-half and vanilla and mix well. Pour the mixture into an ice cream freezer container and add enough milk to reach the fill line. Freeze according to the manufacturer's directions. Yield: 1 gallon.

Betty Jones, Birmingham Life Member Club

Banana Pudding

1 (6-ounce) package vanilla
  instant pudding mix
1½ cups milk
1 (14-ounce) can sweetened
  condensed milk
2 teaspoons vanilla extract

8 ounces whipped topping
1 box vanilla wafers
2 or 3 bananas, sliced
3 egg whites
6 tablespoons sugar
½ teaspoon vanilla extract

Combine the pudding mix and milk in a large mixer bowl and beat at low speed until well blended. Beat in the condensed milk and 2 teaspoons vanilla. Fold in the whipped topping. Layer the vanilla wafers, bananas and pudding in a 9x13-inch baking dish. Beat the egg whites, sugar and ½ teaspoon vanilla in a mixer bowl until very stiff. Spread evenly over the pudding. Bake at 400 degrees until the meringue is golden brown. Yield: 12 to 15 servings.

Lori Ann Avant, Alabama Telco Credit Union

Pecan Kisses

1 egg white
¾ cup packed brown sugar

½ teaspoon vanilla extract
2 cups pecan halves

Beat the egg white in a mixer bowl until soft peaks form. Gradually beat in the brown sugar and vanilla. Fold in the pecans. Place each coated pecan half 1 inch apart on a greased cookie sheet. Bake at 250 degrees for 30 minutes. Turn off the oven and let stand in the oven for 30 minutes. Remove from the oven when completely cool. Place the pecans in an airtight container. Yield: 2 cups.

Donna McNulty, Riverchase Council

Pralines

1 (1-pound) package light
  brown sugar
¾ cup evaporated milk

½ cup (1 stick) margarine
¼ teaspoon cinnamon
1 cup (or more) pecan halves

Combine the brown sugar, evaporated milk, margarine and cinnamon in a saucepan. Cook over medium heat until the mixture begins to boil, stirring constantly. Cook to 234 to 240 degrees on a candy thermometer, soft-ball stage, stirring constantly. Remove from heat and cool slightly. Beat until mixture thickens. Stir in the pecans and drop by teaspoonfuls onto waxed paper. If mixture is too thick, add a few drops of hot water. Yield: 30 to 40 pralines.

Mary W. Martin, Birmingham South Life Member Club

Chocolate Pound Cake

3 cups flour
1/2 cup baking cocoa
1/2 teaspoon baking powder
1/2 teaspoon salt
3 cups sugar
1 cup (2 sticks) margarine,
   softened

1/2 cup vegetable oil
5 eggs
1/4 cup milk
1 teaspoon vanilla extract

Sift the flour, baking cocoa, baking powder and salt into a large bowl. Cream the sugar and margarine in a mixer bowl until light and fluffy. Stir in the oil. Add the eggs 1 at a time, beating well after each addition. Add the flour mixture alternately with the milk, beating well after each addition. Stir in the vanilla. Pour into a greased and floured tube pan. Bake at 325 degrees for 1 1/4 hours or until a wooden pick inserted in the center comes out clean. Yield: 16 servings.

Shirley Crocker, Birmingham Life Member Club

Sour Cream Pound Cake

3 cups sifted flour
1/4 teaspoon baking
   soda
1 teaspoon salt
3 cups sugar

1 cup (2 sticks) butter or
   margarine, softened
6 eggs
1 cup sour cream
1 tablespoon lemon extract

Combine the flour, baking soda and salt in a bowl. Cream the sugar and butter in a mixer bowl until light and fluffy. Add the eggs 1 at a time, beating well after each addition. Add the flour mixture alternately with the sour cream, beating well after each addition. Stir in the lemon extract. Pour into a greased and floured tube pan. Bake at 350 degrees for 1 to 1 1/2 hours or until a wooden pick inserted in the center comes out clean. Yield: 16 servings.

Shirley Crocker, Birmingham Life Member Club

Seven-Up Cake

1 cup (2 sticks) margarine,
  softened
1/2 cup shortening
3 cups sugar

5 eggs
3 cups sifted flour
1 small bottle Seven-Up
2 teaspoons vanilla extract

Cream the margarine and shortening in a bowl until well blended. Beat in the sugar until light and fluffy. Beat in the eggs 1 at a time. Add the flour alternately with the Seven-Up, beating well after each addition. Stir in the vanilla until well blended. Pour into a greased and floured 9x13-inch cake pan. Bake at 350 degrees for 1 hour. Let cool. Yield: 15 to 20 servings.

Susan Poe, Riverchase Council

Apricot Squares

1 (8-ounce) package dried
  apricots, chopped
1 3/4 cups sugar
2 cups sifted flour

1/2 teaspoon baking soda
3/4 cup (1 1/2 sticks) butter
1 1/2 cups flaked coconut
1/2 cup chopped pecans

Combine apricots and enough water to cover in a saucepan. Cook over medium heat for 5 minutes. Remove from heat; drain and reserve liquid. Combine 3/4 cup of the sugar and 1/4 cup reserved apricot liquid in a bowl. Pour over the apricots in the saucepan. Cook over medium heat for 5 minutes. Mash the apricots with a fork and set aside. Combine the remaining 1 cup sugar, flour and baking soda in a large bowl and mix well. Cut in the butter with a pastry blender until crumbly. Stir in the coconut and pecans. Press 3/4 of the flour mixture over the bottom of a 9x13-inch pan. Bake at 350 degrees for 15 minutes. Spread the apricot mixture over the bottom of the prepared pan. Crumble the remaining flour mixture over the top. Bake for 20 minutes longer. Cool before cutting into squares. Yield: 4 dozen squares.

Pat Ramsey, sister of Cathy Kelley,
Birmingham South Cahaba Council

Macadamia Nut Cookies

1 cup (2 sticks) butter,   2¼ cups flour
    softened   1 teaspoon baking soda
¾ cup sugar   1 teaspoon salt
¾ cup packed brown sugar   2 cups white chocolate chips
2 eggs   1 cup macadamia nuts,
1 teaspoon vanilla extract   chopped

Cream the butter, sugar and brown sugar in a large mixer bowl until light and fluffy. Add the eggs and vanilla and beat well. Combine the flour, baking soda and salt in a bowl. Beat the flour mixture gradually into the butter mixture. Stir in the white chocolate chips and macadamia nuts. Drop by spoonfuls onto a cookie sheet. Bake at 350 degrees for 9 to 11 minutes. Yield: 3 dozen cookies.

Karen Tennyson, Riverchase Council

Snowflake Macaroons

2⅔ cups flaked coconut   ¼ teaspoon salt
⅔ cup sugar   4 egg whites, lightly beaten
6 tablespoons flour   1 teaspoon almond extract

Combine the coconut, sugar, flour and salt in a large bowl and mix well. Add the egg whites and almond extract, stirring until well blended. Drop by tablespoonfuls onto a lightly greased and floured cookie sheet. Bake at 325 degrees for 20 minutes or until edges of the cookies are golden brown. Remove the cookies immediately to a wire rack to cool. Yield: 2 dozen cookies.

Betty Etheredge, Bon Secour Life Member Club

Wooden Spoon Cookies

¾ cup blanched almonds,
   ground
½ cup (1 stick) butter or
   margarine

½ cup sugar
1 tablespoon flour
1 tablespoon whipping cream

Combine the almonds, butter, sugar, flour and cream in a 2-quart saucepan. Heat over low heat until the butter melts, stirring occasionally. Drop by spoonfuls 3 inches apart onto a greased and floured cookie sheet. Bake at 350 degrees for 5 to 7 minutes or until the edges are light brown and the centers are just golden brown. Let cookies stand for 30 to 60 seconds on the cookie sheet. Flip the cookies over with a pancake turner or long spatula. Working very quickly, roll each cookie into a cylinder around the handle of a wooden spoon. Remove from the spoon handle and cool on a wire rack. If the cookies become too hard to roll, return to the oven briefly to soften. Yield: 3 dozen cookies.

Brenda Reeves, Birmingham South Cahaba Council

Old-Fashioned Coconut Pie

½ cup (1 stick) margarine
1½ cups sugar
3 eggs, beaten
1 tablespoon vinegar

1 tablespoon vanilla extract
1 cup flaked coconut
1 unbaked (9-inch) pie shell

Melt the margarine in a saucepan. Combine with the sugar and eggs in a bowl and mix well. Stir in the vinegar and vanilla until well blended. Stir in the coconut. Spoon into the pie shell. Bake at 325 degrees for 1 hour. Yield: 8 servings.

Shirley Crocker, Birmingham Life Member Club

Lemon Icebox Pie

1 (14-ounce) can sweetened
  condensed milk
½ cup lemon juice

8 ounces whipped topping
1 (9-inch) graham cracker
  pie shell

Combine the condensed milk and lemon juice in a bowl and mix well. Fold in the whipped topping. Pour the mixture into the pie shell. Chill, covered, until set. Yield: 6 to 8 servings.

Karen Tennyson, Riverchase Council

Lemon Supreme Pie

1 unbaked (9-inch) pie shell
19 ounces cream cheese,
  softened
¾ cup confectioners' sugar
1½ cups whipped topping
1 tablespoon lemon juice
1½ cups sugar
6 tablespoons cornstarch

½ teaspoon salt
1¼ cups water
2 tablespoons butter, softened
2 teaspoons grated lemon zest
4 or 5 drops of yellow food
  coloring
½ cup lemon juice

Line the pie shell with a double thickness of foil. Bake at 450 degrees for 8 minutes. Remove the foil and bake for 5 minutes longer or until light brown. Beat the cream cheese and confectioners' sugar in a bowl until smooth. Fold in the whipped topping and 1 tablespoon lemon juice. Reserve ½ cup for topping. Spread the remaining cream cheese mixture over the bottom of the prepared pie shell. Combine the sugar, cornstarch, salt and water in a saucepan. Bring to a boil over medium heat, stirring occasionally. Reduce the heat and cook for 2 minutes or until thickened. Remove from the heat. Stir in the butter, lemon zest and food coloring. Stir in ½ cup lemon juice gently. Let cool to room temperature. Spread over the cream cheese layer. Spoon the reserved cream cheese mixture into a pastry bag fitted with a star decorator tip. Pipe stars onto the top of the pie. Chill, covered, until serving time. Yield: 6 to 8 servings.

Sam Wesley, Montgomery Council

Lemon Chess Pie

3 eggs
1½ cups sugar
1 tablespoon cornmeal
6 tablespoons margarine,
  melted

5 tablespoons milk
Juice of 1 lemon
1 teaspoon lemon extract
1 unbaked (9-inch) pie shell

Beat the eggs, sugar and cornmeal in a mixer bowl until well blended. Add the margarine and milk and beat well. Beat in the lemon juice and lemon extract. Pour into the pie shell. Bake at 350 degrees for 45 minutes. Yield: 8 servings.

Francis M. Tucker, Selma Life Member Club

Pecan Pie

8 ounces cream cheese,
  softened
½ cup sugar
1 egg
1 teaspoon salt
3 eggs

¼ cup sugar
1 cup corn syrup
1 teaspoon vanilla extract
1 unbaked (9-inch) pie shell
1¼ cups chopped pecans

Beat the cream cheese, ½ cup sugar, 1 egg and salt in a medium mixer bowl until smooth. Combine 3 eggs, ¼ cup sugar, corn syrup and vanilla in a mixer bowl and beat until well blended. Spoon the cream cheese mixture over the bottom of the pie shell and top with the pecans. Pour the corn syrup mixture over the pecans. Bake at 375 degrees for 40 minutes. Yield: 6 to 8 servings.

Jean Mann, Birmingham Life Member Club

SUMMER

Ten-Layer Dip

1 cup sour cream
1 envelope taco seasoning mix
1 (16-ounce) can nonfat
  refried beans
1 cup avocado dip
1/2 head lettuce, shredded
1 medium tomato, chopped
1 (4-ounce) can chopped
  green chiles, drained

1 (4-ounce) can chopped black
  olives, drained
3 medium green onions,
  chopped
2 cups shredded sharp
  Cheddar cheese
Chopped jalapeño chiles

Combine the sour cream and taco seasoning mix in a bowl and mix well. Layer the refried beans, avocado dip, sour cream mixture, lettuce, tomato, green chiles, black olives, green onions and cheese on a large platter. Sprinkle with jalapeño chiles. Chill, covered, in the refrigerator. Serve with corn or tortilla chips.
Yield: 8 to 10 servings.

Marie P. Williams, Mobile Council

Mint Tea

3 cups water
3 family-size tea bags, or
  9 regular-size tea bags
10 fresh mint leaves
3/4 cup sugar
1 (6-ounce) can frozen
  lemonade concentrate,
  thawed

1 (6-ounce) can frozen orange
  juice concentrate, thawed
6 juice cans water

Bring 3 cups water to a boil in a saucepan. Add the tea bags and mint leaves. Remove from heat and cool. Strain into a large pitcher. Add the sugar, lemonade concentrate, orange juice concentrate and 6 cans water and mix well. Yield: 1/2 gallon.

Dot Spencer, Birmingham South Life Member Club

Missionary Salad

1 small jar maraschino
   cherries
1 (29-ounce) can crushed
   pineapple
1 (16-ounce) can sliced
   peaches

2 (15-ounce) cans fruit
   cocktail
1 (15-ounce) can pears
1/2 package miniature
   marshmallows
8 ounces cream cheese, cubed

Drain the cherries, pineapple, peaches, fruit cocktail and pears thoroughly. Combine the drained fruit and marshmallows in a large bowl. Add the cream cheese and toss to mix well. Chill, covered, in the refrigerator. Yield: 10 to 12 servings.

Linda Cunningham, Birmingham Metro Council

Cabbage Slaw

1 medium cabbage, shredded
2 medium onions, sliced
3/4 cup sugar
1 cup vinegar
1 1/2 teaspoons salt

1 teaspoon celery seeds
1 teaspoon mustard
1 teaspoon sugar
3/4 cup vegetable oil

Alternate layers of the cabbage and onions in a large bowl. Sprinkle with 3/4 cup sugar. Combine the vinegar, salt, celery seeds, mustard and 1 teaspoon sugar in a saucepan. Bring to a boil. Stir in the oil. Pour over the layers. Chill, covered, for 8 to 12 hours. Toss before serving. May store in the refrigerator for several days.
Yield: 8 servings.

Elizabeth Cornwell, Birmingham Life Member Club

Coleslaw

2 heads cabbage, shredded
1 carrot, grated
1/4 cup chopped green onions
1/4 cup thinly sliced
  white onion
1/4 cup chopped green bell
  pepper

1 1/2 cups mayonnaise
2 tablespoons sugar
1 tablespoon white vinegar
1 tablespoon pepper
1 tablespoon garlic salt
1 tablespoon seasoned salt

Combine the cabbage, carrot, green onions, white onion and green pepper in a large bowl. Mix the mayonnaise, sugar, vinegar, pepper, garlic salt and seasoned salt in a bowl. Add to the cabbage mixture and toss to mix well. Add additional sugar if needed. Marinate, covered, in the refrigerator for 6 to 24 hours. May reduce the recipe by half. Yield: 12 to 15 servings.

Cheryl Loeffler, Riverchase Council

Country Coleslaw

1 cup vegetable oil
6 tablespoons rice vinegar
1/4 cup sugar
1 tablespoon MSG
1 teaspoon salt
1 teaspoon pepper
2 packages ramen noodles,
  crushed

1 package sliced almonds
1 package sunflower seed
  kernels
1 package coleslaw mix
1/2 package broccoli slaw mix
8 green onions, chopped

Blend the oil, rice vinegar, sugar, MSG, salt and pepper in a bowl. Chill, covered, for 8 to 12 hours. Place the ramen noodles, almonds and sunflower seed kernels on a baking sheet. Bake at 350 degrees for 15 to 20 minutes or until toasted. Combine the coleslaw mix, broccoli slaw mix and green onions in a bowl. Add the toasted almond mixture and toss to mix well. Add the vinaigrette just before serving and toss to mix well. Yield: 8 to 10 servings.

Susan Poe, Riverchase Council

Golden Rule Coleslaw

1 large package coleslaw mix
1 onion, chopped
1 green bell pepper, chopped
½ cup sugar
1 cup vinegar

½ cup vegetable oil
2 teaspoons celery seeds
1 teaspoon dry mustard
1 teaspoon salt

Place the coleslaw mix in a large bowl. Layer the onion and green pepper over the top. Sprinkle with sugar. Combine the vinegar, oil, celery seeds, dry mustard and salt in a saucepan. Bring to a rolling boil. Pour over the layers and toss to mix well. Chill, covered, for 2 hours. Yield: 6 servings.

Don Helms, Birmingham South Cahaba Council

Layered Salad

Shredded lettuce
Chopped cooked bacon
Chopped green onions
1 cup frozen peas

Mayonnaise
Salt and pepper to taste
Grated Parmesan cheese

Layer lettuce, bacon, green onions and frozen peas in a bowl. Spread mayonnaise over the top, sealing to the edge of the bowl. Season with salt and pepper. Sprinkle with Parmesan cheese. Yield: variable.

Cathy Prange, Alabama Telco Credit Union

Chicken Salad

4 boneless skinless chicken
    breasts, cooked, chopped
1 cup green grapes
1 cup red grapes
1 cup chopped pecans
1 cup mayonnaise

¼ cup pickle relish
Salt and pepper to taste
¾ package shell pasta or
    elbow macaroni, cooked,
    drained

Combine the chicken, green grapes, red grapes, pecans, mayonnaise and relish in a bowl and mix well. Season with salt and pepper. Stir in the pasta. Chill, covered, until serving time. Yield: 6 to 8 servings.

Debbie Speaks, Montgomery Council

Shoe Peg Corn Salad

2 (16-ounce) cans Shoe Peg
    corn, drained
1 onion, chopped
1 green bell pepper, chopped
1 (2-ounce) jar pimento,
    drained

½ cup vegetable oil
¼ cup vinegar
¼ teaspoon dry mustard
Minced garlic to taste
Salt to taste

Combine the corn, onion, green pepper and pimento in a bowl and mix well. Mix the oil, vinegar, dry mustard, garlic and salt in a bowl. Add to the corn mixture and mix well. Chill, covered, until serving time. Yield: 5 or 6 servings.

Della Pearl Dukes, Bon Secour Life Member Club

Corn Bread Salad

2 (8-inch) round loaves cold
  corn bread
6 slices bacon, cooked
1/2 cup chopped onion
1/2 cup chopped green bell
  pepper

1/4 cup chopped celery
6 hard-cooked eggs, sliced
1 cup (or more) mayonnaise

Crumble the corn bread and bacon into a large bowl. Add the onion, green pepper, celery and eggs. Stir in just enough mayonnaise to moisten. Chill, covered, for 2 hours.
Yield: 20 servings.

Alice Walski, Birmingham Life Member Club

Fourth-of-July Corn Bread Salad

1 loaf corn bread
Crumbled cooked bacon
Chopped green bell pepper
Chopped purple onion

Chopped green onions
Chopped tomatoes
Chopped celery
Mayonnaise

Crumble the corn bread into a large bowl. Add bacon, green pepper, purple onion, green onions, tomatoes and celery and mix well. Stir in just enough mayonnaise to moisten. Chill, covered with plastic wrap, until ready to serve. May store in the refrigerator for up to several days. Yield: 8 to 10 servings.

Boots Cooper, Opelika Life Member Club

Vegetable Pasta Salad

1 zucchini, sliced
1 red and/or green bell
  pepper, chopped
1 (16-ounce) can red beans,
  drained
1 (16-ounce) can corn,
  drained
1 (14-ounce) can hearts of
  palm, or 1 small jar
  marinated artichoke hearts,
  drained

Black and/or green olives to
  taste
Green onions to taste
Minced fresh garlic to taste
Chopped fresh parsley to taste
Lemon pepper to taste
1/4 bottle Italian salad
  dressing, or to taste
16 ounces pasta noodles

Combine the zucchini, bell peppers, beans, corn, hearts of palm, olives, green onions, garlic, parsley and lemon pepper in a large bowl and mix well. Add the salad dressing and toss to mix. Marinate, covered, in the refrigerator for 8 to 12 hours. Cook the pasta using package directions; drain. Add to the vegetable mixture and toss to mix. May add chopped tomatoes, purple onion, cucumbers, salami, ham and/or pepperoni. Yield: 20 servings.

Gloria Wadsworth, Birmingham South Cahaba Council

Cheesy Potato Salad

5 pounds potatoes
4 hard-cooked eggs, chopped
2 cups mayonnaise
1 (8-ounce) jar sweet pickle
  relish

1 tablespoon prepared mustard
2 1/2 teaspoons salt
1 teaspoon pepper
1 1/2 cups shredded mild
  Cheddar cheese

Peel the potatoes and cut into cubes. Place in cold water to cover in a saucepan. Cook until tender; drain. Add the eggs, mayonnaise, pickle relish, mustard, salt and pepper and mix well. Stir in the cheese. Spoon into a serving bowl. Yield: 30 servings.

Sandra Deason, Birmingham South Cahaba Council

Potato Salad

5 pounds potatoes, cubed,
  cooked
5 hard-cooked eggs, chopped
1 cup chopped celery
2 or 3 onion slices, chopped
12 to 15 pitted olives, chopped

1 small jar pimento, drained
Dill and sweet pickle relish
  to taste
Mayonnaise-type salad
  dressing to taste

Combine the potatoes, hard-cooked eggs, celery, onion, olives, pimento and dill and sweet pickle relish in a large bowl and mix well. Stir in enough mayonnaise-type salad dressing to moisten. Spoon into a large serving bowl. Yield: 18 servings.

Mary Ann Goodson, Birmingham South Life Member Club

Tuscan Potato Salad

3 pounds red potatoes
1 cup ricotta cheese
2/3 cup freshly grated
  Parmesan cheese
1/2 cup thinly sliced red onion

4 garlic cloves, minced
1/2 cup olive oil
6 tablespoons cider vinegar
Salt and pepper to taste
1/2 cup chopped fresh parsley

Peel the potatoes and cut into small cubes. Cook in water to cover in a saucepan until tender; drain. Combine the ricotta cheese, Parmesan cheese, onion and garlic in a medium bowl. Whisk the olive oil, vinegar, salt and pepper in a small bowl. Fold the cheese mixture and olive oil mixture into the potatoes. Spoon into a large serving bowl. Chill, covered, until serving time to enhance the flavor. Sprinkle with parsley just before serving. May store for up to 2 days in the refrigerator. Yield: 8 servings.

Donna Jean Bowman, Birmingham South Cahaba Council

Marinated Vegetable Salad

1 (16-ounce) can whole kernel
  corn
1 (16-ounce) can green beans
1 (16-ounce) can carrots
1 (16-ounce) can green peas
1 (14-ounce) can bean sprouts
1 (8-ounce) can water
  chestnuts
1 medium jar pimentos,
  drained

1 medium red onion, chopped
1 small green bell pepper,
  chopped
Chopped celery to taste
1/2 cup vegetable oil
1/4 cup white vinegar
1 cup sugar
1 teaspoon salt

Drain the corn, green beans, carrots, green peas, bean sprouts and water chestnuts, reserving half the liquid. Combine the corn, green beans, carrots, green peas, bean sprouts, water chestnuts and reserved liquid in a large bowl and mix well. Stir in the pimentos, red onion, green pepper and celery. Whisk the oil, vinegar, sugar and salt in a bowl until the sugar is dissolved. Add to the vegetable mixture and stir to mix well. Marinate, covered, in the refrigerator for 24 hours, stirring occasionally. Yield: 12 to 15 servings.

Judy Howard, Riverchase Council

Barbecued Meatballs

3 pounds ground beef
1 cup rolled oats
1 cup cracker crumbs
1/2 cup chopped onion
1 (12-ounce) can evaporated
  milk
2 eggs
2 teaspoons salt

2 teaspoons chili powder
1/2 teaspoon garlic powder
1/2 teaspoon pepper
2 cups catsup
1 cup packed brown sugar
1/4 cup chopped onion
1/2 teaspoon liquid smoke
1/2 teaspoon garlic powder

Combine the ground beef, oats, cracker crumbs, 1/2 cup onion, evaporated milk, eggs, salt, chili powder, 1/2 teaspoon garlic powder and pepper in a bowl and mix well. Shape into small balls. Place in a single layer on a baking sheet lined with waxed paper. Freeze until firm. Store frozen meatballs in freezer bags until ready to use. Heat the catsup, brown sugar, $1/4$ cup onion, liquid smoke and $1/2$ teaspoon garlic powder in a saucepan until the brown sugar is dissolved, stirring constantly. Place the meatballs in a 9x13-inch baking pan. Pour the sauce over the meatballs. Bake at 350 degrees for 1 hour or until the meatballs are cooked through. Yield: 8 to 10 servings.

Mary G. Crittenden, Huntsville Council

Firecracker Casserole

2 pounds ground beef
1 medium onion, chopped
1 to 2 tablespoons chili
   powder
2 to 3 teaspoons cumin
$1/2$ teaspoon salt
4 (7-inch) flour tortillas

1 (10-ounce) can cream of
   mushroom soup
1 (10-ounce) can diced
   tomatoes and green chiles
1 cup shredded Cheddar
   cheese

Brown the ground beef with the onion in a skillet, stirring until the ground beef is crumbly; drain. Add the chili powder, cumin and salt. Spoon into a greased 9x13-inch baking dish. Arrange the tortillas over the top. Combine the mushroom soup and undrained tomatoes and green chiles in a bowl and mix well. Pour over the tortillas. Sprinkle with Cheddar cheese. Bake, uncovered, at 350 degrees for 25 to 30 minutes or until heated through. Yield: 6 to 8 servings.

Faye Harper, Tuscaloosa Council

Texas Chili Cheese Fries

1 pound ground beef
1 large onion, finely chopped
1 tomato, peeled, finely
  chopped
1/8 teaspoon finely chopped
  garlic
1 (8-ounce) can tomato sauce
1/8 teaspoon chili powder

1/8 teaspoon salt
1/8 teaspoon pepper
1/4 (32-ounce) package frozen
  French-fried potatoes
Creole seasoning to taste
Shredded Cheddar cheese to
  taste

Brown the ground beef in a skillet, stirring until crumbly; drain. Sauté the onion, tomato and garlic in a large nonstick skillet until the onion is translucent. Add the ground beef and tomato sauce and mix well. Season with chili powder, salt and pepper. Simmer until heated through, stirring frequently. Place the frozen potatoes on a baking sheet. Season with Creole seasoning. Bake at 350 to 400 degrees until the potatoes are brown, turning once. Place the French-fried potatoes in a microwave-safe dish. Sprinkle with cheese. Microwave for 5 to 10 seconds or until the cheese is melted. Top with the hot chili. Serve immediately. Yield: 4 to 6 servings.

élan MariKathryn Glenn, Birmingham South Life Member Club

*To keep celery fresh for weeks, wrap it in foil
and store in the refrigerator.*

Easy Barbecued Pork

1 pork roast
2 cups catsup
½ cup packed brown sugar
½ cup Worcestershire sauce

¼ cup vinegar
2 teaspoons garlic powder
1 teaspoon mustard
⅛ teaspoon Tabasco sauce

Cook the pork roast in a slow cooker until cooked through; drain. Cool slightly. Shred the pork into strips, discarding the skin and bones. Place the pork strips in a 9x13-inch glass baking dish. Combine the catsup, brown sugar, Worcestershire sauce, vinegar, garlic powder, mustard and Tabasco sauce in a saucepan. Heat until the brown sugar dissolves, stirring frequently. Pour over the pork. Bake at 350 degrees until bubbly. Yield: 4 to 6 servings.

Sherrie Poynor, Montgomery Council

Smoked Ribs with Honey-Mustard Sauce

Hickory chips
5 pounds pork spareribs
½ cup honey

¼ cup prepared mustard
½ teaspoon maple flavoring

Soak hickory chips in water to cover for 15 minutes or longer; drain. Heat the charcoal in a smoker for 15 to 20 minutes or until the coals are white. Place the hickory chips on the coals. Fill the water pan in the smoker with water. Place the spareribs on a smoker rack. Cover with the smoker lid. Cook for 3 hours. Combine the honey, mustard and maple flavoring in a saucepan. Cook over medium heat until blended, stirring constantly. Baste the ribs with the sauce. Cook, covered, for 30 minutes. Turn over the ribs and baste again with the sauce. Cook, covered, for 30 minutes longer or until cooked through. Yield: 4 to 6 servings.

Narice Sutton, Birmingham Life Member Club

Hot Diggity Dogs

1 medium bottle catsup
1 onion, chopped
1 green bell pepper, chopped
1 tablespoon prepared mustard
1 tablespoon Worcestershire
  sauce

1 tablespoon vinegar
1/4 cup sugar
Sauerkraut (optional)
4 packages jumbo hot dogs

Combine the catsup, onion, green pepper, mustard, Worcestershire sauce, vinegar and sugar in a slow cooker and mix well. Stir in the sauerkraut. Arrange the hot dogs standing up in the mixture. Cook on Low for 3 1/2 to 4 hours or until cooked through.
Yield: 32 servings.

Tara Goodwin, Riverchase Council

Ultimate Baked Chicken

2 garlic cloves, slivered
Sprigs of fresh marjoram
1 (3-pound) chicken

Kosher salt
Freshly ground pepper to taste

Place the garlic and marjoram under the skin of the chicken breast. Coat the chicken liberally with kosher salt. Sprinkle with pepper. Place the chicken on a bed of kosher salt in a pan. Marinate, covered, in the refrigerator for 24 hours. Line a roasting pan with foil and add a small amount of water. Place the chicken breast side up on a wire rack sprayed with olive oil nonstick cooking spray. Place in the prepared pan. Bake at 350 degrees for 25 minutes. Turn over the chicken. Bake for 15 minutes longer or until brown and cooked through. May substitute oregano or tarragon for the marjoram. Yield: 4 to 6 servings.

Donna Jean Bowman, Birmingham South Cahaba Council

Fourth-of-July Chicken

1 bottle soy sauce
1 bottle Dale's steak seasoning
1 cup sugar
½ teaspoon pepper

¼ teaspoon garlic powder
2 (3-pound) chickens, cut up
Seasoned salt to taste

Combine the soy sauce, steak seasoning, sugar, pepper and garlic powder in a large saucepan. Heat until the sugar is dissolved, stirring frequently. Add the chicken. Sprinkle with seasoned salt. Marinate, covered, in the refrigerator for 24 hours. Drain the chicken, discarding the marinade. Place the chicken on a grill rack. Grill over hot coals until cooked through. Yield: 8 to 12 servings.

Larry M. Ryan, Riverchase Council

Fried Chicken

4 skinless chicken breasts
1 cup flour
1 tablespoon salt

Pepper to taste
Vegetable oil for frying

Coat the chicken with a mixture of the flour, salt and pepper. Fry the chicken in hot oil in a skillet over medium heat for 30 minutes or until brown and cooked through, turning several times. Remove to paper towels to drain. Yield: 4 servings.

Lola G. Duffey, Shoals Life Member Club

Honey-Mustard Chicken Nuggets

2 (4-ounce) boneless skinless
  chicken breasts
¼ cup honey
2 tablespoons prepared
  mustard
1 tablespoon reduced-calorie
  margarine

2 teaspoons reduced-sodium
  soy sauce
½ cup cornflake crumbs
1 teaspoon paprika

Cut the chicken into eighteen 1-inch pieces. Combine the honey, mustard, margarine and soy sauce in a microwave-safe bowl and mix well. Microwave on High for 20 seconds or until the margarine melts. Add the chicken and stir to coat. Mix the cornflake crumbs and paprika in a shallow dish. Dredge each chicken piece in the cornflake mixture until coated, using wooden picks. Arrange ½ of the chicken pieces in a circle around the edge of a large heavy-duty paper plate. Cover with waxed paper. Microwave on High for 2 to 2½ minutes or until cooked through. Repeat the process with the remaining chicken pieces. Microwave the remaining honey-mustard mixture on High for 1 to 1½ minutes or until cooked through. Serve with the chicken pieces. Yield: 2 servings.

Susan Currie, Birmingham South Cahaba Council

Pepsi Chicken

5 boneless skinless chicken
  breasts, cut into strips
1 tablespoon vegetable oil
1 cup catsup

1 (12-ounce) can diet Pepsi
3 tablespoons tomatoes with
  green chiles

Cook the chicken in the oil in a large skillet over medium-low heat for 5 minutes. Add the catsup, Pepsi and tomatoes with green chiles. Cook, covered, for 20 minutes. Simmer, uncovered, for 10 minutes or until the chicken is cooked through. *Note:* If you wish to add more chicken, add 1 tablespoon of tomatoes with green chiles for every 2 extra chicken breasts added. Yield: 5 servings.

Judy Howard, Riverchase Council

Barbecued Shrimp

1 pound (4 sticks) margarine
2 teaspoons garlic powder
2 teaspoons salt

1 jar seasoned pepper
Unpeeled jumbo shrimp

Melt the margarine in a Dutch oven. Add the garlic powder, salt and seasoned pepper. Simmer for 3 to 4 minutes, stirring constantly. Add the shrimp. Cook until the shrimp turn pink, stirring constantly. Yield: variable.

Emma Allen, Riverchase Council

Fourth-of-July Baked Beans

8 ounces ground beef
8 ounces sliced bacon
1 cup chopped onion
1 cup chopped green bell
  pepper
1 (28-ounce) can pork and
  beans
1 (17-ounce) can lima beans,
  drained
1 (15-ounce) can red kidney
  beans, drained

½ cup barbecue sauce
½ cup catsup
½ cup packed brown sugar
2 tablespoons prepared
  mustard
2 tablespoons dark corn syrup
1 tablespoon honey
1 teaspoon salt
½ teaspoon chili powder

Brown the ground beef and bacon with the onion and green pepper, stirring until the ground beef is crumbly and the onion is transparent; drain. Combine the ground beef mixture, undrained pork and beans, lima beans and red kidney beans in a large bowl and mix well. Add the barbecue sauce, catsup, brown sugar, mustard, corn syrup, honey, salt and chili powder and mix well. Spoon into a 2½-quart baking dish. Bake, covered, at 350 degrees for 45 minutes. Bake, uncovered, for 15 minutes longer. Yield: 12 servings.

Marie Williams, Mobile Council

Sommor

1/4 cup vegetable oil
4 or 5 potatoes, peeled, cubed
1 small onion, chopped

1 (16-ounce) can pork and
  beans
1/2 cup catsup

Heat the oil in a large skillet. Add the potatoes and onion. Cook until tender. Stir in the pork and beans and catsup. Simmer for 10 minutes or until heated through. May add cooked ground beef. Yield: 4 to 6 servings.

Mike Whitt, Montgomery Council

Barbecued Corn

8 fresh ears of corn
1/2 cup (1 stick) butter,
  softened

1/4 cup barbecue sauce

Remove the husks from the corn. Blend the butter and barbecue sauce in a bowl. Spread generously over the corn. Wrap each ear of corn securely in heavy-duty foil. Place on a grill rack. Grill over hot coals for 15 to 20 minutes or until the corn is cooked through, turning several times. Yield: 8 servings.

Narice Sutton, Birmingham Life Member Club

Shoe Peg Corn Casserole

Bacon to taste
1 medium onion, chopped
2 (11-ounce) cans white
  Shoe Peg corn, drained

1 cup sour cream
Salt and pepper to taste

Fry bacon in a skillet until crisp. Remove the bacon to paper towels to drain. Crumble the bacon. Add the onion to the bacon drippings in the skillet. Sauté until the onion is translucent; drain. Combine the onion, corn and sour cream in a bowl and mix well. Season with salt and pepper. Place in a nonstick baking dish. Top with the crumbled bacon. Bake at 350 degrees for 30 minutes or until bubbly. Yield: 6 to 8 servings.

Aileene Lindsey, Birmingham Life Member Club

Hash Brown Potato Casserole

1 package miniature Tater
  Tots
1 (10-ounce) can cream of
  chicken soup
1 cup sour cream

1 onion, chopped
2 cups sharp Cheddar cheese
½ cup (1 stick) butter, melted
2 cups crushed cornflakes
½ cup (1 stick) butter, melted

Combine the Tater Tots, chicken soup, sour cream, onion, cheese and ½ cup butter in a large bowl and mix well. Spoon into a large baking dish. Bake at 350 degrees for 1 hour. Remove from the oven and stir the mixture. Sprinkle the cornflakes over the top. Pour ½ cup butter over the cornflakes. Bake for 5 to 10 minutes longer or until golden brown. Yield: 8 to 10 servings.

Susan Poe, Riverchase Council

Pineapple Casserole

1 (20-ounce) can juice-pack
   crushed pineapple
1 cup shredded Cheddar
   cheese
1/2 cup sugar

3 tablespoons flour
1 sleeve butter crackers,
   coarsely crushed
1/2 cup (1 stick) butter, melted

Drain the pineapple, reserving 5 tablespoons of the juice. Mix the pineapple and cheese in a bowl. Place in a nonstick baking dish. Combine the sugar and flour in a bowl. Stir in the reserved pineapple juice. Pour over the pineapple mixture. Sprinkle with cracker crumbs. Drizzle with melted butter. Bake at 300 degrees for 30 minutes. Yield: 4 to 6 servings.

Mamie Jewel Posey, Shoals Life Member Club

Barbecue Sauce

4 cups catsup
4 cups water
3/4 cup sugar
1 lemon, quartered

1 small onion, finely chopped
1 garlic clove, minced
1 1/2 teaspoons celery seeds

Combine the catsup, water, sugar, lemon quarters, onion, garlic and celery seeds in a saucepan and mix well. Bring to a boil and reduce heat. Simmer for 30 to 45 minutes. Remove the lemon quarters. Pour into a container with a lid. Store, covered, in the refrigerator. Yield: 2 quarts.

Betty Foshee, Decatur Council

Sweet Barbecue Sauce

8 cups water
4 cups red wine vinegar
4 cups white wine
4 cups catsup
1½ cups Worcestershire sauce

1½ cups packed brown sugar
1½ cups salt
1½ cups prepared mustard
½ cup ground black pepper
½ cup red pepper flakes

Combine the water, red wine vinegar, white wine, catsup, Worcestershire sauce, brown sugar, salt, mustard, black pepper and red pepper flakes in a saucepan and mix well. Bring to a boil and reduce heat. Simmer, covered, for 30 minutes. Yield: 1 gallon.

Donna Jean Bowman, Birmingham South Cahaba Council

Spicy Barbecue Sauce

1 bottle catsup
½ cup vinegar
¼ teaspoon Tabasco sauce
   (optional)
¼ cup (½ stick) butter

1 tablespoon Worcestershire
   sauce
Juice of 1 lemon
Salt and pepper to taste

Combine the catsup, vinegar, Tabasco sauce, butter, Worcestershire sauce, lemon juice, salt and pepper in a saucepan and mix well. Heat until the butter melts, stirring frequently. Add enough water for the desired consistency, stirring constantly. Yield: 2½ cups.

Janice Bass, Riverchase Council

Red Slaw Relish

1/3 cup sugar
1/2 cup red wine
1/2 cup water
1/4 cup vinegar
1 tablespoon mustard seeds
2 teaspoons salt
1 teaspoon celery seeds
Red pepper to taste
1 large head cabbage, cut into
 chunks or shredded

1 large green bell pepper,
 chopped
1 quart tomatoes, cubed,
 drained
1 (6-ounce) jar dill pickles,
 chopped
Cayenne pepper to taste

Combine the sugar, red wine, water, vinegar, mustard seeds, salt, celery seeds and red pepper to taste in a saucepan. Bring to a boil over medium heat and reduce the heat. Simmer, uncovered, for 5 minutes. Cool. Combine the cabbage, green pepper, tomatoes, pickles and cayenne pepper in a large bowl and mix well. Add the vinegar mixture and toss to mix. Chill, covered, until serving time, tossing to mix occasionally. Yield: 8 servings.

Larry Ryan, Riverchase Council

Cheese Garlic Biscuits

2 cups baking mix
2/3 cup milk
1/2 cup shredded Cheddar
 cheese

1/4 cup (1/2 stick) butter or
 margarine, melted
1/4 teaspoon garlic powder

Mix the baking mix, milk and cheese in a bowl to form a soft dough. Beat vigorously by hand for about 30 seconds. Drop by spoonfuls onto an ungreased baking sheet. Bake at 450 degrees for 8 to 10 minutes or until golden brown. Blend melted butter and garlic powder in a bowl. Brush over the hot biscuits. Serve immediately. Yield: 10 to 12 servings.

Susan Poe, Riverchase Council

Blackberry Cobbler

4 cups undrained canned
  sweetened blackberries

1 (10-count) can biscuits
1 pint vanilla ice cream

Bring the blackberries to a boil in a saucepan. Cut each biscuit round into quarters. Add to the blackberries 1 at a time. Cook, covered, until the biscuit quarters are cooked through. Serve with vanilla ice cream. Yield: 4 servings.

Marjorie S. (Francis) Tucker, Selma Life Member Club

Blueberry Cobbler

1 (20-ounce) can crushed
  pineapple, drained
2 cups blueberries
3/4 cup sugar
1 (2-layer) package yellow
  cake mix

1 cup (2 sticks) butter, melted
1 cup chopped pecans
1/4 cup sugar

Layer the pineapple and blueberries in a buttered 9x13-inch baking dish. Sprinkle with 3/4 cup sugar. Spread the cake mix over the layers. Pour the butter over the cake mix. Sprinkle with pecans and 1/4 cup sugar. Bake at 325 degrees for 35 to 40 minutes. Yield: 8 to 10 servings.

Louise Wheeler, Selma Life Member Club

Blueberry Crisp

5 to 6 cups fresh or frozen
   blueberries
2 tablespoons cornstarch
1 tablespoon sugar

1 cup flour
3/4 cup sugar
1/2 cup (1 stick) butter
1/2 cup chopped pecans

Combine the blueberries, cornstarch and 1 tablespoon sugar in a bowl and stir to mix well. Spoon into a large baking dish. Combine the flour and 3/4 cup sugar in a bowl. Cut in the butter until crumbly. Stir in the pecans. Crumble over the blueberry mixture. Bake at 400 degrees for 30 minutes. Yield: 8 servings.

Judy Burrow, Decatur Council

Easy Peach Cobbler

1/2 cup (1 stick) margarine
1 cup sugar
1 cup flour
2 1/2 teaspoons baking powder

3/4 cup milk
1 (29-ounce) can cling
   peaches

Melt the margarine in a 9x13-inch baking dish. Sift the sugar, flour and baking powder into a bowl. Add the milk and mix well. Pour into the prepared dish; do not stir. Pour the undrained peaches over the top; do not stir. Bake at 350 degrees for 40 minutes or until brown. Yield: 8 to 10 servings.

Susan Poe, Riverchase Council

Cinnamon Peach Cobbler

1 cup sugar	1/2 cup (1 stick) butter, melted
1 cup self-rising flour	1 (29-ounce) can peach slices
1 cup milk	in light syrup
1 teaspoon vanilla extract	1/2 teaspoon cinnamon

Mix the sugar and flour in a bowl. Add the milk and vanilla gradually, beating constantly. Stir in the butter. Mix the peaches and cinnamon in a bowl. Pour into a baking dish. Spoon the batter over the peaches; do not stir. Bake at 375 degrees for 35 minutes or until brown. Yield: 8 to 10 servings.

Betty Hyde, Montgomery Council

Strawberry Cobbler

3 cups thawed frozen sliced	3/4 cup flour
strawberries	2 teaspoons baking powder
1/2 cup sugar	1/2 teaspoon salt
1/2 cup (1 stick) butter	3/4 cup milk
1 cup sugar	

Combine the strawberries and 1/2 cup sugar in a bowl and mix well. Melt the butter in a 9x13-inch baking dish. Mix 1 cup sugar, flour, baking powder, salt and milk in a bowl. Pour into the prepared dish; do not stir. Top with the strawberry mixture; do not stir. Bake at 350 degrees for 45 minutes. May use fresh strawberries sweetened with 1 cup sugar. Yield: 8 servings.

Betty Darnell, Gadsden Life Member Club

Homemade Peach Ice Cream

4 cups chopped fresh peaches   Drop of vanilla extract
Sugar to taste   1 (12-ounce) can evaporated
5 eggs   milk
2 cups sugar   2% or whole milk

Mash the peaches in a bowl. Sweeten with sugar to taste. Beat the
eggs in a mixer bowl until light and fluffy. Add 2 cups sugar
gradually, beating constantly until thick. Beat in vanilla. Stir in the
peach mixture and evaporated milk. Pour into an ice cream freezer
container. Add 2% milk to the fill line. Freeze using the
manufacturer's directions. Yield: 1 gallon.

Tom Coffield, Birmingham South Cahaba Council

Rocky Road Ice Cream

2 cups milk   4 cups heavy cream
6 ounces semisweet chocolate   2 cups miniature
1¾ cups sugar   marshmallows
½ teaspoon salt   1½ cups chocolate chips
2 cups half-and-half   1 cup chopped pecans
1 tablespoon vanilla extract

Combine the milk and semisweet chocolate in a saucepan. Cook
over medium heat until the chocolate is melted, stirring constantly.
Remove from heat. Add the sugar and salt and stir until dissolved.
Stir in the half-and-half, vanilla, cream, marshmallows, chocolate
chips and pecans. Chill, covered, for 30 minutes to 12 hours. Pour
into an ice cream freezer container. Freeze using the manufacturer's
directions. Yield: 1 gallon.

Wayne Gentle, Riverchase Council

Easy Vanilla Ice Cream

4 eggs
2½ cups sugar
½ teaspoon salt
1 (14-ounce) can sweetened
   condensed milk

2½ teaspoons vanilla extract
½ gallon milk

Beat the eggs in a mixer bowl until light and fluffy. Add a mixture of the sugar and salt gradually, beating constantly until thick. Stir in the condensed milk and vanilla. Add the milk and mix well. Pour into an ice cream freezer container. Freeze using the manufacturer's directions. Yield: 2 to 3 quarts.

Vicki Weyerbacher, Birmingham South Cahaba Council

Vanilla Pudding Ice Cream

1 (6-ounce) package vanilla
   pudding and pie filling mix
3 cups milk
3 cups sugar

1 tablespoon vanilla extract
½ to ¾ teaspoon salt
6 eggs
Milk

Prepare the pudding using the package directions, using 3 cups milk. Add the sugar gradually, stirring constantly. Stir in the vanilla and salt. Beat the eggs well in a mixer bowl. Add the pudding mixture a small amount at a time, beating constantly. Pour into an ice cream freezer container. Add enough milk to fill ⅔ full. Freeze using the manufacturer's directions. May substitute cream for the milk used to fill the container. Yield: 1½ gallons.

Marjorie S. (Francis) Tucker, Selma Life Member Club

Banana Pudding

2½ cups milk
1½ cups sugar
3 egg yolks, beaten
2 tablespoons cornstarch
1 tablespoon butter
1 teaspoon vanilla extract, or
   to taste

1 small package vanilla wafers
3 or 4 bananas, sliced
3 egg whites
2 tablespoons sugar
1 teaspoon vanilla extract

Combine the milk, 1½ cups sugar, egg yolks, cornstarch, butter and 1 teaspoon vanilla in a heavy saucepan. Cook over medium heat until thickened, stirring constantly. Alternate layers of the vanilla wafers, bananas and pudding in a large baking dish. Beat the egg whites in a mixer bowl until foamy. Add 2 tablespoons sugar and 1 teaspoon vanilla gradually, beating constantly until stiff peaks form. Spread over the pudding, sealing to the edges. Bake at 350 degrees for 10 minutes or until the meringue is light brown.
Yield: 6 to 8 servings.

Eva Hammack, Riverchase Council

Pineapple Pudding

2 (6-ounce) packages vanilla
   instant pudding mix
3 cups milk
1 cup sour cream
12 ounces whipped topping

1 package pecan sandies,
   crumbled
2 (15-ounce) cans pineapple
   tidbits, drained

Whisk the pudding mix and milk in a bowl until thickened. Fold in the sour cream and whipped topping. Spread ¼ of the crumbled cookies in a serving bowl. Reserve some pineapple for topping. Alternate layers of the remaining pineapple, pudding mixture and remaining cookies in the prepared bowl. Top with the reserved pineapple. Chill, covered, for 8 to 12 hours. May reduce the recipe by half and use reduced-fat ingredients. Yield: 25 servings.

Sharon Wolfe, Birmingham South Life Member Club

Creamy Banana Split Dessert

2 cups graham cracker crumbs
1/4 cup sugar
1/2 cup (1 stick) butter, melted
16 ounces cream cheese,
  softened

2 cups confectioners' sugar
4 bananas, split lengthwise
1 cup crushed pineapple
16 ounces whipped topping

Mix the graham cracker crumbs, sugar and butter in a bowl. Press into a 9x13-inch glass dish. Bake at 350 degrees for 5 minutes. Let cool. Beat the cream cheese and confectioners' sugar in a mixer bowl until smooth. Spread over the baked layer. Layer the bananas and pineapple over the cream cheese mixture. Spread the whipped topping over the top. Chill, covered, until serving time. Garnish with blueberries and sliced strawberries to resemble the United States flag, or with chopped pecans and cherry chips.
Yield: 12 servings.

Pat White, Montgomery Council

Banana Split Dessert

1 cup (2 sticks) margarine,
  softened
2 eggs
2 cups confectioners' sugar
1/2 cup (1 stick) margarine
2 cups graham cracker crumbs

5 to 7 bananas, sliced
1 (20-ounce) can crushed
  pineapple, drained
16 ounces whipped topping
1/2 cup pecan pieces
Maraschino cherries

Beat 1 cup margarine in a mixer bowl until light and fluffy. Add the eggs and confectioners' sugar. Beat for 10 minutes. Melt 1/2 cup margarine in a saucepan. Combine with the graham cracker crumbs in a bowl and mix well. Spread in a 9x13-inch glass dish. Pour the egg mixture into the prepared dish. Layer the bananas and pineapple over the egg mixture. Spread whipped topping over the top, sealing to the edges. Sprinkle with pecans and maraschino cherries. Chill, covered, for 4 hours or longer before serving.
Yield: 12 servings.

Cathy Holmes, Mobile Council

Strawberry Cake

1 (2-layer) package white
  cake mix
1 (3-ounce) package
  strawberry gelatin
1 cup vegetable oil
½ cup milk

4 eggs
1 cup thawed frozen
  strawberries
1 cup chopped pecans
Strawberry Frosting
½ cup whipped topping

Combine the cake mix and gelatin in a mixer bowl. Add the oil
and milk and beat well. Add the eggs 1 at a time, beating well after
each addition. Stir in the strawberries and pecans. Pour into three
8-inch greased and floured cake pans. Bake at 350 degrees for 25 to
30 minutes or until the layers test done. Cool in the pans for 10
minutes. Invert onto a wire rack to cool completely. Spread
Strawberry Frosting between the layers and over the top and side of
cake. Spread the whipped topping over the top.
Yield: 12 to 16 servings.

Strawberry Frosting

½ cup (1 stick) margarine,
  softened
1 (1-pound) package
  confectioners' sugar

½ cup drained thawed frozen
  strawberries
4¾ cups whipped topping

Beat the margarine in a mixer bowl until light and fluffy. Add the
confectioners' sugar and beat until creamy. Beat in the strawberries
and whipped topping.

Sarah P. Elam, Montgomery Council

Vanilla Wafer Cake

1 cup (2 sticks) butter,
  softened
2 cups sugar
6 eggs
1/2 cup milk

1 (12-ounce) package vanilla
  wafers, crushed
1 cup chopped nuts
2 cups shredded coconut

Beat the butter and sugar in a mixer bowl until creamy. Add the eggs 1 at a time, beating well after each addition. Add the milk and vanilla wafers and blend well. Stir in the nuts and coconut. Pour into a greased and floured tube pan. Bake at 300 degrees for 1¼ hours. Invert onto a funnel to cool completely. Loosen the cake from the side of the pan. Invert onto a cake plate.
Yield: 16 servings.

Judy Howard, Riverchase Council

Black Walnut Pound Cake

3 cups flour
1 teaspoon baking soda
1/2 teaspoon salt
1 cup chopped black walnuts
Flour for coating
1 1/2 cups shortening

2 1/2 cups sugar
5 eggs
1 cup milk
1 teaspoon black walnut
  flavoring

Sift 3 cups flour, baking soda and salt into a bowl. Coat the walnuts with a small amount of flour in a bowl. Beat the shortening and sugar in a mixer bowl until light and fluffy. Beat in the eggs. Add the milk and flour mixture alternately, beating well after each addition. Beat in the flavoring. Fold in the floured walnuts. Pour into a greased and floured tube pan. Bake at 300 degrees for 1 hour and 20 minutes. Invert onto a funnel to cool completely. Loosen the cake from the side of the pan. Invert onto a cake plate.
Yield: 16 servings.

Mauntez Mayer, Anniston Council

Chewy Charles

1½ cups sugar
⅓ cup baking cocoa
½ teaspoon salt
½ cup milk
¼ cup corn syrup

¼ cup peanut butter
¼ cup (½ stick) butter
1 teaspoon vanilla extract
3 cups rolled oats

Combine the sugar, baking cocoa, salt, milk and corn syrup in a heavy saucepan and mix well. Bring to a boil over medium heat. Boil for 2 to 3 minutes, stirring constantly. Remove from heat. Add the peanut butter, butter and vanilla and stir until smooth. Stir in the oats. Drop by spoonfuls onto a surface lined with waxed paper. Yield: 2 pounds.

Sandra Deason, Birmingham South Cahaba Council

Clinton's Chips

1½ cups flour
1 teaspoon salt
1 teaspoon baking soda
1 cup shortening
1 cup packed light brown
   sugar

½ cup sugar
1 teaspoon vanilla extract
2 eggs
2 cups old-fashioned oats
2 cups semisweet chocolate
   chips

Mix the flour, salt and baking soda together. Beat the shortening, brown sugar, sugar and vanilla in a mixer bowl until creamy. Add the eggs and beat until light and fluffy. Beat in the flour mixture and oats gradually. Stir in the chocolate chips. Drop by rounded teaspoonfuls onto greased cookie sheets. Bake at 350 degrees for 8 to 10 minutes or until golden brown. Cool on cookie sheets for 2 minutes; remove to a wire rack to cool completely. Yield: 7½ dozen.

Judy Boozer, Birmingham South Cahaba Council

Apple Pie in Cheddar Cheese Pie Pastry

2 cups sugar
½ cup (1 stick) butter, melted
2 eggs, beaten
2 teaspoons cinnamon

1 teaspoon vanilla extract
4 large Granny Smith apples,
    peeled, sliced
Cheddar Cheese Pie Pastry

Beat the sugar, butter and eggs in a mixer bowl until blended. Beat in the cinnamon and vanilla. Stir in the apples. Divide the Cheddar Cheese Pie Pastry into 2 equal portions. Roll 1 portion into an 11-inch circle on a lightly floured surface. Fit into a 9-inch pie plate sprayed with nonstick cooking spray. Fill with the apple filling. Roll the remaining Cheddar Cheese Pie Pastry into a circle on a lightly floured surface. Cut into strips. Layer over the top of the pie to form a lattice. Trim and flute the edge. Bake at 425 degrees for 10 minutes. Reduce the oven temperature to 350 degrees. Bake until the pastry is golden brown and the pie filling is set. Yield: 6 to 8 servings.

Betty M. Jones-Moon, Birmingham Life Member Club

Cheddar Cheese Pie Pastry

4 cups flour
2 teaspoons salt
1⅓ cups shortening

½ cup cold water
32 ounces grated Cheddar
    cheese

Process the flour, salt and shortening in a food processor until crumbly. Add the cold water in a fine stream, processing constantly. Add the Cheddar cheese, processing constantly to form a ball. Chill, covered, for up to 2 days. Yield: enough for 2 pastries.

Betty M. Jones-Moon, Birmingham Life Member Club

Dutch Apple Pie

1 (2-crust) pie pastry	3 tart apples, thinly sliced
½ cup flour	½ cup (1 stick) margarine,
½ cup sugar	softened
1 teaspoon cinnamon	1 cup packed brown sugar

Fit 1 of the pastries into a pie plate. Mix the flour, sugar and cinnamon in a bowl. Alternate layers of the apples and cinnamon mixture in the prepared pie plate until all ingredients are used. Mix the margarine and brown sugar in a bowl until crumbly. Sprinkle over the layers. Cut the remaining pie pastry into strips. Layer over the top of the pie to form a lattice. Trim and flute the edge. Bake at 350 degrees for 45 minutes. Yield: 6 to 8 servings.

Sue Woodruff, sister of Cathy Kelley,
Birmingham South Cahaba Council

Pineapple Orange Pie

2 cups graham cracker crumbs	2½ cups boiling water
2 tablespoons sugar	8 ounces cream cheese,
¾ cup margarine, melted	softened
1 (20-ounce) can crushed	½ teaspoon grated orange zest
pineapple	6 tablespoons sugar
1 (6-ounce) package orange or	1 teaspoon vanilla extract
orange pineapple gelatin	2 cups sour cream

Press a mixture of the first 3 ingredients into a greased 9x13-inch baking dish. Bake at 350 degrees for 12 minutes. Drain the pineapple, reserving the syrup. Dissolve the gelatin in the boiling water in a bowl. Stir in the reserved syrup. Cool slightly. Mix 1 cup of the gelatin mixture with the pineapple in a bowl. Beat the cream cheese, orange zest, 6 tablespoons sugar and vanilla in a mixer bowl until blended. Add the remaining gelatin mixture and beat until smooth. Fold in the sour cream. Pour into the prepared graham cracker crust. Chill until partially set. Spoon the pineapple mixture over the top. Chill, covered, until set. Yield: 8 to 10 servings.

Catherine M. Martin, Birmingham Metro Council

Strawberry Pie

1 cup sugar
1 cup water
3 tablespoons cornstarch
1 (3-ounce) package
  strawberry gelatin

2½ cups chopped strawberries
1 (10-inch) graham cracker
  pie shell
8 ounces whipped topping

Combine the sugar, water and cornstarch in a microwave-safe bowl. Microwave on High for 3 minutes; stir. Microwave for 2 minutes longer. Add the gelatin, stirring until dissolved. Stir in the strawberries. Pour into the pie shell. Chill, covered, until set. Spread whipped topping over the top of the pie just before serving. Yield: 6 to 8 servings.

Mona Burdick, Montgomery Council

Fourth-of-July Strawberry Pie

1 (14-ounce) can sweetened
  condensed milk
Juice of 2 lemons
2 cups sliced strawberries

1 cup chopped pecans
8 ounces whipped topping
1 baked (10-inch) pie shell

Combine the condensed milk and lemon juice in a bowl and blend well. Let stand for 5 minutes. Stir in the strawberries and pecans. Fold in the whipped topping. Pour into the baked pie shell. Chill, covered, until set. May prepare the day before and freeze, covered, in the freezer. Yield: 6 to 8 servings.

Nora Carpenter, Birmingham South Cahaba Council

Walking Taco Dip

4 avocados, chopped
Sour cream to taste
Salsa to taste
Pepper to taste
1 (16-ounce) can refried
  beans

1 (16-ounce) jar hot salsa
1 to 2 cups sour cream
Shredded Cheddar cheese
1 tomato, chopped
1 jalapeño chile, sliced
Sliced black olives

Mash the avocados in a bowl. Add sour cream to taste, salsa to taste and pepper and stir until of a creamy consistency. Layer the refried beans, 16 ounces hot salsa, avocado mixture, 1 to 2 cups sour cream, cheese, tomato, jalapeño chile and black olives in the order listed in a shallow dish. Chill, covered, until serving time. Serve with tortilla chips. *Note:* Decrease the fat grams by using nonfat refried beans, nonfat sour cream and reduced-fat Cheddar cheese. Yield: 10 to 12 servings.

Linda A. Tucker, Birmingham South Cahaba Council

Winston Caviar

2 (16-ounce) cans black-eyed
  peas, drained
2 (11-ounce) cans Shoe Peg
  corn, drained
2 (10-ounce) cans tomatoes
  with green chiles
2 large green bell peppers,
  chopped

12 small green onions,
  chopped
3 tomatoes, chopped
1 teaspoon garlic powder
1 teaspoon garlic salt
1 teaspoon parsley flakes
1 (16- to 24-ounce) bottle
  Italian salad dressing

Combine the black-eyed peas, corn, undrained tomatoes, green peppers, green onions, tomatoes, garlic powder, garlic salt and parsley flakes in a bowl and mix gently. Add the salad dressing and toss to coat. Chill, covered, for 12 hours or longer. Serve with tortilla chips. Yield: 25 to 30 servings.

Sue (Joe) Small, Selma Life Member Club

Hot Salsa

2 (28-ounce) cans stewed
whole tomatoes
2 bunches spring onions,
finely chopped
2 medium white onions, finely
chopped
1 (8- to 12-ounce) can
jalapeño chiles, ground

1 (32-ounce) bottle tomato
juice
1/2 to 3/4 cup white vinegar
1/4 cup salt
2 tablespoons minced garlic
1 tablespoon cumin
1 tablespoon cilantro

Process the undrained tomatoes in a blender until puréed. Combine half of the tomatoes, spring onions and white onions in a saucepan and mix well. Stir in the jalapeño chiles. Add the tomato juice and the remaining tomatoes and mix well. Stir in the vinegar, salt, garlic, cumin and cilantro. Bring to a boil over medium heat, stirring occasionally. Let stand until cool. Store, covered, in the refrigerator. Yield: 1 gallon.

Selina Thornton, Alabama Telco Credit Union

Chopped Liver

1 1/4 to 1 1/2 pounds chicken
livers
Chopped onion to taste

2 hard-cooked eggs, chopped
Finely chopped celery
Mayonnaise

Grind the livers, onion and eggs in a meat grinder. Sauté the liver mixture and celery in a nonstick skillet until the livers are cooked through and the vegetables are tender. Let stand until cool. Mix enough mayonnaise with the liver mixture in a bowl to make of a spreading consistency. Chill, covered, until serving time. Serve with celery sticks and/or assorted party crackers.
Yield: 8 to 10 servings.

Margie Stetson, Riverchase Council

Farmhouse Barbecue Muffins

1 (10-count) can biscuits	1 tablespoon vinegar
1 pound ground beef	½ teaspoon chili powder
½ cup catsup	1 cup shredded cheese
3 tablespoons brown sugar	

Separate the biscuits. Flatten each biscuit into a 5-inch circle on a hard surface. Press each dough circle over the bottom and up the side of a greased muffin cup. Brown the ground beef in a skillet, stirring until crumbly; drain. Stir in the catsup, brown sugar, vinegar and chili powder. Spoon some of the ground beef mixture into each of the prepared muffin cups. Sprinkle with the cheese. Bake at 375 degrees for 18 to 20 minutes or until brown and bubbly. Let stand for 5 minutes before serving. Yield: 10 servings.

Mary Gillis, Mobile Council

Zucchini Orange Marmalade

6 cups sugar	Grated zest of 2 oranges
6 cups grated peeled zucchini	1 (6-ounce) package orange
1 (20-ounce) can juice-pack	gelatin
crushed pineapple	

Combine the sugar, zucchini, undrained pineapple and orange zest in a saucepan and mix well. Bring to a boil, stirring occasionally. Cook for 20 minutes, stirring occasionally. Remove from heat. Add the gelatin and stir until dissolved. Pour into hot sterilized jelly jars; seal with 2-piece lids. Yield: 5 to 6 jelly jars.

Eunice T. Henry, Selma Life Member Club

Tomato Sauce

1 quart fresh tomatoes,
    peeled, cut into quarters
1 cup sugar

1 cup vinegar
Hot peppers to taste, chopped

Combine the tomatoes, sugar, vinegar and hot peppers in a stock pot and mix well. Bring to a boil. Cook for several hours or until thickened, stirring occasionally. Spoon into hot sterilized pint jars; seal with 2-piece lids. May store in the refrigerator. Yield: 2 pints.

Betty Darnell, Gadsden Life Member Club

Broccoli Salad

1 (3-ounce) package ramen
    noodles, broken into pieces
1 cup chopped walnuts
1/4 cup (1/2 stick) butter
1 head romaine, chopped
Florets of 1 bunch broccoli,
    chopped

4 green onions, chopped
    (optional)
1 cup sugar
1 cup vegetable oil
1/2 cup red wine vinegar
1 tablespoon soy sauce

Sauté the noodles and walnuts in the butter in a skillet until golden brown. Drain on paper towels. Layer the romaine, broccoli, green onions and noodle mixture in the order listed in a bowl. Combine the sugar, oil, wine vinegar and soy sauce in a saucepan. Cook over low heat until the sugar dissolves, stirring frequently. Cool slightly. Pour the warm dressing over the salad. May substitute chopped red onion for the green onions. Yield: 6 to 8 servings.

Caitlin Wong, Birmingham South Cahaba Council

Corn Bread Salad

1 cup self-rising cornmeal
1 cup sour cream
½ cup (1 stick) margarine,
   melted
1 tablespoon sugar
1 cup chopped onion
1 cup chopped green bell
   pepper

1 cup chopped tomato
1 cup sweet pickle relish
1 cup mayonnaise
1 tablespoon sugar
Shredded Cheddar cheese

Combine the cornmeal, sour cream, margarine and 1 tablespoon sugar in a bowl and mix well. Spoon the batter into a greased cast-iron skillet. Bake at 400 degrees until golden brown. Let stand until cool. Crumble the corn bread. Combine the corn bread, onion, green pepper, tomato and pickle relish in a bowl and mix well. Spread with a mixture of the mayonnaise and 1 tablespoon sugar. Sprinkle with cheese. Chill, covered, until serving time. May store in the refrigerator for several days. Yield: 14 servings.

Jean McBride, Huntsville Council

Seven-Layer Salad

1 large head iceberg lettuce,
   shredded
1 (16-ounce) can tiny peas,
   drained
1 red onion, finely chopped
1 (8-ounce) can sliced water
   chestnuts, drained

1 medium cucumber, sliced
2 cups mayonnaise
2 tablespoons sugar
1 cup shredded cheese
1 (2-ounce) jar bacon bits

Layer the lettuce, peas, onion, water chestnuts and cucumber in the order listed in a salad bowl. Spread with a mixture of the mayonnaise and sugar. Chill, covered, for 8 to 10 hours. Sprinkle with the cheese and bacon bits. Yield: 10 to 12 servings.

Rosa Stodghill, Riverchase Council

Bombay Chicken Salad

1 cup cooked rice
1 tablespoon minced onion
1 tablespoon mayonnaise-type
   salad dressing
1 1/2 teaspoons cider vinegar
1/2 teaspoon curry powder
2 cups chopped cooked
   chicken breasts

1 cup chopped orange
1/2 cup chopped celery
1/3 cup chopped walnuts or
   toasted almonds
2/3 cup mayonnaise
2 tablespoons French salad
   dressing

Combine the rice, onion, mayonnaise-type salad dressing, vinegar and curry powder in a bowl and mix well. Stir in the chicken, orange, celery and walnuts. Add the mayonnaise and French salad dressing and mix gently. Store, covered, in the refrigerator until serving time. Yield: 4 to 6 servings.

Mary Ann Goodson, Birmingham South Life Member Club

Tuna Pasta Salad

12 ounces penne
1 (12-ounce) can water-pack
   tuna, drained, flaked
1 cup chopped celery
1/2 to 1 cup chopped green
   onions
1/2 cup chopped green bell
   pepper
1/2 cup shredded carrot

2 tablespoons minced fresh
   parsley
3/4 cup sour cream
3/4 cup sugar
3/4 cup cider vinegar
6 tablespoons mayonnaise
1 tablespoon celery seeds
1 tablespoon onion powder

Cook the pasta using package directions. Rinse with cold water and drain. Combine the pasta, tuna, celery, green onions, green pepper, carrot and parsley in a bowl and mix well. Combine the sour cream, sugar, vinegar, mayonnaise, celery seeds and onion powder in a bowl and mix well. Add to the salad and toss to coat. Chill, covered, until serving time. Yield: 12 servings.

Frankie (A.T.) Vaughn, Selma Life Member Club

Roast with Gravy

1 (2- to 3-pound) beef roast
1 onion, sliced
1 envelope onion soup mix
1 (10-ounce) can cream of
  mushroom soup

½ soup can water
Pepper to taste

Place the roast in a baking pan. Arrange the onion over the top. Sprinkle with the onion soup mix. Pour a mixture of the mushroom soup and water over the top. Sprinkle with pepper. Bake, covered, at 325 degrees for 2 to 2½ hours or until of the desired degree of doneness. Yield: 6 to 8 servings.

Dot Johnson, Gadsden Life Member Club

Beef and Gravy

3 pounds ground chuck
½ cup rolled oats
Salt and pepper to taste
Flour
Vegetable oil

2 (10-ounce) cans cream of
  mushroom soup
1 envelope onion soup mix
1 soup can water

Combine the ground chuck, oats, salt and pepper in a bowl and mix well. Spread on a baking sheet, pressing down with a spatula. Chill, covered, for 8 to 10 hours. Cut the ground chuck mixture into squares. Coat the squares with flour. Brown the squares on both sides in a small amount of oil in a skillet; drain. Transfer the squares to a baking dish. Pour a mixture of the mushroom soup, onion soup mix and water over the top. Bake at 325 degrees for 30 minutes or until the ground chuck is cooked through. Yield: 6 to 8 servings.

Hazel E. Campbell, Birmingham Life Member Club

Company Beef Casserole

5 ounces macaroni
1 pound ground chuck
2 tablespoons shortening
2 cups chopped canned
  tomatoes
1 medium onion, chopped
½ cup chopped green bell
  pepper
2 tablespoons chopped fresh
  parsley

1 tablespoon catsup
1 tablespoon Worcestershire
  sauce
Salt and pepper to taste
1 (10-ounce) can cream of
  mushroom soup
1 cup shredded Cheddar
  cheese

Cook the macaroni using package directions; drain. Brown the ground chuck in the shortening in a skillet, stirring until crumbly; drain. Stir in the tomatoes, onion, green pepper, parsley, catsup, Worcestershire sauce, salt and pepper. Simmer for 30 minutes. Add the macaroni and mix well. Spoon into a baking dish. Stir in the soup gently, mixing lightly from the bottom. Sprinkle with the cheese. Bake at 350 degrees for 30 minutes. Yield: 4 servings.

Mrs. J.B. (Carol) Raines, Gadsden Life Member Club

Ground Chuck Casserole

1 pound ground chuck
1 medium onion, chopped
1 (16-ounce) package
  Tater Tots

1 (10-ounce) can cream of
  chicken or mushroom soup
1 soup can water
Shredded Cheddar cheese

Brown the ground chuck with the onion in a skillet, stirring until the ground chuck is crumbly; drain. Spoon into a 9x9-inch baking dish. Top with the Tater Tots. Pour a mixture of the soup and water over the prepared layers. Sprinkle with cheese. Bake at 350 degrees until brown and bubbly. Yield: 4 servings.

Hazel E. Campbell, Birmingham Life Member Club

Hamburger Pie

1 cup baking mix
1/4 cup cold water
1 pound ground beef
1 (8-ounce) can tomato sauce
1/2 cup fine bread crumbs
1/2 cup chopped onion
1/4 cup chopped green bell
  pepper
1/2 teaspoon salt

1/2 teaspoon oregano
1/4 teaspoon pepper
1/4 cup milk
1 egg
1/2 teaspoon salt
2 cups shredded Cheddar
  cheese
1/2 teaspoon dry mustard

Combine the baking mix and cold water in a bowl and beat gently for approximately 20 strokes or until a soft dough forms. Knead the dough 5 times on a lightly floured surface. Roll the dough 2 inches larger than a pie plate. Fit the dough into the pie plate; flute the edge. Brown the ground beef in a skillet, stirring until crumbly; drain. Stir in the tomato sauce, bread crumbs, onion, green pepper, 1/2 teaspoon salt, oregano and pepper. Spoon into the prepared pie plate. Whisk the milk, egg and 1/2 teaspoon salt in a bowl until blended. Stir in the cheese and dry mustard. Spoon over the ground beef mixture. Bake at 375 degrees until golden brown.
Yield: 6 servings.

Brenda Smith, Birmingham South Cahaba Council

Lasagna

1 pound ground beef
1 (28-ounce) can crushed
  tomatoes
2 (6-ounce) cans tomato paste
1 medium onion, chopped
2 garlic cloves, minced
2 1/2 teaspoons salt
1 teaspoon celery seeds
1 teaspoon oregano

1/2 teaspoon pepper
3 bay leaves
16 ounces lasagna noodles,
  cooked, drained
4 cups ricotta cheese
1 1/2 pounds mozzarella cheese,
  shredded
Grated Parmesan cheese

Brown the ground beef in a skillet, stirring until crumbly; drain. Stir in the undrained tomatoes, tomato paste, onion, garlic, salt, celery seeds, oregano, pepper and bay leaves and mix well. Bring to a boil; reduce heat. Simmer for 30 minutes, stirring occasionally. Discard the bay leaves. Layer the noodles, ground beef mixture, ricotta cheese and mozzarella cheese 1/2 at a time in 2 greased 9x13-inch baking pans. Sprinkle with Parmesan cheese. Bake, covered, at 350 degrees for 30 minutes; remove the cover. Bake for 15 to 25 minutes longer or until brown and bubbly. Let stand for 10 minutes before serving. Yield: 16 servings.

Laraine McLean, Decatur Council

Cheesy Lasagna

8 ounces lasagna noodles
1 1/2 pounds ground beef
2 (8-ounce) cans tomato sauce
3 tablespoons red wine vinegar
1 1/2 teaspoons parsley flakes
1/2 teaspoon pepper
1/2 teaspoon garlic powder
1/4 teaspoon oregano
1 bay leaf

2 cups cottage cheese
1 1/2 cups sour cream
8 ounces cream cheese, softened
4 cups shredded mozzarella cheese
1/4 cup grated Parmesan cheese

Cook the noodles using package directions, omitting the salt; drain. Brown the ground beef in a skillet, stirring until crumbly; drain. Stir in the tomato sauce, wine vinegar, parsley flakes, pepper, garlic powder, oregano and bay leaf. Simmer for 20 minutes, stirring occasionally. Discard the bay leaf. Combine the cottage cheese, sour cream and cream cheese in a bowl and mix well. Spread 1/2 cup of the sauce in a 9x13-inch baking dish. Layer half the noodles, half the cottage cheese mixture and 2 cups of the sauce in the prepared dish. Sprinkle with the mozzarella cheese. Top with the remaining noodles, cottage cheese mixture and sauce. Sprinkle with the Parmesan cheese. Bake at 350 degrees for 10 minutes or until brown and bubbly. Yield: 8 servings.

Sue Johnston, Birmingham South Cahaba Council

Meat Loaf

1 pound ground chuck
1 onion, chopped
1 green bell pepper, chopped
1 (15-ounce) can tomato
  sauce
1 envelope onion soup mix
1/4 cup Heinz 57 Steak Sauce
1/4 cup milk

2 eggs, beaten
3 tablespoons Worcestershire
  sauce
1 (8-ounce) can tomato sauce
1 tablespoon Worcestershire
  sauce
1 tablespoon hot sauce
  (optional)

Combine the ground chuck, onion, green pepper, 15 ounces tomato sauce, soup mix, steak sauce, milk, eggs and 3 tablespoons Worcestershire sauce in a bowl and mix well. Shape into a loaf and place in a cast-iron skillet, baking dish or loaf pan sprayed with nonstick cooking spray. Bake at 375 degrees for 45 to 55 minutes or until cooked through. Spoon a mixture of 8 ounces tomato sauce, 1 tablespoon Worcestershire sauce and hot sauce over the loaf. Bake for 5 minutes longer. Yield: 4 servings.

Dawn Bowman, Birmingham South Cahaba Council

Microwave Meat Loaf

1 pound ground chuck
6 saltine crackers,
  crushed
1/4 cup minced onion
1/4 cup chopped green bell
  pepper
1/4 cup chopped celery
1 egg, beaten

1/4 cup tomato juice, or
  1 (8-ounce) can tomato
  sauce
1 tablespoon minced parsley
3/4 teaspoon salt
1/4 teaspoon pepper
1 garlic clove, minced
1/4 cup catsup

Combine all the ingredients except the catsup in a bowl and mix well. Shape into a loaf. Arrange the loaf in a microwave-safe dish. Microwave on High for 6 minutes, turning the dish every 2 minutes. Drizzle the catsup over the top. Microwave for 5 minutes longer or until cooked through. Yield: 4 servings.

Flo Watters, Selma Life Member Club

Spaghetti and Meat Sauce

1 pound ground round
1/4 teaspoon fennel seeds
1/4 teaspoon garlic salt
1 package Italian sausage
1 (16-ounce) can whole
   tomatoes

1 large can tomato purée
1 medium can tomato purée
1/4 cup chopped onion
1/8 teaspoon garlic
12 ounces thin spaghetti
1 tablespoon butter

Brown the ground round with the fennel seeds and 1/4 teaspoon garlic salt in a skillet, stirring until the ground round is crumbly; drain. Cook the sausage in a skillet using package directions; drain. Cut into bite-size pieces. Stir the sausage into the ground round mixture. Mix in the next 5 ingredients. Simmer for 30 to 40 minutes or until of the desired consistency, stirring occasionally. Cook the spaghetti using package directions until al dente; drain. Stir in the butter. Add the spaghetti to the ground round mixture and mix well. Yield: 4 to 6 servings.

Grace Franklin, Montgomery Council

Weeknight Pizza Casserole

1 pound ground beef
1 (3-ounce) package sliced
   pepperoni
1 (2-ounce) can sliced black
   olives, drained
1 medium green bell pepper,
   chopped

1 (14-ounce) jar pizza sauce
8 ounces mozzarella cheese,
   shredded
3/4 cup biscuit mix
1 cup milk
2 eggs, lightly beaten

Brown the ground beef in a skillet over medium heat, stirring until crumbly; drain. Stir in the pepperoni, black olives and green pepper. Spoon into a lightly greased 8x8-inch baking dish. Spread with the pizza sauce and sprinkle with the cheese. Combine the biscuit mix, milk and eggs in a bowl and mix well. Spread over the prepared layers. Bake at 400 degrees for 30 to 35 minutes or until brown. Let stand for 5 minutes before serving. Yield: 4 servings.

Donna Daniel, Montgomery Council

Zatoni

4 onions, chopped
2 green bell peppers, chopped
4 garlic cloves, crushed
¼ cup vegetable oil
6 (10-ounce) cans tomato
  soup
2 (6-ounce) cans tomato paste
4 teaspoons salt
Pepper to taste

2 (16-ounce) cans whole
  kernel corn, drained
Juice of 1 lime
4 pounds lean ground beef
24 ounces spaghetti, cooked,
  drained
8 ounces sharp Cheddar
  cheese, shredded

Sauté the first 3 ingredients in the oil in a large saucepan. Stir in
the soup, tomato paste, salt and pepper. Simmer until of the desired
consistency, stirring occasionally. Stir in the corn and lime juice.
Brown the ground beef in a skillet, stirring until crumbly; drain.
Stir into the soup mixture. Layer the spaghetti and ground beef
mixture alternately in 2 or more 9x13-inch baking dishes until
all of the ingredients are used. Sprinkle with the cheese. Bake,
covered, at 325 degrees until bubbly. Yield: 25 to 30 servings.

Sue (Joe) Small, Selma Life Member Club

Corned Beef and Cabbage

2 medium potatoes, thinly
  sliced
1 medium onion, thinly sliced
Salt and pepper to taste
¼ cup water

½ head cabbage, sliced
1 (12-ounce) can corned beef,
  drained, sliced
¼ (½ stick) butter, melted

Layer the potatoes and onion in a microwave-safe dish. Season
with salt and pepper. Pour the water over the top. Microwave,
covered, on High for 8 to 9 minutes. Arrange the cabbage over the
prepared layers. Season with salt and pepper. Top with the corned
beef. Drizzle with the butter. Microwave on High for 12 minutes,
turning once. Let stand for 5 minutes before serving.
Yield: 4 servings.

Brenda Smith, Birmingham South Cahaba Council

Corned Beef Hash

2 red bell peppers, chopped
1½ cups chopped onions
1 teaspoon minced garlic
4 cups chopped cooked
  potatoes
8 ounces corned beef, cut into
  chunks

½ teaspoon pepper
¼ teaspoon salt
½ cup milk
4 eggs, fried or scrambled

Heat a nonstick skillet until hot. Spray with nonstick cooking spray. Sauté the red peppers, onions and garlic in the prepared skillet for 3 minutes. Stir in the potatoes, corned beef, pepper and salt. Sauté for 3 minutes. Press the mixture down with a spatula. Drizzle the milk over the top. Cook for 12 minutes or until crusty, turning and pressing down with a spatula. Top the hash with the eggs. Yield: 4 servings.

Donna Jean Bowman, Birmingham South Cahaba Council

Coriander and Pepper Pork Chops

4 (1-inch-thick) boneless
  pork chops
3 tablespoons soy sauce
1 tablespoon brown sugar
1 tablespoon coarsely ground
  pepper

1 tablespoon crushed
  coriander seeds
2 garlic cloves, crushed

Arrange the pork chops in a shallow dish. Pour a mixture of the soy sauce, brown sugar, pepper, coriander and garlic over the chops and turn to coat. Marinate at room temperature for 30 minutes. Drain, discarding the marinade. Prepare medium-hot coals and bank in the grill bed. Grill the pork chops over indirect heat for 12 to 15 minutes or until cooked through, turning once. May broil or pan broil for 10 minutes or until the juices run clear. Yield: 4 servings.

Judy Boozer, Birmingham South Cahaba Council

Stuffed Pork Chops

4 (1-inch-thick) center cut
  pork chops
2 tablespoons vegetable oil
3 cups (½-inch) dry French
  bread cubes
¼ cup (½ stick) butter or
  margarine, melted

¼ cup chicken broth
2 tablespoons chopped celery
2 tablespoons chopped onion
¼ teaspoon poultry seasoning
1 (10-ounce) can cream of
  mushroom soup
⅓ cup water

Brown the pork chops in the oil in a skillet; drain. Arrange in an ungreased shallow baking pan. Toss the bread cubes, butter, broth, celery, onion and poultry seasoning in a bowl. Mound about ½ cup of the bread mixture on each pork chop. Pour a mixture of the soup and water over the top. Bake, covered, at 350 degrees for 30 minutes; remove the cover. Bake for 10 to 15 minutes longer or until the juices run clear. Yield: 4 servings.

Donna Jean Bowman, Birmingham South Cahaba Council

Italian Meat Loaves

¾ cup cracker or bread
  crumbs
½ cup grated Parmesan
  cheese
½ cup milk
¼ cup finely chopped onion
1 teaspoon Worcestershire
  sauce

2 eggs, beaten
1 teaspoon garlic salt
½ teaspoon Italian seasoning
2 pounds ground pork
¼ cup catsup
2 tablespoons grated
  Parmesan cheese
½ teaspoon Italian seasoning

Mix the cracker crumbs, ½ cup Parmesan cheese, milk, onion, Worcestershire sauce, eggs, garlic salt and ½ teaspoon Italian seasoning in a bowl. Mix in the ground pork. Shape into 10 loaves. Arrange the loaves on a rack in a greased shallow baking pan. Spread the catsup over the tops of the loaves. Sprinkle with the remaining cheese and Italian seasoning. Bake at 350 degrees for 45 to 55 minutes or until the loaves are cooked through. Yield: 10 servings.

Mary Ann Sparks Fulmer, Shoals Life Member Club

Chicken Noodle Casserole

10 ounces fine egg noodles
Chicken stock
1 (3-pound) chicken, cooked
1 (10-ounce) can cream of
  celery soup
1 (10-ounce) can cream of
  chicken soup

1 cup sour cream
½ cup chicken stock
Bread slices, torn into bite-size
  pieces
½ cup (1 stick) margarine,
  melted

Combine the pasta with enough chicken stock to cover in a saucepan. Cook until tender; drain. Chop the chicken into bite-size pieces, discarding the skin and bones. Combine the pasta, chicken, soups, sour cream and ½ cup chicken stock in a bowl and mix well. Spoon into a baking dish. Sprinkle with the bread pieces. Drizzle with the margarine. Bake at 350 degrees for 30 minutes or until golden brown. Yield: 6 servings.

Gail Davis, Montgomery Council

Slow-Cooker Chicken

1 (3½- to 4-pound) chicken
1 (14-ounce) bottle catsup
1 medium onion, chopped

Salt and pepper to taste
3 tablespoons brown sugar
1 (10-ounce) bottle Coca-Cola

Place the chicken in a 3½-quart slow cooker. Add the catsup, onion, salt, pepper, brown sugar and Coca-Cola in the order listed, stirring once. Cook, covered, on Low for 8 to 10 hours. Chop the chicken, discarding the skin and bones. Serve over hot cooked rice. Yield: 3 or 4 servings.

Debbie Speaks, Montgomery Council

To prevent stains on your Tupperware, spray with nonstick cooking spray before adding tomato-based sauces.

Family Chicken Casserole

1 (3-pound) chicken, cooked
1 (10-ounce) can cream of
  chicken soup
1½ cups croutons
1 cup chopped pecans
1 cup mayonnaise

¼ cup chopped onion
3 tablespoons lemon juice
2 tablespoons water
Bread crumbs
Paprika to taste

Chop the chicken, discarding the skin and bones. Combine the chicken, soup, croutons, pecans, mayonnaise, onion, lemon juice and water in a bowl and mix well. Spoon into a 9x13-inch baking dish. Sprinkle with the bread crumbs and paprika. Bake at 325 degrees for 30 minutes. Yield: 6 servings.

Sue Johnston, Birmingham South Cahaba Council

Chicken Breast Supreme

1 jar dried beef
8 boneless skinless chicken
  breasts
8 slices bacon

1 (10-ounce) can cream of
  mushroom soup
1 cup sour cream

Place 2 pieces of the dried beef on top of each chicken breast. Wrap each with 1 slice of bacon and secure with wooden picks. Arrange in a single layer in a greased baking dish. Spoon a mixture of the soup and sour cream over the chicken. Bake at 225 degrees for 3 hours or until the chicken is cooked through. Yield: 8 servings.

Sharon Coffield, Birmingham South Cahaba Council

Richmond Fried Chicken

1 (3-pound) chicken, skinned
1/2 cup flour
1/2 teaspoon salt
1/2 teaspoon paprika
1/4 teaspoon crushed red
   pepper flakes

1/4 teaspoon allspice
1/8 teaspoon ground cloves
1/8 teaspoon nutmeg
2 tablespoons vegetable oil
1 2/3 cups reduced-fat milk

Line a 9x13-inch baking pan with foil and grease lightly. Discard the wing tips of the chicken and cut the chicken into 8 serving pieces. Combine the flour, salt, paprika, red pepper flakes, allspice, cloves and nutmeg in a shallow dish and mix well. Reserve 2 tablespoons of the flour mixture. Coat the chicken with the remaining flour mixture. Brown the chicken in the oil in a skillet over medium-high heat for 6 minutes or until golden brown, turning occasionally. Transfer the chicken to a baking pan using a slotted spoon, reserving 2 tablespoons of the pan drippings in the skillet. Bake at 400 degrees for 20 minutes or until crispy, turning once. Whisk the reserved flour mixture into the reserved pan drippings. Cook over medium heat for 2 minutes or until cinnamon-brown in color, stirring constantly; reduce the heat. Whisk in the milk gradually. Cook over low heat for 5 minutes or until the gravy is slightly thickened, whisking constantly. Serve with the chicken. Yield: 4 servings.

Susan Currie, Birmingham South Cahaba Council

Chicken Stir-Fry

1 whole chicken breast,
   chopped
Vegetable oil

5 cups chopped cabbage
2 cups (1/4-inch) slices celery
Salt and pepper to taste

Sauté the chicken in oil in a skillet until cooked through. Add the cabbage, celery, salt and pepper. Stir-fry until the vegetables are tender-crisp. Serve with corn bread sticks and iced tea.
Yield: 6 servings.

Mayme Holmes, Mobile Council

Quick Chicken Paprika Casserole

1 cup baking mix
¼ cup finely chopped parsley
2 tablespoons paprika
½ teaspoon pepper
4 boneless chicken breasts
1 cup buttermilk
½ cup chopped onion

1 (15-ounce) can chicken
   broth
2 cups sour cream
1 tablespoon Worcestershire
   sauce
8 ounces egg noodle ribbons,
   cooked, drained

Combine the baking mix, parsley, paprika and pepper in a bowl and mix well. Dip the chicken in the buttermilk in a shallow dish. Coat with the baking mix mixture, reserving the remaining baking mix mixture. Brown the chicken in a skillet sprayed with nonstick cooking spray. Transfer the chicken to a platter. Sauté the onion in the skillet until tender. Stir in ⅓ cup of the reserved baking mix mixture. Add the broth and mix well. Cook until thickened, stirring constantly. Stir in the sour cream and Worcestershire sauce. Combine ½ cup of the sauce with the noodles in a bowl and mix well. Spoon into an 8x8-inch baking dish coated with nonstick cooking spray. Arrange the chicken over the noodle mixture. Top with the remaining sauce. Bake at 325 degrees for 30 to 40 minutes or until brown and bubbly. Yield: 4 servings.

Yonna Leigh Bowman Quinn, Birmingham South Cahaba Council

When boiling corn on the cob, add a pinch of sugar to the water to help bring out the corn's natural sweetness.

Sunday Chicken Bake

1 (4-ounce) can mushrooms,
    drained
½ green bell pepper, chopped
1 small onion, chopped
½ cup (1 stick) margarine
1 pound Velveeta cheese,
    shredded
1 (10-ounce) can tomatoes
    with green chiles

1 teaspoon Worcestershire
    sauce
½ teaspoon dry mustard
7 ounces spaghetti, cooked,
    drained
Salt and pepper to taste
4 whole chicken breasts,
    cooked, chopped

Sauté the mushrooms, green pepper and onion in the margarine in a skillet. Stir in the cheese, undrained tomatoes, Worcestershire sauce and dry mustard. Add the spaghetti and mix well. Season with salt and pepper. Stir in the chicken. Spoon into a baking dish. Bake at 350 degrees for 30 to 40 minutes or until brown and bubbly. May be prepared 1 day in advance and stored, covered, in the refrigerator. Bake just before serving. Yield: 6 to 8 servings.

Ilean Moore, Decatur Council

Chicken Casserole

2 cups chopped cooked
    chicken
1 (15-ounce) can macaroni
    and cheese
1 (10-ounce) can chicken
    à la king
1 tablespoon grated onion

1 (4-ounce) can sliced
    mushrooms, drained
1 cup shredded sharp Cheddar
    cheese
12 crackers, crushed
Butter

Combine the chicken, macaroni and cheese, chicken à la king, onion, mushrooms and cheese in a bowl and mix well. Spoon into a 1-quart greased baking dish. Sprinkle with the cracker crumbs. Dot with butter. Bake at 350 degrees for 30 minutes or until brown and bubbly. Yield: 6 servings.

Maureen Wood Sewell, Birmingham Life Member Club

Chicken and Spinach Casserole

2 (10-ounce) packages frozen   1 to 2 cups milk
  spinach or broccoli, cooked,   1 tablespoon garlic salt
  drained   1 teaspoon basil
4 cups chopped cooked   1 teaspoon curry powder
  chicken   2 cups shredded Cheddar
½ cup (1 stick) butter   cheese
1 tablespoon flour   Italian bread crumbs

Squeeze the excess moisture from the spinach. Layer the chicken
and spinach in the order listed in a 9x13-inch baking pan. Heat the
butter in a saucepan until melted. Stir in the flour. Add the milk
gradually, stirring constantly. Cook until of the desired consistency,
stirring constantly. Stir in the garlic salt, basil and curry powder.
Spoon over the prepared layers. Sprinkle with the cheese and bread
crumbs. Bake at 350 degrees for 15 to 20 minutes or until bubbly.
Serve with hot cooked rice. Yield: 6 to 8 servings.

Janet Roberta, Birmingham South Life Member Club

Chicken and Wild Rice Casserole

1 package wild rice, cooked   1 (6-ounce) jar sliced
2 cups chopped cooked   mushrooms, drained
  chicken   1 (2-ounce) jar pimento,
1 cup mayonnaise   drained
1 (10-ounce) can cream of   1 cup shredded Cheddar
  celery soup   cheese
1 (8-ounce) can tiny peas,
  drained

Combine the wild rice, chicken, mayonnaise, soup, peas,
mushrooms and pimento in a bowl and mix well. Spoon into a
9x13-inch baking dish. Sprinkle with the cheese. Bake at 350
degrees for 30 minutes or until bubbly. Yield: 10 to 12 servings.

Pat White, Montgomery Council

Lemon Batter Fish

1 cup flour
1 teaspoon baking powder
3/4 teaspoon salt
1/2 teaspoon sugar
2/3 cup water
1/3 cup lemon juice

1 egg, beaten
1 pound fish fillets
Lemon juice
Flour
Vegetable oil for frying

Combine 1 cup flour, baking powder, salt and sugar in a bowl and mix well. Stir in the water, 1/3 cup lemon juice and egg. Dip the fillets in lemon juice and coat with flour. Dip the fillets in the lemon juice mixture. Fry in hot oil in a skillet until golden brown on both sides; drain. Yield: 3 or 4 servings.

Dorothy Kimbrough, Decatur Council

Tuna Salad Crescent Bake

1 (8-count) can crescent rolls
1 1/3 cups grated Parmesan
  cheese
2 eggs, lightly beaten
1 1/2 cups mayonnaise-type
  salad dressing
1 (9-ounce) can chunk-style
  tuna, drained

6 hard-cooked eggs, chopped
1 cup green peas
1 cup cream-style cottage
  cheese
6 slices processed American
  cheese
1/2 cup soft cracker crumbs
Paprika to taste

Unroll the crescent roll dough. Press the dough over the bottom and 1 1/2 inches up the sides of an 8x12-inch baking dish, pressing the perforations and edges to seal. Whisk the Parmesan cheese and eggs in a bowl. Spoon half the egg mixture into the prepared dish. Combine the salad dressing, tuna, eggs, peas and cottage cheese in a bowl and mix gently. Spread over the egg mixture. Top with the cheese slices. Spoon the remaining egg mixture over the top. Sprinkle with the cracker crumbs and paprika. Bake at 400 degrees for 20 to 30 minutes or until light brown. Serve warm or cold. May use frozen uncooked or canned peas. Yield: 6 to 8 servings.

Sharon Sanders, Riverchase Council

Crawfish Pies

1½ cups chopped onions
1⅓ cups chopped celery
2 garlic cloves, minced
½ cup (1 stick) butter
1 (10-ounce) can cream of
  mushroom soup
1 (5-ounce) can evaporated
  milk
2 pounds peeled crawfish tails

¼ cup chopped fresh parsley
¼ cup chopped green onions
1 teaspoon cornstarch
Salt and pepper to taste
1 pound crab meat
1 (3-ounce) can grated
  Parmesan cheese
6 unbaked (9-inch) pie shells

Sauté the onions, celery and garlic in the butter in a saucepan until tender. Stir in the soup and evaporated milk. Cook over medium heat until mixed, stirring constantly. Add the crawfish tails and mix well. Cook for 15 minutes, stirring occasionally. Stir in the parsley, green onions and cornstarch. Season with salt and pepper. Add the crab meat and cheese and mix well. Cook until thickened, stirring constantly. Spoon the crawfish mixture into 3 of the pie shells. Top with the remaining pie shells, sealing the edges and cutting vents. Cook at 350 degrees for 30 minutes or until brown. Let stand for 15 minutes before serving. *Note:* May freeze for future use. To reheat the frozen pies, thaw in the refrigerator for several hours. Bake at 325 degrees for 15 to 25 minutes. Yield: 18 servings.

Ken Wilson, Birmingham South Cahaba Council

LeBlanc Crawfish Casserole

½ cup (1 stick) margarine
8 ounces cream cheese, cubed
2 pounds peeled crawfish tails
1 large onion, chopped
1 large bell pepper, chopped
8 ounces fresh mushrooms, sliced
2 tablespoons margarine
1 (10-ounce) can cream of mushroom soup

2 cups cooked rice
1 tablespoon garlic powder, or to taste
½ teaspoon red pepper
3 dashes of white pepper
1½ to 2 cups shredded Velveeta cheese
1 cup canned French-fried onions

Heat ½ cup margarine in a double boiler until melted. Add the cream cheese. Cook over low heat until blended, stirring frequently. Sauté the crawfish tails, onion, bell pepper and mushrooms in 2 tablespoons margarine in a skillet until tender. Stir in the soup and rice. Add the garlic powder, red pepper and white pepper and mix well. Stir in the cream cheese mixture. Adjust the seasonings. Spoon into a greased baking dish. Sprinkle with the Velveeta cheese and onions. Bake at 350 degrees for 30 minutes or until bubbly. Note: May be prepared 1 day in advance and stored, covered, in the refrigerator. Bake just before serving or freeze for future use. May substitute shrimp for the crawfish.
Yield: 8 to 10 servings.

Ken Wilson, Birmingham South Cahaba Council

Bundle of Beans

½ cup packed brown sugar
2 tablespoons dry mustard

2 (16-ounce) cans whole
   green beans, drained
Sliced bacon, cut into halves

Combine the brown sugar and dry mustard in a bowl. Add the green beans and toss to coat. Divide the beans into bundles and wrap each bundle with a bacon half. Secure with wooden picks. Arrange the bundles in a single layer in a baking dish. Bake at 350 degrees for 20 minutes. Yield: 6 servings.

Nancy D. Murray, Birmingham South Cahaba Council

Broccoli Casserole

2 (10-ounce) packages frozen
   broccoli
1 (10-ounce) can cream of
   mushroom soup
1 medium onion, chopped
½ cup mayonnaise

2 eggs, beaten
1 cup shredded cheese
Salt and pepper to taste
½ cup bread crumbs
¼ cup (½ stick) butter or
   margarine

Cook the broccoli using package directions; drain. Combine the soup, onion, mayonnaise and eggs in a bowl and mix well. Fold in the broccoli, cheese, salt and pepper. Spoon into a baking dish. Brown the bread crumbs in the butter in a skillet. Sprinkle over the top. Bake at 350 degrees for 45 to 60 minutes or until bubbly. Yield: 6 to 8 servings.

Emma Allen, Riverchase Council

Easy Broccoli Casserole

1 (20-ounce) package frozen
  chopped broccoli
1 (10-ounce) can cream of
  mushroom soup
1 medium onion, chopped
1 cup mayonnaise
2 eggs, beaten

1 cup shredded mild Cheddar
  cheese
½ (8-ounce) package herb-
  seasoned stuffing mix
¼ cup (½ stick) butter or
  margarine, melted

Cook the broccoli using package directions; drain. Combine the
soup, onion, mayonnaise and eggs in a bowl and mix well. Stir in
the broccoli. Spoon into a baking dish. Sprinkle with the cheese.
Top with the stuffing mix and drizzle with the butter. Bake at 350
degrees for 45 minutes. Yield: 6 to 8 servings.

Gloria Wadsworth, Birmingham South Cahaba Council

Italian-Style Broccoli

Florets of 1 bunch broccoli
¾ cup grated Parmesan
  cheese

½ cup bread crumbs
Olive oil

Steam the broccoli in a steamer until tender-crisp; drain. Combine
the broccoli, cheese and bread crumbs in a bowl and mix gently.
Heat a small amount of olive oil in a nonstick skillet until hot. Add
the broccoli mixture to the skillet and press flat with a spatula to
resemble a pancake. Cook until brown on the underside; turn.
Cook until brown on the remaining side. Invert onto a serving
platter. *Note:* Cut into sections to turn if the mixture is too large to
turn as a whole piece. Yield: 4 to 6 servings.

Dorothy Hayes, Riverchase Council

Cabbage Casserole

5 cups coarsely shredded
  cabbage
Salt to taste
3 tablespoons margarine
2 tablespoons flour
½ teaspoon salt
⅛ teaspoon pepper

½ cup chopped yellow bell
  pepper
¼ cup chopped onion
1¼ cups milk
½ cup shredded cheese
4 cups crumbled corn bread

Combine the cabbage and salt to taste with a small amount of water in a saucepan. Cook until the cabbage is tender. Drain for 5 minutes. Heat the margarine in a saucepan until melted. Stir in the flour, ½ teaspoon salt and pepper. Add the yellow pepper and onion and mix well. Stir in the milk. Cook until thickened, stirring constantly. Add the cheese, stirring until melted. Layer 3 cups of the corn bread, cabbage and cheese sauce in a 2-quart baking dish. Sprinkle with the remaining 1 cup corn bread. Sprinkle with additional cheese and drizzle with margarine if desired. Bake at 350 degrees for 35 minutes or until heated through.
Yield: 6 to 8 servings.

Martha L. Bryan, Huntsville Council

Black-Eyed Pea Sausage

2 (16-ounce) cans black-eyed
  peas, drained
1 small onion, chopped
½ cup self-rising flour

1 egg, lightly beaten
½ teaspoon sage
3 tablespoons vegetable oil

Mash the peas in a bowl. Stir in the onion, flour, egg and sage. Heat the oil in a skillet over medium heat until hot. Drop the pea mixture by spoonfuls into the hot oil; flatten slightly to form patties. Fry until golden brown on both sides; drain.
Yield: 4 servings.

Debbie Speaks, Montgomery Council

Italian-Style Black-Eyed Peas

2 (16-ounce) packages frozen black-eyed peas
4 to 5 cups water
½ to ¾ cup hot water
2 (8-ounce) cans tomato sauce
3 cups chopped onions
1 bunch green onions, chopped
1 cup chopped fresh parsley
1 cup chopped green bell pepper
4 garlic cloves, crushed
1 tablespoon Worcestershire sauce
1¼ teaspoons salt
1 teaspoon red pepper
1 teaspoon black pepper
1 teaspoon thyme
½ teaspoon oregano
5 to 6 dashes of hot sauce
2 pounds smoked or Italian sausage, cut into bite-size pieces

Combine the peas and 4 to 5 cups water in a stockpot. Cook over medium-high heat for 30 to 40 minutes, stirring occasionally. Add the hot water and mix well. Stir in the tomato sauce, onions, green onions, parsley, green pepper, garlic, Worcestershire sauce, seasonings and hot sauce. Cook over medium-high heat for 1 hour, stirring occasionally. Add the sausage and mix well. Cook for 1 hour longer, stirring occasionally. Yield: 6 to 8 servings.

Ken Wilson, Birmingham South Cahaba Council

Cheesy Taters

1 (32-ounce) package frozen hash brown potatoes
1½ cups cubed Velveeta cheese
1 (10-ounce) can cream of chicken soup
1 cup sour cream
½ cup finely chopped onion
¼ cup (½ stick) margarine, melted
½ teaspoon salt
2 cups crushed cornflakes
1 cup (2 sticks) butter, melted

Spread the potatoes in a large baking dish. Combine the cheese, soup, sour cream, onion, margarine and salt in a bowl and mix well. Spoon over the potatoes. Sprinkle with the cornflakes. Drizzle with the butter. Bake at 350 degrees for 30 minutes. Yield: 8 servings.

Linda J. Stough, Birmingham South Cahaba Council

Jalapeño Potatoes

5 or 6 potatoes, peeled,
  chopped
1 bell pepper, chopped
2 tablespoons chopped
  jalapeño chile
1/4 cup (1/2 stick) butter
2 tablespoons flour

1 1/2 cups milk
1 (2-ounce) jar pimento
1 tablespoon parsley
1 teaspoon garlic
2 cups shredded sharp
  Cheddar cheese

Combine the potatoes with enough water to cover in a saucepan. Cook until tender-crisp; drain. Spoon into a lightly greased shallow baking dish. Sauté the bell pepper and chile in the butter in a saucepan until tender-crisp. Stir in the flour. Add the milk and mix well. Stir in the pimento, parsley and garlic. Cook until slightly thickened, stirring constantly. Pour over the potatoes. Bake at 375 degrees for 20 to 30 minutes or until heated through. Sprinkle with the cheese. Cook until the cheese is bubbly. Add additional milk if the potatoes become too dry; do not stir. Yield: 6 to 8 servings.

Jan Williams, Riverchase Council

Savory Grilled Potatoes

1/2 cup mayonnaise-type salad
  dressing
3 garlic cloves, minced
1/2 teaspoon paprika
1/4 teaspoon salt

1/4 teaspoon pepper
3 baking potatoes, cut into
  1/4-inch slices
1 large onion, sliced

Cut six 12-inch squares of heavy-duty foil. Combine the salad dressing, garlic, paprika, salt and pepper in a bowl and mix well. Stir in the potatoes and onion. Spoon 1/6 of the potato mixture in the center of each foil square; seal tightly. Arrange the foil packets on a grill rack over medium-hot coals. Grill, covered, for 25 to 30 minutes or until the potatoes are tender. Yield: 6 servings.

Susan Poe, Riverchase Council

Spinach and Artichoke Casserole

2 (10-ounce) packages frozen
   chopped spinach
½ cup chopped green onions
½ cup (1 stick) butter
1 (10-ounce) can artichoke
   hearts, drained, cut into
   quarters

1 cup sour cream
¼ teaspoon garlic powder
Salt and pepper to taste
½ cup grated Parmesan
   cheese

Cook the spinach using package directions; drain well. Sauté the green onions in the butter in a skillet. Combine the spinach, green onions, artichokes, sour cream, garlic powder, salt and pepper in a bowl and mix well. Spoon into a baking dish. Sprinkle with the cheese. Bake at 350 degrees for 30 minutes. Yield: 6 servings.

Linda A. Tucker, Birmingham South Cahaba Council

Squash Casserole

6 to 8 yellow squash
1 large onion, chopped
2 cups shredded sharp
   Cheddar cheese
½ cup evaporated milk
3 wedges corn bread,
   crumbled

2 slices sandwich bread, torn
¼ cup (½ stick) butter,
   melted
2 eggs, lightly beaten
Salt and pepper to taste

Combine the squash and onion with enough water to cover in a saucepan. Cook until tender; drain. Mash the squash and onion in a bowl. Stir in the cheese, evaporated milk, corn bread, sandwich bread, butter, eggs, salt and pepper. Spoon into a baking dish. Sprinkle with additional cheese if desired. Bake at 350 degrees for 45 minutes. Yield: 4 servings.

Di Riccio, Riverchase Council

Vegetable Casserole

1 (15-ounce) can Veg-All,   1 onion, chopped
  drained   Crushed butter crackers
1 cup mayonnaise   1/2 cup (1 stick) margarine,
1 cup shredded Cheddar   melted
  cheese

Combine the Veg-All, mayonnaise, cheese and onion in a bowl and
mix well. Spoon into a baking dish. Bake at 350 degrees for 20 to
25 minutes or until bubbly. Sprinkle with the cracker crumbs and
drizzle with the margarine. Broil until light brown. *Note:* Add a can
or cans of corn, lima beans or peas according to the size of the
crowd you will be serving. Yield: 4 to 6 servings.

Mickey Deal, Birmingham South Cahaba Council

Veg-All Casserole

2 (15-ounce) cans Veg-All   1/2 cup mayonnaise
2 cups shredded cheese   Crushed crackers
1/2 to 3/4 cup chopped onion   1/2 cup (1 stick) margarine,
1 (8-ounce) can water   melted
  chestnuts, drained, chopped

Drain 1 can of the Veg-All. Combine the drained Veg-All and
undrained Veg-All in a bowl. Stir in the cheese, onion, water
chestnuts and mayonnaise. Spoon into a 2-quart baking dish. Top
with a mixture of the crackers and margarine. Bake at 350 degrees
until brown. Yield: 6 to 8 servings.

Martha L. Bryan, Huntsville Council

Mixed Vegetable Casserole

2 (15-ounce) cans Veg-All,
  drained
1 cup shredded Cheddar
  cheese
1 cup mayonnaise

½ cup chopped onion
1 sleeve butter crackers,
  crushed
½ cup (1 stick) margarine,
  melted

Combine the Veg-All, cheese, mayonnaise and onion in a bowl and
mix well. Spoon into a baking dish sprayed with nonstick cooking
spray. Top with a mixture of the crackers and margarine. Bake at
350 degrees for 30 minutes. Yield: 6 to 8 servings.

Fay Clark, Riverchase Council

Corn Bread Dressing

1 (3-pound) chicken
2½ teaspoons vegetable oil
2 cups self-rising cornmeal
1 cup self-rising flour
1 to 2 cups buttermilk
5 eggs, lightly beaten
1 cup cream of chicken or
  mushroom soup

1 cup chopped onion
1 cup water
¾ cup chopped celery
½ cup (1 stick) margarine,
  softened
Salt and pepper to taste
Sage to taste

Combine the chicken with enough water to cover in a stockpot.
Cook until tender. Drain, reserving the broth. Chop the chicken,
discarding the skin and bones. Heat the oil in a cast-iron skillet at
475 degrees until hot. Combine the cornmeal, flour, buttermilk and
eggs in a bowl and mix well. Spoon into the prepared skillet. Bake
until brown and crisp; crumble. Combine the corn bread, chicken,
soup, onion, water, celery, margarine, salt, pepper and sage in a
bowl and mix well. Add the reserved broth until of the desired
consistency. Spoon into a slow cooker. Cook on High for 3 hours;
reduce the heat. Cook on Low for 2 to 3 hours.
Yield: 8 to 10 servings.

Nancy Conner, Anniston Council

Pasta with Artichokes and Basil

4 ounces fettuccini, penne or
   fusilli
1 tablespoon olive oil
3 (6-ounce) cans artichoke
   hearts, drained
2 green bell peppers, chopped
½ cup chopped onion

½ teaspoon garlic powder, or
   2 garlic cloves, minced
1 (14-ounce) can diced
   tomatoes, drained
2 tablespoons basil
Grated Parmesan cheese

Cook the pasta using package directions; drain. Heat the olive oil in a skillet until hot. Add the artichokes, green peppers, onion and garlic powder. Cook until the vegetables are tender, stirring frequently. Stir in the tomatoes and basil. Cook for 2 minutes longer, stirring constantly. Spoon over the pasta on a serving platter. Sprinkle with cheese. *Note:* Top with grilled chicken strips for variety. Yield: 4 servings.

Marty Johnson, Birmingham South Cahaba Council

Garlic Pasta

5 garlic cloves, chopped
2 green onions, chopped
¼ cup olive oil
2 cups fresh or canned
   mushrooms

1 cup water
16 ounces noodles, cooked,
   drained

Sauté the garlic and green onions in the olive oil in a skillet until tender. Stir in the mushrooms. Add the water and mix well. Simmer until of the desired consistency, stirring occasionally. Combine with the noodles in a bowl. Yield: 4 to 6 servings.

MaMa Rita, Riverchase Council

Macaroni and Cheese

8 ounces macaroni, cooked,
   drained
2 cups shredded cheese
1 (10-ounce) can cream of
   chicken soup

1 cup mayonnaise
1 (2-ounce) jar pimento,
   drained

Combine the macaroni, cheese, soup, mayonnaise and pimento in a bowl and mix well. Spoon into a baking dish. Bake at 350 degrees for 25 minutes. Yield: 6 to 8 servings.

Marjorie S. (Francis) Tucker, Selma Life Member Club

Shrimp Fried Rice

1 pound shrimp, peeled,
   deveined
3 tablespoons vegetable oil
1 (10-ounce) package frozen
   peas and carrots

1 onion, chopped
1 egg
3 cups cooked rice
Soy sauce to taste

Stir-fry the shrimp in 1 tablespoon of the oil in a wok or large skillet until cooked through. Remove the shrimp to a serving bowl. Heat 1 tablespoon of the oil in the wok. Add the peas and carrots. Stir-fry for several minutes. Transfer the vegetables to the serving bowl with a slotted spoon. Heat the remaining tablespoon of oil in the wok. Stir-fry the onion in the hot oil until tender-crisp. Transfer the onion to the serving bowl. Scramble the egg in the wok. Add to the shrimp mixture. Stir in the rice. Drizzle with the desired amount of soy sauce. Serve immediately. Yield: 6 servings.

Don Helms, Birmingham South Cahaba Council

Zucchini Bread

3 cups flour
1 teaspoon salt
1 teaspoon baking soda
1 teaspoon cinnamon
1/2 teaspoon baking powder
3 eggs

2 cups sugar
1 cup vegetable oil
1 teaspoon vanilla extract
Chopped nuts to taste
2 cups grated zucchini

Mix the flour, salt, baking soda, cinnamon and baking powder in a bowl. Beat the eggs in a mixer bowl until blended. Add the sugar, oil, vanilla and nuts and beat until mixed. Stir in the flour mixture. Fold in the zucchini. Spoon the batter into 2 greased 5x9-inch loaf pans. Bake at 325 degrees for 1 hour. Cool in pans for 10 minutes. Invert onto a wire rack to cool completely. Yield: 2 loaves.

Sherrie Poynor, Montgomery Council

Dinner Rolls

2 envelopes dry yeast
1 cup lukewarm water
1 cup milk
6 tablespoons shortening

6 tablespoons sugar
1 1/2 teaspoons salt
5 cups flour
Melted butter

Dissolve the yeast in the lukewarm water. Scald the milk, shortening, sugar and salt in a saucepan. Let stand until cool. Combine with the yeast mixture in a bowl and mix well. Add the flour gradually, mixing constantly. Chill, covered with a damp cloth, for up to 2 days. Knead the dough 5 or 6 times on a lightly floured surface 1 1/2 hours before the baking process. Cut or shape the dough into the desired shapes. Dip in melted butter. Arrange the rolls on a baking sheet. Let rise until doubled in bulk. Bake at 350 degrees for 25 minutes or until brown. Yield: 2 to 3 dozen rolls.

Mary Ann Sparks Fulmer, Shoals Life Member Club

Blueberry Crunch

1 (20-ounce) can crushed
   pineapple in syrup
3 cups fresh or frozen
   blueberries
¾ cup sugar

½ cup (1 stick) margarine
1 (2-layer) package yellow
   cake mix
¼ cup sugar
1 cup chopped pecans

Layer the undrained pineapple, blueberries and ¾ sugar in the order listed in a 9x13-inch baking dish. Cut the margarine into the cake mix in a bowl until crumbly. Spread over the prepared layers. Sprinkle with ¼ cup sugar and pecans. Bake at 350 degrees for 45 minutes. Yield: 8 servings.

Pat Prestridge, Birmingham Metro Council

Blueberry Dump Dessert

1 (20-ounce) can crushed
   pineapple
3 cups blueberries
1 (2-layer) package yellow
   cake mix

¾ cup (1½ sticks) butter,
   melted
1 cup chopped pecans

Layer the undrained pineapple and blueberries in the order listed in a 9x13-inch baking pan sprayed with nonstick cooking spray. Sprinkle with the cake mix. Drizzle with the butter. Top with the pecans. Bake at 350 degrees for 40 to 45 minutes or until golden brown. Yield: 8 servings.

Pat White, Montgomery Council

Calypso Dessert

½ gallon vanilla ice cream,   12 ounces whipped topping
   softened   1 cup chopped pecans, toasted
1 package chocolate sandwich   Chocolate syrup
   cookies, crushed

Combine the ice cream, cookie crumbs, whipped topping and
pecans in a bowl and mix well. Spread in a 9x13-inch dish. Freeze,
covered, until firm. Cut into squares. Drizzle each serving with
chocolate syrup. Yield: 15 servings.

Susan Smalley, Alabama Telco Credit Union

Creamy Cheesecake

1 cup graham cracker crumbs   ½ cup sugar
¼ cup sugar   ¾ cup milk
¼ cup (½ stick) margarine,   ¼ cup lemon juice
   melted   1 cup whipping cream,
1 envelope unflavored gelatin   whipped
¼ cup cold water   Strawberries, cut into halves
8 ounces cream cheese,
   softened

Combine the graham cracker crumbs, ¼ cup sugar and margarine
in a bowl and mix well. Press the crumb mixture over the bottom
of a 9-inch springform pan. Soften the gelatin in the cold water in
a saucepan. Cook over low heat until dissolved, stirring constantly.
Combine the cream cheese and ½ cup sugar in a mixer bowl. Beat
at medium speed until blended. Add the gelatin, milk and lemon
juice. Beat until smooth. Chill, covered, until slightly thickened.
Fold in the whipped cream. Spoon into the prepared pan. Chill
until firm. Top with the strawberries just before serving.
Yield: 8 servings.

Susan Poe, Riverchase Council

Pineapple Cheesecake

1¼ cups graham cracker
　crumbs
⅓ cup sugar
⅓ cup margarine, melted
8 ounces cream cheese,
　softened
½ cup sugar

1 (8-ounce) can crushed
　pineapple
½ cup sour cream
2 tablespoons margarine,
　softened
2 tablespoons flour
1 egg

Combine the graham cracker crumbs, ⅓ cup sugar and ⅓ cup margarine in a bowl and mix well. Reserve ½ cup of the crumb mixture. Press the remaining crumb mixture over the bottom of an 8-inch round baking pan or baking dish. Beat the cream cheese and ½ cup sugar in a mixer bowl until blended. Add the undrained pineapple, sour cream, 2 tablespoons margarine, flour and egg and beat until smooth. Spoon into the prepared pan. Bake at 350 degrees for 15 minutes. Let stand until cool. Sprinkle with the reserved crumbs. Chill, covered, for 8 to 10 hours.
Yield: 6 to 8 servings.

Louise Wheeler, Selma Life Member Club

Chocolate Eclairs

2 (4-ounce) packages French
　vanilla instant pudding mix
3 cups milk
16 ounces whipped topping

1 (16-ounce) package graham
　crackers
1 (16-ounce) can chocolate
　frosting

Combine the pudding mixes and milk in a mixer bowl. Beat at low speed for 2 minutes. Chill for 15 minutes. Fold in the whipped topping. Cover the bottom of a buttered 9x13-inch dish with graham crackers. Spread with half the pudding mixture. Top with another layer of graham crackers and the remaining pudding mixture. Layer with graham crackers. Spread with the frosting. Chill, covered, for 8 to 10 hours. Yield: 15 servings.

Celia Stephens, Montgomery Council

Cobbler à la Mode

3 cups undrained fresh or
  frozen sliced peaches,
  apples or cherries
2 tablespoons vanilla extract

1 (2-layer) package butter
  cake mix
½ cup (1 stick) butter, melted

Combine the peaches and vanilla in a bowl and mix gently. Spoon into a baking dish. Sprinkle with the cake mix. Drizzle with the butter. Bake at 350 degrees for 50 minutes or until brown. Let stand for 10 minutes before serving. Serve topped with vanilla ice cream. Yield: 6 servings.

Mildred Choice, Birmingham South Cahaba Council

Easy Fruit Cobbler

½ cup (1 stick) margarine,
  melted
1 cup sugar
1 cup flour

¾ cup milk
1 (21-ounce) can strawberry
  or any flavor pie filling

Pour the margarine into a baking dish, tilting the dish to coat the bottom. Combine the sugar, flour and milk in a bowl and mix well. Spoon over the margarine; do not mix. Spread the pie filling over the top; do not stir. Bake at 350 degrees for 1 hour or until the cobbler tests done. Yield: 6 servings.

Faye S. King, Huntsville Council

Peach Cobbler

2 cups sliced peeled peaches
1 cup sugar
6 tablespoons butter or
  margarine

1 cup sugar
¾ cup flour
¾ cup milk

Combine the peaches and 1 cup sugar in a bowl and mix well. Let stand for 5 to 10 minutes. Heat the butter in a 2-quart baking dish until melted. Stir in the peaches. Combine 1 cup sugar and flour in a bowl and mix well. Stir in the milk. Spoon over the peaches. Bake at 350 degrees for 30 minutes or until brown. Yield: 6 servings.

Sally Burttram, Riverchase Council

Peach Delight

½ cup (1 stick) butter or
  margarine, sliced
1 cup sugar
1 cup self-rising flour

½ cup whole milk
1 (16-ounce) can cling
  peaches
Sugar and cinnamon to taste

Arrange the butter slices over the bottom of a 5x7-inch baking pan. Combine the sugar and flour in a bowl and mix well. Stir in the milk. Spoon over the butter. Top with the undrained peaches. Bake at 350 degrees until brown. Sprinkle with sugar and cinnamon. May substitute your favorite pie filling for the peaches. Yield: 6 servings.

Ella Asberry, Birmingham Metro Council

Fried Peach Pies

4 ounces dried apricots	1/4 teaspoon salt
1 peach, peeled, sliced	1/4 cup shortening
1/4 cup water	3 ounces cream cheese
2 tablespoons sugar	2/3 cup (or more) milk
2 1/2 cups self-rising flour	5 cups corn oil for frying

Combine the apricots, peach and water in a saucepan. Simmer for 12 to 15 minutes or until the fruit is tender, stirring occasionally. Process the apricot mixture and sugar in a blender until smooth. Combine the flour and salt in a bowl. Cut in the shortening and cream cheese until crumbly. Add the milk gradually, stirring until the mixture adheres. Add an additional 1 tablespoon milk if needed to form a ball. Roll the dough 1/3 inch thick on a lightly floured surface. Cut into 3-inch circles. Gather the scraps of dough and roll and cut into more circles. Spoon about 2 teaspoons of the apricot mixture in the center of each circle. Fold over to enclose the filling. Crimp the edges to seal. Heat the corn oil in a skillet to 375 degrees. Fry the pies 5 at a time in the hot oil for 3 to 5 minutes or until golden brown; drain. Yield: 2 dozen.

Donna Jean Bowman, Birmingham South Cahaba Council

Pineapple Twinkie Dessert

1 (6-ounce) package vanilla instant pudding mix	1 (20-ounce) can juice-pack crushed pineapple
2 1/2 cups milk	Whipped topping
1 (10-count) package Twinkies, cut into halves	Chopped pecans

Combine the pudding mix and milk in a mixer bowl. Prepare using package directions. Arrange the Twinkies cut side up in a shallow dish. Spread with the undrained pineapple. Top with the pudding. Spread with whipped topping and sprinkle with pecans. Chill, covered, until serving time. Yield: 15 servings.

Mrs. Bob H. Henson, Birmingham South Life Member Club

Punch Bowl Dessert

1 (6-ounce) package
  vanilla instant
  pudding mix
1 angel food cake, torn into
  bite-size pieces

1 (15-ounce) can crushed
  pineapple
1 (21-ounce) can strawberry
  pie filling
16 ounces whipped topping

Prepare the pudding mix using package directions. Layer the cake, undrained pineapple, pudding and pie filling ½ at a time in a trifle bowl. Spread with the whipped topping, sealing to the edge. Chill, covered with plastic wrap, for 8 to 10 hours. Yield: 8 to 10 servings.

Brenda Freeman, Birmingham Metro Council

Quick and Easy Banana Pudding

1 cup sugar
3 tablespoons cornstarch
2 cups milk
3 egg yolks, lightly beaten
1 teaspoon vanilla extract

24 vanilla wafers
3 bananas, sliced
3 egg whites
1 teaspoon cream of tartar
3 tablespoons sugar

Combine 1 cup sugar and cornstarch in a microwave-safe dish. Stir in the milk, egg yolks and vanilla. Microwave on High for 5 minutes; stir. Layer the vanilla wafers, bananas and pudding alternately in a round baking dish until all of the ingredients are used, ending with the pudding. Beat the egg whites and cream of tartar in a mixer bowl until foamy. Add 3 tablespoons sugar gradually, beating constantly until stiff peaks form. Spread over the pudding, sealing to the edge. Bake at 450 degrees until light brown. Yield: 4 to 6 servings.

Lola Duffey, Shoals Life Member Club

Banana Pudding

2¼ cups sugar
6 tablespoons flour
⅛ teaspoon salt
3 cups milk
6 egg yolks
¾ cup (1½ sticks) margarine
1 tablespoon vanilla extract

1 (16-ounce) package vanilla
  wafers
12 large bananas, sliced
6 egg whites
⅛ teaspoon salt
½ cup sugar

Combine 2¼ cups sugar, flour and ⅛ teaspoon salt in a bowl and mix well. Whisk the milk and egg yolks in a saucepan until blended. Add the sugar mixture and mix well. Add the margarine. Cook until thickened, stirring constantly. Let stand until cool. Stir in the vanilla. Alternate layers of wafers and bananas in a heatproof bowl until all of the ingredients are used. Pour the pudding over the top. Beat the egg whites and ⅛ teaspoon salt in a mixer bowl until foamy. Add ½ cup sugar gradually, beating constantly until stiff peaks form. Spread over the top, sealing to the edge. Bake at 400 degrees for 10 minutes or until light brown. Yield: 12 servings.

Kitty Logan Brown, Gadsden Life Member Club

Chocolate Praline Torte

1 cup packed brown sugar
1/2 cup (1 stick) butter
1/4 cup whipping cream
3/4 cup chopped pecans
1 (2-layer) package devil's
   food cake mix

3/4 cup whipping cream
1/4 cup confectioners' sugar
1/4 teaspoon vanilla extract

Combine the brown sugar, butter and 1/4 cup whipping cream in a saucepan. Cook over low heat until the butter melts, stirring frequently. Pour into 2 greased 9-inch cake pans. Sprinkle with the pecans. Prepare the cake mix using package directions. Spoon the batter into the prepared pans. Bake at 325 degrees for 35 to 45 minutes or until the layers test done. Cool in pans for 10 minutes. Beat 3/4 cup whipping cream in a mixer bowl until soft peaks form. Add the confectioners' sugar and vanilla. Beat until stiff peaks form. Arrange 1 layer pecan side up on a cake plate. Spread with half the whipped cream mixture. Top with the remaining layer pecan side up. Spread with the remaining whipped cream topping. Garnish with chocolate curls. Store, covered, in the refrigerator. Yield: 8 to 10 servings.

Doris Yaber, Shoals Life Member Club

Texas Sheet Cake

1 cup (2 sticks) butter
1 cup water
1 teaspoon baking cocoa
2 cups flour
2 cups sugar
1 teaspoon salt

½ cup sour cream
2 eggs, lightly beaten
1 teaspoon baking soda
1 teaspoon vanilla extract
Chocolate Icing

Combine the butter, water and baking cocoa in a saucepan. Bring to a boil, stirring occasionally. Add the flour, sugar and salt and mix well. Stir in the sour cream, eggs, baking soda and vanilla. Pour the batter into a 10x15-inch cake pan. Bake at 350 degrees for 22 minutes. Spread the hot cake with the Chocolate Icing.
Yield: 12 to 15 servings.

Chocolate Icing

½ cup (1 stick) butter or
   margarine
6 tablespoons milk
¼ cup baking cocoa

1 (1-pound) package
   confectioners' sugar
1 teaspoon vanilla extract
Chopped nuts (optional)

Bring the butter, milk and baking cocoa to a boil in a saucepan, stirring frequently. Pour over the confectioners' sugar in a bowl and whisk until smooth. Stir in the vanilla and nuts.

Sherry Johnson, Birmingham South Cahaba Council

Texas Chocolate Sheet Cake

2 cups flour
2 cups sugar
1 cup (2 sticks) margarine
1 cup water
3 tablespoons baking cocoa

1/2 cup buttermilk
2 eggs, lightly beaten
1 teaspoon baking soda
1 teaspoon vanilla extract
Chocolate Frosting

Combine the flour and sugar in a bowl and mix well. Bring the margarine, water and baking cocoa to a boil in a saucepan, stirring frequently. Pour over the flour mixture and mix well. Stir in the buttermilk, eggs, baking soda and vanilla. Pour the batter into a greased 9x13-inch cake pan. Bake at 350 degrees for 45 minutes. Spread the Chocolate Frosting over the hot cake.
Yield: 15 servings.

Chocolate Frosting

1/2 cup (1 stick) margarine
6 tablespoons buttermilk
2 tablespoons baking cocoa
1 (1-pound) package
    confectioners' sugar

1 teaspoon vanilla extract
1 cup chopped pecans

Bring the margarine, buttermilk and baking cocoa to a boil in a saucepan, stirring frequently. Pour over the confectioners' sugar and vanilla in a bowl and stir until blended. Stir in the pecans.

Janis Swaim, Alabama Telco Credit Union

Honey Bun Cake

1 (2-layer) yellow cake mix
1 cup buttermilk
¾ cup vegetable oil
½ cup sugar
4 eggs
¾ cup packed brown sugar
4 teaspoons cinnamon

½ cup chopped nuts
¼ cup raisins or chopped
   dates
2 cups confectioners' sugar
2 tablespoons milk
1 teaspoon vanilla extract

Combine the cake mix, buttermilk, oil, sugar and eggs in a mixer bowl. Beat for 2 minutes. Spoon the batter into a greased 9x13-inch cake pan. Combine the brown sugar and cinnamon in a bowl and mix well. Stir in the nuts and raisins. Sprinkle over the prepared layer and swirl with a knife. Bake at 350 degrees until the cake tests done. Combine the confectioners' sugar, milk and vanilla in a bowl and mix well. Spread over the hot cake. Yield: 15 servings.

Margarette Russell, Decatur Council

Apple Pie

1 recipe (2-crust) pie pastry
6 cups sliced peeled apples
1 tablespoon lemon juice
1¼ cups sugar

1 tablespoon flour
½ teaspoon nutmeg
½ teaspoon cinnamon
1 tablespoon butter

Line a 9-inch pie plate with half the pastry. Toss the apples with the lemon juice in a bowl. Add a mixture of the sugar, flour, nutmeg and cinnamon. Spoon the apple mixture into the pastry-lined pie plate. Dot with the butter. Top with the remaining pastry, crimping the edge and cutting vents. Bake at 375 degrees for 40 to 45 minutes or until brown. Yield: 8 servings.

Faith Kirby Richardson, Gadsden Life Member Club

Blueberry Pie

¾ cup sugar
3 tablespoons cornstarch
⅛ teaspoon salt
¼ cup cold water
5 cups blueberries

1 tablespoon margarine
1 tablespoon lemon juice
1 (9-inch) graham cracker
   pie shell

Combine the sugar, cornstarch and salt in a saucepan and mix well. Stir in the cold water. Cook over medium heat until smooth, stirring frequently. Stir in 3 cups of the blueberries. Bring to a boil. Cook until thickened, stirring frequently. Remove from heat. Add the remaining 2 cups of blueberries, margarine and lemon juice, stirring gently until the margarine melts. Spoon into the pie shell. Top with whipped cream or whipped topping if desired. Chill until serving time. Yield: 8 servings.

Margaret Hare, Gadsden Life Member Club

Chocolate Pie

1 cup sugar
¼ cup flour
2 tablespoons (rounded)
   baking cocoa
1¾ cups whole milk
¼ cup (½ stick) margarine

2 egg yolks, beaten
1 teaspoon vanilla extract
1 baked (9-inch) pie shell
2 egg whites
⅛ teaspoon cream of tartar
¼ cup sugar

Combine 1 cup sugar, flour and baking cocoa in a saucepan and mix well. Add the milk, margarine and egg yolks. Cook over medium heat until thickened, stirring constantly. Remove from heat. Stir in the vanilla. Spoon into the pie shell. Beat the egg whites and cream of tartar in a mixer bowl until foamy. Add ¼ cup sugar gradually, beating constantly until stiff peaks form. Spread over the filling, sealing to the edge. Bake at 400 degrees until light brown.
Yield: 6 to 8 servings.

Mrs. J.B. (Carol) Raines, Gadsden Life Member Club

Favorite Chocolate Pie

1 (5-ounce) can evaporated
  milk
Milk
¾ cup sugar
3 tablespoons cornstarch
2 tablespoons baking cocoa
2 egg yolks, beaten

1 tablespoon margarine
1 teaspoon vanilla extract
1 baked (9-inch) pie shell
2 egg whites
¼ teaspoon cream of tartar
⅛ teaspoon salt
¼ cup sugar

Combine the evaporated milk with enough milk to measure 2 cups. Combine ¾ cup sugar, cornstarch and baking cocoa in a saucepan and mix well. Stir in the egg yolks. Add the milk mixture and mix well. Cook until thickened, stirring constantly. Remove from heat. Stir in the margarine and vanilla. Spoon into the pie shell. Beat the egg whites, cream of tartar and salt in a mixer bowl until foamy. Add ¼ cup sugar gradually, beating constantly until stiff peaks form. Spread over the filling, sealing to the edge. Bake at 250 degrees until brown. Yield: 8 servings.

Dorthy Yaber, Shoals Life Member Club

Coconut Pie

1½ cups sugar
2 eggs
¼ cup (½ stick) butter or
  margarine, melted
1 can shredded coconut

1 (5-ounce) can evaporated
  milk
1 tablespoon vanilla extract
1 unbaked (9-inch) pie shell

Beat the sugar and eggs in a mixer bowl until creamy. Add the butter and mix well. Stir in ¾ of the coconut, evaporated milk and vanilla. Spoon into the pie shell. Sprinkle with the remaining coconut. Bake at 350 degrees for 30 to 45 minutes or until set. Yield: 6 to 8 servings.

Eulene Miller, Birmingham South Cahaba Council

Delicious Coconut Dream Pie

1 (14-ounce) can sweetened
   condensed milk
8 to 12 ounces whipped
   topping
8 ounces cream cheese,
   softened

1 cup shredded coconut
1 cup pecan pieces
1/2 cup (1 stick) butter
1 (9-inch) graham cracker
   pie shell

Beat the condensed milk, whipped topping and cream cheese in a mixer bowl until blended. Chill, covered, until ready to use. Brown the coconut and pecans in the butter in a skillet, stirring frequently. Spoon the cream cheese mixture into the pie shell. Sprinkle with the coconut mixture. Chill, covered, until serving time.
Yield: 6 servings.

Angie Bolton, Montgomery Council

Fudge Pies

1 cup (2 sticks) margarine
2 cups sugar
1/2 cup baking cocoa
1/2 cup flour

4 eggs, lightly beaten
1 teaspoon vanilla extract
2 unbaked (9-inch) pie shells

Heat the margarine in a saucepan until melted. Add the sugar, baking cocoa, flour, eggs and vanilla in the order listed, mixing well after each addition. Spoon into the pie shells. Bake at 325 degrees for 25 minutes or until firm. Yield: 16 servings.

Linda McKee, Decatur Council

Lemon Pie

1 (14-ounce) can sweetened   ½ cup lemon juice
  condensed milk   1 (9-inch) graham cracker
8 ounces frozen whipped   pie shell
  topping, thawed

Combine the condensed milk, whipped topping and lemon juice in a bowl and mix well. Spoon into the pie shell. Chill until serving time. Garnish with lemon zest. Yield: 6 to 8 servings.

Brenda Reeves, Birmingham South Cahaba Council

Oatmeal Pie

⅔ cup sugar   2 tablespoons brown sugar
⅔ cup light corn syrup   1 teaspoon vanilla extract
⅔ cup margarine, melted   ⅔ cup rolled oats
2 eggs, lightly beaten   1 unbaked (9-inch) pie shell

Combine the sugar, corn syrup, margarine, eggs, brown sugar and vanilla in a bowl and mix well. Stir in the oats. Spoon into the pie shell. Bake at 350 degrees for 45 minutes. Yield: 6 servings.

Fay Clark, Riverchase Council

Mandarin Orange Pies

1 (14-ounce) can sweetened
   condensed milk
½ cup lemon juice
12 ounces whipped topping
2 cans mandarin oranges,
   drained

1 cup chopped nuts
2 (9-inch) graham cracker pie
   shells

Combine the condensed milk and lemon juice in a bowl and mix well. Let stand until set. Fold in the whipped topping, oranges and nuts. Spoon into the pie shells. Chill until serving time.
Yield: 12 servings.

Mrs. J.B. (Carol) Raines, Gadsden Life Member Club

Peanut Butter Pie

12 ounces whipped topping
8 ounces cream cheese,
   softened
1 cup confectioners' sugar

½ cup peanut butter
¼ cup half-and-half
1 (9-inch) graham cracker
   pie shell

Beat the whipped topping, cream cheese, confectioners' sugar, peanut butter and half-and-half in a mixer bowl until blended. Spoon into the pie shell. Freeze until firm. Let stand at room temperature for several minutes before serving.
Yield: 6 to 8 servings.

Opal Norton, Shoals Life Member Club

Spicy Shrimp Dip

32 ounces cream cheese
1½ pounds boiled or steamed
  shrimp, chopped
1 large can chopped tomatoes,
  drained, or 1 large tomato,
  chopped, drained

2 small cans chopped green
  chiles, drained
1 cup chopped jalapeño chiles

Melt the cream cheese in a slow cooker. Add the shrimp, tomatoes, green chiles and jalapeño chiles, stirring gently to mix. Cook on Low until serving time. Serve with tortilla chips. The flavor will get stronger the longer the dip heats. Yield: 10 cups.

Sharon Sanders, Riverchase Council

Barbecue Chicken Wings

2 bottles barbecue sauce
1½ cups Worcestershire sauce
½ cup honey
1 bottle hot sauce
1 teaspoon garlic powder

2 cups flour
¼ cup seasoning salt
Pepper to taste
5 pounds frozen chicken wings
Vegetable oil for deep-frying

Mix the barbecue sauce, Worcestershire sauce, honey, hot sauce and garlic powder in a bowl and set aside. Combine the flour, seasoning salt and pepper in a large bowl. Coat the chicken wings with the flour mixture. Deep-fry in the oil until cooked through and crispy; drain well. Dip the chicken wings in the reserved barbecue sauce mixture. Arrange on a foil-lined baking sheet. Bake at 375 degrees for 30 to 45 minutes or until cooked to taste. May make hotter by mixing in additional hot sauce or sweeter by adding additional honey. Yield: 50 to 60 servings.

Donna Jean Bowman, Birmingham South Cahaba Council

Easy Apricot Preserves

1 (8-ounce) package dried
   apricots
1/2 cup sugar

4 cups water
1/2 lemon, peeled, finely
   chopped

Combine the dried apricots, sugar, water and lemon in a saucepan
and mix well. Cook, uncovered, over medium heat for 20 minutes
or until apricots are plump. Mash coarsely with a potato masher.
Serve with buttered biscuits. Yield: 1 1/2 to 2 cups.

Betty M. Jones-Moon, Birmingham Life Member Club

Red Beans and Rice Soup

1 pound lean ground beef
1 tablespoon vegetable oil
1 small onion, chopped
1 small green bell pepper,
   chopped
1 envelope chili seasoning mix

4 to 6 cans red beans
1 package cocktail smokies
1 large can tomatoes
1 can tomato sauce
1 small bag rice

Brown the ground beef in the oil in a skillet, stirring until the
ground beef is crumbly. Stir in the onion and green pepper. Simmer
over medium heat for 5 minutes; drain. Stir in the chili seasoning
mix. Heat the red beans in a saucepan over medium-low heat for 5
to 10 minutes. Add the ground beef mixture, cocktail smokies,
tomatoes and tomato sauce and mix well. Cook over medium heat
for 20 minutes, stirring frequently. Cook the rice using the package
directions. Ladle the soup over the rice in soup bowls.
Yield: 12 servings.

Ella Asberry, Birmingham Metro Council

Apple Salad

3 Red Delicious apples,
   chopped
3 Golden Delicious apples,
   chopped
1 large can crushed pineapple,
   drained
2 cans mandarin oranges,
   drained

White grapes to taste, cut into
   halves
2 cups chopped pecans
1 (6-ounce) package frozen
   coconut
3/4 to 1 cup mayonnaise
1 to 1 1/2 cups whipped topping

Combine the apples, pineapple, mandarin oranges, grapes, pecans
and coconut in a large bowl and mix well. Stir in a mixture of the
mayonnaise and whipped topping. Chill until serving time.
Yield: 25 to 30 servings.

Jan Williams, Riverchase Council

Corn Bread Salad

4 cups crumbled corn bread
1 green bell pepper, chopped
1 large tomato, chopped
2 hard-cooked eggs, chopped
1 can Mexican corn, drained

1 small onion, chopped
1 can green peas, drained
Chopped bacon to taste
Mayonnaise

Combine the corn bread, green pepper, tomato, eggs, Mexican
corn, onion, green peas, bacon and enough mayonnaise to make of
the desired consistency in a large bowl and mix well. Chill until
serving time. Yield: 6 to 8 servings.

Debbie Speaks, Montgomery Council

Green Bean Salad

1 (16-ounce) can French-style
    green beans, drained
1/2 cup chopped green bell
    pepper
1/2 cup chopped celery
1/2 cup chopped onion

1 medium or large cucumber,
    chopped
1 (2-ounce) jar pimento
1/2 cup vinegar
10 to 12 packets artificial
    sweetener

Mix the French-style green beans, green pepper, celery, onion, cucumber and pimento in a large bowl. Stir in a mixture of the vinegar and artificial sweetener. Marinate, covered, in the refrigerator for 8 to 12 hours. *Note:* This is low in calories.
Yield: 6 to 8 servings.

Brenda Reeves, Birmingham South Cahaba Council

Macaroni Salad

8 ounces elbow macaroni
1 cup chopped celery
1/2 cup chopped fresh parsley
1/2 cup chopped green bell
    pepper
6 green onions with tops,
    chopped
1 cup shredded sharp Cheddar
    cheese

1 (2-ounce) jar pimento,
    drained
1/2 cup mayonnaise
1/2 cup sour cream
1 tablespoon red wine vinegar
1/2 teaspoon seasoning salt
1/4 teaspoon pepper
Paprika to taste

Cook the macaroni using the package directions; drain. Let stand until cool. Combine with the celery, parsley, green pepper, green onions, Cheddar cheese and pimento in a large bowl and mix well. Mix the mayonnaise, sour cream, wine vinegar, seasoning salt and pepper in a bowl. Fold into the macaroni mixture. Spoon into a serving bowl. Sprinkle with paprika. Chill, covered, for 8 to 10 hours before serving. Yield: 10 to 12 servings.

Cheryl Loeffler, Riverchase Council

Potato Salad

½ cup mayonnaise
½ cup nonfat sour cream
3 tablespoons vinegar
2 tablespoons sugar
1 teaspoon salt, or to taste
½ teaspoon white pepper

4 cups chopped cooked
   potatoes, cooled
½ cup chopped onion
½ cup chopped pickles
¼ cup chopped olives

Mix the mayonnaise, nonfat sour cream, vinegar, sugar, salt and white pepper in a large bowl. Add the potatoes, onion, pickles and olives, tossing gently to mix. Chill, covered, for 8 to 10 hours before serving. Yield: 10 to 12 servings.

Betty Darnell, Gadsden Life Member Club

Barbecue Spareribs

Lemon juice
Apple cider vinegar

Spareribs
Barbecue sauce

Mix 1 part lemon juice, 2 parts vinegar and 1 part water in a bowl. Trim fat and skin from the spareribs. Cook over hot coals and hickory chips for 2½ to 3 hours or until cooked through, basting often with the lemon juice mixture. Push the spareribs to the side of the grill rack away from the coals. Mop the spareribs with barbecue sauce. Close the grill. Let the spareribs stand for 45 minutes. *Note:* Marinade may be used on other types of pork and on veal. Yield: variable.

Sly Childress, Birmingham South Cahaba Council

Coca-Cola Ham

1 (10- to 12-pound) ham   Brown sugar
1 package fresh cloves   1 (12-ounce) bottle Coca-Cola

Cut several 1- to 1½-inch-deep slits 2 inches apart in a diamond pattern across the top of the ham. Place in a baking pan. Bake at 325 degrees just until heated through. Press the cloves into each intersection of the slits. Spread a generous amount of brown sugar over the ham. Pour the Coca-Cola in the bottom of the baking pan. Bake at 325 degrees until done to taste, basting every 45 minutes. Remove from the oven. Let stand to cool slightly, basting occasionally. Yield: 30 to 36 servings.

Larry Ryan, Riverchase Council

Sausage and Noodles

1 pound Italian or smoked
     sausage, sliced
½ green bell pepper, chopped
1 small onion, chopped
1 jar Sicilian-flavor pasta
     sauce

2 teaspoons sugar
½ teaspoon crushed fennel
     seeds
8 ounces rigatoni
1 tablespoon olive oil

Cook the sausage, green pepper and onion in a skillet until the sausage is cooked through and the green pepper and onion are tender; drain. Stir in the pasta sauce, sugar and fennel seeds. Simmer, uncovered, for 10 minutes. Cook the rigatoni using the package directions. Toss with the olive oil in a bowl. Serve the sausage mixture over the rigatoni. Serve with garlic bread. Yield: 4 to 6 servings.

Donna McNulty, Riverchase Council

Grilled Lemon Pepper Chicken

½ cup (1 stick) margarine
1 cup lemon juice
2 tablespoons Worcestershire
  sauce

2 tablespoons lemon pepper
Salt to taste
6 to 8 boneless skinless
  chicken breasts

Melt the margarine in a saucepan over medium heat. Stir in the lemon juice, Worcestershire sauce, lemon pepper and salt. Pour over the chicken in a nonreactive dish. Marinate, covered, in the refrigerator for 1 hour, stirring every 15 minutes. Remove the chicken from the marinade, discarding the marinade. Grill the chicken over low heat for 25 to 30 minutes or until cooked through and golden brown. Yield: 6 to 8 servings.

Debbie Speaks, Montgomery Council

Grilled Cornish Hens

Cornish game hens
Garlic powder

Thin barbecue sauce

Rinse the game hens and pat dry. Sprinkle the inside cavity of each game hen with ¼ to ½ teaspoon garlic powder. Grill bottom side down over low heat for 30 minutes. Turn the game hens over. Grill for 15 minutes longer. Baste with barbecue sauce. Grill for 15 minutes longer. Serve immediately. Yield: variable.

Maria Goodson, Birmingham South Cahaba Council

Chiles Rellenos Casserole

½ pound ground turkey
1 cup chopped onion
1¾ teaspoons cumin
1½ teaspoons oregano
½ teaspoon garlic powder
¼ teaspoon salt
¼ teaspoon pepper
1 (16-ounce) can nonfat
  refried beans
2 (4-ounce) cans whole green
  chiles, drained

1 cup shredded Colby-Jack
  cheese
1 cup frozen whole kernel
  corn, thawed, drained
⅓ cup flour
¼ teaspoon salt
1⅓ cups skim milk
⅛ teaspoon hot sauce
2 large eggs, lightly beaten
2 large egg whites, lightly
  beaten

Brown the ground turkey with the onion in a nonstick skillet over medium-high heat, stirring until the ground turkey is crumbly. Remove from the heat. Stir in the cumin, oregano, garlic powder, ¼ teaspoon salt, pepper and refried beans. Cut the green chiles lengthwise into quarters. Arrange half the green chiles in a 7x11-inch baking dish. Sprinkle with ½ cup of the Colby-Jack cheese. Spread the turkey mixture evenly over the cheese, leaving a ¼-inch border. Layer with the corn, remaining green chiles and remaining ½ cup Colby-Jack cheese. Combine the flour and ¼ teaspoon salt in a small bowl. Whisk in the milk, hot sauce, eggs and egg whites. Pour over the layers. Bake at 350 degrees for 1 hour and 5 minutes or until set. Let stand for 5 minutes before serving. May substitute two 4-ounce cans chopped green chiles for the whole green chiles if desired. Yield: 6 servings.

Susan Currie, Birmingham South Cahaba Council

Carrots in Horseradish Sauce

8 slices dry bread
8 medium carrots, sliced
Salt to taste
½ cup mayonnaise
2 tablespoons prepared
   horseradish

1 tablespoon grated onion
¼ cup (½ stick) butter,
   melted

Process the bread in batches in a blender until fine and set aside. Cook the carrots in salted water to cover for 10 minutes. Drain the carrots, reserving the liquid. Combine the mayonnaise, horseradish, onion and 2 tablespoons or more of the reserved liquid in a bowl and mix well. Pour over the carrots in a baking dish. Mix the bread crumbs with the butter in a bowl. Sprinkle over the carrots. Bake at 350 degrees for 15 to 20 minutes or until hot and bubbly. Yield: 4 to 6 servings.

Martha Bush, Birmingham South Cahaba Council

Basil Green Beans

2 pounds fresh young green
   beans
½ to 1 cup water
2 beef bouillon cubes
2 green onions with tops,
   chopped

1 teaspoon chopped fresh leaf
   basil
Garlic powder to taste

Rinse and snap the green beans, discarding the ends and strings. Bring the water to a boil in a large saucepan. Add the bouillon cubes and cook until dissolved, stirring constantly. Add the green beans. Simmer for 20 to 30 minutes or until almost cooked to taste. Stir in the green onions, basil and garlic powder. Simmer for 5 to 10 minutes longer or just until the green beans are cooked to the desired crispness but still bright green. Yield: 6 servings.

Maria Goodson, Birmingham South Cahaba Council

Pineapple Casserole

2 large cans pineapple
  chunks, drained
1/2 cup (1 stick) margarine,
  melted
1/2 cup sugar
5 1/2 tablespoons self-rising
  flour

1 cup shredded cheese
3/4 cup crushed butter crackers
1/2 cup (1 stick) margarine,
  melted

Spread the pineapple in a greased 8x12-inch baking dish. Combine
1/2 cup margarine, sugar, flour and cheese in a bowl and mix well.
Spoon evenly over the pineapple. Top with a mixture of the butter
crackers and 1/2 cup margarine. Bake at 325 degrees for 30 minutes.
Yield: 4 to 6 servings.

Martha Bush, Birmingham South Cahaba Council

Excellent Mashed Potatoes

6 medium potatoes, peeled,
  cut into pieces
2 tablespoons butter or
  margarine
1/2 teaspoon salt

Garlic powder to taste
1/2 cup whole or skim milk
1 to 2 tablespoons mayonnaise
Pepper to taste
Seasoning salt to taste

Boil the potatoes in water to cover in a saucepan until tender;
drain. Beat the potatoes, 1 1/2 tablespoons of the butter, salt and
garlic powder in a mixer bowl. Add enough of the milk to make of
the desired consistency. Beat in the mayonnaise. Spoon the potato
mixture into a serving dish. Dot with the remaining 1/2 tablespoon
butter. Sprinkle with pepper and seasoning salt. Yield: 6 servings.

Maria Goodson, Birmingham South Cahaba Council

Hash Brown Potato Casserole

2 cups shredded American or
  Cheddar cheese
1 (10-ounce) can cream of
  chicken soup
1 cup sour cream
1/2 cup finely chopped onion
1/4 cup (1/2 stick) butter, melted

1/4 teaspoon salt
1/4 teaspoon pepper
1 (32-ounce) package frozen
  loose-pack hash brown
  potatoes, thawed
1 cup cornflakes
1 tablespoon butter, melted

Combine the cheese, soup, sour cream, onion, 1/4 cup butter, salt
and pepper in a large bowl and mix well. Fold in the hash brown
potatoes. Spoon into a greased 9x13-inch baking dish. Top with a
mixture of the cornflakes and 1 tablespoon butter. Bake at 350
degrees for 1 hour or until golden brown. Yield: 12 to 15 servings.

Sherry Sullivan, Riverchase Council

Banana Nut Bread

1 cup (2 sticks) butter
1 1/2 cups sugar
3 or 4 bananas, mashed
2 eggs

2 cups cake flour
1 teaspoon vanilla extract
1 cup chopped pecans

Cream the butter and sugar in a mixer bowl. Beat in the bananas.
Beat in the eggs and flour 1/2 at a time. Beat in the vanilla. Stir in
the pecans. Spoon into a greased loaf pan or tube pan. Bake at 350
degrees for 1 hour. Yield: 12 to 16 servings.

Flo Watters, Selma Life Member Club

Cantaloupe with Ice Cream

1 cantaloupe   1/2 gallon vanilla ice cream

Cut the cantaloupe into bite-size pieces in individual serving bowls.
Top each serving with a scoop of ice cream. Yield: 8 to 10 servings.

Maria Goodson, Birmingham South Cahaba Council

Chocolate Icebox Dessert

2 cups semisweet chocolate
   chips
3 tablespoons water
3 tablespoons sugar
5 egg yolks, lightly beaten
2 cups whipping cream

1 teaspoon vanilla extract
5 egg whites
1 (12-ounce) angel food cake,
   cut into 1-inch cubes
½ cup whipped cream

Cook the chocolate chips, water and sugar in the top of a double boiler over low heat until the chocolate chips are melted, stirring constantly. Remove to a large bowl. Let stand until cool. Stir in the egg yolks. Beat the whipping cream until stiff peaks form. Fold into the chocolate mixture. Stir in the vanilla. Beat the egg whites until stiff peaks form. Fold into the chocolate mixture. Line a loaf pan with waxed paper. Add layers of angel food cake and chocolate mixture until all is used. Chill, covered, until firm. Invert onto a serving plate. Remove waxed paper. Spread with ½ cup whipped cream. Garnish with shaved chocolate. Yield: 6 to 8 servings.

Betty Jo Campbell, Montgomery Council

Dirt Dessert

1 (16-ounce) package
   chocolate sandwich cookies,
   crushed
8 ounces cream cheese,
   softened
½ cup (1 stick) margarine,
   softened

1 cup confectioners' sugar
8 ounces whipped topping
2 (3-ounce) packages vanilla
   or chocolate instant
   pudding mix
3 cups milk
1 teaspoon vanilla extract

Sprinkle half the cookie crumbs over the bottom of a 9x13-inch pan. Beat the cream cheese and margarine until smooth. Mix in the confectioners' sugar. Fold in the whipped topping. Mix the next 3 ingredients in a large bowl. Fold in the cream cheese mixture. Spoon into the prepared pan. Sprinkle with the remaining cookie crumbs. Chill, covered, until set. Yield: 10 servings.

Jan Williams, Riverchase Council

Super Fig Cobbler

5 cups fresh figs, cut into
   halves
2 teaspoons lemon juice
3/4 cup sugar
3 tablespoons flour
1/2 teaspoon cinnamon
1/2 teaspoon nutmeg
3/4 cup water

1 tablespoon margarine
1 cup flour
1/4 teaspoon salt
1/3 cup shortening
1/4 cup shredded Cheddar
   cheese
2 tablespoons cold water

Arrange the figs evenly in a lightly greased 6x10-inch baking dish. Sprinkle with the lemon juice. Mix the sugar, 3 tablespoons flour, cinnamon, nutmeg and 3/4 cup water in a bowl. Pour evenly over the figs. Dot with the margarine. Combine 1 cup flour and salt in a large bowl. Cut in the shortening until crumbly. Stir in the Cheddar cheese. Sprinkle with the cold water. Stir with a fork until moistened. Shape into a ball. Roll 1/8 inch thick on a lightly floured surface. Cut into 1/2x10-inch strips. Arrange the strips lattice fashion over the figs, trimming the ends. Bake at 350 degrees for 40 to 45 minutes or until hot and bubbly. Yield: 6 servings.

Debbie Hughes, Birmingham South Cahaba Council

Easy Cobbler

6 slices bread, torn
3 cups fruit of choice
1 tablespoon sugar
3 tablespoons butter, melted

3/4 cup sugar
1/2 cup (1 stick) butter, melted
1 egg

Arrange half the bread evenly over the bottom of a greased baking pan. Spoon the fruit evenly over the bread. Sprinkle with 1 tablespoon sugar. Drizzle with 3 tablespoons butter. Arrange the remaining bread evenly over the fruit. Top with a mixture of 3/4 cup sugar, 1/2 cup butter and egg. Bake at 350 degrees for 30 minutes or until brown. *Note:* If using apples, add 1 tablespoon cinnamon. Yield: 6 to 8 servings.

Sonia East, Alabama Telco Credit Union

Peach Delight

3/4 cup (1 1/2 sticks) margarine, melted
2 cups self-rising flour
1 cup nuts
8 ounces cream cheese
2 1/4 cups confectioners' sugar
8 ounces whipped topping

1 quart fresh peaches, peeled, sliced
1 cup sugar
1 cup water
2 tablespoons cornstarch
3 tablespoons apricot or peach gelatin

Mix the margarine, flour and nuts in a bowl. Press over the bottom of a 9x13-inch baking pan. Bake at 350 degrees for 15 minutes. Let stand until cool. Beat the cream cheese, confectioners' sugar and whipped topping in a mixer bowl until well mixed. Spread over the prepared crust. Spread with a mixture of the peaches and sugar. Mix the water, cornstarch and gelatin in a saucepan. Cook over medium heat until thickened, stirring constantly. Let stand until cool. Pour over the peaches. Chill, covered, until set. Yield: 12 to 15 servings.

Donna McNulty, Riverchase Council

Chocolate Cake

2 cups flour
2/3 cup baking cocoa
1 1/4 teaspoons baking soda
1/4 teaspoon baking powder
1 2/3 cups sugar

3 eggs
1 teaspoon vanilla extract
1 cup mayonnaise
1 1/3 cups water

Mix the first 4 ingredients in a bowl. Beat the sugar, eggs and vanilla in a mixer bowl at high speed for 3 minutes or until light and fluffy, scraping the bowl occasionally. Add the mayonnaise and beat at low speed until blended. Beat in the flour mixture alternately with the water, ending with the flour mixture. Pour into 2 greased and floured 9-inch cake pans. Bake at 350 degrees for 30 to 35 minutes or until a wooden pick inserted in the center comes out clean. Cool on wire racks. Remove to a serving plate. Frost as desired. Garnish with sliced almonds. Yield: 12 to 16 servings.

Eileen Smaha, Birmingham South Cahaba Council

German Chocolate Upside-Down Cake

1 cup chopped pecans
1 cup flaked coconut
1 (2-layer) package chocolate
  cake mix
8 ounces cream cheese

½ cup (1 stick) margarine,
  melted
1 (1-pound) package
  confectioners' sugar

Grease a 9x13-inch cake pan. Sprinkle the pecans and coconut over the bottom of the cake pan. Prepare the cake batter using the package directions. Pour the batter over the pecans and coconut. Beat the remaining ingredients in a mixer bowl. Drop by spoonfuls over the batter. Bake at 350 degrees for 30 to 40 minutes or until cake tests done. Yield: 15 servings.

John Kemp, Birmingham South Life Member Club

Blackberry Wine Cake

1 (2-layer) package white
  cake mix
1 (3-ounce) package
  blackberry gelatin
4 eggs
½ cup vegetable oil

1 cup blackberry wine
½ cup chopped pecans
½ cup (1 stick) butter or
  margarine
½ cup confectioners' sugar
½ cup blackberry wine

Beat the first 5 ingredients in a mixer bowl at low speed just until moistened. Beat at medium speed for 2 minutes, scraping the sides of the bowl frequently. Grease and flour a tube pan. Sprinkle the pecans in the bottom of the tube pan. Add the batter. Bake at 325 degrees for 45 to 50 minutes or until cake tests done. Melt the butter in a saucepan over medium heat. Stir in the confectioners' sugar and ½ cup wine. Bring to a boil, stirring constantly. Remove 3 tablespoons of the glaze to a small bowl. Pour the remaining glaze over the warm cake in the tube pan. Let stand for 30 minutes. Invert onto a serving plate. Let stand until cool. Stir enough additional confectioners' sugar into the reserved glaze to make of the desired consistency. Spoon over the cake. Yield: 16 servings.

Judy Buster, Riverchase Council

Walnut Pound Cake

1 cup (2 sticks) butter,
  softened
½ cup shortening
2 cups packed light brown
  sugar
1 cup sugar
5 eggs
3 cups flour

½ teaspoon baking powder
1 cup milk
1 teaspoon vanilla extract
1 cup chopped English
  walnuts
Brown Sugar Frosting
English walnuts to taste

Cream the butter and shortening in a mixer bowl. Beat in the brown sugar and sugar until light and fluffy. Beat in the eggs 1 at a time. Add a mixture of the flour and baking powder and beat well. Mix in the milk and vanilla. Fold in 1 cup English walnuts. Spoon into a tube pan. Bake at 350 degrees for 60 to 70 minutes or until cake tests done. Invert onto a wire rack to cool. Remove to a serving plate. Frost with the Brown Sugar Frosting. Sprinkle with English walnuts to taste. Yield: 16 servings.

Brown Sugar Frosting

½ cup (1 stick) butter
1 cup packed light brown
  sugar

⅓ cup half-and-half
1¼ cups confectioners' sugar
1 teaspoon vanilla extract

Melt the butter in a saucepan over medium-high heat. Stir in the brown sugar. Bring to a boil. Boil for 2 minutes. Let stand until cooled slightly. Add the half-and-half and mix well. Return to a boil. Cool to room temperature. Beat in the confectioners' sugar and vanilla.

Emma Allen, Riverchase Council

*To determine whether an egg is fresh, immerse it in a
pan of cool, salted water. If it sinks, it is fresh; if
it rises to the surface, throw it away.*

Sour Cream Pound Cake

3 cups sugar
1 cup (2 sticks) butter,
  softened
6 egg yolks
3 cups sifted flour

1/4 teaspoon baking soda
1/4 teaspoon salt
1 cup sour cream
2 teaspoons vanilla extract
6 egg whites

Cream the sugar and butter in a mixer bowl. Beat in the egg yolks
1 at a time. Mix the flour, baking soda and salt. Add to the creamed
mixture and beat well. Beat in the sour cream and vanilla. Beat the
egg whites until stiff peaks form. Fold into the batter. Spoon into a
greased tube pan. Bake at 350 degrees for 1 hour and 15 minutes or
until cake tests done. Invert onto a wire rack to cool.
Yield: 16 servings.

Sharron James Wordell, Riverchase Council

Microwave Fudge

3 cups sugar
3/4 cup (1 1/2 sticks) margarine
1 (5-ounce) can evaporated
  milk

2 cups chocolate chips
1 (7-ounce) jar marshmallow
  creme
2 cups nuts

Combine the sugar, margarine and evaporated milk in a
microwave-safe dish. Microwave on High for 10 1/2 minutes or until
the sugar is dissolved, stirring 2 times. Add the chocolate chips,
marshmallow creme and nuts. Stir until the chocolate chips are
melted. Spoon into a well-greased dish. Chill, covered, until set.
Cut into squares. Yield: 3 pounds.

Jan Williams, Riverchase Council

Microwave Peanut Brittle

2 cups peanuts, shelled
1 cup sugar
½ cup light corn syrup
⅛ teaspoon salt

1 teaspoon butter
1 teaspoon vanilla extract
1 teaspoon baking soda

Mix the peanuts, sugar, corn syrup and salt in a microwave-safe bowl. Microwave on high for 8 minutes, stirring after 4 minutes. Mix in the butter and vanilla. Microwave for 2 minutes longer. Add the baking soda and stir quickly until light and foamy. Pour immediately onto a lightly greased pan, spreading until very thin. Let stand until cool. Break into small pieces. Store in an airtight container. Yield: 1 pound.

Jan Williams, Riverchase Council

Fool's Toffee

36 saltines
1 cup butter
1 cup packed dark brown
  sugar

2 cups (scant) vanilla chips
½ cup chopped pecans

Line a large pan with foil. Spray with nonstick cooking spray. Arrange the saltines in a single layer on the prepared pan. Melt the butter and brown sugar in a small saucepan over medium heat. Bring to a boil. Boil for 4 minutes. Pour the butter mixture evenly over the saltines. Bake at 375 degrees for 5 minutes. Sprinkle with the vanilla chips and pecans immediately. Chill until cool. Break into small pieces. Store, covered, in the refrigerator.
Yield: 36 servings.

Susan Poe, Riverchase Council

Pralines

2 cups sugar
1 cup buttermilk
1 teaspoon baking soda

1 teaspoon butter
1 teaspoon vanilla extract
2 cups pecan halves

Mix the sugar, buttermilk and baking soda in a saucepan. Cook over medium heat until the mixture turns brown and reaches soft-ball stage, stirring constantly. Beat in the butter and vanilla. Arrange the pecan halves 2 inches apart on waxed paper. Drop the sugar mixture by teaspoonfuls over the pecan halves. Let stand until cool. Store in an airtight container. Yield: 100 to 120 pralines.

Donna McNulty, Riverchase Council

Lemon Squares

2 cups flour
1 cup confectioners' sugar
1 cup (2 sticks) butter, melted
4 eggs
¼ cup flour

4 teaspoons lemon juice
Grated lemon zest to taste
2 cups sugar
1 teaspoon baking powder

Mix 2 cups flour, confectioners' sugar and butter in a bowl. Press over the bottom of a 9x13-inch baking pan. Bake at 350 degrees for 20 minutes. Combine the eggs, ¼ cup flour, lemon juice, lemon zest, sugar and baking powder in a bowl and mix well. Spoon over the prepared crust. Bake at 350 degrees for 25 minutes. Sprinkle with additional confectioners' sugar. Yield: 15 servings.

Cheryl Loeffler, Riverchase Council

Chocolate Cookies

1½ cups (3 sticks) margarine	½ teaspoon baking powder
1½ cups sugar	½ teaspoon baking soda
2 eggs	¼ teaspoon salt
1 tablespoon vanilla extract	⅔ cup baking cocoa
3¼ cups flour	2 cups chopped nuts

Beat the margarine in a mixer bowl. Add sugar gradually, beating constantly at medium speed. Beat in the eggs and vanilla. Stir in a mixture of the flour, baking powder, baking soda, salt and baking cocoa. Fold in the nuts. Drop by teaspoonfuls 2 inches apart onto a cookie sheet. Bake at 350 degrees for 8 minutes. Cool on the cookie sheet for 2 minutes. Remove to a wire rack to cool completely. Yield: 6 dozen cookies.

Jan Williams, Riverchase Council

Peanut Butter Cookies

1 cup shortening	1 cup peanut butter
1 cup sugar	2 cups flour
1 cup packed brown sugar	2 teaspoons baking soda
1 teaspoon vanilla extract	1 teaspoon salt
2 eggs, beaten	

Beat the shortening, sugar, brown sugar and vanilla in a mixer bowl. Beat in the eggs. Add the peanut butter and mix well. Stir in a mixture of the flour, baking soda and salt. Drop by teaspoonfuls 2 inches apart onto a cookie sheet. Flatten in a crisscross pattern with a fork dipped in flour. Bake at 350 degrees for 10 minutes or until light brown. Cool on the cookie sheet for 2 minutes. Remove to a wire rack to cool completely. Yield: 6 dozen cookies.

Jan Williams, Riverchase Council

Easy Peanut Butter Cookies

1 cup crunchy or smooth   1 egg, beaten
   peanut butter   ½ teaspoon vanilla extract
1 cup sugar   (optional)

Combine the peanut butter, sugar, egg and vanilla in a mixer bowl
and mix well. Shape into 1-inch balls. Arrange on a greased cookie
sheet. Flatten in a crisscross pattern with a fork dipped in sugar.
Bake at 325 degrees for 8 minutes for chewy cookies or 10 to 11
minutes for crunchy cookies. Cool on the cookie sheet for 2
minutes. Remove to a wire rack to cool completely.
Yield: 2 dozen cookies.

Ruth P. Apperson, Decatur Council

Potato Chip Cookies

1 cup (2 sticks) margarine   1 teaspoon baking soda
1 cup sugar   ⅛ teaspoon salt
1 egg, beaten   ¾ cup chopped pecans
2 cups flour   ¾ cup crushed potato chips

Beat the margarine, sugar and egg in a mixer bowl. Mix in the flour,
baking soda, salt, pecans and potato chips. Shape with floured
hands by teaspoonfuls into balls. Arrange 2 inches apart on a
cookie sheet. Flatten slightly with a fork. Bake at 375 degrees for 10
to 12 minutes or until light brown, watching carefully as these do
burn easily. Cool on the cookie sheet for 2 minutes. Remove to a
wire rack to cool completely. Yield: 2 to 3 dozen cookies.

Joyce Thomas, Birmingham South Cahaba Council

Sugar-Free Blueberry Pie

1 cup blueberries
1½ cups water
3 tablespoons cornstarch
6 teaspoons artificial
  sweetener

⅓ cup water
1 (9-inch) graham cracker pie
  shell

Combine the blueberries and 1½ cups water in a saucepan. Bring to a boil over medium-high heat. Boil for 2 minutes. Combine the cornstarch, artificial sweetener and ⅓ cup water in a bowl and stir until artificial sweetener is dissolved. Add to the blueberry mixture. Cook until thickened, stirring constantly. Spoon into the pie shell. Serve with whipped topping. Yield: 8 servings.

Christine Diggs, Gadsden Life Member Club

Caramel Pecan Pie

1 (14-ounce) can sweetened
  condensed milk
½ cup packed brown sugar

1 cup toasted pecan halves
1 baked pie shell

Cook the condensed milk and brown sugar in a saucepan over medium-low heat until thick, stirring constantly. Remove from the heat. Let stand to cool for 5 minutes. Stir in the pecans. Spoon into the pie shell. Let stand to cool completely. Serve with whipped topping. May top with toasted coconut. Yield: 8 servings.

Faith Kirby Richardson, Gadsden Life Member Club

Heavenly Pie

1¼ cups finely crushed
   graham crackers
⅓ cup butter, melted
1 tablespoon sugar
2 ripe bananas

1 cup sugar
⅛ teaspoon salt
2 egg whites
⅛ teaspoon almond extract

Mix the graham cracker crumbs, butter and 1 tablespoon sugar in a bowl. Press over the bottom and side of a greased 9-inch pie plate. Mash the bananas with 1 cup sugar and salt in a bowl. Beat the egg whites in a mixer bowl until stiff peaks form. Add the banana mixture. Beat until stiff peaks form. Mix in the almond extract. Spoon into the prepared piecrust. Bake at 350 degrees for 15 minutes. Reduce oven temperature to 300. Bake for 15 to 20 minutes longer or until hot and bubbly. Chill until serving time. Serve with whipped cream. Yield: 8 servings.

Lillian Jones, Riverchase Council

Chocolate Pie

½ cup (1 stick) margarine
2 cups water
1¼ cups sugar
½ cup flour

2 tablespoons baking cocoa
1 egg, beaten
1 teaspoon vanilla extract
1 baked pie shell

Melt the margarine in the top of a double boiler. Stir in the water, sugar, flour, baking cocoa, egg and vanilla. Cook until thickened, stirring constantly. Let stand until cool. Spoon into the pie shell. Serve with whipped topping. Yield: 8 servings.

Hazel E. Campbell, Birmingham Life Member Club

FALL

Chutney Cheese Ball

16 ounces cream cheese,
   softened
Crushed pecans
Flaked coconut

1 (9-ounce) jar chutney
1 bunch green onions,
   chopped

Shape the cream cheese into a ball. Roll in pecans and sprinkle with coconut. Place on a serving plate. Pour the chutney over the cheese ball. Top with the chopped green onions. Serve with assorted crackers. Yield: 12 servings.

Catherine M. Martin, Birmingham Metro Council

Hot Wings

Vegetable oil for deep-frying
5 pounds chicken wings
12 ounces Louisiana
   hot sauce

1½ cups Dale's steak
   seasoning
½ cup (1 stick) butter
4 to 6 garlic cloves, crushed

Heat the oil in a deep fryer or large skillet. Deep-fry the chicken until golden brown, but not cooked completely through. Drain on paper towels. Combine the steak seasoning, hot sauce, butter and garlic in a saucepan and cook until heated through. Dip the chicken wings in the hot sauce mixture and place in a baking dish. Pour the remaining mixture over the chicken wings. Bake at 350 degrees until the chicken is cooked through. Serve with bleu cheese dressing and celery sticks. Yield: 4 to 6 servings.

Betsy Mickle, Birmingham South Cahaba Council

Sweet-and-Sour Meatballs

2 slices bread
2 pounds ground chuck
1½ envelopes onion soup mix
1 cup catsup
½ cup vinegar
1 cup apricot nectar

½ cup packed brown sugar
4 teaspoons prepared mustard
4 teaspoons prepared
  horseradish
2 teaspoons Worcestershire
  sauce

Moisten the bread with water and squeeze dry. Combine the bread, ground chuck and soup mix in a bowl and mix well. Roll into small balls. Brown the meatballs in a nonstick skillet over medium heat and drain on paper towels. Combine the catsup, vinegar and apricot nectar in a bowl and mix well. Mix in the brown sugar, mustard, horseradish and Worcestershire sauce. Pour into a saucepan and simmer over medium heat for 10 minutes. Add the meatballs and simmer for an 10 minutes longer. Transfer to a chafing dish to serve. Yield: 8 servings.

Donna McNulty, Riverchase Council

Spiced Nut Mix

3 egg whites
2 teaspoons water
2 (12-ounce) cans salted
  peanuts
1 cup whole blanched almonds
1 cup walnut halves

1¾ cups sugar
3 tablespoons pumpkin
  pie spice
¾ teaspoon salt
1 cup raisins

Beat the egg whites and water in a mixer bowl until frothy. Add the peanuts, almonds and walnuts, stirring gently to coat. Combine the sugar, pumpkin pie spice and salt in a bowl. Stir into the nut mixture. Fold in the raisins. Spread the mixture in 2 greased 10x15-inch baking pans. Bake at 300 degrees for 20 to 25 minutes or until light brown, stirring every 10 minutes. Let stand until cool. Store in an airtight container. Yield: 10 cups.

Frankie (A.T.) Vaughn, Selma Life Member Club

Seafood Gumbo Creole

1 green bell pepper, minced	1½ teaspoons salt
1 onion, minced	1 teaspoon pepper
2 ribs celery, chopped	2 bay leaves
1 garlic clove, crushed	1 tablespoon hot sauce
2 tablespoons bacon drippings	1 tablespoon thyme
2 tablespoons flour	1 tablespoon MSG
1 (15-ounce) can tomatoes	1 (14-ounce) can chicken
2 (6-ounce) cans tomato paste	broth
2 cans mushroom sauce for	2 pounds cooked shrimp
steak	2 pounds cooked crab meat
1 (10-ounce) can cream of	1 chicken, cooked, cut into
mushroom soup	bite-size pieces
1 pound okra, chopped	1 tablespoon filé powder

Sauté the green pepper, onion, celery and garlic in the bacon drippings in a saucepan over low to medium heat for 5 minutes. Stir in the flour and cook for several minutes. Add the tomatoes, tomato paste, mushroom sauce and soup. Add the okra, salt, pepper, bay leaves, hot sauce, thyme and MSG. Stir in the chicken broth and simmer for 10 minutes. Remove the bay leaves. Add the shrimp, crab meat and chicken and mix well. Stir in the filé powder. Simmer for 5 minutes; do not boil. Serve over rice. *Note:* To cook the shrimp, combine with boiling water and crab boil seasoning in a saucepan and cook for 2 minutes. This recipe may be doubled or tripled; do not increase the chicken.
Yield: 8 servings.

Mrs. R.N. Autry, Birmingham South Life Member Club

Idiot-Proof Chili

1 to 1½ pounds ground beef
½ cup flour
¼ cup chili powder
1 (24-ounce) jar salsa
⅓ salsa jar water
2 (15-ounce) cans chili beans
1 bean can water
Salt to taste

Brown the ground beef in a large skillet, stirring until crumbly; drain. Stir in a mixture of the flour and chili powder. Stir in the salsa and ⅓ jar water. Add the beans and 1 can water and mix well. Bring to a boil, stirring occasionally. Add salt if needed. May add more water for thinner chili. Yield: 8 servings.

Connie Willoughby, Birmingham Metro Council

Crimson Tide Congealed Salad

1 (6-ounce) package
   strawberry gelatin
1 (21-ounce) can strawberry
   pie filling
1 (20-ounce) can crushed
   pineapple, drained
1 cup sour cream
6 ounces cream cheese,
   softened
½ teaspoon lemon juice
½ teaspoon sugar
½ teaspoon salt
1 cup chopped nuts

Prepare the gelatin according to the package directions. Stir in the pie filling and the crushed pineapple. Pour into an 8x12-inch dish. Chill until set. Beat the sour cream, cream cheese, lemon juice, sugar and salt in a mixer bowl until smooth. Fold in ½ cup nuts. Spread over the congealed salad. Sprinkle with the remaining nuts. Yield: 15 servings.

Sharron James Wordell, Riverchase Council

Coleslaw

5 cups shredded cabbage   Mayonnaise
3 eggs, hard-cooked, grated   Salt and pepper to taste
Sweet pickle relish to taste

Combine the cabbage, eggs and pickle relish in a large bowl and
mix well. Stir in enough mayonnaise to make of the desired
consistency. Season with salt and pepper. Chill, covered, in the
refrigerator until serving time. May substitute chopped sweet
pickles for the pickle relish. Yield: 8 servings.

Sherry Bircheat, Birmingham South Cahaba Council

German Slaw

1½ large heads cabbage   2 cups sugar
1 (2-ounce) jar pimento   1½ teaspoons celery seeds
2 green bell peppers, chopped   1½ teaspoons dry mustard
1 large onion, chopped   1½ teaspoons salt
2 cups white vinegar   1½ teaspoons turmeric
⅓ cup vegetable oil

Shred the cabbage. Combine with the pimento, bell peppers and
onion in a bowl and mix well. Combine the vinegar, oil, sugar,
celery seeds, dry mustard, salt and turmeric in a saucepan. Bring
to a boil and simmer for 3 to 5 minutes. Pour over the cabbage
mixture and stir until well coated. Yield: 12 to 15 servings.

Donna Lee, Birmingham South Cahaba Council

Montana Potato Salad

4 to 5 pounds potatoes,
  chopped
1 (16-ounce) bottle Italian
  salad dressing
1 onion, chopped
1/4 cup chopped dill pickles
2 eggs, hard-cooked, minced

1/2 cup diced green bell pepper
1/4 cup chopped celery
1 (16-ounce) bottle ranch
  salad dressing
1 cup mayonnaise
1/4 cup prepared mustard
Salt and pepper to taste

Boil the potatoes in water to cover in a saucepan until tender; drain. Combine the potatoes and Italian dressing in a large bowl. Marinate, covered, for 2 to 12 hours in the refrigerator. Add the onion, pickles, eggs, bell pepper and celery to the potato mixture and mix well. Blend the ranch dressing, mayonnaise, mustard, salt and pepper in a bowl. Add to the potato mixture, stirring until well coated. Garnish with fresh parsley and paprika. Yield: 8 servings.

Donna Jean Bowman, Birmingham South Cahaba Council

Stacked Chicken Salad

2 cups chopped cooked
  chicken breasts
1/4 teaspoon salt
1/4 teaspoon paprika
1/8 teaspoon lemon pepper
4 cups (1 medium head)
  shredded lettuce
1 (8-ounce) can sliced water
  chestnuts, drained

1 cup tiny peas
1 cup cooked macaroni
1 1/2 cups shredded Cheddar
  cheese
3 eggs, hard-cooked, chopped
1 cup mayonnaise
1 cup sour cream
1 envelope ranch-style salad
  dressing mix

Combine the first 4 ingredients in a bowl and toss gently. Layer the lettuce, chicken mixture, water chestnuts, peas, macaroni, cheese and eggs in a large bowl. Mix the mayonnaise, sour cream and dressing mix in a bowl. Spread over the top of the salad, sealing to the edge. Chill, covered, for 24 hours. Toss before serving. Serve with fruit and Kit Rolls (page 300). Yield: 8 servings.

Sherrie Poynor, Montgomery Council

Easy Lasagna

1 pound ground beef
1 (32-ounce) jar spaghetti
   sauce
12 ounces lasagna noodles,
   cooked, drained

8 ounces mozzarella cheese,
   shredded
8 ounces cottage cheese

Brown the ground beef in a skillet, stirring until crumbly, drain.
Alternate layers of the spaghetti sauce, noodles, ground beef and
cheeses in a 9x13-inch baking dish until all ingredients are used.
Bake at 350 degrees for 35 to 40 minutes or until bubbly.
Yield: 8 to 12 servings.

Billie Harrison, Shoals Life Member Club

Mexican Casserole

1 pound ground beef
1 medium onion, chopped
1 small green bell pepper,
   chopped
1 (10-ounce) can cream of
   mushroom soup
1 (10-ounce) can tomatoes
   with green chiles

1 (15-ounce) can hot chili
   beans
Doritos, crushed
Shredded Cheddar cheese to
   taste
5 or 6 pats of butter

Brown the ground beef with the onion and bell pepper in a large
skillet, stirring until the ground beef is crumbly; drain. Combine
the soup, tomatoes with green chiles and chili beans in a bowl and
mix well. Layer the crushed Doritos, ground beef mixture and bean
mixture in a 9x13-inch baking dish. Top with the cheese and dot
with the butter. Bake at 350 degrees until hot and bubbly.
Yield: 6 servings

Laraine McLean, Decatur Council

Pizza Casserole

1 pound ground beef
Chopped onion
Chopped green bell pepper
Sliced mushrooms
Sliced olives
1 (14-ounce) jar pizza sauce

10 ounces shredded mozzarella
  cheese
2 eggs, beaten
¾ cup baking mix
1½ cups milk

Brown the ground beef in a skillet, stirring until crumbly; drain. Spoon into a 9x13-inch baking dish. Top with the onion, bell pepper, mushrooms and olives. Pour the pizza sauce over the ground beef and vegetables. Top with the cheese. Combine the eggs, baking mix and milk in a bowl and mix well. Pour over the top. Bake at 400 degrees for 30 minutes. May substitute or add any of your favorite pizza toppings. Yield: 6 servings.

Laraine McLean, Decatur Council

Beefy Pork and Bean Casserole

1 pound ground beef
1 (15-ounce) can pork and
  beans
1 (16-ounce) can kidney
  beans
1 cup catsup

1 envelope onion soup mix
3 tablespoons vinegar
2 tablespoons prepared
  mustard
1 teaspoon Tabasco sauce

Brown the ground beef in a skillet, stirring until crumbly; drain. Combine the ground beef, pork and beans and kidney beans in a bowl. Stir in the catsup, onion soup mix, vinegar, mustard and Tabasco sauce. Spoon into a baking dish. Bake at 400 degrees for 30 minutes or until hot and bubbly. Yield: 6 servings.

Elba Skinner, Selma Life Member Club

Red Beans and Rice

1 package smoked sausage,
  chopped
1 (6-count) package hot
  sausage links, chopped
1 large onion, chopped
1 green bell pepper, chopped
2 ribs celery with tops,
  chopped
1 tablespoon sugar

2 (16-ounce) cans New
  Orleans-style kidney beans
1 tablespoon minced garlic
2 tablespoons chopped parsley
Cayenne pepper to taste
Salt and pepper to taste
1 bean can water
3 bay leaves
1 cup rice, cooked

Brown the sausage and sausage links in a large heavy saucepan over
low heat; drain. Add the onion, green pepper and celery. Sauté
until tender, stirring constantly. Add the sugar, kidney beans,
garlic, parsley, cayenne pepper, salt and pepper and mix well. Stir
in the water and place the bay leaves on top. Simmer for one hour,
adding additional water if needed to prevent sticking. Remove the
bay leaves and stir in the rice. Yield: 8 servings.

Jan Williams, Riverchase Council

Sour Cream Cheese Potatoes

1 (32-ounce) package frozen
  hash brown potatoes,
  thawed
1/2 cup chopped onion
1 (10-ounce) can cream of
  chicken soup
2 cups sour cream

2 cups shredded Cheddar
  cheese
1 tablespoon seasoned salt
1/8 teaspoon garlic salt
2 cups cornflakes
1/2 cup (1 stick) margarine,
  melted

Mix the potatoes, onion, soup and sour cream in a large bowl. Stir
in the cheese, seasoned salt and garlic salt. Spoon the mixture into
a 9x13-inch baking dish. Combine the cornflakes and melted
margarine in a bowl and mix until the cornflakes are well coated.
Spread over the potato mixture. Bake at 350 degrees for 1 1/4 hours.
Yield: 8 servings.

Laraine McLean, Decatur Council

Squash Casserole

1½ pounds squash, finely
  chopped
2 carrots, finely grated
1 medium onion, finely grated
Salt to taste
1 cup sour cream

1 (10-ounce) can cream of
  chicken soup
½ cup (1 stick) butter, melted
1½ cups cornbread stuffing
  mix

Cook the squash, onions and carrots in salted water to cover in a
saucepan for 10 minutes; drain. Combine with the sour cream and
soup in a large bowl and mix well. Mix the melted butter and
stuffing in a bowl. Alternate layers of the vegetable mixture and
stuffing mixture in a baking dish until all ingredients are used,
ending with the stuffing mixture. Bake at 350 degrees for 30 to 40
minutes or until golden brown. Yield: 6 servings.

Donna McNulty, Riverchase Council

Sweet Potato Muffins

⅓ cup margarine, softened
1 cup sugar
2 eggs
1¼ cups mashed cooked sweet
  potatoes
1½ cups flour
2 teaspoons baking powder

1 teaspoon cinnamon
¼ teaspoon salt
¼ teaspoon nutmeg
1 cup milk
¼ cup chopped pecans
¼ cup raisins

Beat the margarine, sugar and eggs until a mixer bowl until light
and fluffy. Add the sweet potatoes and beat until creamy. Sift the
flour, baking powder, cinnamon, salt and nutmeg together. Add to
the sweet potato mixture alternately with the milk, mixing just
until moistened after each addition; do not overmix. Fold in the
pecans and raisins. Spoon into greased muffin cups. Bake at 400
degrees until muffins test done. Yield: 6 muffins.

Flo Watters, Selma Life Member Club

Kit Rolls

1 cup self-rising flour   ½ cup (1 stick) margarine,
1 cup sour cream   softened

Combine the self-rising flour, sour cream and margarine in a mixer bowl and beat until well blended. Spoon into muffin cups. Bake at 425 degrees for 20 to 25 minutes or until light brown. May bake in miniature muffin cups. Yield: 6 muffins.

Sherrie Poynor, Montgomery Council

Apricot Walnut Swirl Coffee Cake

2⅓ cups reduced-fat baking   1 egg
   mix   ⅔ cup skim milk
12 packets artificial sweetener ⅓ cup nonfat sour cream
2 tablespoons margarine,   Apricot Walnut Filling
   melted   ⅓ cup light apricot preserves

Combine the baking mix and artificial sweetener in a mixer bowl. Beat in the margarine, egg, milk and sour cream until well blended. Spread ⅓ of the batter in a greased and floured 6-cup bundt pan. Layer the Apricot Walnut Filling and remaining coffee cake batter ½ at a time in the prepared pan. Bake at 375 degrees for 25 minutes or until golden brown and a wooden pick comes out clean. Cool in the pan for 5 minutes; invert onto a wire rack to cool for 5 to 10 minutes. Spoon the apricot preserves over the top of the cake. Serve warm. Yield: 12 servings.

Apricot Walnut Filling

½ cup light apricot preserves   4 teaspoons cinnamon
18 packets artificial sweetener ½ cup chopped walnuts

Combine the apricot preserves, artificial sweetener, cinnamon and walnuts in a small bowl and mix well.

Susan Poe, Riverchase Council

Orange Cake

2 cups cake flour
1/2 teaspoon salt
1 3/4 cups sugar

1 cup shortening
5 eggs
5 tablespoons orange juice

Sift the cake flour and salt into a bowl. Set aside. Cream the sugar and shortening in a mixer bowl until light and fluffy. Add the eggs alternately with the cake flour mixture, beating well after each flour addition and for 5 minutes after adding each egg. Mix in the orange juice. Pour the batter into a greased and floured tube or bundt pan. Bake at 325 degrees for 1 hour or until a wooden pick comes out clean. Cool in the pan for 10 minutes. Remove to a wire rack to cool completely. Yield: 16 servings.

Betty C. Gray, Montgomery Life Member Club

Crusty Cream Cheese Pound Cake

1 cup (2 sticks) butter or
  margarine, softened
1/2 cup shortening
3 cups sugar
8 ounces cream cheese,
  softened

3 cups sifted cake flour
6 eggs
1 tablespoon vanilla extract

Cream the butter and shortening in a large mixer bowl. Beat in the sugar gradually at medium speed. Add the cream cheese and beat until light and fluffy. Add the flour and eggs alternately, beginning and ending with the flour and beating well after each addition. Stir in the vanilla. Pour the batter into a greased and floured tube pan. Bake at 325 degrees for 1 1/4 hours or until a wooden pick comes out clean. Cool in the pan for 10 minutes. Remove to a wire rack to cool completely. Yield: 16 servings.

Susan Poe, Riverchase Council

Peanut Cupcakes

4 pounds raw peanuts
1 (2-layer) package white
   cake mix
1 (1-pound) package
   confectioners' sugar

½ cup (1 stick) butter,
   softened
1 (12-ounce) can evaporated
   milk
1 tablespoon vanilla extract

Roast the peanuts on a baking sheet in the oven. Let stand until cool. Shell the peanuts and remove the thin skins. Chop the peanuts in a food processor. Prepare the cake mix using the package directions for cupcakes; cool. Combine the confectioners' sugar, butter, evaporated milk and vanilla in a mixer bowl and beat until smooth. Frost the cupcakes with the confectioners' sugar mixture and roll in the peanuts. Let stand for several hours.
Yield: 16 servings.

Sonia East, in memory of June Vines, Alabama Telco Credit Union

Boiled Cookies

2 cups sugar
½ cup milk
½ cup (1 stick) butter
¼ cup baking cocoa
2½ cups quick-cooking oats

½ cup peanut butter
1 teaspoon vanilla extract
1 cup chopped pecans
   (optional)

Mix the sugar, milk, butter and baking cocoa in a saucepan. Bring to a boil over medium heat, stirring constantly. Boil for 1½ minutes. Remove from the heat and stir in the oats, peanut butter, vanilla and pecans. Drop by teaspoonfuls onto waxed paper. Let stand until cool. Yield: 2 to 3 dozen cookies.

Cindy Johnson, Birmingham South Cahaba Council

Barbara Bush's Cookies

2 cups flour
1 teaspoon baking soda
1 teaspoon salt
1 cup (2 sticks) unsalted
  butter, softened
1 cup packed light brown
  sugar

2 eggs
2 teaspoons vanilla extract
2 cups quick-cooking oats
2 cups semisweet chocolate
  chips

Sift the flour, baking soda and salt together. Beat the butter, brown sugar, eggs and vanilla in a mixer bowl until light and fluffy. Add the flour mixture, stirring until well blended. Stir in the oats and chocolate chips. Drop by rounded tablespoonfuls 2 inches apart onto cookie sheets. Bake at 350 degrees for 10 minutes or until light brown. Yield: 4 dozen cookies.

Judy Boozer, Birmingham South Cahaba Council

Easy Cookies

1 (2-layer) package yellow
  cake mix
1 egg

¾ cup vegetable oil
1 cup chopped nuts

Combine the cake mix, egg and oil in a large mixer bowl and beat until well blended. Stir in the chopped nuts. Drop by teaspoonfuls onto a cookie sheet. Bake at 350 degrees for 10 to 15 minutes or until golden brown. May substitute any flavor cake mix for the yellow cake mix. Yield: 4 dozen cookies.

Mrs. Hoyt Powell, Gadsden Life Member Club

Maple Syrup Cookies

¾ cup shortening
½ cup packed brown sugar
1 egg
½ cup maple syrup
1 teaspoon maple flavoring
2¼ cups flour

2 teaspoons baking powder
½ teaspoon baking soda
½ teaspoon salt
½ cup chopped walnuts
3½ dozen walnut halves
  (optional)

Cream the shortening, brown sugar and egg in a mixer bowl until light and fluffy. Add the maple syrup and maple flavoring and mixwell. Combine the flour, baking powder, baking soda and salt in a bowl. Stir into the maple syrup mixture. Fold in the chopped walnuts. Drop by rounded teaspoonfuls onto a cookie sheet. Press a walnut half into each cookie. Bake at 400 degrees for 8 minutes or until light brown. Cool on a wire rack. Yield: 3½ dozen cookies.

Susan Poe, Riverchase Council

Old-Fashioned Tea Cakes

1 teaspoon baking soda
⅓ cup milk
1 cup (2 sticks) butter,
  softened
2¼ cups sugar

2 eggs, beaten
5 cups flour
1 teaspoon baking powder
2 teaspoons nutmeg
2 teaspoon vanilla extract

Dissolve the baking soda in the milk in a small bowl. Cream the butter and sugar in a large mixer bowl until light and fluffy. Add the eggs and beat well. Sift the flour, baking powder and nutmeg together. Add to the creamed mixture alternately with the milk, mixing well after each addition. Chill, covered, until firm. Roll to desired thickness on a floured surface. Cut out as desired with cookie cutters or a knife and place on a cookie sheet. Bake at 325 degrees for 15 to 20 minutes or until light brown. Cool on a wire rack. May substitute 2 teaspoons of lemon flavoring and the zest of 2 lemons for the nutmeg and vanilla. Yield: 7 dozen cookies.

Sue (Joe) Small, Selma Life Member Club

Rice Krispies Squares

1 cup light corn syrup
1 cup packed brown sugar
1 cup peanut butter
6 cups crisp rice cereal

Combine the corn syrup and brown sugar in a saucepan. Bring to a boil and cook until the brown sugar is dissolved. Add the peanut butter and stir until melted. Add the cereal, stirring until well coated. Pour into a greased pan and press firmly. Let stand until firm. Cut into squares to serve. Yield: 4 dozen squares.

Betty Foshee, Decatur Council

Chocolate Pecan Pie

1 unbaked (9-inch) pie shell
1 cup sugar
1/2 cup flour
1/2 cup (1 stick) butter, melted
2 eggs, beaten
1 teaspoon vanilla extract
1/8 teaspoon salt
1 cup chocolate chips
1 cup chopped pecans

Bake the pie shell at 350 degrees until partially cooked. Mix the sugar and flour in a bowl. Combine the melted butter, eggs, vanilla and salt in a large mixer bowl and mix well. Add the sugar mixture and beat until well blended. Fold in the chocolate chips and pecans. Pour into the prepared pie shell. Bake at 350 degrees for 30 minutes. Yield: 6 to 8 servings.

Betty Foshee, Decatur Council

Run your hands under cold water before pressing
Rice Krispie treats in the pan. This keeps the marshmallow
from sticking to your hands.

Cheesy Deviled Egg Mice

6 large eggs, hard-cooked,
   chilled
1/3 cup shredded Cheddar
   cheese
2 tablespoons cream cheese,
   softened
1 tablespoon mayonnaise

1/4 teaspoon salt
4 radishes, thinly sliced
24 dried currants
1/2 cup alfalfa sprouts
1 (1-ounce) log string cheese,
   separated into 12 strands

Peel the eggs and cut into halves lengthwise. Scoop out the yolks. Combine the yolks with the Cheddar cheese, cream cheese, mayonnaise and salt in a bowl and mash with a fork to blend. Spoon the yolk mixture into the egg whites, leveling with a knife, and reserving any remaining yolk mixture. Arrange the stuffed eggs cut side down on a work surface. Cut 2 small slits in the egg whites for the ears. Insert a radish slice in each slit. Make holes for the eyes and nose with a wooden pick. Insert a currant for each eye. Cut small pieces of radish and insert in the remaining holes for noses. Arrange the eggs on a bed of alfalfa sprouts on a serving plate. Place a strand of the cheese for each tail. Shape the reserved yolk mixture into small balls to represent cheese for the mice. Yield: 12 servings.

Brenda Reeves, Birmingham South Cahaba Council

*Cure for headaches: Take a lime, cut it into halves and rub it
on your forehead. The throbbing will go away.*

Halloween Party Mix

1 (11-ounce) package pretzels
1 (10-ounce) package
   miniature peanut butter-
   filled butter crackers
1 cup dry-roasted peanuts
1 cup sugar
1/2 cup (1 stick) butter or
   margarine

1/2 cup corn syrup
2 tablespoons vanilla extract
1 teaspoon baking soda
1 (10-ounce) package
   "M&M's" Chocolate
   Candies
1 (18-ounce) package candy
   corn

Mix the pretzels, crackers and peanuts in a bowl. Combine the sugar, butter and corn syrup in a large saucepan. Bring to a boil over medium heat, stirring constantly. Boil for 5 minutes, stirring constantly. Remove from the heat. Stir in the vanilla and baking soda; mixture will foam. Pour over the pretzel mixture and stir until coated. Spoon into a greased 10x15-inch baking pan. Bake at 250 degrees for 45 minutes, stirring every 10 to 15 minutes. Break into pieces while warm. Toss with the "M&M's" and candy corn in a bowl. Let stand until cool. Store in an airtight container.
Yield: 16 cups.

Donna Jean Bowman, Birmingham South Cahaba Council

Gruesome Brew-Some

2 quarts 2% milk
1 cup instant hot
   chocolate mix
2 teaspoons ground cinnamon

1/4 cup frozen orange juice
   concentrate, thawed
1 pint chocolate ice cream
1 orange, sliced

Mix the milk, hot chocolate mix and cinnamon in a large saucepan. Bring to a boil over medium heat. Reduce the heat to low. Stir in the orange juice concentrate. Cook just until heated through. Ladle into cups. Top with a small scoop of ice cream. Cut the orange slices into halves and add 1 to each cup.
Yield: 8 servings.

Brenda Reeves, Birmingham South Cahaba Council

Spiced Cider

2 quarts apple cider
1 cup lemon juice
1 cup packed light brown
   sugar

8 cloves
2 cinnamon sticks

Combine the apple cider, lemon juice, brown sugar, cloves and cinnamon sticks in a large saucepan and mix well. Bring to a boil over medium heat. Reduce the heat to low and simmer for 10 minutes. Remove the cloves and cinnamon sticks. Serve hot or cold. May garnish with sliced apples or fresh cinnamon sticks if desired. Yield: 8 servings.

Debbie Speaks, Montgomery Council

Wormy Orange Punch

1 gallon orange sherbet,
   softened
1 quart pineapple juice,
   chilled

2 liters lemon-lime soda,
   chilled
Gummy worms

Combine the orange sherbet and pineapple juice in a punch bowl and stir well. Add the soda, stirring until most of the sherbet is melted. Decorate the bowl with gummy worms. Serve immediately. Yield: 20 servings.

Donna Jean Bowman, Birmingham South Cahaba Council

White Chili

2 pounds boneless chicken
  breasts
2 medium onions, chopped
1 tablespoon olive oil
4 garlic cloves, minced
1 (10-ounce) can tomatoes
  with green chiles
2 teaspoons ground cumin
2 teaspoons chili powder
1/4 teaspoon ground cloves

1 1/2 teaspoons dried oregano,
  crumbled
1/4 teaspoon cayenne pepper
6 cups chicken stock or broth
2 (16-ounce) cans great
  Northern beans
1 cup shredded Monterey
  Jack cheese
1 cup sour cream
Salt and pepper to taste

Combine the chicken with cold water to cover in a large saucepan.
Bring to a simmer. Simmer for 15 minutes or just until tender;
drain. Let stand until cool. Chop the chicken, discarding the skin.
Sauté the onions in the olive oil in a large saucepan over medium-
high heat for 10 minutes or until translucent. Add the garlic,
tomatoes with green chiles, cumin, chili powder, cloves, oregano
and cayenne pepper. Sauté for 2 minutes. Add the chicken stock
and beans and mix well. Bring to a boil. Reduce the heat to low and
simmer for 2 hours, stirring occasionally. Add the chicken, cheese
and sour cream. Simmer to blend flavors, stirring until the cheese
melts. Season with salt and pepper. Serve with additional cheese
and sour cream, salsa and chopped fresh cilantro. May prepare 1
day in advance. Add the beans, cover and refrigerate. Bring to a
simmer, adding the chicken, cheese and sour cream to serve. May
substitute 1 pound of cooked dried beans for the canned beans.
Yield: 8 servings.

Jennifer McAllister, Birmingham South Cahaba Council

Orange Congealed Salad

1 (6-ounce) package orange
   gelatin
2 cups hot water

2 (8-ounce) cans mandarin
   oranges
8 ounces whipped topping

Dissolve the gelatin in the hot water in a bowl. Drain the mandarin oranges, reserving the juice. Combine the juice with enough water to measure 2 cups. Add the juice to the gelatin. Chill, covered, until partially set. Mix in the whipped topping. Fold in the oranges. Spoon into a 9x13-inch dish. Chill, covered, until set. Cut into squares. Serve on lettuce leaves. Yield: 24 servings.

Betty C. Gray, Montgomery Life Member Club

Goblin's Gook Chili Dogs

½ medium onion, chopped
2 teaspoons vegetable oil
1 garlic clove, crushed
1 teaspoon chili powder
½ teaspoon ground cumin

1 (16-ounce) can red kidney
   beans, rinsed, drained
1 cup mild salsa
10 hot dogs
10 hamburger buns

Sauté the onion in the oil in a medium saucepan over medium heat for 3 minutes or until tender. Add the garlic, chili powder and cumin and sauté for 1 minute longer. Stir in the kidney beans and salsa. Reduce the heat to low and simmer for 10 minutes to blend the flavors. Cut slits at ½-inch intervals in the hot dogs. Bend the hot dogs into circles and secure with wooden picks. Broil until cooked through. Remove the wooden picks. Place on the hamburger buns and top with the bean mixture. Yield: 10 servings.

Brenda Reeves, Birmingham South Cahaba Council

Chicken Spaghetti

1 chicken
1 green bell pepper, chopped
2 onions, chopped
¼ cup (½ stick) butter
1 pound uncooked spaghetti
1 large jar pimentos

2 (10-ounce) cans tomatoes
  with green chiles
1 can mushrooms
2 pounds Velveeta cheese, cut
  into cubes

Cook the chicken in water to cover in a large saucepan until tender; drain, reserving the broth. Chop the chicken, discarding the skin and bones. Sauté the green pepper and onions in the butter in a skillet until tender; set aside. Cook the spaghetti in the reserved chicken broth using the package directions; drain. Combine the chicken, hot spaghetti, sautéed vegetables, pimentos, tomatoes with green chiles and mushrooms in a large bowl and mix well. Add the Velveeta cheese and mix well. Serve immediately. Yield: 8 servings.

Betty J. Goins, Shoals Life Member Club

Chicken Rotel

8 chicken breasts
Salt and pepper to taste
1 large onion, chopped
1 green bell pepper, chopped
6 tablespoons margarine

6 ounces vermicelli, cooked
1 pound Velveeta cheese,
  cut into cubes
1 (4-ounce) can mushrooms,
  drained

Combine the chicken with water to cover in a large saucepan. Season with salt and pepper. Bring to a boil over high heat and cook until tender. Chop the chicken, discarding the skin and bones. Sauté the onion and green pepper in the margarine in a skillet until tender. Mix with the chicken, vermicelli, Velveeta cheese and mushrooms in a large bowl. Spoon into a baking dish. Bake at 350 degrees for 35 to 45 minutes or until bubbly. Yield: 8 servings.

Mauntez Mayer, Anniston Council

Broccoli Casserole

1 cup uncooked instant rice
2 (10-ounce) packages frozen
   chopped broccoli, thawed
1 onion, chopped
¼ cup (½ stick) margarine
½ cup milk

8 ounces Velveeta cheese,
   cut into cubes
1 (10-ounce) can cream of
   chicken soup
Shredded cheese

Cook the rice using the package directions. Combine with the broccoli in a bowl. Sauté the onion in the margarine in a skillet until tender. Add to the rice mixture and mix well. Combine the milk, cubed Velveeta cheese and soup in a saucepan. Cook over medium heat until the cheese melts, stirring constantly. Add to the broccoli mixture and mix well. Spoon into a baking dish. Bake at 350 degrees for 30 to 35 minutes or until hot and bubbly. Sprinkle with shredded cheese. Bake for 5 minutes longer or until the cheese is melted. May substitute cooked fresh broccoli for the frozen broccoli. Yield: 10 servings.

Kitty Logan Brown, Gadsden Life Member Club

Baked Corn

1 can cream-style corn
1 can whole kernel corn
½ (9-ounce) package corn
   muffin mix
2 eggs, beaten

½ cup (1 stick) margarine,
   melted
1 cup sour cream
Salt and pepper to taste

Mix the cream-style corn, undrained whole kernel corn, muffin mix, eggs, margarine, sour cream, salt and pepper in a bowl. Spoon into a baking dish. Bake at 350 degrees for 45 to 50 minutes or until light brown. Yield: 6 servings.

Marjorie S. (Francis) Tucker, Selma Life Member Club

Squash Croquettes

8 medium yellow crookneck
  squash, chopped
2 medium onions, chopped
2 ribs celery, chopped
½ cup (1 stick) butter
6 eggs, beaten

1 teaspoon salt
1 teaspoon pepper
2 pounds white bread crumbs
2 pounds corn bread crumbs
Vegetable oil for deep-frying

Cook the squash in water to cover in a saucepan until tender; drain. Sauté the onions and celery in the butter in a skillet until tender. Combine with the squash, eggs, salt and pepper in a large bowl. Add the bread crumbs gradually, mixing well after each addition. Shape into oblong croquettes. Deep-fry in the oil until golden brown. Yield: 24 servings.

Susan Poe, Riverchase Council

Scrumptious Dessert

2 cups flour
1 tablespoon sugar
1 cup (2 sticks) margarine,
  softened
1 cup chopped pecans
8 ounces cream cheese,
  softened

1 (1-pound) package
  confectioners' sugar
12 ounces whipped topping
2 (16-ounce) cans peaches
2 tablespoons cornstarch

Mix the flour, sugar, margarine and pecans in a bowl. Press over the bottom of a 9x13-inch baking pan. Bake at 350 degrees for 15 minutes; cool. Beat the cream cheese and confectioners' sugar in a mixer bowl until light and fluffy. Fold in the whipped topping. Spread over the prepared crust. Drain the peaches, reserving the juice. Chop the peaches. Combine the peaches with the cornstarch and reserved juice in a saucepan. Bring to a boil over medium heat. Cook for 5 minutes or until thickened, stirring constantly. Let stand until cool. Spoon over the cream cheese layer. Chill, covered, until serving time. Yield: 10 servings.

Ilean Moore, Decatur Council

Butter Pecan Cake

1 (2-layer) package butter
  pecan cake mix
¾ cup vegetable oil
5 eggs

1 (16-ounce) can coconut
  pecan frosting
1 cup water
1 cup chopped pecans

Beat the cake mix and oil in a mixer bowl until blended. Beat in the eggs 1 at a time. Add the frosting and water and mix well. Stir in the pecans. Spoon into a greased and floured tube pan. Bake at 350 degrees for 1 hour. Cool in the pan for 10 minutes. Remove to a wire rack to cool completely. Serve topped with whipped cream or whipped topping. Store in an airtight container; cake will stay moist for several days. Yield: 12 servings.

Jean Phillips, Decatur Council

Chewy Cake

½ cup (1 stick) margarine
1 (1-pound) package light
  brown sugar
2 cups self-rising flour

3 eggs, beaten
1½ teaspoons vanilla extract
1 cup chopped pecans or
  walnuts

Cook the margarine and brown sugar in a saucepan over medium heat until melted and bubbly, stirring constantly. Stir in the flour, eggs, vanilla and pecans. Spoon into a greased 9x13-inch cake pan. Bake at 350 degrees for 20 to 25 minutes or until cake tests done. Yield: 15 servings.

Mrs. J.B. (Carol) Raines, Gadsden Life Member Club

Autumn Pumpkin Cake

1 (2-layer) package yellow
  cake mix
¾ cup sugar
1 teaspoon cinnamon
⅛ teaspoon nutmeg

½ cup vegetable oil
4 eggs
1 cup cooked pumpkin
¼ cup water
Cream Cheese Frosting

Combine the cake mix, sugar, cinnamon and nutmeg in a mixer bowl. Beat in the oil and eggs. Add the pumpkin and water and beat for 5 minutes. Spoon into a greased and floured tube pan. Bake at 350 degrees for 35 minutes or until cake tests done. Cool in the pan for 10 minutes. Remove to a wire rack to cool completely. Frost with the Cream Cheese Frosting. May omit the sugar if desired. Yield: 16 servings.

Cream Cheese Frosting

3 ounces cream cheese,
  softened
½ cup (1 stick) margarine,
  softened

1 (1-pound) package
  confectioners' sugar
1 teaspoon vanilla extract

Beat the cream cheese and margarine in a mixer bowl until blended. Add the confectioners' sugar and beat until smooth. Mix in the vanilla.

Della Pearl Dukes, Bon Secour Life Member Club

Halloween Pumpkin Cake

2 (2-layer) packages devil's
  food cake mix
½ teaspoon red food coloring
½ teaspoon yellow food
  coloring

2 (16-ounce) cans white
  frosting
1 (3-inch) sugar cookie
½ chocolate candy bar

Bake the 2 cakes using the package directions for bundt pans. Cool in the pans for 10 minutes. Remove to wire racks to cool completely. Combine the red and yellow food coloring with the frosting in a bowl and mix well. Trim the flat side of each cake to make level. Place 1 of the cakes flat side up on a serving platter. Spread the top with the orange frosting. Place the second cake flat side down over the first cake, lining up the edges. Place the cookie over the hole of the cake. Frost the entire surface of the cake with the orange frosting; ridges should still be visible. Place the candy bar cut side down at the top to represent the pumpkin stem, securing with orange frosting. Serve immediately or store, loosely covered, until serving time. *Note:* Reserve a small amount of the white frosting to mix with green food coloring to frost the stem green. Use candy corn, gumdrops, raisins, miniature marshmallows and/or chocolate chips to decorate the pumpkin to look like a jack-o-lantern. Yield: 20 to 24 servings.

Brenda Reeves and Sandy Tribble, Birmingham South Cahaba Council

Mini Cupcake Fright Bites

1 (2-layer) package yellow
  cake mix
1 (16-ounce) can white
  frosting
Red food coloring
Yellow food coloring

Black gumdrops
Orange gumdrops
Black licorice laces
Chocolate chips
Miniature marshmallows

Prepare the cake mix using the package directions for miniature cupcakes, baking in paper-lined muffin cups. Cool in the pan on a wire rack. Reserve ¼ cup of the frosting. Divide the remaining frosting into 2 equal portions in 2 medium bowls. Add 6 drops of red food coloring and 6 drops of yellow food coloring to 1 portion of frosting and mix well to make orange frosting. Frost half the cupcakes with the orange frosting and the remaining cupcakes with the white frosting.

To make a cat cupcake, cut a gumdrop lengthwise into 3 slices. Cut ears from the middle slice. Use the bottom slice for the body and the top slice for the head. Cut a narrow strip from the licorice to use for a tail.

To make a spider cupcake, use a slice of gumdrop for the body, a chocolate chip for the head and 8 pieces of licorice for the legs.

To make a ghost cupcake, use the reserved white frosting to hold 2 marshmallows together. Place on top of the cupcake. Spread with additional frosting. Use 2 tiny pieces of licorice for the eyes. Yield: 7 to 8 dozen.

Brenda Reeves, Birmingham South Cahaba Council

Molasses Cookies

½ cup shortening, melted
1 egg
¼ cup molasses
¾ cup rolled oats
1½ cups flour

1 cup sugar
1 teaspoon baking soda
1 teaspoon ginger
½ teaspoon ground cloves
½ teaspoon salt

Mix the shortening, egg, molasses and oats in a bowl. Stir in a mixture of the flour, sugar, baking soda, ginger, cloves and salt. Dip with an ice cream scoop and place 3 inches apart on a greased cookie sheet. Flatten with the bottom of a glass dipped in additional sugar. Bake at 375 degrees for 12 minutes. Yield: 1 dozen cookies.

Bernice Moore, Birmingham South Cahaba Council

Orange Finger Cookies

2 cups flour
18 orange slice candies,
  chopped
½ cup chopped pecans

4 eggs, beaten
2½ cups packed brown sugar
¼ cup confectioners' sugar

Mix the flour, orange slice candies and pecans in a bowl. Add the eggs and brown sugar and mix well. Spread ½ inch thick in a buttered 9x13-inch baking pan. Bake at 350 degrees for 30 to 40 minutes or until golden brown. Let stand until cool. Cut into fingers. Roll in the confectioners' sugar. Yield: 2½ dozen cookies.

Alice Walski, Birmingham Life Member Club

Peanut Butter Creepy Crawlies

2½ cups flour
1 teaspoon baking powder
¼ teaspoon salt
¾ cup sugar
¾ cup (1½ sticks) unsalted
  butter, softened
¾ cup creamy peanut butter

1 egg
1 teaspoon vanilla extract
Mini pretzel twists
Mini chocolate chips
Black, brown and orange
  sprinkles (optional)

Mix the flour, baking powder and salt together. Beat the sugar, butter and peanut butter at medium speed in a mixer bowl until light and fluffy. Beat in the egg and vanilla. Add the dry ingredients gradually, beating at low speed until blended after each addition. Shape the dough into 2 logs. Wrap in plastic wrap. Chill for 2 hours or longer.

To make snakes, shape the dough into 1½-inch balls. Shape the balls into 5-inch-long snakes, making the head ends slightly larger than the tail ends. Place on an ungreased cookie sheet. Press markings along the snakes with a fork. Use small pieces of pretzel for the tongues and chocolate chips for the eyes. Decorate with sprinkles. Bake at 375 degrees for 8 to 10 minutes or until golden brown.

To make beetles, shape the dough into 1-inch balls and flatten slightly. Place 2 pretzels with pointed ends touching on a work surface for each beetle. Press 1 ball over the pointed ends. Make heads with small balls of dough. Use small pieces of pretzels to make antennae and chocolate chips for the eyes. Place on an ungreased cookie sheet. Make ridges in the body with a fork. Bake at 375 degrees for 10 to 12 minutes or until golden brown. Yield: 3 dozen.

Brenda Reeves, Birmingham South Cahaba Council

Pumpkin Cheesecake Bars

1 (16-ounce) package pound
  cake mix
1 egg
2 tablespoons margarine,
  melted
2 teaspoons pumpkin pie spice
8 ounces cream cheese,
  softened

1 (14-ounce) can sweetened
  condensed milk
2 eggs
1 (16-ounce) can pumpkin
2 teaspoons pumpkin pie spice
1/2 teaspoon salt
1 cup chopped nuts

Beat the cake mix, 1 egg, margarine and 2 teaspoons pumpkin pie spice at low speed in a mixer bowl until crumbly. Press over the bottom of a 10x15-inch baking pan. Beat the cream cheese at high speed in a mixer bowl until fluffy. Beat in the sweetened condensed milk gradually. Mix in 2 eggs, pumpkin, 2 teaspoons pumpkin pie spice and salt. Spoon over the prepared crust. Sprinkle with the nuts. Bake at 350 degrees for 30 to 35 minutes or until set. Let stand until cool. Chill, covered, until serving time. Cut into bars. Store, covered, in the refrigerator. Yield: 3 dozen.

Mrs. Bob H. Henson, Birmingham South Life Member Club

Seven-Layer Magic Bars

½ cup (1 stick) margarine
1½ cups graham cracker
  crumbs
1 (14-ounce) can sweetened
  condensed milk

1 cup butterscotch chips
1 cup semisweet chocolate
  chips
1⅓ cups flaked coconut
1 cup chopped nuts

Melt the margarine in a 9x13-inch baking pan in a 350-degree oven. Sprinkle with the graham cracker crumbs. Pour the sweetened condensed milk evenly over the crumbs. Sprinkle with the butterscotch chips, chocolate chips, coconut and nuts; press with the back of a spoon. Bake at 350 degrees for 25 minutes or until light brown. Let stand until cool. Cut into bars. Store, covered, at room temperature. Yield: 2 dozen.

Pat Griffin, Montgomery Council

Apple Pie

½ cup sugar
3 tablespoons sifted flour
⅛ teaspoon nutmeg
⅛ teaspoon cinnamon
¼ cup orange juice
1½ tablespoons light corn
  syrup

2½ tablespoons butter,
  melted
8 medium Rome or Granny
  Smith apples, peeled, sliced
1 recipe (2-crust) pie pastry

Combine the sugar, flour, nutmeg, cinnamon, orange juice, corn syrup and butter in a bowl and mix well. Stir in the apples until well coated. Spoon into a pastry-lined pie plate. Top with the remaining pastry, fluting the edge to seal and cutting vents. Bake at 375 degrees for 15 minutes. Reduce the oven temperature to 300 degrees. Bake for 45 minutes longer, covering the edge with foil if necessary to prevent overbrowning. Cool completely before slicing. May add additional nutmeg and/or cinnamon for a spicier taste. Yield: 6 to 8 servings.

Sam Wesley, Montgomery Council

Grandma's Butterscotch Pie

2 cups sugar
1/2 cup (1 stick) butter
4 egg yolks
1 cup sugar

5 tablespoons flour
2 cups milk
1 baked (9-inch) pie shell

Cook 2 cups sugar and butter in an iron skillet until golden brown, stirring constantly. Beat the egg yolks, 1 cup sugar and flour in a mixer bowl until well mixed. Add the milk gradually, beating well after each addition. Stir in the sugar and butter mixture. Let stand until thickened. Spoon into the pie shell. Serve immediately. Store, covered, in the refrigerator. Yield: 6 to 8 servings.

Betty Foshee, Decatur Council

Skillet Chocolate Pie

1 1/2 cups sugar
3 tablespoons cornstarch
3 tablespoons baking cocoa
2 cups milk
3 egg yolks, beaten
1/4 cup (1/2 stick) margarine,
    melted

1 1/2 teaspoons vanilla extract
1 baked (9-inch) pie shell
3 egg whites
1/8 teaspoon salt
1/2 teaspoon cream of tartar
1/4 cup sugar
1/2 teaspoon vanilla extract

Mix 1 1/2 cups sugar, cornstarch and baking cocoa in an iron skillet. Add the milk and egg yolks gradually, mixing well after each addition. Cook over medium heat until thickened, stirring constantly. Remove from the heat. Add the margarine and 1 1/2 teaspoons vanilla and mix well. Spoon into the pie shell. Beat the egg whites, salt and cream of tartar in a mixer bowl until stiff peaks form. Fold in 1/4 cup sugar and 1/2 teaspoon vanilla. Spread over the chocolate mixture. Bake at 400 degrees until golden brown.
Yield: 6 to 8 servings.

Fay Clark, Riverchase Council

Chili Cheese Ball

2 pounds Velveeta cheese
16 ounces cream cheese
1/2 teaspoon garlic powder

Salt to taste
1 cup chopped nuts
Chili powder

Cut the Velveeta cheese and cream cheese into cubes and place in a large bowl. Let stand at room temperature until softened. Mix until well blended. Add the garlic powder, salt and nuts and mix well. Shape into 1 or 2 balls and roll in chili powder to coat. Wrap in foil and chill until firm. Unwrap and place on a serving plate. Serve with assorted party crackers. Yield: 25 to 30 servings.

Marjorie S. (Francis) Tucker, Selma Life Member Club

Honey Sticks

1/2 loaf sliced bread
1/2 cup honey
1/2 cup shortening

1 cup peanut butter
1/2 cup confectioners' sugar

Trim the crusts from the bread using a sharp knife and reserve the crusts. Cut the bread slices into sticks. Place the bread sticks and the reserved crusts on a baking sheet. Bake at 200 degrees for 1 hour or until crisp, turning occasionally. Crush the dried crusts into fine crumbs and place in a shallow dish. Combine the honey, shortening and peanut butter in a saucepan. Heat over low heat until well blended, stirring frequently; do not boil. Blend in the confectioners' sugar. Dip the dried bread sticks into the peanut butter mixture and roll in the crumbs to coat well. Place on waxed paper. Let stand until firm. Yield: variable.

Doris Dean, Birmingham Life Member Club

Thanksgiving Punch

1 cup cranberry-apple juice	2 strips orange zest
1 cup cranberry-raspberry	2 whole cloves
juice	1 cinnamon stick
½ cup orange juice	

Combine the juices, orange zest, cloves and cinnamon in a saucepan. Simmer for 20 minutes. Discard the cloves and cinnamon. Ladle into mugs and add a slice of orange or lime for garnish. May prepare by simmering in a slow cooker for several hours or prepare in a traditional coffee pot. Yield: 2½ cups.

Eunice Henry, Selma Life Member Club

Apple Salad

4 tart apples	½ to 1 cup drained pineapple
½ cup red cherries	chunks
½ cup shredded coconut	½ cup mayonnaise
½ cup chopped pecans	Whipped topping to taste
½ cup raisins	

Peel, core and chop the apples. Combine the apples with the cherries, coconut, pecans, raisins and pineapple in a bowl. Blend the mayonnaise with the desired amount of whipped topping and add to the fruit mixture, mixing gently. Chill until serving time. Adjust the amounts of ingredients to taste. The salad does not keep well after the first day. *Note:* Rinse the apples with lemon juice, Fruit Fresh or other ascorbic acid product to prevent browning. Yield: 6 to 8 servings.

Betty Darnell, Gadsden Life Member Club

Cranberry Mold

1 (3-ounce) package raspberry gelatin	1 cup whole cranberry sauce
½ teaspoon salt	½ cup crushed pineapple, drained
1 cup boiling water	½ cup chopped celery
½ cup cold water	½ cup chopped apple
2 teaspoons lemon juice	¼ cup chopped nuts

Dissolve the gelatin and salt in the boiling water in a medium bowl. Add the cold water and lemon juice. Chill until partially set. Fold in the cranberry sauce, pineapple, celery, apple and nuts. Spoon into a gelatin mold. Chill until firm. Invert onto a serving plate. Yield: 5 to 6 servings.

Pat White, Montgomery Council

Cranberry Salad

2 (3-ounce) packages cherry gelatin	1 (16-ounce) can whole cranberry sauce
2 cups boiling water	1 cup chopped pecans
1 medium can juice-pack crushed pineapple	1 cup sour cream
	¼ cup mayonnaise

Dissolve the gelatin in the boiling water. Chill until partially set. Reserve a small amount of pineapple juice. Mix the remaining undrained pineapple, cranberry sauce and pecans in a bowl. Blend the sour cream and mayonnaise in a small bowl, adding the reserved pineapple juice. Fold the sour cream mixture into the cranberry mixture. Fold the mixture into the gelatin. Chill, covered, for 8 to 10 hours. May store in the refrigerator for up to 1 week. Yield: 12 servings.

Jean Phillips, Decatur Council

Festive Cranberry Salad

1 (14-ounce) can sweetened
   condensed milk
¼ cup lemon juice
1 (20-ounce) can crushed
   pineapple, drained
1 (16-ounce) can whole
   cranberry sauce

2 cups miniature
   marshmallows
½ cup chopped pecans
8 ounces whipped topping

Blend the condensed milk and lemon juice in a large bowl. Add the pineapple, cranberry sauce, marshmallows and pecans and mix well. Fold in the whipped topping. Spoon into a 9x13-inch dish. Freeze for 4 to 10 hours or until firm. Cut into squares.
Yield: 12 to 16 servings.

Frankie (A.T.) Vaughn, Selma Life Member Club

Cranberry and Orange Salad

2 (3-ounce) packages cherry
   gelatin
2 cups boiling water
½ cup sugar
1 tablespoon lemon juice
½ cup chopped celery

½ cup chopped pecans
1 (13-ounce) can crushed
   pineapple, drained
1 (16-ounce) can whole or
   jellied cranberry sauce
2 oranges, peeled, chopped

Dissolve the gelatin in the boiling water in a large bowl. Add the sugar and lemon juice and stir until the sugar dissolves. Chill until partially set. Fold in the celery, pecans, pineapple, cranberry sauce and oranges. Chill, covered, until set. Yield: 6 to 8 servings.

Hazel E. Campbell, Birmingham Life Member Club

Holiday Cranberry Salad

2 cups cranberries
1½ cups water
1 cup sugar
1 (3-ounce) package cherry
    gelatin

1 (8-ounce) can crushed
    pineapple, partially drained
1 Granny Smith apple, peeled,
    chopped
1½ cups chopped pecans

Combine the cranberries and water in a large saucepan. Simmer until the cranberries pop and become tender. Stir in the sugar and gelatin. Cook until the sugar and gelatin dissolve completely, stirring frequently. Chill until partially set. Fold in the pineapple, apple and pecans. Spoon into a gelatin mold. Chill until set. Invert onto a serving plate. Yield: 4 to 6 servings.

Tom Coffield, Birmingham South Cahaba Council

Orange Buttermilk Salad

1 (6-ounce) package orange
    gelatin
1 (20-ounce) can crushed
    pineapple

2 cups buttermilk
Shredded coconut to taste
Chopped pecans to taste
16 ounces whipped topping

Combine the gelatin and pineapple in a saucepan. Bring to a boil, stirring constantly. Remove from heat. Let stand until cool. Combine the buttermilk, coconut, pecans and whipped topping in a large bowl and mix well. Stir in the gelatin mixture. Spoon into a serving bowl. Chill until serving time. Yield: 8 servings.

Gloria Wadsworth, Birmingham South Cahaba Council

Grape Salad

8 ounces cream cheese,   3 tablespoons sugar
  softened   1 teaspoon vanilla extract
¼ cup sour cream   2 pounds seedless grapes
¼ cup mayonnaise   1 cup chopped pecans

Combine the cream cheese, sour cream, mayonnaise, sugar and vanilla in a bowl and blend well. Stem the grapes, rinse and drain well. Place in a bowl. Add the cream cheese mixture and mix gently. Mix in the pecans. Yield: 8 servings.

Judy Burrow, Decatur Council

Mandarin Orange Salad

3 (11-ounce) cans mandarin   1 cup chopped nuts (optional)
  oranges   1 cup drained maraschino
1 (20-ounce) can juice-pack   cherries (optional)
  pineapple chunks   1 cup shredded coconut
1 (10-ounce) package   (optional)
  miniature marshmallows   1 cup sour cream

Drain the juice from the oranges and pineapple and reserve the juice for another purpose such as punch or gelatin. Combine the oranges, pineapple, marshmallows, nuts, cherries and coconut in a bowl and mix well. Add the sour cream and mix well. Chill, covered, for 1 to 10 hours. Yield: 8 servings.

Myra Davis, Alabama Telco Credit Union

Broccoli Salad

Florets of 2 bunches broccoli
2 bunches green onions,
  chopped
1 cup raisins
1 cup chopped pecans or
  peanuts

1½ cups mayonnaise
¼ cup apple cider vinegar
½ cup sugar
6 slices crisp-fried bacon,
  crumbled

Combine the broccoli, green onions, raisins and pecans in a large bowl. Blend the mayonnaise, vinegar and sugar in a small bowl. Add to the broccoli mixture and mix gently. Spoon into a crystal serving bowl. Sprinkle with the bacon. Salad will keep for several days in the refrigerator. Yield: 6 servings.

Betty J. Goins, Shoals Life Member Club

Thanksgiving Slaw

½ head cabbage, chopped
1 green bell pepper, chopped
½ bunch green onions,
  chopped
1 package sliced almonds
1 (3-ounce) package chicken
  ramen noodles
1 (7-ounce) package sunflower
  seed kernels

½ cup olive oil
¼ cup vinegar
3 tablespoons sugar
1½ tablespoons Dijon mustard
½ teaspoon pepper
1 packet ramen noodle
  flavoring

Combine the cabbage, green pepper and green onions in a bowl. Chill, covered, in the refrigerator. Add the almonds, ramen noodles and sunflower kernels. Combine the olive oil, vinegar, sugar, Dijon mustard, pepper and ramen noodle flavoring packet in a small bowl and mix well. Pour over the cabbage mixture and mix well. Serve immediately. Yield: 6 to 8 servings.

Sharon Coffield, Birmingham South Cahaba Council

Green Bean Salad

1 (20-ounce) can French-style green beans, drained
1 (8-ounce) can peas, drained
4 large ribs celery, chopped
1 medium onion, minced
1 (2-ounce) jar chopped pimento
1 green bell pepper, chopped
1/4 cup vegetable oil
1/2 cup vinegar
1/3 cup Italian salad dressing (optional)
3/4 cup sugar
1 teaspoon salt

Combine the green beans, peas, celery, onion, pimento and green pepper in a large bowl and mix gently. Combine the oil, vinegar, salad dressing, sugar and salt in a small bowl and mix well. Pour over the vegetable mixture and toss to coat. Chill, tightly covered, for 8 to 10 hours; drain. Spoon into a serving bowl. Chill, covered, until serving time. Yield: 10 servings.

E.B. Thornton, Tuscaloosa Council

Relish Salad

1 (16-ounce) can French-style green beans
1 (16-ounce) can tiny green peas
1 (15-ounce) can whole kernel white corn
1 cup each chopped green bell pepper and celery
1 cup chopped purple onion
1 (2-ounce) jar pimento
1/2 cup vegetable oil
3/4 cup red vinegar
1 tablespoon water
1 cup sugar
1 teaspoon salt
1/4 teaspoon pepper

Drain the green beans, peas and corn and place in a large bowl. Add the green pepper, celery, onion and pimento. Combine the oil, vinegar, water, sugar, salt and pepper in a saucepan. Bring the mixture to a boil, stirring occasionally. Let stand until cool. Pour over the vegetables and mix gently. Marinate, covered, in the refrigerator for 8 to 10 hours or for up to 2 weeks.
Yield: 10 to 12 servings.

Jamima Edney, Birmingham Life Member Club

Delicious Baked Chicken

1 cup uncooked rice
6 boneless skinless chicken
  pieces

1 (10-ounce) can cream of
  mushroom soup
1 cup sour cream

Spread the rice evenly in a baking dish. Arrange the chicken over the rice. Mix the soup and sour cream in a bowl and pour over the chicken. Bake, covered, at 350 degrees for 1¼ hours or until the chicken and rice are tender. Yield: 4 to 6 servings.

Margaret Copelin, Montgomery Life Member Club

Chicken Corn Bread Casserole

1 (10-inch) skillet corn bread
1 cup finely chopped celery
1 onion, finely chopped
2 eggs, beaten
2 (14-ounce) cans chicken
  broth

1 tablespoon ground sage
Salt and pepper to taste
4 chicken breasts, cooked,
  shredded

Crumble the corn bread into a large bowl. Add the celery, onion, eggs, broth, sage, salt and pepper and chicken and mix well. Spoon into a greased baking dish. Bake at 350 degrees for 1 hour or until brown. May prepare the day before baking but do not add the eggs and onion until just before baking. Yield: 8 servings.

Donna Jean Bowman, Birmingham South Cahaba Council

Deep-Fried Marinated Turkey

½ bottle hot barbecue sauce
½ bottle Dale's steak
 seasoning
½ bottle Italian salad dressing

Cayenne pepper to taste
2 tablespoons Tony Chachere's
 Cajun seasoning
1 (10- to 12-pound) turkey

Combine the barbecue sauce, Dale's steak seasoning, salad dressing, cayenne pepper and Cajun seasoning in a bowl and mix well. Insert the mixture with a basting needle into the turkey. Marinate, tightly wrapped, in the refrigerator for 2 days. Deep-fry the turkey as desired. Yield: 15 to 20 servings.

Bernice Adams, Huntsville Council

Asparagus Casserole

2 (15-ounce) cans asparagus,
 drained
1 (8-ounce) can green peas,
 drained
1 (10-ounce) can cream of
 mushroom soup

1 (8-ounce) jar Cheez Whiz
½ teaspoon garlic salt
1 teaspoon Worcestershire
 sauce
1 large package sliced almonds

Combine the asparagus, peas and soup in a bowl and mix gently. Add the Cheez Whiz, garlic salt and Worcestershire sauce and mix gently. Spoon into a greased baking dish. Sprinkle the almonds over the top. Bake at 350 degrees until brown.
Yield: 4 to 6 servings.

Sharon Coffield, Birmingham South Cahaba Council

Green Bean Bundles

2 cans whole green beans
Bacon slices
1 small onion, finely chopped

1 bottle Catalina salad
   dressing

Drain the beans and separate into 15- to 20-bean portions. Cut the bacon lengthwise into thin strips. Wrap each bean bundle with bacon and arrange in a baking dish. Sprinkle with the onion and pour the salad dressing over the bundles. Bake at 350 degrees for 30 minutes or until the bacon is cooked through. Yield: 8 servings.

Susan Friday, Montgomery Council

Broccoli Casserole

1 (9-ounce) package frozen
   chopped broccoli, thawed
1 cup instant rice
1 (10-ounce) can cream of
   mushroom soup
1 (10-ounce) can cream of
   chicken soup

1 cup chopped onion
¼ cup (½ stick) butter,
   melted
1 (8-ounce) jar jalapeño
   Cheez Whiz

Combine the broccoli, rice, soups, onion, butter and Cheez Whiz in a bowl and mix well. Spoon into a greased baking dish. Bake at 350 degrees for 30 to 45 minutes or until bubbly.
Yield: 6 to 8 servings.

Nora Carpenter, Birmingham South Cahaba Council

Corn Casserole

4 slices bacon
1 large onion, chopped
1 cup sour cream

2 (16-ounce) cans whole
   kernel corn, drained

Fry the bacon in a skillet until crisp. Drain, reserving the pan drippings. Crumble the bacon. Add the onion to the reserved drippings in the skillet. Sauté until tender. Combine the sour cream, corn and onion with drippings in a bowl and mix well. Stir in the bacon. Spoon into a baking dish. Bake at 350 degrees for 30 minutes. Yield: 4 to 6 servings.

Donna McNulty, Riverchase Council

Corn Bread Casserole

1 medium onion, chopped
Butter
2 (17-ounce) cans cream-style
   corn
1 (16-ounce) can whole kernel
   corn, drained

2 eggs, beaten
⅔ cup vegetable oil
1 package honey golden corn
   bread mix

Sauté the onion in a small amount of butter in a skillet until tender. Combine the cream-style corn, whole kernel corn, eggs, oil, corn bread mix and onion in a large bowl and mix well. Spoon into a greased 2-quart baking dish. Bake at 350 degrees for 40 to 45 minutes or until golden brown. Yield: 8 to 10 servings.

Sherry A. Liles, Huntsville Council

Creamy Potato Casserole

8 medium potatoes
Salt to taste
1 (10-ounce) can cream of
  chicken soup
1/4 cup (1/2 stick) margarine,
  melted
1/4 cup water

1/2 cup chopped green onions
2 cups sour cream
1 cup shredded Cheddar
  cheese
2 1/2 cups crushed cornflakes
1/4 cup (1/2 stick) margarine,
  melted

Peel the potatoes and cut into cubes. Cook in boiling salted water
in a saucepan until tender. Drain the potatoes and place in a
greased baking dish. Combine the soup, 1/4 cup margarine and water
in a bowl and mix well. Add the green onions, sour cream and
cheese and mix well. Pour over the potatoes. Mix the cornflakes
with 1/4 cup margarine and sprinkle over the top. Bake at 350
degrees until bubbly. Yield: 8 servings.

Ila M. Skidmore, Shoals Life Member Club

Sour Cream Potatoes

6 medium potatoes
1/2 cup (1 stick) margarine
2 cups shredded sharp
  Cheddar cheese

1 cup sour cream
2/3 cup chopped onion
Paprika to taste

Peel the potatoes and cut into halves. Cook in water to cover in a
saucepan just until cooked through. Drain and cut into slices.
Combine the margarine and cheese in a double boiler. Heat over
hot water until melted and well blended, stirring frequently. Blend
in the sour cream. Add the onion and mix well. Alternate layers of
the potato slices and cheese sauce in a 9x13-inch baking dish until
all of the ingredients are used. Sprinkle with paprika. Chill,
covered, for 8 to 10 hours. Bake, uncovered, at 350 degrees for 30
minutes. Yield: 4 to 6 servings.

Dee Ann H. Weaver, Birmingham Life Member Club

Squash Casserole

5 or 6 medium yellow squash
½ cup mayonnaise
2 eggs
1½ cups shredded Cheddar
   cheese
3 tablespoons chopped onion

1 teaspoon sugar
Salt and pepper to taste
1½ to 2 cups cracker crumbs
½ cup (1 stick) margarine,
   melted

Slice the squash and place in a large saucepan. Add water to cover. Cook until tender; drain. Place in a mixer bowl and beat until mashed. Beat in the mayonnaise and eggs. Add the cheese, onion, sugar, salt and pepper and stir until well mixed. Spoon into a buttered 1-quart baking dish. Toss the cracker crumbs with the melted butter in a bowl and sprinkle over the squash mixture. Bake at 350 degrees for 35 to 40 minutes or until golden brown.
Yield: 6 servings.

Betty Foshee, Decatur Council

Baked Squash

3 or 4 yellow squash, chopped
¼ cup chopped onion
½ teaspoon salt

½ teaspoon pepper
¼ cup cornmeal

Combine the squash, onion, salt, pepper and cornmeal in a large bowl and toss until well mixed. Spoon the mixture into a baking dish sprayed with nonstick cooking spray. Bake at 375 degrees for 30 minutes. Yield: 4 servings.

Ila M. Skidmore, Shoals Life Member Club

Candied Sweet Potatoes

4 pounds sweet potatoes
½ cup packed dark brown
  sugar
¼ cup (½ stick) margarine
¾ teaspoon salt

¼ teaspoon coarsely ground
  pepper
Nutmeg to taste
¼ cup water
Marshmallows (optional)

Peel and cut the sweet potatoes into 1-inch-thick rounds. Place in a large saucepan and add water to cover. Bring to a boil; reduce the heat. Simmer for 5 minutes or until the sweet potatoes are slightly underdone; drain. Arrange the sweet potatoes in a shallow 2-quart baking dish. Combine the next 5 ingredients in a skillet. Add the water. Cook over medium heat for 3 minutes or until the margarine melts and the mixture is well blended, stirring frequently. Drizzle over the sweet potatoes. Bake at 400 degrees for 20 minutes, basting occasionally with the brown sugar mixture. Turn the slices over and bake for 20 minutes longer, basting occasionally. Top with marshmallows. Bake for 10 minutes longer. Yield: 12 servings.

Brenda Reeves, Birmingham South Cahaba Council

Sweet Potato Balls

4 cups mashed cooked sweet
  potatoes
3 tablespoons brown sugar
3 tablespoons margarine,
  melted

2 eggs, beaten
⅛ teaspoon salt
16 to 20 large marshmallows
1 cup (or more) crushed
  cornflakes

Combine the sweet potatoes, brown sugar, margarine, eggs and salt in a bowl and mix well. Chill the mixture until very cold. Shape a small amount of the sweet potato mixture around each marshmallow and roll in the cornflakes to coat. Arrange on a greased baking sheet. Bake at 350 degrees for 20 to 30 minutes or until golden brown. Yield: 16 to 20 balls.

Ruth P. Apperson, Decatur Council

Thanksgiving Sweet Potatoes

4 medium sweet potatoes,
  peeled, sliced
½ cup packed brown sugar
1 tablespoon cornstarch
¼ teaspoon salt

1 cup orange juice
½ cup raisins
¼ cup (½ stick) margarine
½ teaspoon grated orange zest
½ cup chopped nuts

Cook the sweet potatoes in water to cover in a saucepan until tender; drain. Place in a greased baking dish. Combine the brown sugar, cornstarch and salt in a saucepan. Stir in the orange juice. Bring to a boil, stirring constantly. Stir in the raisins, margarine, orange zest and nuts. Pour over the sweet potatoes. Bake at 350 degrees for 30 minutes or until bubbly. Yield: 10 to 12 servings.

Gloria Wynne, Mobile Council

Individual Sweet Potato Casseroles

4 cups cubed peeled sweet
  potatoes
¼ cup unsweetened apple
  juice
1½ tablespoons brown sugar
2 tablespoons buttermilk
2 tablespoons nonfat sour
  cream

1 teaspoon grated orange zest
¼ teaspoon orange extract
⅛ teaspoon each cinnamon,
  coriander and nutmeg
2 egg whites
1 teaspoon gingersnap cookie
  crumbs
1 teaspoon chopped pecans

Cook the sweet potatoes in water to cover in a large saucepan until tender; drain. Process the sweet potatoes in a food processor until smooth. Place in a bowl. Add the next 9 ingredients and mix well. Beat the egg whites in a mixer bowl until stiff peaks form. Fold into the sweet potato mixture gently. Spoon into four ³/₄-cup ramekins sprayed with nonstick cooking spray. Sprinkle with the cookie crumbs and pecans. Place the ramekins in a 9-inch square baking pan. Add hot water to the pan to a depth of 1 inch. Bake at 325 degrees for 30 minutes. Serve immediately. Yield: 4 servings.

Susan Currie, Birmingham South Cahaba Council

Orange-Glazed Yams

4 medium yams
1½ cups sugar
1½ cups light corn syrup
¾ cup orange juice
3 tablespoons butter

1 tablespoon grated orange
   zest
1 teaspoon salt
1 large orange

Boil the yams in water to cover in a saucepan just until cooked through; do not overcook. Peel and cut into halves lengthwise. Combine the sugar, corn syrup, orange juice, butter, orange zest and salt in a large saucepan. Bring to a full rolling boil, stirring constantly. Slice the orange into ¼-inch slices. Add the sweet potatoes and orange slices to the hot syrup. Cook over low heat until the yams are glazed and the syrup is thickened, turning the yams frequently. Yield: 6 servings.

Mrs. Bob H. Henson, Birmingham South Life Member Club

Cheesy Apples

1 (16-ounce) can sliced apples
½ cup sugar
½ cup flour
½ cup (1 stick) butter, melted

¼ cup milk
8 ounces Velveeta cheese,
   cubed

Place the undrained apples in a greased 1½-quart baking dish. Combine the sugar and flour in a saucepan and mix well. Add the butter and milk and mix well. Add the cheese and cook until the cheese melts and the mixture is well blended, stirring constantly. Spread the cheese mixture over the apples. Bake at 350 degrees for 30 to 40 minutes or until light brown. Yield: 6 to 8 servings.

Emily Coburn, Selma Life Member Club

Apple Cranberry Casserole

2 cups cranberries
3 cups chopped unpeeled
   apples
1¼ cups sugar
1½ cups quick-cooking oats

½ cup packed brown sugar
⅓ cup flour
⅓ cup chopped pecans
½ cup (1 stick) margarine,
   melted

Combine the cranberries and apples in a 9x13-inch baking dish. Sprinkle the sugar over the fruit. Combine the oats, brown sugar, flour and pecans in a bowl. Add the margarine and toss to mix. Sprinkle over the top. Bake at 350 degrees for 1½ hours. Yield: 6 to 8 servings.

Janice Bass, Riverchase Council

Cranberry Butter

1 cup (2 sticks) butter,
   softened
1 cup jellied or whole
   cranberry sauce

Chopped pecans (optional)

Beat the butter in a mixer bowl until light and fluffy. Add the cranberry sauce. Beat at medium speed until well blended. Spoon into a serving bowl and sprinkle with pecans. Store, covered, in the refrigerator. Serve at room temperature with muffins, bagels or pancakes. Yield: 2 cups.

Mary Smith and Donna Frederick,
Birmingham South Cahaba Council

Cranberry Chutney

1 cup water
3/4 cup sugar
1 (12-ounce) package
   cranberries
1 cup chopped peeled apple
1/2 cup cider vinegar

1/2 cup raisins
1 teaspoon cinnamon
1/4 teaspoon ginger
1/4 teaspoon allspice
1/8 teaspoon ground cloves

Bring the water and sugar to a boil in a saucepan, stirring until the sugar dissolves. Add the cranberries, apple, vinegar, raisins and spices. Bring to a boil; reduce the heat. Simmer for 10 minutes, stirring frequently. Pour into a bowl. Place plastic wrap directly on the surface. Cool to room temperature. Store in the refrigerator. Serve at room temperature. Yield: 2 3/4 cups.

Martha Bolling, Birmingham Life Member Club

Grandma's Fresh Cranberry Relish

1 (12-ounce) package
   cranberries
1 medium Granny Smith
   apple, peeled, chopped
1 medium Gala apple, peeled,
   chopped

1 small unpeeled navel
   orange, chopped
2/3 cup sugar

Combine the cranberries, apples, orange and sugar in a food processor. Pulse until the fruit is finely chopped. Pour into a serving bowl. Chill, covered, for 3 hours to 4 days. Yield: 4 cups.

Brenda Reeves, Birmingham South Cahaba Council

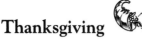
Cranberry Apple Relish

1 orange	1 (20-ounce) can crushed
5 or 6 apples	pineapple, drained
1 pound cranberries	½ cup chopped pecans
2 cups sugar	

Cut the orange and apples into quarters. Seed the orange and core the apples. Process the orange, apples and cranberries in a food processor or blender until coarsely ground. Pour into a large bowl. Add the sugar, pineapple and pecans and mix well. Chill, covered, for 8 to 10 hours. Yield: 2 quarts.

Francis M. Tucker, Selma Life Member Club

Creole Corn Bread Dressing

2 or 3 (7-ounce) packages	Crushed pepper to taste
corn bread mix	3 garlic cloves, minced
¼ cup sugar	2 teaspoons butter
3 large onions, chopped	1 pound smoked sausage,
Chopped fresh parsley to taste	chopped

Prepare and bake the corn bread mix using package directions and adding the sugar. Let stand until cool. Crumble and set aside. Sauté the onions, parsley, pepper and garlic in the butter in a large saucepan until tender. Stir in the sausage. Cook over medium heat for several minutes, stirring frequently. Add the crumbled corn bread and mix well. Cook for 1 to 2 minutes and add additional butter if the mixture is dry. Spoon into a serving dish. Serve immediately. Yield: 8 to 10 servings.

Kathleen B. Hamrick, Birmingham South Cahaba Council

Mama Bee's Dressing

1 chicken
Sage, poultry seasoning, salt
  and pepper to taste
2 recipes Corn Bread
6 dry hamburger buns or
  equivalent bread
4 eggs, beaten
1 medium onion, chopped

3 ribs celery, chopped
1 (10-ounce) can cream of
  chicken soup
1 (10-ounce) can cream of
  mushroom soup
1 (10-ounce) can cream of
  celery soup

Cook the chicken in a generous amount of water in a stockpot, adding the sage, poultry seasoning, salt and pepper. Strain the broth and reserve. Chop the chicken, discarding the skin and bones. Crumble the corn bread and buns into a large bowl. Add the eggs, onion, celery, chicken and soups. Stir in enough of the reserved broth a small amount at a time. Add additional water if necessary. A potato masher works well for mixing but do not overmix. The consistency should be well mixed, not too thick and not mushy. Chill, covered, for 8 to 10 hours. Place in a large greased baking pan. Bake, covered, at 400 degrees for 2 hours; remove the cover. Bake until brown and a knife inserted in the center comes out clean. Yield: 12 to 15 servings.

Corn Bread

2 cups self-rising cornmeal
1 cup self-rising flour
1 tablespoon sugar

1 egg
1 cup buttermilk
Melted shortening

Combine the cornmeal, flour and sugar in a bowl. Add the egg and buttermilk and mix well. Preheat a cast-iron skillet in a 400-degree oven. Pour in enough shortening to cover the bottom of the skillet. Pour the batter into the hot skillet. Bake for 30 to 35 minutes or until a knife inserted in the center comes out clean. Let stand until cool.

Myra Davis, Alabama Telco Credit Union

Macaroni and Cheese

12 to 16 ounces macaroni
1/4 cup (1/2 stick) margarine
Salt and pepper to taste
3 cups (or more) shredded
   Cheddar cheese

1 (12-ounce) can evaporated
   milk
1 egg, beaten

Cook the macaroni using package directions; drain. Add the margarine, salt and pepper. Stir in 1 cup of the cheese, evaporated milk and egg. Spoon about half the macaroni mixture into a baking pan sprayed with nonstick cooking spray. Sprinkle with half the remaining cheese. Top with the remaining macaroni mixture and remaining cheese. Bake at 365 degrees for 25 to 30 minutes or until golden brown. Yield: 6 to 8 servings.

Elizabeth S. Hatcher, Riverchase Council

Baked Rice

1/2 cup (1 stick) butter
1 (10-ounce) can French
   onion soup

1 (4-ounce) can mushrooms
1 cup uncooked rice
1/4 cup water

Melt the butter in a 2-quart baking dish. Stir in the soup, undrained mushrooms, rice and water. Bake, covered, at 350 degrees for 1 hour, stirring every 15 minutes. Yield: 4 to 6 servings.

Susan Y. May, Shoals Life Member Club

Tender Biscuit Rolls

2 1/4 cups baking mix
1 cup sour cream

1/2 cup (1 stick) butter, melted

Combine the baking mix, sour cream and butter in a bowl and mix well. Drop by spoonfuls into greased muffin cups. Bake at 400 degrees for 15 to 20 minutes or until golden. Yield: 1 dozen.

Hannah M. Segrest, Montgomery Life Member Club

Pumpkin Bread

4 cups sugar
4 cups canned pumpkin
1 cup vegetable oil
1 teaspoon vanilla extract
5 cups flour

4 teaspoons baking soda
4 teaspoons cinnamon
1 teaspoon salt
1 teaspoon ground cloves
1 cup chopped pecans

Combine the sugar, pumpkin, oil and vanilla in a large bowl and mix well. Sift in the flour, baking soda, cinnamon, salt and cloves and mix well. Stir in the pecans. Divide the batter among 4 greased coffee cans. Bake at 350 degrees for 1 hour or until the loaves test done. Remove to wire racks to cool. Serve with cream cheese. Yield: 4 loaves.

Vicki Weyerbacher, Birmingham South Cahaba Council

Apple Crunch

⅓ cup flour
¾ packed brown sugar

⅓ cup margarine
5 or 6 medium tart apples

Mix the flour and brown sugar in a bowl. Cut in the margarine until crumbly and set aside. Peel and thinly slice enough of the apples to measure 4 cups. Place the apple slices in a buttered 6x10-inch baking dish. Sprinkle the brown sugar mixture over the top. Bake at 375 degrees for 30 minutes or until the apples are tender and the topping is golden brown and crunchy. Yield: 5 servings.

Betty M. Jones-Moon, Birmingham Life Member Club

Apple Dumplings

2 Granny Smith apples
½ cup sugar
½ cup packed brown sugar
1 (8-count) can crescent rolls

½ cup sugar
½ cup packed brown sugar
1 cup orange juice
¼ cup (½ stick) margarine

Peel the apples, cut into quarters and discard the cores. Mix ½ cup sugar and ½ cup brown sugar in a shallow dish. Separate the roll dough into triangles. Roll each apple quarter in the sugar mixture and wrap in a triangle, sealing tightly. Arrange in a baking dish. Combine the remaining ½ cup sugar and ½ cup brown sugar in a saucepan. Blend in the orange juice and margarine. Heat until the sugars dissolve completely, stirring constantly. Pour over the wrapped apples. Bake at 350 degrees for 35 to 40 minutes or until the apples are tender. Yield: 8 servings.

Ila M. Skidmore, Shoals Life Member Club

Blueberry Fluff

2 cups self-rising flour
1 cup chopped pecans
1 cup (2 sticks) butter, melted
8 ounces cream cheese,
  softened

3 cups confectioners' sugar
1 envelope whipped topping
  mix
2 (21-ounce) cans blueberry
  pie filling

Mix the flour and pecans in a small bowl. Add the butter and mix well. Press evenly into a 9x13-inch baking dish. Bake at 350 degrees for 15 to 20 minutes or until golden brown. Let stand until completely cool. Cream the cream cheese and confectioners' sugar in a mixer bowl until light and fluffy. Prepare the whipped topping mix using package directions. Fold into the cream cheese mixture. Spread evenly over the cooled crust. Top with a layer of the pie filling. Chill until serving time. May substitute apple, strawberry or peach pie filling for the blueberry. Yield: 15 servings.

Kathryn Morgan, Gadsden Life Member Club

Praline Cheesecake

1 cup graham cracker crumbs

3 tablespoons sugar

3 tablespoons margarine,
  melted

24 ounces cream cheese,
  softened

1¼ cups packed dark brown
  sugar

2 tablespoons flour

3 eggs

1½ teaspoons vanilla extract

½ cup finely chopped pecans

Maple syrup

Pecan halves

Mix the crumbs and sugar in a bowl. Add the margarine and mix well. Press evenly over the bottom of a 9-inch springform pan. Bake at 350 degrees for 10 minutes. Combine the cream cheese, brown sugar and flour in a mixer bowl. Beat at medium speed until well blended. Add the eggs 1 at a time, beating well after each addition. Beat in the vanilla. Add chopped pecans and stir until well mixed. Pour over the crumb crust. Bake at 350 degrees for 50 to 55 minutes or until set. Cool for several minutes. Loosen the cheesecake from the side of the pan. Let stand until completely cooled. Remove the side of the pan. Chill until serving time. Brush the cheesecake with maple syrup and arrange the pecan halves decoratively over the top. Yield: 10 to 12 servings.

Kay Atkisson, Montgomery Life Member Club

Pumpkin Cheesecake

1¼ cups graham cracker
  crumbs
¼ cup sugar
1 teaspoon ground cinnamon
¼ cup (½ stick) butter,
  melted
32 ounces cream cheese,
  softened
1½ cups sugar

3 eggs
1 cup whipping cream
2 (16-ounce) cans pumpkin
2 teaspoons vanilla extract
1 tablespoon pumpkin pie
  spice
2 cups sour cream
½ cup sugar
2 teaspoons vanilla extract

Mix the crumbs, ¼ cup sugar and cinnamon in a bowl. Add the butter and mix well. Press the crumb mixture evenly over the bottom of a buttered 10-inch springform pan. Bake at 350 degrees for 10 minutes. Beat the cream cheese and 1½ cups sugar in a mixer bowl until light and fluffy. Add the eggs 1 at a time, beating well after each addition. Add the whipping cream, pumpkin, 2 teaspoons vanilla and the pumpkin pie spice and beat until well blended. Pour over the crust. Bake at 300 degrees for 1½ hours or until set. Cool in the pan for 10 minutes. Blend the sour cream, ½ cup sugar and 2 teaspoons vanilla in a bowl. Pour the sour cream mixture over the top. Let stand until completely cool. Loosen the cheesecake from the side of the pan. Remove the side of the pan. Chill until serving time. Yield: 10 to 12 servings.

Janet Hanel, Montgomery Life Member Club

Log Cabin Pudding

2 envelopes unflavored gelatin
1/3 cup cold water
1 cup maple syrup
2 cups milk

1 cup whipping cream
1 cup pecans, toasted,
  chopped
30 vanilla wafers, crushed

Sprinkle the gelatin over the cold water in a small saucepan. Let stand for 1 minute or until softened. Heat over low heat for 2 to 3 minutes or until dissolved, stirring constantly; do not boil. Remove from the heat and blend in the maple syrup. Pour the milk into a medium bowl. Blend in the gelatin mixture with a wire whisk. Place the bowl in a larger bowl of ice water and stir for 15 minutes or until the mixture thickens. Whip the whipping cream in a large bowl. Fold in the gelatin mixture. Fold in the pecans. Sprinkle half the vanilla wafer crumbs into a shallow 2½-quart dish. Spread the gelatin mixture over the crumbs and top with the remaining crumbs. Chill, covered, for 6 to 10 hours. Yield: 16 servings.

Brenda Reeves, Birmingham South Cahaba Council

Pumpkin Dessert

1 (2-layer) package yellow
  cake mix
1 egg
1/2 cup (1 stick) butter, melted
1 cup canned pumpkin
2 eggs

1/2 cup packed brown sugar
2/3 cup evaporated milk
2 teaspoons cinnamon
1/4 teaspoon nutmeg
1/2 cup sugar
1/4 cup (1/2 stick) butter, melted

Reserve 1 cup of the cake mix for topping. Combine the remaining cake mix, 1 egg and ½ cup butter in a bowl and mix well. Press over the bottom and partway up the sides of a 9x13-inch baking pan. Combine the next 6 ingredients in a medium bowl and mix well. Pour into the prepared pan. Combine the reserved cake mix with the sugar and ¼ cup butter in a small bowl and mix until crumbly. Sprinkle over the pumpkin mixture. Bake at 350 degrees for 1 hour. Yield: 10 to 12 servings.

Milly Frakes, Montgomery Council

Holiday Pumpkin Treats

1 1/4 cups flour
1/4 cup sugar
1/4 cup packed brown sugar
1 cup (2 sticks) butter
1 cup chopped nuts
1 (27-ounce) jar mincemeat
1 (16-ounce) can pumpkin

1 (14-ounce) can sweetened
    condensed milk
2 eggs
1 teaspoon cinnamon
1/2 teaspoon allspice
1/2 teaspoon salt

Mix the flour, sugar and brown sugar in a bowl. Cut in the butter until crumbly. Mix in the nuts. Reserve 1 1/2 cups of the mixture for topping. Press the remaining mixture over the bottom and halfway up the sides of a 9x13-inch baking pan. Spread with the mincemeat. Combine the pumpkin, condensed milk, eggs, cinnamon, allspice and salt in a bowl and blend well. Pour over the mincemeat. Top with the reserved crumb mixture. Bake at 425 degrees for 15 minutes. Reduce the oven temperature to 350 degrees. Bake for 40 minutes longer or until golden brown around the edges. Cool for several minutes. Cut into squares. Serve warm or at room temperature. Store the leftovers in the refrigerator. Yield: 10 to 12 servings.

Susan Currie, Birmingham South Cahaba Council

Fresh Apple Cake

1 1/2 cups vegetable oil
1 1/2 cups sugar
1 teaspoon vanilla extract
3 eggs

3 cups flour
1 teaspoon baking soda
3 cups finely chopped apples
1 cup nuts (optional)

Combine the oil, sugar, vanilla and eggs in a large bowl and mix well. Add a mixture of the flour and baking soda and mix well. Stir in the apples and nuts. Pour into a greased bundt pan. Bake at 350 degrees for 1 hour. Cool in the pan for 10 to 15 minutes. Invert onto a wire rack to cool completely. Yield: 16 servings.

Lillian Weaver, Huntsville Council

Autumn Apple Cake

2 cups sugar	1 teaspoon baking soda
1⅓ cups vegetable oil	½ teaspoon baking powder
2 eggs, beaten	½ teaspoon salt
1 large banana, mashed	3 cups finely chopped apples
1 tablespoon vanilla extract	½ cup chopped pecans
3 cups sifted flour	Cream Cheese Frosting

Combine the sugar and oil in a large bowl and blend well. Add the eggs, banana and vanilla and mix well. Mix the flour, baking soda, baking powder and salt together. Add to the banana mixture and mix well. Stir in the apples and pecans. The batter will be stiff. Divide the batter among 3 greased and floured cake pans. Bake at 350 degrees for 30 to 40 minutes or until the layers test done. Cool in the pans for 10 minutes. Remove to wire racks to cool completely. Spread Cream Cheese Frosting between the layers and over the top and side of the cake. Yield: 12 servings.

Cream Cheese Frosting

½ cup (1 stick) margarine, softened	1 teaspoon vanilla extract
8 ounces cream cheese, softened	1½ cups sifted confectioners' sugar
	1 cup finely chopped pecans

Beat the margarine and cream cheese in a mixer bowl until light and fluffy. Beat in the vanilla. Add the confectioners' sugar and beat until smooth. Stir in the pecans.

Betty M. Jones-Moon, Birmingham Life Member Club

Brandied Fresh Apple Cake

2 cups flour	2 eggs
1½ teaspoons salt	2 cups sugar
1 teaspoon nutmeg	1 teaspoon vanilla extract
1 teaspoon cinnamon	½ cup apricot brandy
1 teaspoon baking soda	2 cups chopped apples
1¼ cups vegetable oil	1 cup nuts

Combine the flour, salt, nutmeg, cinnamon and baking soda in a large bowl and mix well. Combine the oil, eggs, sugar, vanilla and brandy in a bowl and mix well. Stir in the apples and nuts. Pour the apple mixture into the flour mixture and mix well. The batter will be stiff. Pour into a lightly greased 9x13-inch cake pan. Bake at 350 degrees for 45 minutes or until the cake tests done.
Yield: 15 servings.

Brenda Reeves, Birmingham South Cahaba Council

Jewish Apple Cake

2 cups sugar	2 teaspoons baking powder
1½ cups vegetable oil	1 teaspoon baking soda
2 eggs	1 teaspoon salt
1 teaspoon vanilla extract	3 cups chopped apples
2½ cups sifted flour	1 cup chopped pecans

Combine the sugar, oil, eggs and vanilla in a large bowl and beat until well blended. Sift in the flour, baking powder, baking soda and salt and beat well. Stir in the apples and pecans. Pour into a greased and floured 9x13-inch cake pan. Bake at 350 degrees for 1 hour or until the cake tests done. Serve warm topped with ice cream or whipped topping. Yield: 15 servings.

Judy Howard, Riverchase Council

Blackberry Cake

2 cups blackberries	2 teaspoons baking soda
1 cup shortening	1/2 teaspoon salt
2 cups sugar	1 teaspoon ground cloves
2 eggs	1 teaspoon cinnamon
1 teaspoon vanilla extract	1 cup raisins
3 cups flour	1 cup chopped pecans

Put the blackberries through a food mill to remove the seeds and set aside. Cream the sugar and shortening in a mixer bowl until light and fluffy. Add the eggs and vanilla and beat until smooth. Combine the flour, baking soda, salt, cloves and cinnamon and mix well. Add to the creamed mixture alternately with the blackberry pulp, mixing well after each addition. Stir in the raisins and pecans. Pour the batter into a greased and floured bundt or tube pan. Bake at 300 degrees for 1 hour and 25 minutes or until the cake tests done. Cool in the pan for 10 to 15 minutes. Invert onto a wire rack to cool completely. Yield: 15 servings

Joann Ford, Anniston Council

Mandarin Orange Cake

1 (2-layer) package yellow cake mix	1 (4- to 6-ounce) package vanilla instant pudding mix
1 (11-ounce) can mandarin oranges	1 (20-ounce) can crushed pineapple, drained
1 cup vegetable oil	16 ounces whipped topping
4 eggs	

Beat the cake mix, undrained mandarin oranges, oil and eggs in a large mixer bowl until well mixed. Pour into 4 greased and floured layer cake pans. Bake at 350 degrees for 15 minutes or until the layers test done. Cool in the pans for 10 minutes. Cool on wire racks. Combine the remaining ingredients in a large bowl and mix well. Spread between the cake layers and over the top and side of the cake. Chill until serving time. Yield: 12 to 16 servings.

Mona Burdick, Montgomery Council

Butternut Cake

1 cup shortening
2 cups sugar
4 eggs
2½ cups sifted all-purpose
  flour
½ cup self-rising flour

½ teaspoon baking powder
1 cup milk
1 tablespoon butternut
  flavoring
Butternut Frosting

Combine the shortening, sugar and eggs in a large mixer bowl. Beat at high speed for 10 minutes. Add 1 cup of the all-purpose flour. Beat at medium speed for 1 minute. Add the remaining 1½ cups all-purpose flour, self-rising flour, baking powder and milk. Beat for 1 minute. Stir in the flavoring. Divide the batter among 3 greased and floured cake pans. Bake at 350 degrees until the layers test done. Cool in the pans for 10 minutes. Remove to wire racks to cool completely. Spread the Butternut Frosting between the layers and over the top and side of the cake. Yield: 12 servings.

Butternut Frosting

½ cup (1 stick) margarine,
  softened
8 ounces cream cheese,
  softened
1 tablespoon butternut
  flavoring

1 (1-pound) package
  confectioners' sugar
1 cup chopped pecans

Cream the margarine and cream cheese in a mixer bowl until light and fluffy. Add the flavoring and confectioners' sugar. Beat until smooth and creamy. Stir in the pecans.

Ramona Minor, Montgomery Council

Carrot Cake

2 cups sugar	1 teaspoon salt
1½ cups vegetable oil	1 teaspoon cinnamon
4 eggs	2 cups grated carrots
2 cups cake flour	1 cup chopped pecans
1 teaspoon baking soda	Cream Cheese Frosting

Combine the sugar, oil and eggs in a large bowl and beat until well blended. Mix the flour, baking soda, salt and cinnamon together. Add to the sugar mixture and mix well. Stir in the carrots and pecans. Pour into 3 greased and floured cake pans. Bake at 350 degrees for 25 to 30 minutes or until the layers test done. Cool in the pans for 10 minutes. Remove to wire racks to cool completely. Spread Cream Cheese Frosting between the layers and over the top and side of the cake. Top with additional pecans. Yield: 12 servings.

Cream Cheese Frosting

½ cup (1 stick) margarine, softened	2 teaspoons vanilla extract
8 ounces cream cheese, softened	1 (1-pound) package confectioners' sugar

Beat the margarine, cream cheese and vanilla in a mixer bowl until well blended. Add the confectioners' sugar and beat until smooth and creamy.

Mrs. Bob H. Henson, Birmingham South Life Member Club

Not the Usual Fruitcakes

2½ cups sugar
2 cups flour
2½ teaspoons baking powder
1 teaspoon ground cloves
1 teaspoon cinnamon
½ teaspoon salt
8 ounces pitted prunes,
   finely chopped

1 cup cranberries
4 ounces dried apricots, finely
   chopped
¾ cup chopped pecans
1 cup vegetable oil
2 (4-ounce) jars strained baby
   food plums with tapioca
3 eggs

Grease two 6-cup fluted tube pans generously. Sprinkle each pan with ¼ cup of the sugar and tilt and rotate the pans to coat well with the sugar; shake out the excess sugar and set the pans aside. Combine the remaining 2 cups sugar, flour, baking powder, cloves, cinnamon and salt in a large bowl. Add the prunes, cranberries, apricots and pecans and mix with a wooden spoon until the fruit is coated with the flour mixture. Combine the oil, baby food plums and eggs in a medium bowl and whisk until well blended. Add to the flour mixture and mix with the wooden spoon just until well mixed. Divide the batter between the prepared pans. Bake at 375 degrees for 50 to 60 minutes or until the cakes pull from the sides of the pans and a wooden pick inserted in the center comes out clean. Let stand in the pans on wire racks until completely cooled. Loosen the cakes from the sides of the pans and invert onto the wire racks. Store the cakes in airtight containers at room temperature for up to 1 week or in the freezer for up to 3 months. May bake in one 12-cup tube pan for 1 hour and 20 minutes.
Yield: 12 to 16 servings.

Judy Buster, Riverchase Council

Old-Fashioned Three-Pound Fruitcake

⅔ cup butter, softened
⅔ cup packed brown sugar
2 eggs
1½ cups flour
1 teaspoon baking powder
½ teaspoon baking soda
2 teaspoons cinnamon
½ teaspoon salt
1 cup fruit juice or water
¼ cup molasses

8 ounces candied pineapple
8 ounces candied red cherries
4 ounces candied green
    cherries
4 ounces candied lemon peel
4 ounces candied orange peel
4 ounces candied citron
1 cup raisins
½ cup chopped pecans
½ cup flour

Grease a tube pan or large loaf pan generously and line with waxed paper. Cream the butter and brown sugar in a large mixer bowl until light and fluffy. Add the eggs and beat until blended. Sift 1½ cups flour, baking powder, baking soda, cinnamon and salt together. Add to the creamed mixture alternately with the fruit juice, mixing well after each addition. Mix in the molasses. Combine the candied fruit, raisins and pecans in a bowl. Add ½ cup flour and mix until well coated. Stir into the batter. Spoon into the prepared pan. Bake at 275 degrees for 2 to 3 hours or until a wooden pick inserted in the center comes out clean. A pan of water placed in the oven during baking will provide for a moister fruitcake. Cool the fruitcake in the pan on a wire rack. Invert onto the wire rack. Store in an airtight container. May substitute mixed candied fruit for the individual candied fruit. Yield: 16 servings.

Louise Morrison, Tuscaloosa Council

Caramel Pound Cake

1 cup (2 sticks) butter,
   softened
1/2 cup shortening
1 (1-pound) package dark
   brown sugar
1 cup sugar
5 eggs

3 cups flour
1/2 teaspoon baking powder
1 cup milk
1 teaspoon vanilla extract
1 cup chopped nuts
Caramel Icing

Cream the butter, shortening, brown sugar and sugar in a large mixer bowl until light and fluffy. Add the eggs 1 at a time, beating well after each addition. Sift the flour and baking powder together. Add to the creamed mixture alternately with the milk, beating well after each addition. Beat in the vanilla. Stir in the nuts. Pour into greased and floured tube pan. Bake at 325 degrees for 1 1/2 hours or until the cake tests done. Cool in the pan for 10 to 15 minutes. Invert onto a serving plate. Pour the hot icing over the warm cake. Yield: 16 servings.

Caramel Icing

1 1/2 cups packed light brown
   sugar
1 cup sugar
1 cup (2 sticks) butter

1/2 cup evaporated milk
1 teaspoon vanilla extract
10 large marshmallows

Combine the brown sugar, sugar, butter and evaporated milk in a saucepan. Heat until the butter melts and the mixture is well blended, stirring constantly. Bring to a boil. Boil for 5 minutes. Remove from heat. Stir in the vanilla. Place the marshmallows in a large mixer bowl. Add the hot mixture and beat until smooth.

Catherine M. Martin, Birmingham Metro Council

Pumpkin Cake

2 cups sugar
4 eggs
1 cup vegetable oil
2 cups sifted flour
2 teaspoons baking soda

2 teaspoons cinnamon
½ teaspoon salt
1 (16-ounce) can pumpkin
Cream Cheese Frosting

Combine the sugar and eggs in a large mixer bowl and beat until blended. Add the oil and beat for 1 minute. Sift in the flour, baking soda, cinnamon and salt. Beat until blended. Stir in the pumpkin. Pour into 3 greased and floured 8-inch cake pans. Bake at 350 degrees for 25 minutes or until the layers test done. Cool in the pans for 10 minutes. Remove to a wire rack to cool completely. Spread the Cream Cheese Frosting between the layers and over the top and side of the cake. Yield: 12 servings.

Cream Cheese Frosting

8 ounces cream cheese,
   softened
½ cup (1 stick) butter,
   softened

1 (1-pound) package
   confectioners' sugar
2 teaspoons vanilla extract
1 cup chopped pecans

Beat the cream cheese and butter in a mixer bowl until blended. Add the confectioners' sugar and vanilla and beat until smooth and creamy. Stir in the pecans.

Kay R. (Tom) Mingus, Opelika Life Member Club

Pumpkin Cake Roll

3 eggs
1 cup sugar
2/3 cup canned pumpkin
1 teaspoon lemon juice
2/3 cup flour
1 teaspoon baking powder
1/2 teaspoon salt
2 teaspoons cinnamon
1/2 teaspoon pumpkin pie spice

1/2 teaspoon nutmeg
1 cup chopped pecans
Confectioners' sugar
8 ounces cream cheese,
  softened
1/4 cup (1/2 stick) butter,
  softened
2 teaspoons vanilla extract
1 cup confectioners' sugar

Beat the eggs in a large mixer bowl. Beat in the sugar gradually. Add the pumpkin and lemon juice and beat until blended. Combine flour, baking powder, salt, cinnamon, pumpkin pie spice and nutmeg in a bowl and mix well. Add to the pumpkin mixture and beat until blended. Spread the batter evenly in a greased 10x15-inch cake pan. Sprinkle with the pecans. Bake at 325 degrees for 15 minutes. Invert the cake onto a tea towel sprinkled generously with confectioners' sugar. Roll as for a jelly roll in the tea towel. Let stand until completely cool. Combine the cream cheese, butter, vanilla and 1 cup confectioners' sugar in a small bowl and beat until smooth and creamy. Unroll the cake carefully. Spread with the cream cheese mixture and reroll. Place seam side down on a serving plate. Chill, covered, until serving time.
Yield: 8 to 12 servings.

Ann Sellers, Tuscaloosa Council

Yam Cake Roll

3 eggs	½ teaspoon nutmeg
1 cup sugar	1 cup finely chopped nuts
⅔ cup mashed yams	Confectioners' sugar
1 teaspoon lemon juice	6 ounces cream cheese,
¾ cup flour	softened
1 teaspoon baking powder	¼ cup (½ stick) butter,
½ teaspoon salt	softened
2 teaspoons cinnamon	½ teaspoon vanilla extract
1 teaspoon ginger	1 cup confectioners' sugar

Beat the eggs in a large mixer bowl for 5 minutes. Beat in the sugar gradually. Stir in the yams and lemon juice. Mix the flour, baking powder, salt, cinnamon, ginger and nutmeg together. Fold into the egg mixture. Spread the batter evenly in a greased and floured 10x15-inch cake pan. Sprinkle with the nuts. Bake at 375 degrees for 15 minutes. Invert the cake onto a tea towel sprinkled generously with confectioners' sugar. Roll as for a jelly roll in the tea towel. Let stand until completely cooled. Combine the cream cheese, butter and vanilla in a small mixer bowl and beat until blended. Beat in 1 cup confectioners' sugar until smooth and creamy. Unroll the cake carefully. Spread with the cream cheese mixture to within 1 inch of the edges and reroll. Place seam side down on a serving plate. Chill for 2 to 3 hours before serving.
Yield: 8 to 12 servings.

Judy Howard, Riverchase Council

Chess Squares

1 (2-layer) package yellow
  cake mix
½ cup (1 stick) butter,
  softened
1 egg
1 package chopped pecans

8 ounces cream cheese,
  softened
2 eggs
1 (1-pound) package
  confectioners' sugar

Combine the cake mix, butter and 1 egg in a large bowl and mix until crumbly. Mix in the pecans. Pat into a 9x13-inch baking pan. Combine the cream cheese and 2 eggs in a mixer bowl and beat until blended. Add the confectioners' sugar and beat until smooth. Spread over the pecan layer. Bake at 350 degrees for 20 to 30 minutes or until light golden brown. Let stand until cool. Cut into squares. Yield: 2 to 3 dozen squares.

Susan Deal, Birmingham South Cahaba Council

Holiday Oatmeal Cookies

1 cup quick-cooking oats
¾ cup flour
½ teaspoon baking soda
½ teaspoon salt
½ cup packed brown sugar

¼ cup sugar
½ cup shortening
1 egg
½ teaspoon vanilla extract

Combine the oats, flour, baking soda, salt, brown sugar and sugar in a large mixer bowl. Add the shortening, egg and vanilla. Beat with a mixer at medium speed until well mixed, scraping the bowl occasionally. Drop by spoonfuls 1 inch apart onto a nonstick cookie sheet. Bake at 375 degrees for 12 minutes or until light brown. Cool on cookie sheet for 2 minutes. Remove to a wire rack to cool. Yield: 4 dozen cookies.

JoAnn Thomas, Selma Life Member Club

Praline Cookies

1 egg, beaten
6 tablespoons butter, melted
1¼ cups packed dark brown
  sugar

1 teaspoon vanilla extract
1 cup plus 2 tablespoons flour
¼ teaspoon salt
1¼ cups pecan halves

Combine the egg, butter, brown sugar and vanilla in a bowl and mix well. Add the flour and salt and mix well. Stir in the pecans. Drop by tablespoonfuls onto a greased cookie sheet. Bake at 350 degrees for 10 minutes. Cool on cookie sheet for 1 to 2 minutes. Remove to a wire rack to cool completely.
Yield: 1 to 2 dozen cookies.

Diana Shepherd, Birmingham South Cahaba Council

Pumpkin Cookies

1 cup sugar
¾ cup vegetable oil
1½ cups mashed cooked
  pumpkin
2¼ cups flour
4 teaspoons baking powder
¼ teaspoon salt

1 teaspoon cinnamon
¼ teaspoon ginger
¼ teaspoon nutmeg
½ teaspoon vanilla extract
1 cup raisins
1 cup pecans

Combine the sugar and oil in a large bowl and mix well. Add the pumpkin and mix until blended. Add the flour, baking powder, salt and spices and mix well. Stir in the vanilla, raisins and pecans. Drop by teaspoonfuls onto a lightly greased cookie sheet. Bake at 350 degrees for 10 minutes or until golden brown. Cool on cookie sheet for 1 to 2 minutes. Remove to a wire rack to cool completely.
Yield: 3 dozen cookies.

Alice Walski, Birmingham Life Member Club

Egg Custard Pie

1½ cups milk
2 tablespoons plus 2 teaspoons
  butter
3 eggs

¾ cup sugar
1 tablespoon flour
1 teaspoon vanilla extract
1 unbaked (9-inch) pie shell

Scald the milk in a saucepan. Add the butter and stir until melted. Beat the eggs, sugar, flour and vanilla in a bowl until well blended. Stir a small amount of the hot mixture into the egg mixture. Stir the egg mixture into the hot mixture. Pour into the pie shell. Bake at 375 degrees for 25 minutes or until the center is set.
Yield: 8 servings.

Masinah S. Hawkins, Birmingham Life Member Club

Fruit Pie

1½ cups apple slices, peach
  slices or blueberries
1 cup water
3 tablespoons cornstarch
4 teaspoons artificial
  sweetener

1 teaspoon ground cinnamon
⅓ cup water
1 tablespoon lemon juice
1 tablespoon margarine
1 recipe (2-crust) pie pastry

Combine the apple slices and 1 cup water in a saucepan. Bring to a boil. Boil for 2 minutes. Blend the cornstarch, sweetener and cinnamon in ⅓ cup water and add the lemon juice. Stir into the apple mixture. Cook until thickened, stirring constantly. Add the margarine. Pour into a pastry-lined pie plate. Top with the remaining pastry, sealing the edge and cutting vents. Bake at 350 degrees until brown. Yield: 6 servings.

Christine Diggs, Gadsden Life Member Club

Peanut Butter Pie

¾ cup chocolate fudge topping
1 (9-inch) graham cracker
  pie shell
8 ounces whipped topping

½ cup creamy peanut butter
1¼ cups cold milk
2 (4-ounce) packages vanilla
  instant pudding mix

Spoon half the fudge topping into the pie shell. Spread with half
the whipped topping. Freeze for 10 minutes. Blend the peanut
butter and milk in a large bowl. Add the pudding mixes. Whisk for
2 minutes or until blended. Blend in the remaining whipped
topping. Spread over the whipped topping in the pie shell. Chill for
3 hours or until set. Drizzle the remaining fudge topping over the
top. Yield: 8 servings.

Eula Mae Watson, Gadsden Life Member Club

Pecan Pie

3 eggs, beaten
½ cup sugar
1 cup light corn syrup
¼ cup (½ stick) butter,
  melted

¼ teaspoon salt
1 cup chopped pecans
1 unbaked (9-inch) pie shell

Combine the eggs, sugar, corn syrup, butter and salt in a bowl and
mix until blended. Stir in the pecans. Pour into the pie shell. Bake
at 425 degrees for 10 minutes. Reduce the oven temperature to 350
degrees. Bake for 40 minutes longer or until set. May use 1 cup
sugar, ½ cup light corn syrup and omit the salt. Yield: 6 servings.

Susan Y. May, Shoals Life Member Club
Linda Wong, Birmingham South Cahaba Council

Sunday Pecan Pie

2 eggs, beaten
1/2 cup sugar
1 cup corn syrup
2 tablespoons flour
2 tablespoons margarine,
  melted

1 tablespoon milk
1 tablespoon vanilla extract
1 cup pecans
1 unbaked (9-inch) pie shell

Combine the eggs, sugar, corn syrup, flour, margarine, milk and vanilla in a bowl and mix well. Stir in the pecans. Pour into the pie shell. Bake at 350 degrees for 1 hour or until set. Yield: 6 servings.

Gail Davis, Montgomery Council

Company Pecan Pie

1/2 cup sugar
1 cup corn syrup
3 eggs, beaten
3 tablespoons margarine,
  melted

1/2 teaspoon salt
1 teaspoon vanilla extract
1 cup pecans
1 unbaked (9-inch) pie shell

Blend the sugar and corn syrup in a bowl. Add the eggs, margarine, salt and vanilla and mix well. Pour into the pie shell. Bake at 325 degrees for 50 minutes or until set. Yield: 6 servings.

Marjorie S. (Francis) Tucker, Selma Life Member Club

Pecan Tarts

¾ cup sugar
1 tablespoon cornstarch
1 cup corn syrup
3 eggs, beaten
1 teaspoon vanilla extract

1 cup chopped pecans
2 (4-count) packages frozen
   party pie shells
Melted butter

Mix the sugar and cornstarch in a bowl. Add the corn syrup and blend well. Add the eggs and vanilla and mix well. Fill each small shell about half full. Add 2 tablespoons pecans to each and stir carefully. Top each with a small amount of melted butter. Bake at 400 degrees for 10 minutes. Reduce the oven temperature to 300 degrees. Bake for 30 minutes longer or until set. Yield: 8 tarts.

Catherine M. Martin, Birmingham Metro Council

Double-Layer Pumpkin Pie

4 ounces cream cheese,
   softened
1 tablespoon milk or half-and-
   half
1 tablespoon sugar
1½ cups whipped topping
¼ cup chopped pecans
1 (9-inch) graham cracker
   pie shell

1 cup cold milk or
   half-and-half
1 (16-ounce) can pumpkin
2 (4-ounce) packages vanilla
   instant pudding mix
1 teaspoon cinnamon
½ teaspoon ginger
¼ teaspoon ground cloves

Combine the cream cheese, 1 tablespoon milk and sugar in a small bowl and whisk until smooth. Stir in the whipped topping gently. Mix in the pecans. Spread in the pie shell. Combine 1 cup milk, pumpkin, pudding mix and spices in a large bowl and beat until smooth and well mixed. Spread over the cream cheese layer. Chill, covered, for 4 hours or until set. Garnish with additional whipped topping. Yield: 8 servings.

Betty Etheredge, Bon Secour Life Member Club

Pumpkin Chiffon Pie

1½ cups mashed cooked   1 envelope unflavored gelatin
    pumpkin   ¼ cup cold water
½ cup milk   3 egg whites
½ cup sugar   ½ cup sugar
3 egg yolks, beaten   1 teaspoon vanilla extract
2 teaspoons pumpkin pie spice   1 (9-inch) graham cracker
⅛ teaspoon salt   pie shell

Combine the pumpkin, milk, ½ cup sugar, egg yolks, pumpkin pie spice and salt in a saucepan and mix well. Cook over low heat until thickened, stirring constantly. Soften the gelatin in the cold water. Add to the hot pumpkin mixture and stir until dissolved. Let stand until cool. Beat the egg whites in a mixer bowl until soft peaks form. Add ½ cup sugar gradually, beating constantly until stiff peaks form. Fold the egg whites and vanilla into the pumpkin mixture. Pour into the pie shell. Chill until firm. Serve with whipped cream. Yield: 7 servings.

Betty Yancy, Birmingham Life Member Club

*For perfectly shaped pancakes every time, use a meat baster
to squeeze your pancake batter onto the hot griddle.*

Sweet Tater Pie

½ cup (1 stick) butter,
   softened
1 cup sugar
2 eggs, beaten
½ cup evaporated milk

2 cups mashed cooked sweet
   potatoes
1 teaspoon vanilla extract
¼ teaspoon salt
1 unbaked (9-inch) pie shell

Cream the butter and sugar in a large bowl. Add the eggs, evaporated milk, sweet potatoes, vanilla and salt and mix well. Pour into the pie shell. Bake at 375 degrees for 40 minutes or until set. Yield: 6 servings.

Susan Poe, Riverchase Council

Sweet Potato Pie

2 eggs
1 cup sugar
1 teaspoon salt
⅛ teaspoon nutmeg
1 teaspoon cinnamon

1 cup milk
2 tablespoons butter, melted
1½ cups mashed cooked sweet
   potatoes
1 unbaked (8-inch) pie shell

Beat the eggs in a bowl. Add the sugar, salt, nutmeg, cinnamon and milk and mix well. Blend the butter into the sweet potatoes. Add to the egg mixture and mix well. Pour into the pie shell. Bake at 450 degrees for 10 minutes. Reduce the oven temperature to 350 degrees. Bake for 30 to 40 minutes longer or until set. Store in the refrigerator. Yield: 6 servings.

Brenda Reeves, Birmingham South Cahaba Council

Sweet Potato Pies

1 (14-ounce) can sweetened
　condensed milk
2 cups mashed cooked sweet
　potatoes
2 cups sugar
3 eggs, beaten

½ cup (1 stick) margarine,
　melted
1 teaspoon vanilla extract
1 teaspoon cinnamon
2 unbaked (9-inch) pie shells

Combine the condensed milk, sweet potatoes, sugar, eggs, margarine, vanilla and cinnamon in a large bowl and mix until blended. Pour into the pie shells. Bake at 350 degrees for 30 to 45 minutes or until set. Yield: 12 servings.

Marjorie S. (Francis) Tucker, Selma Life Member Club

Southern Sweet Potato Pie

¾ cup sugar
½ teaspoon salt
1 teaspoon cinnamon
1 teaspoon ginger
½ teaspoon ground cloves
2 cups mashed cooked hot
　sweet potatoes

2 tablespoons butter
3 eggs
1¼ cups milk
1 tablespoon grated lemon zest
1 unbaked (9-inch) pie shell

Combine the sugar, salt, cinnamon, ginger and cloves in a large bowl. Add the hot sweet potatoes and butter and mix well. Let stand until cool. Add the eggs and beat until blended. Stir in the milk and lemon zest. Pour into the pie shell. Bake at 400 degrees for 40 to 50 minutes or until set. Yield: 8 servings.

Joann Ford, Anniston Council

Cheese Dip

1 pound ground beef
32 ounces Velveeta cheese,
  cubed

8 ounces Mexican Velveeta
  cheese, cubed
Salsa

Brown the ground beef in a skillet, stirring until crumbly; drain.
Combine the ground beef, the cheese cubes and the salsa in a slow
cooker. Cook on Low until the cheese is melted. Serve with tostado
chips. Yield: 20 to 30 servings.

Diana Casey, Alabama Telco Credit Union

Corn Dip

1 (12-ounce) can Mexican
  corn, drained
8 ounces Cheddar cheese,
  shredded

½ cup sour cream
½ cup mayonnaise
½ cup chopped green onions
½ teaspoon salt

Combine the corn, cheese, sour cream, mayonnaise, green onions
and salt in a bowl and mix well. Chill, covered, until serving time.
Serve with butter crackers. Yield: 10 servings.

Sue (Joe) Small, Selma Life Member Club

Cheese Ball

16 ounces cream cheese,
  softened
2 teaspoons seasoned salt
2 tablespoons chopped bell
  pepper

2 tablespoons chopped onion
¼ cup drained crushed
  pineapple
1 cup chopped pecans or sliced
  almonds

Mix the cream cheese and seasoned salt in a bowl. Add the bell
pepper, onion and pineapple and mix well. Shape into a ball. Roll
in the pecans. Chill, covered, for several hours. Serve with
crackers. Yield: 20 to 25 servings.

Donna McNulty, Riverchase Council

Shrimp and Cheese Ball

1 package shredded Cheddar
  or Colby cheese
Crushed parsley
1 can chopped shrimp
3 ounces cream cheese,
  softened

¼ cup chopped pecans
1 small garlic clove, chopped
1 teaspoon lemon juice
1 teaspoon A.1. steak sauce
Paprika to taste

Spray a sheet of waxed paper with nonstick cooking spray. Sprinkle half the Cheddar cheese and the parsley on the waxed paper and set aside. Mix the shrimp, cream cheese and remaining Cheddar cheese in a bowl. Add the pecans and the garlic gradually and mix well. Add the lemon juice and steak sauce and mix well. Shape into a ball. Roll in the Cheddar cheese mixture on the waxed paper. Chill, covered, overnight. Sprinkle with paprika just before serving. Serve with wheat or butter crackers. Yield: 8 to 10 servings.

Helen Smith, Birmingham Metro Council

Cheese Logs

8 ounces mild Cheddar
  cheese, shredded
8 ounces medium Cheddar
  cheese, shredded
8 ounces sharp Cheddar
  cheese, shredded

8 ounces cream cheese,
  softened
Garlic salt or garlic powder
  to taste
Chopped pecans
Chili powder

Combine the Cheddar cheese and cream cheese in a bowl and blend well. Mix in the garlic salt and pecans. Shape into logs. Sprinkle the chili powder on waxed paper. Roll the cheese logs in the chili powder. Yield: 20 to 30 servings.

Jennifer McAllister, Birmingham South Cahaba Council

Texas Cheese Roll

2 to 3 jalapeño chiles
16 ounces Velveeta cheese
8 ounces cream cheese,
   softened

1 envelope onion soup mix
½ cup chopped pecans

Chop the jalapeños; do not drain. Place the Velveeta cheese between sheets of waxed paper and roll ½ inch thick. Remove the top sheet of waxed paper. Spread the cream cheese over the Velveeta cheese. Combine the soup mix, pecans and undrained jalapeños in a bowl and mix well. Spread over the cream cheese. Roll as for a jelly roll. Chill, covered, until firm. Cut into slices. Serve with crackers. Yield: 12 to 15 servings.

Earline Weaver, Shoals Life Member Club

Olive Spread

1 cup chopped salad olives
6 ounces cream cheese,
   softened

½ cup mayonnaise
½ cup chopped pecans
⅛ teaspoon pepper, or to taste

Drain the olives, reserving 2 tablespoons of the liquid. Combine the cream cheese and mayonnaise in a bowl and mash with a fork. Add the olives, reserved liquid, pecans and pepper and mix well. Spoon into a 1-pint jar. Chill, covered, for 24 hours. Serve with butter crackers or use as a sandwich spread on toasted white bread. Yield: 20 to 30 servings.

Betty Yancy, Birmingham Life Member Club

Christmas "Catsup" Cranberry Sauce

1 (16-ounce) can jellied
  cranberry sauce or whole
  cranberry sauce
3/4 cup sugar
1/4 cup white vinegar
1/4 teaspoon cinnamon

1/8 teaspoon pepper
1 tablespoon minced fresh
  gingerroot
1 tablespoon flour
2 tablespoons water

Combine the cranberry sauce, sugar, vinegar, cinnamon, pepper and gingerroot in a medium saucepan and mix well. Combine the flour and water in a small bowl, stirring until smooth. Stir into the cranberry sauce mixture. Bring to a boil, stirring constantly; reduce the heat. Simmer for 5 minutes or until thickened and bubbly. Remove from the heat and let cool. Store in an airtight container in the refrigerator. Serve with cream cheese and gourmet crackers or with meat. Yield: 2 cups.

Mary Smith and Donna Frederick,
Birmingham South Cahaba Council

Pepper Jelly

1/4 cup chopped seeded green
  chiles or hot red chiles
1 1/2 cups chopped green bell
  peppers

6 1/2 cups sugar
1 1/2 cups vinegar
1 bottle pectin

Grind the green chiles and green peppers. Combine the ground peppers, sugar and vinegar in a saucepan. Boil for 3 minutes. Add the pectin and boil for 1 minute. Let stand for 5 minutes. Pour into hot sterilized jars; seal with 2-piece lids. Process in a boiling water bath for 10 minutes. Serve on butter crackers spread with cream cheese or serve with meat. *Note:* Wear rubber gloves when working with the chiles. Yield: 3 to 4 pints.

Joyce Thomas, Birmingham South Cahaba Council

Cheese Wafers

1 cup (2 sticks) margarine,
  softened
2 cups flour
2 cups shredded mild Cheddar
  cheese

1 teaspoon salt
⅛ teaspoon Tabasco sauce, or
  to taste
2 cups crisp rice cereal

Combine the margarine, flour, cheese, salt and Tabasco sauce in a
bowl and mix well. Work in the cereal. Shape into tiny balls and
place on baking sheets. Flatten with a fork. Bake at 325 degrees for
8 to 10 minutes or until crisp. Yield: 7 to 8 dozen.

Doris Dean, Birmingham Life Member Club

Olive Appetizers

1 small bottle pimento-stuffed
  olives
2 tablespoons butter, softened
6 ounces cream cheese,
  softened

1 cup (about) finely chopped
  pecans

Drain the olives and place on paper towels to drain completely.
Cream the butter and cream cheese in a mixer bowl. Press a small
amount of the cream cheese mixture around each olive, completely
covering the olive. Roll in the pecans. Chill overnight. Cut into
halves to serve. Yield: 15 to 20 servings.

Mary Smith and Donna Frederick,
Birmingham South Cahaba Council

Ranch Pinwheels

16 ounces cream cheese,
softened
1 package ranch salad
dressing mix
2 green onions, minced
4 (12-inch) flour tortillas
1 (4-ounce) jar chopped
pimentos, drained,
patted dry

1 (4-ounce) can chopped
green chiles, drained,
patted dry
1 (2-ounce) can sliced black
olives, drained, patted dry

Mix the cream cheese, salad dressing mix and green onions in a bowl. Spread on each tortilla. Sprinkle the pimentos, green chiles and olives over the cream cheese mixture. Roll the tortillas up tightly. Chill for 2 hours or longer. Cut each tortilla into 1-inch pieces, discarding the end pieces. *Note:* Rolls can be frozen for easier slicing. Yield: 3 dozen.

Jennifer McAllister, Birmingham South Cahaba Council

Ranch Oyster Crackers

1 package ranch salad
dressing mix
1/2 teaspoon dillweed
1/4 teaspoon lemon pepper
(optional)

1/4 teaspoon garlic powder
(optional)
3/4 cup vegetable oil
5 cups plain oyster crackers

Combine the salad dressing mix, dillweed, lemon pepper, garlic powder and oil in a bowl and mix well. Place the oyster crackers on a baking sheet. Pour the dressing over the crackers and stir to coat. Bake at 250 degrees for 15 to 20 minutes or until heated through, stirring gently halfway through baking process.
Yield: 15 to 20 servings.

Jennifer McAllister, Birmingham South Cahaba Council

Sugared Pecans

1 egg white   2½ to 3 cups pecan halves
1 cup packed brown sugar

Beat the egg white in a mixer bowl until soft peaks form. Add the brown sugar and beat until thick and creamy. Add the pecans 1 cup at a time. Mix well with a fork. Place small clusters of pecans on a baking sheet. Bake at 300 degrees for 15 minutes. Cool on a wire rack. Store in an airtight container. Yield: 5 dozen.

Edith Schlechty, Montgomery Life Member Club

Yummy Pecans

1 egg white   ½ teaspoon vanilla extract
¾ cup packed brown sugar   2 cups (or more) pecan halves

Beat the egg white in a mixer bowl until soft peaks form. Beat in the brown sugar and vanilla gradually. Fold in the pecans. Place single pecan halves on a greased baking sheet. Bake at 250 degrees for 30 minutes. Turn off the oven. Let stand with the oven door closed for 30 minutes. Remove from the oven. Cool to room temperature. Store in an airtight container. Yield: 4 dozen.

Judy Howard, Riverchase Council

Holiday Eggnog

6 eggs   1 cup golden rum, or 1 to
1 cup sugar   2 tablespoons rum extract
½ teaspoon salt   Nutmeg to taste
1 quart light cream

Beat the eggs in a large mixer bowl until foamy. Add the sugar and salt and beat until thick and pale yellow. Stir in the cream and rum. Chill, covered, for 3 hours or longer. Sprinkle each serving with nutmeg just before serving. Yield: 12 servings

Jennifer McAllister, Birmingham South Cahaba Council

Rich Holiday Eggnog

12 large eggs
1¼ cups sugar
½ teaspoon salt
1 quart milk
1 cup dark rum (optional)

2 tablespoons vanilla extract
1 teaspoon ground nutmeg
1 quart milk
1 cup whipping cream

Whisk the eggs, sugar and salt in a heavy 4-quart saucepan until blended. Stir in 1 quart milk gradually. Cook over low heat for 25 minutes or until the custard is thick, stirring constantly; do not boil. Pour into a large bowl. Stir in the rum, vanilla, nutmeg and 1 quart milk. Chill, covered, for 3 hours or longer. Beat the whipping cream at medium speed in a mixer bowl until soft peaks form. Fold the whipped cream into the custard. Pour into a chilled 5-quart punch bowl. Garnish with additional nutmeg.
Yield: 32 servings.

Brenda Reeves, Birmingham South Cahaba Council

Red Punch

3 envelopes raspberry drink
  mix
3 cups sugar
4 quarts water
1 (46-ounce) can pineapple
  juice

1 quart ginger ale
2 pints pineapple sherbet
  (softened)

Combine the drink mix, sugar and water in a large punch bowl, stirring until the drink mix and sugar are dissolved. Add the pineapple juice, ginger ale and ice cream just before serving.
Yield: 24 servings.

JoAnn Thomas, Selma Life Member Club

Hot Holiday Fruit Punch

1 (48-ounce) can
  unsweetened apple juice
	1 (46-ounce) can
	  unsweetened orange juice

1 teaspoon ground nutmeg	1/4 cup sugar
1 cinnamon stick	2 medium oranges
1 (46-ounce) can unsweetened pineapple juice	2 teaspoons whole cloves

Combine the apple juice, nutmeg and cinnamon stick in a large saucepan. Cook, covered, over low heat for 20 minutes. Add the pineapple juice, orange juice and sugar and mix well. Stud the oranges with the cloves. Add the oranges to the punch. Cook for 5 minutes; do not boil. Serve immediately. Yield: about 4½ quarts.

Narice Sutton, Birmingham Life Member Club

Russian Tea

1 orange, cut into halves	1/2 cup sugar
30 whole cloves	1 teaspoon cinnamon
1 large bottle apple juice	3 (single-serving size) tea bags
1 large can pineapple juice	

1 large can orange juice, or
  1 large can frozen orange
  juice concentrate, thawed	

Stud the orange with the cloves. Combine the apple juice, pineapple juice, orange juice, sugar, cinnamon and tea bags in a slow cooker or large saucepan. Simmer until heated through; do not boil. Remove the tea bags. Yield: variable.

Elizabeth Cornwell, Birmingham Life Member Club

Wassail

2 quarts sweet apple cider
2 (20-ounce) cans pineapple
   juice
1 teaspoon whole cloves
2 cups orange juice

1 cup lemon juice
1 cinnamon stick
Sugar or honey to taste
1 fifth of applejack

Bring the apple cider, pineapple juice, cloves, orange juice, lemon juice, cinnamon stick and sugar to a simmer in a large saucepan. Add the brandy. Strain into a punch bowl. Serve hot.
Yield: 20 to 25 servings.

Rosa Merriwether, Montgomery Council

Ambrosia

1 (20-ounce) can juice-packed
   pineapple chunks, drained
1 (11-ounce) can mandarin
   oranges, drained
1 banana, sliced
1½ cups seedless grapes

1 cup miniature
   marshmallows
½ cup flaked coconut
¼ cup chopped almonds
1 cup vanilla yogurt

Combine the pineapple, mandarin oranges, banana, grapes, marshmallows, coconut and almonds in a bowl and mix well. Fold in the yogurt. Spoon into a 9x13-inch dish. Cover and chill thoroughly. Yield: 10 to 12 servings.

Eunice Henry, Selma Life Member Club

Apricot Salad

1 (3-ounce) package orange
   gelatin
1 (3-ounce) package apricot
   gelatin
⅔ cup sugar
⅔ cup water
1 cup sour cream

2 small jars baby food apricots
1 (8-ounce) can crushed
   pineapple
½ cup (or more) chopped
   pecans or walnuts
8 ounces whipped topping

Combine the gelatin, sugar and water in a saucepan. Bring to a boil, stirring until the gelatin and sugar are dissolved. Remove from the heat. Let stand until cool. Mix the sour cream and baby food in a bowl. Add the undrained pineapple. Stir in the pecans. Fold in the gelatin mixture and whipped topping. Freeze until serving time. Yield: 12 servings.

Jeraldean R. Morris, Birmingham South Life Member Club

Congealed Salad

1 (5-ounce) can evaporated
   milk
1 can pineapple chunks
1 (3-ounce) package lime
   gelatin

Juice of ½ lemon
8 ounces cream cheese,
   softened
1 small jar cherries, chopped
1 cup chopped pecans

Chill the evaporated milk for 1 hour. Drain the pineapple, reserving the juice. Combine the gelatin and reserved juice in a saucepan. Bring to a boil, stirring until the gelatin is dissolved. Remove from the heat. Let stand until cool. Beat the evaporated milk in a mixer bowl. Add the lemon juice. Blend in the cream cheese. Stir in the gelatin mixture gradually. Fold in the cherries and pecans. Spoon into a shallow 2½-quart dish. Chill until set. Yield: 10 to 12 servings.

Alma G. Galloway, Huntsville Council

Cranberry Salad

1 package raspberry gelatin
¾ cup sugar
1 cup hot water
1 (16-ounce) can whole
 cranberry sauce

½ cup crushed pineapple
½ cup pecans
Grated zest of 1 orange

Dissolve the gelatin and sugar in the hot water. Pour into a 9x13-inch dish. Chill until partially set. Fold in the cranberry sauce, pineapple, pecans and orange zest. Chill until set.
Yield: 10 to 12 servings.

Sue Woodruff, sister of Cathy Kelly,
Birmingham South Cahaba Council

Cranberry Nut Salad

1 (16-ounce) can whole
 cranberry sauce
1 (3-ounce) package red,
 yellow or orange gelatin
1 cup boiling water
¼ teaspoon salt

1 tablespoon lemon juice
½ cup mayonnaise
1 apple or orange, peeled,
 chopped
1 cup chopped walnuts

Heat the cranberry sauce in a saucepan. Strain the sauce, reserving the cranberries. Dissolve the gelatin in the hot cranberry sauce and boiling water in a bowl. Add the salt and lemon juice. Chill until partially set. Beat in the mayonnaise until light and fluffy. Fold in the apple, walnuts and reserved cranberries. Chill for 4 hours or longer. Yield: 10 to 12 servings.

Betty Darnell, Gadsden Life Member Club

Fruit Salad

1 can flaked coconut
1 can pineapple chunks
1 can mandarin oranges
½ jar cherries, chopped

½ package miniature
  marshmallows
1 cup sour cream
½ cup chopped pecans

Combine the coconut, pineapple, mandarin oranges, cherries, marshmallows, sour cream and pecans in a bowl and mix well. Chill, covered, for 8 to 12 hours. Yield: 10 to 12 servings.

Louise Morrison, Tuscaloosa Council

Wonderful Fruit Salad

2 cans fruit cocktail, drained
1 can peaches, drained
Fresh strawberries or kiwifruit
1 can pineapple chunks

3 tablespoons Tang
1 (6-ounce) package vanilla
  instant pudding mix
2 to 3 bananas

Combine the fruit cocktail, peaches and strawberries in a large bowl. Drain the pineapple, reserving ½ cup juice. Mix the reserved juice, Tang and pudding mix in a medium bowl. Pour over the fruit and mix well. Chill until serving time. Slice bananas on top of the salad just before serving. Yield: 10 to 12 servings.

Dorothy Kimbrough, Decatur Council

Heavenly Hash

16 ounces large curd cottage
  cheese
1 (20-ounce) can crushed
  pineapple, drained

1 (6-ounce) package red or
  green gelatin
16 ounces whipped topping
½ cup chopped pecans

Combine the cottage cheese, pineapple, gelatin, whipped topping and pecans in a bowl and mix well. Spoon into a 9x13-inch dish. Cover and chill thoroughly. Yield: 10 to 12 servings.

Sue Walton, Birmingham Life Member Club

Heavenly Hash Salad

2 eggs, beaten
¾ cup sugar
3 tablespoons lemon juice
1 (20-ounce) can pineapple
   chunks, drained
2 (10-ounce) jars maraschino
   cherries, drained

2 cups whipping cream,
   chilled
2 tablespoons sugar
1 (16-ounce) package
   miniature marshmallows
1 cup chopped pecans

Combine the eggs, ¾ cup sugar and lemon juice in a saucepan. Cook until thick, stirring frequently. Chill thoroughly. Beat the whipping cream and 2 tablespoons sugar in large bowl. Add the egg mixture and mix well. Fold in the marshmallows and pecans. Cover and chill thoroughly. Yield: 10 to 12 servings.

Doris Yarber, Shoals Life Member Club

Pink Arctic Salad

6 ounces cream cheese,
   softened
2 tablespoons sugar
2 tablespoons mayonnaise
1 (16-ounce) can whole
   cranberry sauce

1 (8-ounce) can crushed
   pineapple, drained
½ cup chopped pecans
8 ounces whipped topping

Combine the cream cheese, sugar and mayonnaise in a large bowl and mix well. Crush the cranberry sauce. Mix the cranberry sauce, pineapple and pecans in a bowl. Add to the cream cheese mixture and mix well. Fold in the whipped topping. Freeze in a square glass dish or in paper muffin cup liners placed on a baking sheet. Let stand for 5 minutes before serving. Serve on lettuce leaves. Yield: 12 servings.

Betty Yancy, Birmingham Life Member Club

Red Congealed Salad

1 (20-ounce) can crushed
  pineapple
1 (6-ounce) package
  strawberry gelatin

8 ounces whipping topping
1 cup chopped pecans

Combine the undrained pineapple and gelatin in a saucepan and mix well. Boil for 2 minutes. Remove from the heat. Let stand until cool. Combine with the whipped topping and pecans in a bowl. Chill, covered, until set. Yield: 8 to 10 servings.

Opal Norton, Shoals Life Member Club

Strawberry Cloud

1 (14-ounce) can sweetened
  condensed milk
1 (21-ounce) can strawberry
  pie filling
2 cans crushed pineapple,
  drained

1 cup sour cream
16 ounces whipped topping
2 cups chopped pecans
1/2 package miniature
  marshmallows

Combine the condensed milk and pie filling in a blender container. Process until mixed. Pour into a large bowl. Add the pineapple, sour cream, whipped topping, pecans and marshmallows and mix well. Chill, covered, for 2 to 3 hours. Serve in a large clear punch bowl. Yield: 12 to 15 servings.

Cathy Holmes, Mobile Council

Strawberry Salad

2 (3-ounce) packages
  strawberry gelatin
2 cups boiling water
1 (10-ounce) package frozen
  strawberries, thawed

1 (8-ounce) can crushed
  pineapple
½ cup chopped pecans
1 cup sour cream

Dissolve the gelatin in the boiling water in a bowl. Add the strawberries, pineapple and pecans. Spoon half the mixture into a mold or 9x13-inch dish. Chill, covered, until set. Spread sour cream over the congealed layer. Spoon the remaining gelatin mixture over the top. Chill, covered, until set.
Yield: 10 to 12 servings.

Sherrie Poynor, Montgomery Council

Mixed Greens with
Bleu Cheese Vinaigrette

3 cups torn iceberg lettuce
3 cups torn romaine

3 cups torn Bibb lettuce
Bleu Cheese Vinaigrette

Combine all the greens in a large bowl and toss to mix. Divide evenly among 6 serving plates. Drizzle with the Bleu Cheese Vinaigrette. Yield: 6 servings.

Bleu Cheese Vinaigrette

¼ cup water
3 tablespoons vegetable oil
2 tablespoons lemon juice
2 tablespoons Dijon mustard

1 teaspoon dried whole
  oregano
½ teaspoon pepper
⅓ cup crumbled bleu cheese

Combine the water, oil, lemon juice, Dijon mustard, oregano, pepper and cheese in a jar with a tight-fitting lid. Cover and shake to mix well. Chill thoroughly.

Betty M. Jones-Moon, Birmingham Life Member Club

Veggie Christmas Tree

1 (8-ounce) bottle ranch salad   3 to 4 cups cauliflowerets
  dressing mix   4 to 5 cherry tomatoes, cut
4 cups broccoli florets   into quarters
1 broccoli stem   1 medium carrot, sliced

Cover the bottom of a 9x13-inch dish with salad dressing. Arrange
the broccoli in a tree shape in the dish, using the stem as the trunk.
Arrange cauliflowerets around the "tree." Add tomatoes and carrot
slices as ornaments. Yield: 20 servings.

Wanda Plunkett, Anniston Council

Holiday Pasta Salad

2 cups chopped red apples   2 tablespoons lemon juice
1 cup chopped celery   1 teaspoon sugar
½ cup walnut pieces   2 cups uncooked pasta
1 cup mayonnaise

Combine the apples, celery, walnuts, mayonnaise, lemon juice and
sugar in a large bowl and mix well. Cook the pasta using the
package directions; drain well. Rinse the pasta with cold water
until cooled. Add the pasta to the apple mixture and toss gently.
Yield: 4 servings.

Susan Currie, Birmingham South Cahaba Council

Holiday Porter Pot Roast

1 (4- to 5-pound) chuck,
   bottom round or rump roast,
   boned, tied
Salt and pepper to taste
Thyme and sage to taste
3 tablespoons olive oil
2 pounds onions, peeled,
   thinly sliced
1 carrot, chopped

1 rib celery, chopped
6 garlic cloves, chopped
1 tablespoon molasses
4 bay leaves
1 (12-ounce) bottle porter or
   other dark ale or beer
2 tablespoons Dijon mustard
1 tablespoon malt vinegar or
   red wine vinegar

Season the roast generously with salt, pepper, thyme and sage. Heat the olive oil in a large Dutch oven over medium-high heat. Add the roast. Sear on all sides. Remove the roast to a platter. Add the onions, carrot, celery, garlic and molasses to the Dutch oven. Cook, covered, over medium heat for 10 to 12 minutes or just until the onions are tender and beginning to brown. Return the roast to the Dutch oven. Add the bay leaves and porter. Cook, covered, over low heat for 1½ to 2 hours or until the roast is tender. Remove the roast to a warm platter. For the sauce, skim the fat from the liquid in the Dutch oven. Stir in the Dijon mustard and vinegar. Boil until syrupy. Discard the bay leaves. Cut the roast into slices. Spoon some of the sauce and the vegetables over the roast. Serve the remaining sauce on the side. Yield: 6 to 8 servings.

Brenda Reeves, Birmingham South Cahaba Council

Eye-of-Round Creole

1 eye-of-round roast	Worcestershire sauce
(8 to 12 ounces per person)	Creole Meat Seasoning

Moisten all sides of the roast with Worcestershire sauce. Cover with Creole Meat Seasoning. Place the roast on a rack in a broiler pan. Bake at 500 degrees for 7 minutes per pound. Turn off the oven. Let stand with the oven door closed for 1 hour.
Yield: variable.

Creole Meat Seasoning

1 (26-ounce) package salt	1 ounce garlic powder
1½ ounces black pepper	1 ounce MSG
2 ounces cayenne pepper	1 ounce chili powder

Combine the salt, black pepper, cayenne pepper, garlic powder, MSG and chili powder in a bowl and mix well. Store in a 2-quart jar.

Pat White, Montgomery Council

Shepherd's Pie

1 pound ground beef	Hot mashed potatoes
Sliced onions (optional)	Cheese of choice

Brown the ground beef with the onions in a skillet, stirring until the ground beef is crumbly; drain well. Alternate layers of ground beef, mashed potatoes and cheese in a baking pan until all ingredients are used. Bake at 350 degrees until the cheese melts.
Yield: 4 to 6 servings.

Diana Casey, Alabama Telco Credit Union

Breakfast Casserole

1 pound sausage
2 cups cooked grits
6 eggs

½ teaspoon salt
Pepper to taste

Brown the sausage in a nonstick skillet, stirring until crumbly; drain. Add the grits and mix well. Spoon into a casserole. Beat the eggs, salt and pepper in a bowl. Pour over the sausage mixture. Bake at 400 degrees for 45 minutes. Serve with cinnamon-raisin toast and your favorite hot beverage. Yield: 6 to 8 servings.

Mayme Holmes, Mobile Council

Holiday Roast Chicken Jarlsberg

3 slices bacon, chopped
1 cup sliced mushrooms
1 medium onion, chopped
2 cups chopped fresh spinach,
    or 1 (10-ounce) package
    frozen spinach, thawed,
    drained
⅓ cup chopped parsley
⅓ cup minced celery

2 cups cooked mixed wild and
    white rice, or brown rice
1½ cups shredded Jarlsberg
    cheese
⅓ cup sliced almonds
1 (8-pound) chicken
Salt and pepper to taste
3 tablespoons butter or
    margarine

Cook the bacon in a large skillet until crisp. Crumble the bacon and set aside. Sauté the mushrooms and onion in the bacon drippings in the skillet until the onion is tender. Remove from the heat. Stir in the bacon, spinach, parsley, celery, rice, cheese and almonds. Stuff loosely into the chicken cavity. Place the chicken breast side up in a shallow roasting pan. Truss with skewers or kitchen string. Season with salt and pepper. Dot with butter. Bake at 325 degrees for 25 minutes per pound or until the chicken is cooked through and golden brown, basting occasionally with the pan drippings. *Note:* Stuffing may be baked separately in a pan at 350 degrees for about 45 minutes. Stuffing recipe may be doubled for a 16-pound turkey. Yield: 8 servings.

Kathryn Morgan, Gadsden Life Member Club

Chicken Holiday Wreath

2 (8-count) packages
  crescent rolls
½ cup chopped red bell pepper
½ cup chopped fresh broccoli
¼ cup drained chopped water
  chestnuts
2 tablespoons chopped onion

1 cup shredded Colby-Jack
  cheese
1 (5-ounce) can chunk
  chicken, drained, flaked
⅔ cup canned condensed
  cream of chicken soup

Unroll the roll dough and separate into triangles. Arrange the triangles in a circle on a greased 14-inch pizza pan, overlapping the wide ends in the center and with the points facing outward. Mix the red pepper, broccoli, water chestnuts, onion, cheese, chicken and soup in a bowl. Scoop evenly onto the widest end of each triangle. Bring the outside points of the triangles down over the filling; tuck the wide ends of dough at the center. Bake at 350 degrees for 25 minutes or until golden brown. Serve warm. Yield: 6 servings.

Brenda Reeves, Birmingham South Cahaba Council

Individual Chicken Bake

2 cups chopped cooked
  chicken breast
¾ cup chopped celery
¼ cup chopped onion
1 (4-ounce) can sliced
  mushrooms, drained
1 cup evaporated skim milk

¼ cup egg substitute
½ teaspoon salt
¼ teaspoon pepper
1 tablespoon Worcestershire
  sauce
⅓ cup whole cranberry sauce

Combine the chicken, celery, onion, mushrooms, evaporated milk, egg substitute, salt, pepper and Worcestershire sauce in a bowl and mix well. Spoon evenly into six 6-ounce custard cups coated with nonstick cooking spray. Cover loosely with foil. Bake at 350 degrees for 50 minutes or until a knife inserted near the center comes out clean. Let stand, uncovered, for 5 minutes. Remove the chicken to plates. Top each serving with cranberry sauce. Yield: 6 servings.

Betty M. Jones-Moon, Birmingham Life Member Club

Baked Apples à l'Orange

6 medium cooking apples
¼ cup unsweetened apple
   juice
1 tablespoon lemon juice
¼ cup water
2 whole cloves

1 (4-inch) cinnamon stick,
   broken into halves
⅓ cup reduced-calorie orange
   marmalade
6 small gingersnaps, crushed

Core the apples to within ½ inch of the bottom. Peel the top ⅓ of each apple. Place the apples in a shallow 8x12-inch baking dish. Add a mixture of the apple juice, lemon juice, water, cloves and cinnamon stick. Bake at 350 degrees for 30 minutes, basting frequently with the cooking liquid. Remove the apples from the oven. Spoon equal amounts of marmalade and gingersnap crumbs over each apple. Bake for 5 minutes longer or until the apples are tender. Yield: 6 servings.

Betty M. Jones-Moon, Birmingham Life Member Club

Cranberry Apple Casserole

3 cups fresh cranberries
3 cups chopped peeled apples
2 tablespoons flour
1 cup sugar
3 (1½-ounce) packages
   instant apple-cinnamon oats

½ cup chopped walnuts or
   pecans
½ cup flour
½ cup packed brown sugar
½ cup (1 stick) margarine,
   melted

Combine the cranberries, apples and 2 tablespoons flour in a bowl, tossing to coat. Add the sugar and mix well. Spoon into a 2-quart casserole. Mix the oats, walnuts, ½ cup flour and brown sugar in a small bowl. Add the margarine and mix well. Spoon over the fruit mixture. Bake at 325 degrees for 45 minutes. Yield: 8 to 10 servings.

Margarette Russell, Decatur Council

Garlic Grits Casserole

1 cup grits
3½ cups water
1 teaspoon salt
½ cup (1 stick) margarine

1 roll garlic cheese
2 eggs
Milk

Combine the grits, water and salt in a saucepan. Cook according to the package directions. Add the margarine and garlic cheese and mix well. Mix the eggs with enough milk to measure 2 cups; beat well. Add the egg mixture to the grits and mix well. Spoon into a buttered casserole. Bake at 350 degrees for 30 minutes or until set. Recipe can be doubled. Reheats well in the microwave.
Yield: 6 servings.

Betty (Bob) Passet, Mobile Council

Puffy Cheddar Grits

2 tablespoons margarine or
  butter
1 teaspoon salt
1½ cups milk
2 cups water
1¼ cups quick-cooking grits

8 ounces shredded Cheddar
  cheese
1 teaspoon hot pepper sauce
¼ teaspoon pepper
5 large eggs
2 cups milk

Combine the margarine, salt, 1½ cups milk and water in a 3-quart saucepan. Bring to a boil over medium-high heat. Add the grits gradually, whisking constantly. Reduce the heat to low. Cook, covered, for 5 minutes, stirring occasionally (the grits will be very stiff). Remove from the heat and stir in the cheese. Whisk the hot pepper sauce, pepper, eggs and 2 cups milk in a large bowl. Add the grits mixture gradually, whisking after each addition. Spoon into a greased shallow 2½-quart casserole. Bake at 325 degrees for 45 minutes or until a knife inserted near the center comes out clean.
Yield: 12 servings.

Brenda Reeves, Birmingham South Cahaba Council

Potato Casserole

8 medium potatoes, boiled,
  grated
1½ cups sharp cheese,
  shredded
⅓ to ½ cup chopped green
  onions or minced onion

1½ teaspoons salt
2 cups sour cream
½ cup (1 stick) margarine,
  melted

Combine the potatoes, cheese, green onions, salt, sour cream and margarine in a bowl and mix well. Spoon into a greased 8x8-inch baking pan. Bake at 350 degrees for 35 to 40 minutes or until bubbly and heated through. Yield: 10 to 12 servings.

Mrs. Bob H. Henson, Birmingham South Life Member Club

New Potato Medley

1 tablespoon reduced-calorie
  margarine
3 cups chopped new potatoes
1½ cups diagonally sliced
  carrots

1 cup chopped onion
¼ teaspoon salt
¼ teaspoon pepper

Melt the margarine in a large saucepan over medium heat. Add the potatoes, carrots, onion, salt and pepper and toss gently. Reduce the heat. Cook, covered, for 20 minutes or until the vegetables are tender, stirring once. Yield: 6 servings.

Betty M. Jones-Moon, Birmingham Life Member Club

Sweet Potato Casserole

3 cups mashed cooked sweet
  potatoes
1 cup sugar
2 eggs
1 teaspoon vanilla extract
½ cup (1 stick) butter,
  softened

⅓ cup milk
1 cup packed light brown
  sugar
⅓ cup flour
⅓ cup butter, softened
⅓ cup chopped pecans

Combine the sweet potatoes, sugar, eggs, vanilla, ½ cup butter and milk in a mixer bowl and beat well. Spoon into a greased casserole. Combine the brown sugar, flour and ⅓ cup butter in a bowl and mix well. Spread over the sweet potato mixture. Sprinkle with the pecans. Bake at 350 degrees for 25 to 35 minutes or until heated through. Yield: 6 to 8 servings.

Mary D. Palmer, Birmingham Life Member Club

Sweet Potato Bake

3 medium sweet potatoes,
  cooked, peeled
1 cup packed dark brown
  sugar
2 eggs, beaten
1 teaspoon vanilla extract

¼ cup flour
1 cup chopped pecans
½ cup packed dark brown
  sugar
¼ cup (½ stick) butter or
  margarine, melted

Mash the sweet potatoes in a bowl. Add 1 cup brown sugar, eggs and vanilla and mix well. Spoon into a casserole. Mix the flour, pecans and ½ cup brown sugar in a bowl. Spoon onto the sweet potato mixture. Drizzle with the butter. Bake at 350 degrees for 25 minutes. Yield: 6 to 8 servings.

Donna Jean Bowman, Birmingham South Cahaba Council

Banana Bread

½ cup shortening	½ teaspoon salt
1 cup sugar	1 teaspoon baking soda
2 eggs, beaten	¼ cup chopped pecans
3 bananas, mashed	¼ cup chopped cherries
2 cups flour	¼ cup chocolate chips

Cream the shortening and sugar in a mixer bowl until light and fluffy. Add the eggs and beat well. Add the bananas, flour, salt and baking soda and mix well. Fold in the pecans, cherries and chocolate chips. Spoon into a greased loaf pan. Bake at 350 degrees for 1 hour. Yield: 12 servings.

Vicki Weyerbacher, Birmingham South Cahaba Council

Cranberry Fruit Bread

12 ounces fresh or thawed frozen cranberries, cut into halves	4 cups flour
	2 cups sugar
	1 tablespoon baking powder
2 cups pecan halves	1 teaspoon baking soda
1 cup chopped mixed fruit	¼ teaspoon salt
1 cup chopped dates	2 eggs
1 cup golden raisins	1 cup orange juice
1 tablespoon grated orange zest	¼ cup shortening, melted
	¼ cup warm water

Combine the cranberries, pecans, mixed fruit, dates, raisins, orange zest and ¼ cup of the flour in a bowl and toss to mix well. Mix the remaining 3¾ cups flour, sugar, baking powder, baking soda and salt together. Beat the eggs in a large mixer bowl. Add the orange juice, shortening and water and mix well. Add the sugar mixture and stir just until mixed. Fold in the cranberry mixture. Spoon into 3 greased and waxed paper-lined 5x9-inch loaf pans. Bake at 350 degrees for 60 to 65 minutes or until the loaves test done. Yield: 36 servings.

Jean Escott, Montgomery Council

Blueberry Muffins

2 cups baking mix
1/3 cup sugar
2/3 cup milk
2 tablespoons vegetable oil

1 egg, beaten
3/4 cup fresh or thawed frozen
    blueberries, drained

Line 12 muffin cups with paper liners or grease the bottoms only of the muffin cups. Combine the baking mix, sugar, milk, oil and egg in a bowl, stirring just until moistened. Stir in the blueberries. Spoon into the prepared pan. Bake at 400 degrees for 13 to 18 minutes or until golden brown. Yield: 12 servings.

Susan Currie, Birmingham South Cahaba Council

Sweeter Muffins

1 1/2 cups flour
1/2 cup sugar
1/2 teaspoon salt
2 teaspoons baking powder

1 egg, lightly beaten
1/2 cup milk
1/4 cup vegetable oil

Grease the bottoms only of 12 muffin cups. Combine the flour, sugar, salt and baking powder in a bowl and mix well. Blend the egg and milk in a small bowl. Stir in the oil. Add the flour mixture gradually, stirring just until moistened. Fill each muffin cup 2/3 full. Bake at 400 degrees for 20 to 25 minutes or until the muffins test done. Yield: 12 servings.

Janet T. Streeter, Montgomery Council

Candy Cane Coffee Breads

2 cups sour cream
2 envelopes dry yeast
1/2 cup warm water
1/4 cup (1/2 stick) butter or
  margarine, softened
1/3 cup sugar
2 teaspoons salt
2 eggs

6 cups flour
1 1/2 cups finely chopped dried
  apricots
1 1/2 cups drained finely
  chopped maraschino
  cherries
2 cups confectioners' sugar
2 tablespoons (about) water

Heat the sour cream in a saucepan over low heat just until lukewarm. Remove from the heat. Dissolve the yeast in the warm water in a large bowl. Stir in the sour cream, 1/4 cup butter, sugar, salt, eggs and 2 cups of the flour. Beat until smooth. Add enough of the remaining flour gradually to make a soft dough. Knead on a floured work surface for 10 minutes or until smooth and elastic. Place in a greased bowl, turning to grease the surface of the dough. Let rise, covered, in a warm place for 1 hour or until doubled in bulk. Punch down the dough. Divide into 3 equal portions. Roll each portion into a 6x15-inch rectangle. Place on a greased baking sheet. Make 2-inch cuts at 1/2-inch intervals on the long sides of each rectangle. Mix the apricots and cherries in a bowl. Spread 1/3 of the mixture down the center of each rectangle. Crisscross strips over the filling. Stretch the dough until it measures 22 inches. Curve to form a cane. Bake at 375 degrees for 15 to 20 minutes or until golden brown. Blend the confectioners' sugar and water in a bowl until of desired consistency, adding a few additional drops of water if the icing is too stiff. Brush the warm canes with additional butter and drizzle with icing. Decorate with cherry halves and pieces if desired. Yield: 36 servings.

Janet Hanel, Montgomery Life Member Club

Easy Yeast Rolls

2¼ cups warm water
3 tablespoons sugar
1½ teaspoons salt
⅓ cup vegetable oil

2 envelopes dry yeast
3 cups all-purpose flour
3 cups self-rising flour
Melted butter

Mix the warm water, sugar, salt, oil and yeast in a bowl. Let rise for 15 minutes or until foamy. Add the flour gradually, mixing until a smooth dough forms. Place in a greased bowl, turning to coat the surface. Chill, covered, until ready to bake (up to 3 days). Roll the dough on a floured work surface. Cut with a biscuit cutter. Place 1 inch apart on a greased baking sheet. Let rise in a warm place for 1½ hours. Brush the tops of the rolls with butter. Bake at 400 degrees for 15 to 20 minutes or until golden brown. Remove from the oven. Brush the tops with butter. Yield: 2 dozen rolls.

Bernice Moore, Birmingham South Cahaba Council

Christmas Cigars

2 cups chopped pecans
1 cup chopped almonds
2 tablespoons sugar
1 tablespoon cinnamon
1 (16-ounce) package phyllo

Melted butter
3 cups sugar
2 cups water
3 cinnamon sticks
Juice of 1 lemon

Mix the first 4 ingredients in a bowl. Cut the phyllo into quarters. Brush 1 sheet of phyllo with butter. Top with another sheet of phyllo and brush with butter, keeping the remaining phyllo sheets covered with a damp cloth. Place 1 tablespoon of the pecan mixture at 1 end of the phyllo stack. Turn in the sides and roll up. Place in a buttered baking dish. Brush with butter. Repeat with the remaining phyllo sheets and pecan mixture. Bake at 350 degrees for 25 to 30 minutes or until brown. Combine 3 cups sugar, water, cinnamon sticks and lemon juice in a saucepan. Bring to a boil and reduce heat. Simmer for 10 minutes. Cool. Pour over the hot rolls. Cover and let stand until the syrup is absorbed. Yield: 3 dozen.

Vicki Weyerbacher, Birmingham South Cahaba Council

Chocolate Eclair Dessert

1 (16-ounce) package graham
  crackers
2 (4-ounce) packages French
  vanilla instant pudding mix

3 cups milk
16 ounces whipped topping
1 teaspoon almond extract
Chocolate Frosting

Line the bottom of a buttered 9x13-inch dish with graham crackers. Beat the pudding mix and milk in a large bowl until thick. Add the whipped topping and flavoring and blend well. Layer the pudding and remaining graham crackers ½ at a time in the prepared dish, ending with graham crackers. Spread the Chocolate Frosting over the top. Chill, covered, for 24 hours before serving. Yield: 12 to 15 servings.

Chocolate Frosting

½ cup baking cocoa
3 tablespoons butter, softened
3 tablespoons milk

2 tablespoons light corn syrup
1 teaspoon vanilla extract
1½ cups confectioners' sugar

Combine the baking cocoa, butter, milk, corn syrup and vanilla in a mixer bowl and beat until smooth. Add the confectioners' sugar and beat until thick.

Susan Deal, Birmingham South Cahaba Council

To get the most juice out of fresh lemons, bring them to room temperature and roll them under your palm against the kitchen counter before squeezing.

Miniature Fruitcake Loaves

1 pound candied cherries
1 pound candied pineapple
1 pound chopped dates
1 cup flour

2 cups shredded coconut
2 cups sweetened condensed
  milk
7 cups pecan halves

Combine the cherries, pineapple, dates and flour in a large bowl and mix well. Add the coconut, condensed milk and pecan halves and stir to mix well. Spoon into 7 miniature loaf pans. Bake at 300 degrees for 30 minutes or until the loaves test done. Cool in the pans for 10 minutes. Invert onto wire racks to cool completely. Yield: 7 miniature loaves.

Shirley W. Crocker, Birmingham Life Member Club

Fruitcake

1½ cups flour
1 teaspoon baking powder
1 pound candied cherries
1 pound candied pineapple
4 cups coarsely chopped
  pecans
¼ cup flour

1 cup (2 sticks) margarine,
  softened
1½ cups sugar
5 eggs, beaten
1 tablespoon vanilla extract
1 tablespoon lemon extract

Line a tube pan with waxed paper and grease with shortening. Sift 1½ cups flour and baking powder together. Combine the cherries, pineapple, pecans and ¼ cup flour in a bowl and toss to coat. Beat the margarine and sugar in a mixer bowl until creamy. Add the eggs 1 at a time, beating well after each addition. Add the flour mixture and flavorings and mix well. Stir in the fruit mixture. Press into the prepared pan. Bake at 250 degrees for 2 hours and 45 minutes. Cool in the pan for 10 minutes. Invert onto a serving plate. Store wrapped in foil. Yield: 16 servings.

Dorothy Yarbe, Shoals Life Member Club

The Best Fruitcake

1 pound candied cherries, finely chopped
1 pound candied pineapple, finely chopped
1 pound dates, finely chopped
1½ cups flour

1 teaspoon baking powder
8 cups chopped pecan halves
1 (14-ounce) package flaked coconut
2 (14-ounce) cans sweetened condensed milk

Combine the cherries, pineapple, dates, flour and baking powder in a large bowl and toss to coat. Stir in the pecans and coconut. Add the condensed milk and mix well. Press into a 10-inch tube pan sprayed with nonstick cooking spray. Bake at 275 degrees for 1¼ hours. Increase the oven temperature to 300 degrees. Bake for 15 minutes longer. Cool in the pan for 10 minutes. Invert onto a serving plate. Yield: 16 servings.

Glenda Golden, Mobile Council

Mystery Fruitcake

1 (2-layer) package yellow or spice cake mix
4 cups mixed candied fruit
½ cup candied cherries

1½ cups raisins or dates
4½ cups chopped pecans
1 package fluffy white frosting mix, prepared

Prepare and bake the cake using the package directions for a 9x13-inch cake pan. Cool on a wire rack. Crumble the cooled cake into a large bowl. Add the fruit, cherries, raisins and pecans and mix well. Add the frosting and mix well. Pack into a foil-lined loaf pan. Chill, covered, in the refrigerator. Yield: 12 servings.

Frankie (A.T.) Vaughn, Selma Life Member Club

No-Bake Holiday Fruitcake

1 (16-ounce) package graham
   crackers, crushed
1 (6-ounce) container red
   candied cherries, coarsely
   chopped
1 (6-ounce) container green
   candied cherries, coarsely
   chopped

1 (6-ounce) container candied
   pineapple, coarsely chopped
2 (14-ounce) cans sweetened
   condensed milk
1½ cups coarsely chopped
   pecans

Line a 5x9-inch loaf pan with plastic wrap, allowing the plastic
wrap to overhang the edges by a few inches. Combine the graham
cracker crumbs, red cherries, green cherries, pineapple, condensed
milk and pecans in a large bowl and mix well using clean hands.
Press into the prepared loaf pan. Cover with the plastic wrap.
Freeze for 8 to 12 hours before serving. Uncover and invert onto a
serving plate, removing the pan and plastic wrap. Cut into slices.
Store any remaining fruitcake in the freezer. May use mixed
candied fruit instead of the cherries and pineapple.
Yield: 18 to 20 servings.

Brenda Reeves, Birmingham South Cahaba Council

Fruit Dump Cake

1 (21-ounce) can cherry pie
   filling
1 (20-ounce) can crushed
   pineapple
1 (2-layer) package yellow
   cake mix

1 cup chopped pecans
½ cup (1 stick) butter or
   margarine, melted
Whipped topping

Layer the cherry pie filling and pineapple in a 9x13-inch cake pan.
Sprinkle the dry cake mix and pecans over the fruit. Pour melted
butter over the top. Bake at 350 degrees for 1 hour or until brown.
Serve with whipped topping. Yield: 15 servings.

Marcelle Kelley, mother-in-law of Cathy Kelley,
Birmingham South Cahaba Council

Applesauce Cake

1½ cups self-rising flour
1 cup packed brown sugar
2 eggs, beaten
1 jar chunky applesauce

1 cup chopped nuts
½ cup raisins (optional)
1 teaspoon vanilla extract

Mix the flour and brown sugar in a large bowl. Add the eggs, applesauce, nuts, raisins and vanilla. Stir until all the ingredients are blended. Pour into a floured tube pan. Bake at 350 degrees for 1 hour. Cool in the pan for 10 minutes. Invert onto a serving plate. Yield: 16 servings.

Donna Jean Bowman, Birmingham South Cahaba Council

Banana Chocolate Chip Pound Cake

1 (2-layer) package banana
  supreme cake mix
½ cup sugar
1 (4-ounce) package chocolate
  instant pudding mix
¾ cup vegetable oil
¾ cup water
4 eggs

½ cup sour cream
2 teaspoons vanilla extract
1 cup semisweet chocolate
  chips
½ cup chopped pecans
  (optional)
Sifted confectioners' sugar

Combine the cake mix, sugar and pudding mix in a large bowl and whisk with a wire whisk to remove any lumps. Add the oil, water, eggs and sour cream and stir until smooth. Fold in the vanilla, chocolate chips and pecans. Spoon into a greased and floured 10-inch tube pan. Bake at 350 degrees for 1 hour. Cool in the pan for 15 minutes. Invert onto a serving plate. Sprinkle with confectioners' sugar. Yield: 16 servings.

Hannah M. Segrest, Montgomery Life Member Club

Country Butter Cream Ribbon Chocolate Fudge Cake

8 ounces cream cheese,
  softened
1 egg
1/4 cup sugar
3 tablespoons milk
2 tablespoons butter or
  margarine, softened
1 tablespoon cornstarch
1/2 teaspoon vanilla extract
4 ounces unsweetened
  chocolate

2 cups flour
1 teaspoon baking powder
1/2 teaspoon baking soda
1/4 teaspoon salt
1/2 cup (1 stick) butter,
  softened
2 cups sugar
2 eggs
1 1/3 cups milk
1 teaspoon vanilla extract
Fudge Frosting

Combine the cream cheese, 1 egg and 1/4 cup sugar in a medium mixer bowl. Beat at high speed until smooth. Add 3 tablespoons milk, 2 tablespoons butter, cornstarch and 1/2 teaspoon vanilla gradually, beating well after each addition. Place the chocolate in a double boiler over boiling water. Reduce the heat to low. Cook until the chocolate is melted, stirring occasionally. Remove from the heat and cool. Mix the flour, baking powder, baking soda and salt together. Beat 1/2 cup butter in a large mixer bowl until creamy. Add 2 cups sugar gradually, beating constantly at medium speed. Beat in 2 eggs 1 at a time. Add the flour mixture and 1 1/3 cups milk alternately, beating well after each addition and beginning and ending with the flour mixture. Stir in the melted chocolate and 1 teaspoon vanilla. Spread 1/2 of the batter into a greased and floured 9x13-inch cake pan. Spread the cream cheese mixture evenly over the batter. Top with the remaining batter. Bake at 350 degrees for 55 to 60 minutes or until a wooden pick inserted in the center comes out clean. Cool in the pan on a wire rack. Spread Fudge Frosting over the cooled cake. Yield: 15 servings.

Fudge Frosting

2 ounces unsweetened
  chocolate
¼ cup (½ stick) butter or
  margarine

3½ cups sifted confectioners'
  sugar
⅓ cup milk
1 teaspoon vanilla extract

Combine the chocolate and butter in a double boiler over boiling water. Reduce the heat to low. Cook until melted, stirring occasionally. Remove from heat and cool. Add confectioners' sugar and milk. Beat at medium speed until smooth. Stir in vanilla.

Pat Griffin, Montgomery Council

Chocolate Sheet Cake

1 cup (2 sticks) margarine
1 cup water
3 tablespoons baking cocoa
2 cups flour
2 cups sugar
½ teaspoon salt
½ cup buttermilk
2 eggs
1 teaspoon baking soda

1 teaspoon vanilla extract
6 tablespoons (¾ stick) butter
3 tablespoons baking cocoa
6 tablespoons milk
1 teaspoon vanilla extract
1 (1-pound) package
  confectioners' sugar
½ cup chopped pecans
  (optional)

Combine the margarine, water and 3 tablespoons baking cocoa in a saucepan. Bring to a boil and remove from the heat. Add the flour, sugar and salt and mix well. Add the buttermilk, eggs, baking soda and 1 teaspoon vanilla and mix well. Spoon into a greased and floured 9x13-inch cake pan. Bake at 400 degrees for 20 minutes or until cake tests done. Cool slightly. Combine the butter, 3 tablespoons baking cocoa and milk in a saucepan. Bring to a boil, stirring constantly. Remove from the heat. Add 1 teaspoon vanilla, confectioners' sugar and mix until smooth. Stir in the pecans. Spread over the warm cake. Yield: 15 servings.

Sherry A. Liles, Huntsville Council

Quick Coconut Cake

1 (2-layer) package yellow
 cake mix
4 eggs
1/2 cup sweetened condensed
 milk
1 (4-ounce) package vanilla
 instant pudding mix

1 1/3 cups water
1/3 cup canola oil
1 teaspoon coconut flavoring
Sour Cream Coconut Frosting
6 ounces frozen coconut

Combine the cake mix, eggs, condensed milk, pudding mix, water, canola oil and coconut flavoring in a mixer bowl and beat until smooth. Pour into 3 greased and floured 8- or 9-inch cake pans. Bake at 350 degrees for 30 to 35 minutes or until the layers test done. Cool in the pans for 10 minutes. Invert onto wire racks to cool completely. Spread Sour Cream Coconut Frosting between the layers and over the top and side of cake. Sprinkle with coconut. Yield: 12 to 16 servings.

Sour Cream Coconut Frosting

2 cups sugar
1 cup sour cream

1 teaspoon coconut flavoring
2 1/2 to 6 ounces frozen coconut

Blend the sugar, sour cream and flavoring in a bowl. Stir in the coconut.

Louise Wheeler, Selma Life Member Club

Moist and Creamy Coconut Cake

1 (2-layer) package yellow or
 white cake mix
1 1/2 cups milk

1/2 cup sugar
2 cups flaked coconut
8 ounces whipped topping

Prepare and bake the cake using the package directions for a 9x13-inch cake pan. Cool in the pan for 15 minutes. Poke holes into the warm cake. Combine the milk, sugar and 1/2 cup of the coconut in a saucepan. Bring to a boil and reduce the heat. Simmer for 1 minute. Spoon over the warm cake, letting the mixture soak into the holes. Cool completely. Fold ½ cup of the remaining coconut into the whipped topping in a bowl. Spread over the cake. Sprinkle with the remaining 1 cup coconut. Chill, covered, for 8 to 12 hours. Store in the refrigerator. Yield: 15 servings.

Mrs. Bob H. Henson, Birmingham South Life Member Club

Creole Christmas Cake

1 pound chopped dates
1 pound glacé cherries
1 pound chopped mixed fruit
8 ounces dried apricots, chopped
8 ounces prunes, chopped
8 ounces Brazil nuts, chopped
8 ounces pecans, chopped
½ cup rum
½ cup brandy
½ cup port
½ cup cherry brandy
1 tablespoon vanilla extract
1 teaspoon cinnamon
1 teaspoon nutmeg
1 teaspoon salt
1 teaspoon ground cloves
2 cups (4 sticks) butter, softened
10 eggs
3 cups sugar
4 cups self-rising flour

Combine the dates, cherries, mixed fruit, apricots, prunes, Brazil nuts and pecans in a large bowl and toss well. Combine the rum, brandy, port, cherry brandy, vanilla, cinnamon, nutmeg, salt and cloves in a bowl and mix well. Pour over the fruit mixture. Let stand, covered, for 2 to 7 days, stirring daily. Beat the butter and eggs in a mixer bowl. Add the sugar and flour and beat until smooth. Stir into the fruit mixture. Pour into 2 greased bundt pans. Bake at 275 degrees for 3 to 3½ hours or until the cakes test done. The cakes will be moist in the center. Cool in the pans for 10 minutes. Invert onto wire racks to cool completely. Store wrapped in foil. Yield: 32 servings.

Frankie (A.T.) Vaughn, Selma Life Member Club

Japanese Fruitcake

3 cups flour	1 cup chopped pecans
1 tablespoon baking powder	1 cup raisins
1 cup (2 sticks) butter,	1 teaspoon cinnamon
softened	1 teaspoon ground cloves
2 cups sugar	1 teaspoon nutmeg
4 eggs	1 teaspoon allspice
1 cup milk	Orange Coconut Filling
1 teaspoon vanilla extract	

Sift the flour and baking powder together. Beat the butter and sugar in a mixer bowl until creamy. Add the eggs 1 at a time, beating well after each addition. Add the flour mixture and milk alternately, beating well after each addition. Beat in the vanilla. Divide the batter into 2 equal portions. Stir the pecans into 1 portion of the batter. Pour the pecan batter into 2 greased and floured 9-inch cake pans. Add the raisins, cinnamon, cloves, nutmeg and allspice to the remaining batter and mix well. Pour the raisin batter into 2 additional greased and floured 9-inch cake pans. Bake at 350 degrees for 20 to 25 minutes or until the 4 cake layers test done. Cool in the pans for 10 minutes. Remove to wire racks to cool completely. Alternate the pecan cake layers and raisin cake layers on a serving plate, spreading Orange Coconut Filling between the layers and on top of the cake. Yield: 12 to 16 servings.

Orange Coconut Filling

2 cups sugar	3 tablespoons cornstarch
Grated zest of 1 orange	1 cup coconut milk
2 oranges, peeled, torn into	1 cup boiling water
small pieces	1 fresh coconut, grated

Combine the sugar, orange zest, oranges, cornstarch, coconut milk and boiling water in a saucepan. Cook over medium heat for 10 minutes. Stir in the coconut. Cook for 5 minutes longer. Remove from the heat and cool.

Susan Poe, Riverchase Council

Holiday Cake

1 (2-layer) package butter-
  recipe yellow cake mix
1 (20-ounce) can juice-pack
  crushed pineapple
1 orange, thinly sliced
1 cup orange juice

1 cup chopped pecans
1/2 cup maraschino cherries
1/2 cup shredded coconut
1 cup sugar
2 tablespoons cornstarch
1/4 cup (1/2 stick) margarine

Prepare and bake the cake using the package directions for a 9x13-inch cake pan. Drain the pineapple, reserving 1 cup of the juice. Mix the pineapple, reserved pineapple juice and remaining ingredients in a saucepan. Cook over low heat until thickened, stirring constantly. Pour over the warm or cool cake.
Yield: 15 servings.

Celia Hoy and Ethel Tillery, Riverchase Council

Orange Slice Cake

1 pound chopped dates
1 pound orange slice candy,
  cut into small pieces
1 (3-ounce) can flaked
  coconut
2 cups chopped pecans
3 1/2 cups flour
2 cups sugar

1 cup (2 sticks) margarine,
  softened
4 eggs
1 teaspoon baking soda
1/2 cup buttermilk
2 cups confectioners' sugar
1 cup fresh orange juice

Mix the dates, orange candy, coconut, pecans and flour in a bowl. Beat the sugar and margarine in a mixer bowl until creamy. Add the eggs 1 at a time, beating well after each addition. Stir the baking soda into the buttermilk. Add to the creamed mixture and blend well. Stir in the date mixture. Spoon into a greased and floured tube pan. Bake at 275 degrees for 2 1/2 to 3 hours or until the cake tests done. Cool in the pan for 10 minutes. Remove to a serving plate. Combine the confectioners' sugar and orange juice in a bowl and blend well. Drizzle over the cake. Yield: 16 servings.

Joann Ford, Gadsden Life Member Club

Patience Cake

1 (2-layer) package German
  chocolate cake mix
8 ounces whipped topping
1 cup sour cream
1 cup confectioners' sugar
1 (8-ounce) can crushed
  pineapple, drained

1 cup chopped pecans
1 small can flaked coconut
1 jar maraschino cherries,
  drained, chopped

Prepare and bake the cake using the package directions for two 9-inch cake pans. Cut each cooled cake layer horizontally into 2 layers. Combine the whipped topping, sour cream and confectioners' sugar in a bowl and blend well. Stir in the pineapple, pecans, coconut and maraschino cherries. Spread between the cake layers. Store, covered, in the refrigerator. May substitute frozen coconut for the flaked coconut. Yield: 12 to 16 servings.

Kathryn Morgan, Gadsden Life Member Club

Piña Colada Cake

1 (2-layer) package yellow
  cake mix
¾ (8-ounce) can cream of
  coconut

1 (14-ounce) can sweetened
  condensed milk
16 ounces whipped topping
Shredded coconut to taste

Prepare and bake the cake using the package directions for a 9x13-inch cake pan. Cool in the pan on a wire rack. Punch holes in the cake. Combine the cream of coconut and condensed milk in a bowl and blend well. Pour over the cake. Spread whipped topping over the top. Sprinkle with coconut. Yield: 15 servings.

Brenda Freeman, Birmingham Metro Council

White Chocolate Butter Pecan Cake

3¼ cups sifted flour
½ teaspoon (heaping) nutmeg
1 teaspoon baking powder
½ teaspoon baking soda
1 cup (2 sticks) butter,
  softened
2¼ cups sugar
5 extra-large eggs

1 egg white
1 cup buttermilk
6 ounces Nestlé Premier white
  baking bars, melted
2 cups coarsely chopped
  pecans
White Chocolate Glaze
Pecan meal (optional)

Sift the flour, nutmeg, baking powder and baking soda together. Combine the butter, sugar, eggs and egg white in a large mixer bowl. Beat at high speed for 5 minutes or until light and fluffy. Add the flour mixture alternately with the buttermilk, stirring with a wooden spoon after each addition. Stir in the melted baking bars and pecans. Pour into a greased 10-inch tube pan. Bake at 325 degrees for 1¼ hours or until the center springs back when lightly touched. Cool in the pan on a wire rack for 10 minutes. Loosen the cake from the side of the pan. Remove to a wire rack to cool completely. Drizzle White Chocolate Glaze over the top of the cake, letting the glaze run down the side. Sprinkle with pecan meal. *Note:* Do not substitute bark, which contains paraffin, for the white baking bars. Yield: 16 servings.

White Chocolate Glaze

2 tablespoons water
2 tablespoons light corn syrup
1½ cups confectioners' sugar

6 ounces Nestlé Premier white
  baking bars

Combine the water, corn syrup and confectioners' sugar in a medium bowl and blend well. Stir in the baking bars. Set the bowl over hot but not boiling water. Heat until the baking bars melt and the mixture is of a glaze consistency, stirring frequently. Do not substitute bark, which contains paraffin, for the white baking bars.

Gussie M. Evans, Mobile Council

Poppy Seed Cake

1 (2-layer) package pecan   1 cup hot water
  cake mix   ½ cup vegetable oil
1 (4-ounce) package coconut   3 tablespoons poppy seeds
  instant pudding mix   1 teaspoon vanilla extract
4 eggs   ½ cup chopped pecans

Combine the cake mix, pudding mix, eggs, water, oil, poppy seeds and vanilla in a large mixer bowl and beat until smooth. Stir in the pecans. Pour into a greased and floured bundt pan. Bake at 350 degrees for 35 to 45 minutes or until the cake tests done. Cool in the pan for 10 minutes. Invert onto a serving plate to cool completely. Yield: 16 servings.

Sarah Elam, Montgomery Council

Christmas Rum Cake

1 cup chopped pecans   ½ cup vegetable oil
1 (2-layer) package yellow   ½ cup dark rum
  cake mix   ½ cup (1 stick) butter
1 (4-ounce) package vanilla   ¼ cup water
  instant pudding mix   1 cup sugar
4 eggs   ½ cup dark rum
½ cup cold water

Grease and flour a 10-inch tube pan or 12-cup bundt pan. Sprinkle pecans in the pan. Beat the cake mix, pudding mix, eggs, ½ cup water, oil and ½ cup rum in a mixer bowl until smooth. Pour into the prepared pan. Bake at 325 degrees for 1 hour. Cool in the pan for 10 minutes. Melt the butter in a saucepan. Stir in ¼ cup water and sugar. Boil for 5 minutes, stirring constantly. Remove from the heat. Stir in ½ cup rum. Invert the cake onto a serving plate. Prick the top with a fork. Drizzle the glaze a small amount at a time evenly over the top and side of the cake until all the glaze is absorbed. Yield: 16 servings.

Patricia Newton, Huntsville Council

Yellow Cake with Caramel Icing

2¾ cups flour
2½ teaspoons baking powder
½ teaspoon salt
⅔ cup butter-flavor shortening
2 cups sugar

3 eggs
1½ teaspoons vanilla extract
1½ cups milk
Caramel Icing

Mix the flour, baking powder and salt together. Beat the shortening and sugar in a mixer bowl until creamy. Add the eggs and vanilla and beat until light and fluffy. Add the flour mixture and milk. Beat at low speed until blended, scraping the side of the bowl constantly. Beat at medium speed for 2 minutes, scraping the side of the bowl constantly. Spoon into 2 greased and floured 9-inch cake pans. Bake at 350 degrees for 35 to 45 minutes or until the centers spring back when lightly touched. Cool in the pans for 5 minutes. Invert onto wire racks to cool completely. Spread Caramel Icing between the layers and over the top and side of cake.
Yield: 12 to 16 servings.

Caramel Icing

3½ cups sugar
1½ cups evaporated milk

1 teaspoon vanilla extract

Place ½ cup of the sugar in a small cast-iron skillet. Cook over low heat until caramelized, stirring constantly. Combine the remaining 3 cups sugar and evaporated milk in a saucepan. Heat until the sugar is dissolved. Add the caramel syrup gradually, stirring constantly. Bring just to the boiling point. Cook to 234 to 240 degrees on a candy thermometer, soft-ball stage. Remove from the heat. Cool to lukewarm. Add the vanilla and beat until creamy and of spreading consistency.

Nell D. Bell, Birmingham Life Member Club

Buttermilk Candy

2 cups sugar
1 cup buttermilk
½ cup (1 stick) butter
2 tablespoons light corn syrup

1 teaspoon baking soda
¼ teaspoon salt
1 cup chopped nuts

Combine the sugar, buttermilk, butter, corn syrup, baking soda and salt in a heavy saucepan. Cook, uncovered, over medium heat to 234 to 240 degrees on a candy thermometer, soft-ball stage, stirring constantly. Remove from the heat. Beat until thick. Stir in the nuts. Drop by spoonfuls onto a surface lined with waxed paper. Let stand until cool. Store in an airtight container. Do not use reduced-fat buttermilk in this recipe. Yield: 1¾ pounds.

Sue (Joe) Small, Selma Life Member Club

Candy Wreath

1 wire coat hanger
1 (⅛- to ¼-inch) roll curly
    ribbon, cut into pieces
5 pounds (about) individually-
    wrapped candy

1 large bow
1 bell
1 pair small scissors

Shape the wire hanger into a circle. Tie a piece of ribbon onto one end of each piece of candy. Tie the candy to the wire hanger. Continue until the hanger is completely full. Attach the bow and bell to the top of the wreath. Tie the scissors to the wreath using a piece of ribbon long enough to enable the candy to be cut. Hang on the front door and let guests cut the candy from the wreath. Yield: 5 pounds.

Janet T. Streeter, Montgomery Council

Chocolate Nut Balls

1 (1-pound) package
  confectioners' sugar
1 cup flaked coconut
1 cup chopped pecans
1 cup graham cracker crumbs
1/2 cup crunchy peanut butter

1 cup vegetable oil
1 teaspoon vanilla extract
2 ounces paraffin
2 1/2 cups semisweet chocolate
  chips

Combine the confectioners' sugar, coconut, pecans, cracker crumbs, peanut butter, oil and vanilla in a large bowl and mix well. Shape into balls. Microwave the paraffin and chocolate chips in a microwave-safe bowl on High until melted. Dip the balls into the chocolate mixture and place on a surface lined with waxed paper. Let stand until firm. May reheat the chocolate mixture in the microwave if needed. Yield: 2 pounds.

Jean Escott, Montgomery Council

Chocolate Rum Balls

1 cup semisweet chocolate
  chips
1 (7-ounce) jar marshmallow
  creme
1 tablespoon rum extract

3 cups crisp rice cereal
1/2 cup shredded coconut
1/2 cup chopped pecans
Shredded coconut or chopped
  pecans for coating

Melt the chocolate chips in a double boiler over hot water. Combine the marshmallow creme and flavoring in a small bowl and mix well. Stir into the chocolate. Add the cereal, 1/2 cup coconut and 1/2 cup pecans and mix well. Shape into small balls. Roll in additional coconut or pecans. Place in a single layer in containers. Chill until firm. Yield: 4 dozen.

Mary Crittenden, Huntsville Council

Date Balls

1 cup (2 sticks) margarine
8 ounces dates, chopped
1 cup sugar
1 teaspoon vanilla extract

1 cup finely chopped pecans
2 cups crisp rice cereal
Confectioners' sugar for
coating

Melt the margarine in a heavy saucepan. Stir in the dates and sugar. Cook until thickened, stirring constantly. Remove from the heat. Add the vanilla, pecans and cereal and mix well. Cool completely. Shape into small balls. Roll in confectioners' sugar. Store in a tightly covered container or freeze. Yield: about 4 dozen.

Marie Hartley, Birmingham South Life Member Club

Date Nut Balls

½ cup (1 stick) margarine
¾ cup sugar
8 ounces dates, chopped
1 cup chopped pecans or
walnuts

2½ cups crisp rice cereal
Confectioners' sugar for
coating

Melt the margarine in a heavy saucepan. Stir in the sugar and dates. Cook until thickened, stirring constantly. Stir in the pecans. Pour over the cereal in a large bowl and mix well. Shape into small balls. Sprinkle with confectioners' sugar. Place several balls at a time in confectioners' sugar in a nonrecyled paper bag and shake until coated. Yield: about 4 dozen.

Lynn Gray, Montgomery Council

No-Bake Chocolate Kahlúa Balls

1 (10-ounce) package teddy
  bear-shaped chocolate
  graham cracker cookies
⅔ cup finely chopped pitted
  dates
¼ cup instant nonfat dry milk
  powder

3 tablespoons Kahlúa or other
  coffee liqueur
2 tablespoons skim milk
⅓ cup finely chopped pecans

Process the cookies in a food processor fitted with a knife blade to a fine powder. Add the dates, milk powder, Kahlúa and milk, processing constantly until smooth. Shape into ¾-inch balls. Roll in the pecans. Place in a single layer in containers. Chill, covered, in the refrigerator. Yield: 4 dozen.

Kay Atkisson, Montgomery Life Member Club

Divinity

2 cups sugar
½ cup light corn syrup
¼ cup hot water
¼ teaspoon salt

2 egg whites
Vanilla extract to taste
Chopped pecans to taste

Combine the sugar, corn syrup, hot water and salt in a heavy saucepan. Bring to a boil over medium heat, stirring constantly. Cook to 250 to 268 degrees on a candy thermometer, hard-ball stage; do not stir. Beat the egg whites in a mixer bowl until stiff peaks form. Add the hot syrup mixture gradually, beating constantly. Beat at high speed until thick. Fold in the vanilla and pecans. Drop by teaspoonfuls onto a surface lined with waxed paper. Let stand until cool. Yield: about 1½ pounds.

Mary W. Martin, Birmingham South Life Member Club

Never-Fail Microwave Divinity

4 cups sugar
1 cup light corn syrup
¾ cup water
Dash of salt

3 egg whites
1 teaspoon vanilla extract
2 cups chopped nuts

Combine the sugar, corn syrup, water and salt in a large microwave-safe bowl. Microwave on High for 19 minutes, stirring every 5 minutes. Beat the egg whites in a mixer bowl until stiff peaks form. Add the hot syrup gradually, beating constantly at high speed. Continue beating for 12 minutes or until the mixture is thick and begins to lose its gloss. Fold in the vanilla and nuts. Drop by spoonfuls onto a surface lined with waxed paper. Let stand until cool. Yield: about 3 pounds.

Jan Williams, Riverchase Council

Nutty Fudge

4½ cups sugar
1 (14-ounce) can sweetened
  condensed milk
1 cup (2 sticks) margarine
3 cups chocolate chips

1 (9-ounce) jar marshmallow
  creme
1 tablespoon vanilla extract
4 cups chopped nuts

Combine the sugar and condensed milk in a double boiler. Bring to a boil over medium heat, stirring constantly. Continue to cook for 10 minutes, stirring constantly. Remove from the heat. Stir in the margarine immediately. Add the chocolate chips and marshmallow creme and beat until smooth. Stir in the vanilla and nuts. Pour immediately into four 8x8-inch glass dishes. Let stand until cool. Cut into squares. Yield: 5 pounds.

Brenda Reeves, Birmingham South Cahaba Council

Fudge

3 cups sugar
1/4 cup baking cocoa
1 1/2 cups milk
1/4 teaspoon salt

1 tablespoon light corn syrup
1/2 cup (1 stick) margarine
1 teaspoon vanilla extract
1/2 cup chopped nuts (optional)

Combine the sugar and baking cocoa in a heavy saucepan. Add the milk gradually, stirring constantly. Stir in the salt and corn syrup. Cook over medium heat until 240 to 248 degrees on a candy thermometer, hard-ball stage. Remove from the heat. Add the margarine and vanilla and stir until smooth. Cool for 15 minutes. Beat with a wooden spoon until the mixture loses its gloss. Stir in the nuts. Pour into a buttered dish. Let stand until firm. Cut into squares. Yield: 2 1/2 pounds.

Edith Schlechty, Montgomery Life Member Club

Chocolate Fudge

4 1/2 cups sugar
1/2 teaspoon salt
2 ounces unsweetened
  chocolate
1 cup (2 sticks) margarine
1 (12-ounce) can evaporated
  milk

3 cups chocolate chips
1 (7-ounce) jar marshmallow
  creme
1 tablespoon vanilla extract
4 cups chopped nuts

Combine the sugar, salt, chocolate, margarine and evaporated milk in a large heavy saucepan and mix well. Bring to a boil. Boil for 7 minutes, stirring constantly. Remove from the heat. Add the chocolate chips, marshmallow creme and vanilla and mix until smooth. Stir in the nuts. Beat until the mixture begins to harden. Pour into square pans lined with waxed paper. Cool completely. Cut into squares. Yield: 4 pounds.

Sue (Joe) Small, Selma Life Member Club

Creamy Gift Fudge

6 ounces cream cheese,
   softened
4 cups confectioners' sugar,
   sifted

1 tablespoon vanilla extract
2½ ounces unsweetened
   chocolate, melted
1 cup chopped pecans

Beat the cream cheese and confectioners' sugar in a bowl until smooth. Add the vanilla, melted chocolate and pecans and mix well. Press into an 8x8-inch dish sprayed lightly with nonstick cooking spray. Chill until firm. Cut into small squares.
Yield: about 5 dozen.

Betty C. Gray, Montgomery Life Member Club

Chocolate Fudge

6 ounces white chocolate
2 cups chocolate chips

1½ cups chopped pecans

Place the white chocolate and chocolate chips in a 3- to 4-quart microwave-safe bowl. Microwave for 3 minutes or until melted; mix well. Add the pecans and mix well. Pour into an 8x9-inch buttered dish. Let stand until cool. Cut into squares. Store in an airtight container. Yield: 16 servings.

Maureen Sewell, Birmingham Life Member Club

Peanut Butter Fudge

2 cups sugar
½ cup milk
1⅓ cups peanut butter

1 (7-ounce) jar marshmallow
   creme

Bring the sugar and milk to a boil in a heavy saucepan. Boil for 3 minutes. Add the peanut butter and marshmallow creme and mix well. Pour immediately into a buttered 8x8-inch dish. Chill until set. Cut into small squares. Yield: 3 to 4 dozen.

Virginia S. Killian, Gadsden Life Member Club

Orange Candy Balls

1 pound orange slice candy,
  cut into small pieces
2 (14-ounce) cans sweetened
  condensed milk
2 cups shredded coconut

1 teaspoon orange extract
1 teaspoon vanilla extract
2 cups chopped pecans
Confectioners' sugar for
  coating

Combine the candy, condensed milk, coconut and flavorings in a bowl and mix well. Stir in the pecans. Pour into an ungreased 9x13-inch baking pan. Bake at 325 degrees until light golden brown. Let stand until cool. Shape into balls. Roll in confectioners' sugar to coat. Store in an airtight container. Yield: about 2 pounds.

Nancy Conner, Anniston Council

Peanut Brittle Candy

2 cups raw peanuts
1 cup sugar
1/2 cup light corn syrup

2 tablespoons margarine
1 teaspoon baking soda

Place the peanuts on a baking sheet. Bake at 350 degrees for 5 minutes. Mix the sugar and corn syrup in a 2 1/2-quart microwave-safe dish. Microwave on High for 4 minutes. Stir in the peanuts. Microwave on High for 5 minutes. Stir in the margarine. Microwave on High for 2 minutes. Add the baking soda and mix well. Pour into a pizza pan sprayed with nonstick cooking spray. Let stand until cool. Break into pieces. Yield: about 1 pound.

Flo Watters, Selma Life Member Club

Peanut Clusters

1 cup semisweet chocolate chips	2 cups butterscotch chips
	1 (6-ounce) jar peanuts

Place the chocolate chips and butterscotch chips in a microwave-safe bowl. Microwave on High for 5 minutes or until melted. Stir in the peanuts. Drop by spoonfuls onto a surface lined with waxed paper. Let stand for 30 minutes or until firm. Yield: about 2 pounds.

Susan Currie, Birmingham South Cahaba Council

Sweet Tooth Candy

5 cups sugar	1½ pounds milk chocolate
1 (12-ounce) can evaporated milk	1 (7-ounce) jar marshmallow creme
½ cup (1 stick) butter	3 to 6 cups chopped pecans

Combine the sugar, evaporated milk and butter in a heavy saucepan and mix well. Bring to a boil. Cook for 5 minutes. Remove from the heat. Add the chocolate and stir until melted. Stir in the marshmallow creme. Stir in the pecans. Drop by spoonfuls onto a surface lined with waxed paper or pour into two 9x13-inch dishes. Yield: 8 dozen.

Michael Whisenant, Riverchase Council

Pralines

1 cup heavy cream	2 tablespoons margarine, softened
1 (1-pound) package brown sugar	2 cups pecan halves

Mix the cream and brown sugar in a 4-quart microwave-safe bowl. Microwave on High for 13 minutes. Stir in the margarine and pecans. Drop by teaspoonfuls onto a surface lined with foil. Let stand until firm. Store in an airtight container. Yield: 2 dozen.

Susan Currie, Birmingham South Cahaba Council

Southern Pralines

2 cups sugar
1 cup packed light brown sugar
1/4 teaspoon salt
2/3 cup evaporated milk

1 tablespoon butter or
  margarine
1 teaspoon vanilla extract
2 cups pecan halves

Combine the sugar, brown sugar, salt and evaporated milk in a heavy saucepan and mix well. Cook over medium heat to 234 to 240 degrees on a candy thermometer, soft-ball stage. Remove from the heat and beat lightly. Add the butter and vanilla and mix well. Stir in the pecans. Drop by tablespoonfuls onto a surface lined with waxed paper. Let stand until cool. Yield: about 2 pounds.

Marcelle Kelley, mother-in-law of Cathy Kelley,
Birmingham South Cahaba Council

Praline Pecan Crunch

8 cups oat square cereal
2 cups pecan pieces
1/2 cup light corn syrup
1/2 cup packed brown sugar

1/4 cup (1/2 stick) margarine
1 teaspoon vanilla extract
1/2 teaspoon baking soda

Combine the cereal and pecans in a 9x13-inch baking pan. Combine the corn syrup, brown sugar and margarine in a 2-cup microwave-safe bowl. Microwave on High for 1 1/2 minutes; stir. Microwave for 30 to 90 seconds longer or until the mixture boils. Stir in the vanilla and baking soda. Pour over the cereal mixture. Stir until the cereal mixture is evenly coated. Bake at 250 degrees for 1 hour, stirring every 20 minutes. Spread on a baking sheet to cool. Break into pieces. Yield: 10 cups.

Marilyn Aldridge, Birmingham Life Member Club

Cap'n Crunch Munch

2 cups Cap'n Crunch Cereal	2 cups salted peanuts
2 cups crisp rice cereal	24 ounces almond bark,
2 cups broken pretzels	melted

Combine the cereals, pretzels and peanuts in a large bowl and mix well. Add the almond bark and mix until coated. Spread in a large pan lined with waxed paper. Let stand until cool. Break into pieces. Store in an airtight container. May place in the freezer for a few minutes to harden. Yield: about 4 dozen.

Betty Hyte, Montgomery Council

Candy Cane Cookies

1 cup (2 sticks) butter, softened	2½ cups flour
1 cup confectioners' sugar	¼ teaspoon salt
1 egg	1 cup finely crushed candy canes
½ teaspoon peppermint extract	3 tablespoons sugar
½ teaspoon vanilla extract	

Beat the butter and confectioners' sugar in a mixer bowl until light and fluffy. Add the egg and flavorings and beat until well blended. Add a mixture of the flour and salt gradually, beating well after each addition. Chill, tightly covered with plastic wrap, for 1 hour. Combine the candy canes and sugar in a shallow dish and mix well. Shape the dough into 1-inch balls. Coat with the candy cane mixture. Arrange on a cookie sheet. Bake at 375 degrees for 10 to 12 minutes or until brown. Remove to a wire rack to cool.
Yield: 4 dozen cookies.

Brenda Reeves, Birmingham South Cahaba Council

Prize-Winning Chocolate Chip Cookies

5 cups rolled oats
2 cups (4 sticks) butter,
  softened
2 cups sugar
2 cups packed brown sugar
4 eggs
2 teaspoons vanilla extract
4 cups flour

2 teaspoons baking soda
2 teaspoons baking powder
1 teaspoon salt
4 cups chocolate chips
1 (7-ounce) chocolate candy
  bar, chopped
3 cups chopped nuts

Process the oats in a blender until of a flour consistency. Cream the butter, sugar and brown sugar in a mixer bowl. Beat in the eggs and vanilla. Add a mixture of the flour, oats, baking soda, baking powder and salt and mix well. Stir in the chocolate chips, candy bar and nuts. Shape into small balls. Arrange 2 inches apart on a cookie sheet. Bake at 375 degrees for 10 minutes. Cool on the cookie sheet for 2 minutes; remove to a wire rack to cool completely. May divide recipe in half. Yield: 10 dozen cookies.

Chrys Gibbs, Birmingham South Cahaba Council

Easy Chocolate Chip Cookies

2 eggs
1/2 cup vegetable oil
1 (2-layer) package yellow
  cake mix

1 cup chopped pecans
1 cup semisweet chocolate
  chips

Combine the eggs and oil in a large bowl and mix well. Stir in the cake mix, pecans and chocolate chips. Drop by spoonfuls 2 inches apart onto an ungreased cookie sheet. Bake at 325 degrees for 15 minutes. Cool on the cookie sheet for 2 minutes; remove to a wire rack to cool completely. Yield: 3 to 4 dozen cookies.

Sybil Bynum, Gadsden Life Member Club

Coconut Fruitcake Cookies

16 ounces mixed candied fruit
1/2 cup plain or self-rising flour
1 (3-ounce) can shredded
   coconut

2 cups chopped pecans
1 (14-ounce) can sweetened
   condensed milk
1/8 teaspoon salt

Coat the fruit with the flour in a large bowl. Add the coconut, pecans, condensed milk and salt and mix well. Drop by spoonfuls 2 inches apart onto a greased cookie sheet. Bake at 275 degrees for 20 to 30 minutes. Cool on the cookie sheet for 2 minutes; remove to a wire rack to cool completely. Store in an airtight container for 5 days before serving. Yield: 4 dozen cookies.

Joyce Thomas, Birmingham South Cahaba Council

Fruitcake Cookies

1 cup flour
1/2 teaspoon cinnamon
1/2 teaspoon nutmeg
1/2 teaspoon baking soda
1 1/2 tablespoons milk
1/2 cup orange juice
12 ounces golden raisins
8 ounces candied cherries
8 ounces candied pineapple

8 ounces chopped dates
1/2 cup flour
1/4 cup (1/2 stick) butter,
   softened
1/2 cup packed brown sugar
2 egg yolks
3 cups nuts
2 egg whites

Sift 1 cup flour, cinnamon and nutmeg together. Dissolve the baking soda in the milk. Stir in the orange juice. Toss the raisins, cherries, pineapple and dates with 1/2 cup flour. Cream the butter and brown sugar in a mixer bowl. Beat in the egg yolks. Beat in the flour mixture alternately with the orange juice mixture. Stir in the raisin mixture and nuts. Beat the egg whites in a mixer bowl until stiff peaks form. Fold into the batter. Drop by spoonfuls 2 inches apart onto a greased cookie sheet. Bake at 300 degrees for 15 to 20 minutes or until brown. Cool on the cookie sheet for 2 minutes; remove to a wire rack to cool completely. Yield: 5 to 6 dozen cookies.

Mrs. Bob H. Henson, Birmingham South Life Member Club

Claxton Fruitcake Cookies

1 (1-pound) Claxton
   Fruitcake, crumbled
1 (2-layer) package yellow
   cake mix

2 eggs
1/3 cup vegetable oil
1/2 teaspoon rum extract
1 1/2 cups chopped pecans

Combine the fruitcake and cake mix in a bowl and toss to mix well. Stir in the eggs, oil, flavoring and pecans. Drop by spoonfuls 2 inches apart onto a greased cookie sheet. Bake at 350 degrees for 10 minutes. Cool on the cookie sheet for 2 minutes; remove to a wire rack to cool completely. Yield: 8 to 9 dozen cookies.

Patsi Holmes, Birmingham South Cahaba Council

Fruit Rocks

16 cups chopped pecans
32 ounces candied pineapple
8 ounces red candied cherries
8 ounces green candied
   cherries
1 1/2 cups flour
1 cup bourbon
2 cups flour
2 teaspoons cinnamon

2 teaspoons ground cloves
2 teaspoons allspice
2 teaspoons nutmeg
1/2 teaspoon salt
1 cup (2 sticks) margarine,
   softened
1 1/2 cups sugar
5 eggs
2 teaspoons vanilla extract

Coat the pecans, pineapple and cherries with 1 1/2 cups flour in a large nonreactive bowl. Add the bourbon and mix well. Let stand, covered, for 10 to 12 hours. Mix 2 cups flour, cinnamon, cloves, allspice, nutmeg and salt together. Cream the margarine and sugar in a mixer bowl. Beat in the eggs and vanilla. Stir in the pecan mixture. Drop by spoonfuls 2 inches apart onto a greased cookie sheet. Bake at 325 degrees for 15 to 20 minutes. Cool on the cookie sheet for 2 minutes; remove to a wire rack to cool completely. Note: May divide recipe in half. Yield: 25 dozen cookies.

Joe Small, Selma Life Member Club

Molasses Cookies

2 cups flour
2 teaspoons baking soda
1 teaspoon allspice
½ teaspoon salt

1 cup sugar
¼ cup molasses
¾ cup peanut oil
1 egg

Sift the flour, baking soda, allspice and salt together. Combine the sugar, molasses, peanut oil and egg in a large bowl and mix well. Stir in the flour mixture. Chill, covered, until firm. Shape into 1-inch balls. Coat with additional sugar. Arrange 2 inches apart on an ungreased cookie sheet. Bake at 350 degrees for 10 minutes or until brown. Cool on the cookie sheet for 2 minutes; remove to a wire rack to cool completely. Yield: 2 to 3 dozen cookies.

Betty B. Bush, Montgomery Council

Nut Butter Balls

2 cups sifted flour
¼ cup sugar
½ teaspoon salt
1 cup (2 sticks) butter,
   softened

2 teaspoons vanilla extract
2½ cups finely chopped
   pecans
Confectioners' sugar

Sift the flour, sugar and salt into a bowl. Add the butter and vanilla and mix with fingers. Mix in the pecans. Shape into small balls. Arrange 2 inches apart on a cookie sheet. Bake at 350 degrees for 20 minutes or until golden brown. Coat with confectioners' sugar while warm. Yield: 2 to 3 dozen cookies.

Mrs. Bob H. Henson, Birmingham South Life Member Club

Oatmeal Cookies

3 cups rolled oats
1½ cups flour
1 teaspoon salt
1 teaspoon baking soda
1 teaspoon cinnamon
1 cup chopped pecans

1 cup (2 sticks) butter, melted
1 cup packed brown sugar
1 cup sugar
2 eggs, beaten
1 teaspoon vanilla extract

Combine the oats, flour, salt, baking soda, cinnamon and pecans in a large bowl and mix well. Stir in the butter, brown sugar, sugar, eggs and vanilla. Let stand, covered, for 1 hour. Drop by teaspoonfuls 2 inches apart onto an ungreased cookie sheet. Bake at 325 degrees for 10 to 12 minutes or until golden brown, watching carefully to prevent burning. Cool on the cookie sheet for 1 minute; remove to a wire rack to cool completely.
Yield: 5 to 6 dozen cookies.

Sandra Deason, Birmingham South Cahaba Council

Oatmeal Nut Cookies

1½ cups sifted flour
1 teaspoon baking soda
1 teaspoon salt
1 cup shortening
¾ cup sugar
¾ cup packed light brown
    sugar

2 eggs
1 teaspoon vanilla extract
2 cups quick-cooking oats
1 cup chopped pecans

Sift the flour, baking soda and salt together. Beat the shortening, sugar, brown sugar, eggs and vanilla in a mixer bowl at medium speed until light and fluffy. Mix in the flour mixture and oats. Stir in the pecans; mixture will be stiff. Drop by rounded teaspoonfuls 2 inches apart onto a lightly greased cookie sheet. Bake at 375 degrees for 10 to 12 minutes or until golden brown. Cool on the cookie sheet for 1 minute; remove to a wire rack to cool completely.
Yield: 6 dozen cookies.

Mrs. Bob H. Henson, Birmingham South Life Member Club

Quick and Easy Chocolate Oatmeal Cookies

2 cups sugar
1/4 cup baking cocoa
1/2 cup (1 stick) butter
1/2 cup milk

2 teaspoons vanilla extract
3 cups quick-cooking oats
1/2 cup peanut butter
1/2 cup nuts (optional)

Combine the sugar, baking cocoa, butter and milk in a saucepan over medium-high heat. Cook until the mixture comes to a rolling boil, stirring constantly. Boil for 2 minutes, stirring constantly. Remove from the heat. Stir in the vanilla, oats, peanut butter and nuts. Drop by teaspoonfuls 2 inches apart onto waxed paper. Let stand until firm. Yield: 3 to 4 dozen cookies.

Donna Lynn Pike, Birmingham South Cahaba Council

Peanut Butter Elf Bites

1/2 cup sugar
1/2 cup light corn syrup

1 cup peanut butter
2 cups crisp rice cereal

Cook the sugar and corn syrup in a saucepan over medium heat until the mixture comes to a boil, stirring constantly. Remove from the heat. Add the peanut butter and stir until smooth. Stir in the cereal. Drop by tablespoonfuls 2 inches apart onto waxed paper. Let stand until cool. Yield: 3 dozen cookies.

Marilyn Aldridge, Birmingham Life Member Club

Wrap chocolate in foil before putting it in the refrigerator, and it will not turn white.

Persimmon Cookies

2 cups flour
1 teaspoon baking soda
½ teaspoon cinnamon
½ teaspoon ground cloves
½ teaspoon nutmeg
1 cup sugar

½ cup (1 stick) butter,
    softened
1 egg
1 cup persimmon pulp
1 cup raisins
1 cup chopped nuts

Mix the flour, baking soda, cinnamon, cloves and nutmeg together. Cream the sugar and butter in a mixer bowl. Beat in the egg. Add the flour mixture and mix well. Stir in the persimmon pulp, raisins and nuts. Drop by rounded teaspoonfuls 2 inches apart onto a cookie sheet. Bake at 350 degrees for 12 to 15 minutes or just until light brown. Cool on the cookie sheet for 2 minutes; remove to a wire rack to cool completely. Yield: 3 dozen cookies.

Pat White, Montgomery Council

Thumbprint Cookies

1 cup (2 sticks) butter or
    margarine
¼ cup sugar
2 cups flour
¼ teaspoon salt

1 teaspoon vanilla extract
1 cup finely chopped nuts
1 cup confectioners' sugar
½ teaspoon almond extract
Red and green food coloring

Cream the butter and sugar in a mixer bowl. Mix in the flour, salt and vanilla. Stir in the nuts. Drop by teaspoonfuls 2 inches apart onto an ungreased cookie sheet. Make an indentation in each cookie with thumb. Bake at 300 degrees for 20 to 30 minutes. Cool on the cookie sheet for 2 minutes; remove to a wire rack to cool completely. Mix the confectioners' sugar, almond extract and enough water to make of glaze consistency in a bowl. Divide the glaze evenly between 2 bowls. Add 2 drops of red food coloring to 1 portion of the glaze and mix well. Add 2 drops of green food coloring to the remaining glaze and mix well. Spoon a small amount of glaze onto the center of each cookie. Yield: 3 dozen cookies.

Pat Ramsey, sister of Cathy Kelley, Birmingham South Cahaba Council

Grandma's Christmas Cookie Bars

1 cup (2 sticks) butter,
  softened
1½ cups sugar
2 tablespoons sour cream
1 teaspoon sugar
1 teaspoon vanilla extract
1 large egg
3 cups flour
¼ teaspoon baking soda

¼ teaspoon baking powder
1½ cups ground pecans
2 tablespoons sugar
½ cup packed brown sugar
1 large egg
1 teaspoon vanilla extract
Red sprinkles
Green sprinkles

Cream the butter and 1½ cups sugar in a mixer bowl. Combine the sour cream, 1 teaspoon sugar, 1 teaspoon vanilla and 1 egg in a bowl and mix well. Add the butter mixture and mix well. Mix the flour, baking soda and baking powder together. Add to the sour cream mixture and mix well. Stir in additional flour if mixture is too sticky. Chill, covered, for 3 hours or longer. Divide the dough into 2 equal portions. Pat 1 portion of the dough over the bottom of a buttered 9x13-inch baking pan. Combine the pecans, 2 tablespoons sugar, brown sugar, 1 egg and 1 teaspoon vanilla in a bowl and stir until of a paste consistency. Spread evenly over the dough in the baking pan. Roll the remaining portion of dough until thin. Cut into strips. Arrange the strips lattice-fashion over the pecan mixture. Top with red and green sprinkles. Bake at 350 degrees for 30 minutes, covering with foil when brown to prevent the top from burning. Yield: 3 to 4 dozen bars.

Debra Lawyer, Birmingham South Cahaba Council

Festive Cranberry Cheese Squares

2 cups flour
1 1/2 cups rolled oats
1/4 cup packed brown sugar
1 cup (2 sticks) butter or
  margarine, softened
8 ounces cream cheese,
  softened
1 (14-ounce) can sweetened
  condensed milk

2 eggs
1 (27-ounce) jar mincemeat
2 tablespoons cornstarch
1 tablespoon brown sugar
1 (16-ounce) can whole
  cranberry sauce

Combine the flour, oats, 1/4 cup brown sugar and butter in a mixer bowl and beat until crumbly. Reserve 1 1/2 cups of the crumb mixture. Press the remaining crumb mixture evenly over the bottom of a 10x15-inch cookie sheet with sides. Bake at 350 degrees for 15 minutes or until light brown. Beat the cream cheese in a mixer bowl until light and fluffy. Add the condensed milk and beat until smooth. Beat in the eggs. Spread over the prepared crust. Spread with the mincemeat. Mix the cornstarch and 1 tablespoon brown sugar in a bowl. Stir in the cranberry sauce. Spoon over the mincemeat. Sprinkle with the reserved crumb mixture. Bake at 350 degrees for 40 minutes or until golden brown. Let stand until cool. Chill, covered, until serving time. Cut into squares. Store, covered, in the refrigerator. Yield: 16 to 20 bars.

Susan Currie, Birmingham South Cahaba Council

Chocolate Coconut Bars

2 cups graham cracker crumbs
½ cup (1 stick) butter or
   margarine, melted
¼ cup sugar
2 cups flaked coconut
1 (14-ounce) can sweetened
   condensed milk

½ cup chopped pecans
1 (7-ounce) chocolate candy
   bar
2 tablespoons creamy peanut
   butter

Mix the graham cracker crumbs, butter and sugar in a bowl. Press over the bottom of a 9x13-inch baking pan. Bake at 350 degrees for 10 minutes. Combine the coconut, condensed milk and pecans in a bowl and mix well. Spread over the prepared crust. Bake at 350 degrees for 15 minutes. Let stand until cool. Melt the candy bar in a small saucepan over low heat. Add the peanut butter and stir until well mixed. Spread over the coconut mixture. Let stand until chocolate is set. Cut into bars. Yield: 3 dozen bars.

Virginia S. Killian, Gadsden Life Member Club

Fruit Bars

¾ cup sifted flour
1½ teaspoons baking powder
1 teaspoon salt
2 eggs
1 cup confectioners' sugar

3 tablespoons melted
   shortening
1 cup nuts
1 cup chopped dates
¾ cup mixed fruit

Sift the flour, baking powder and salt together. Beat the eggs in a mixer bowl until foamy. Add the confectioners' sugar gradually, beating well after each addition. Mix in the shortening. Add the dry ingredients and mix well. Stir in the nuts, dates and fruit. Spoon into a greased 8x8-inch baking pan. Bake at 325 degrees for 30 to 35 minutes or until golden brown. Cut into squares while warm. Remove from the baking pan. Yield: 16 squares.

Earline Weaver, Shoals Life Member Club

Unbaked Cherry Pies

1 (21-ounce) can cherry pie
　filling
1 (8-ounce) can crushed
　pineapple
1½ cups flaked coconut
1 (14-ounce) can sweetened
　condensed milk

1½ cups miniature
　marshmallows
1½ cups chopped pecans
12 ounces whipped topping
2 baked (9-inch) pie shells

Combine the cherry pie filling, pineapple, coconut, condensed milk and marshmallows in a large bowl and mix well. Fold in the chopped pecans and whipped topping. Pour into the prepared pie shells. Chill until serving time. Yield: 12 servings.

Ilean Moore, Decatur Council

Sandy's Delicious Chocolate Pie

1 cup sugar
2 tablespoons flour or
　cornstarch
3 tablespoons baking cocoa
2 egg yolks

2 cups milk
2 tablespoons butter
½ teaspoon vanilla extract
1 baked (9-inch) pie shell
Whipped topping

Combine the sugar, flour and baking cocoa in a large mixer bowl. Add the egg yolks and milk and beat well. Pour the mixture into a saucepan and cook over medium heat, stirring constantly, until thickened. Add the butter and vanilla, stirring until the butter is melted. Pour into the prepared pie shell. Chill until set. Top with whipped topping. Yield: 6 to 8 servings.

Margaret Copelin, Montgomery Life Member Club

Chocolate Chip Pie

1 cup sugar
½ cup flour
2 eggs, beaten
½ cup (1 stick) margarine,
   softened

1 teaspoon vanilla extract
1 cup chocolate chips
1 cup chopped pecans
1 unbaked (9-inch) pie shell

Combine the sugar, flour, eggs and margarine in a large mixer bowl and beat until well blended. Stir in the vanilla. Fold in the chocolate chips and pecans. Pour into the pie shell. Bake at 350 degrees for 1 hour. Yield: 6 to 8 servings.

Debbie Speaks, Montgomery Council

Buttermilk Coconut Pie

1½ cups sugar
2 tablespoons flour
3 eggs, well beaten
½ cup (1 stick) margarine,
   melted

½ cup buttermilk
1 teaspoon vanilla extract
1 (3-ounce) can flaked
   coconut
1 unbaked (9-inch) pie shell

Combine the sugar and flour in a large bowl and mix well. Add the eggs, margarine, buttermilk and vanilla and mix until well blended. Fold in ⅔ of the coconut. Pour into the pie shell. Sprinkle with the remaining coconut. Bake at 325 degrees for 1 hour.
Yield: 6 to 8 servings.

Kathryn Morgan, Gadsden Life Member Club

Jeff Davis Pie

3 eggs, separated
1/4 cup (1/2 stick) butter,
  softened
1/2 cup packed brown sugar
1/2 cup sugar

1/2 cup milk
1 tablespoon flour
1 teaspoon vanilla extract
1 unbaked (9-inch) pie shell
Sugar to taste

Beat the egg yolks, butter, brown sugar and sugar in a large mixer bowl until light and fluffy. Beat in the milk, flour and vanilla until blended. Pour into the pie shell. Bake at 350 degrees for 35 to 40 minutes. Beat the egg whites in a mixer bowl until stiff peaks form, adding sugar to taste. Spread over the pie and return to the oven until the meringue is golden brown. Yield: 6 to 8 servings.

Janet T. Streeter, Montgomery Council

Pecan Pies

1/2 cup (1 stick) margarine,
  softened
1 cup dark corn syrup
1 cup sugar

3 eggs, beaten
1 teaspoon vanilla extract
2 1/2 cups chopped pecans
2 unbaked (9-inch) pie shells

Cream the margarine, corn syrup and sugar in a mixer bowl until light and fluffy. Add the eggs and vanilla, stirring until well blended. Fold in the pecans. Pour into the pie shells. Bake at 350 degrees for 45 minutes. Yield: 12 to 16 servings.

Marie Hartley, Birmingham South Life Member Club

Golden Eagle Pecan Pie

3 eggs, slightly beaten
½ cup sugar
1 cup Golden Eagle syrup
1 teaspoon vanilla extract

¼ teaspoon salt
1 cup pecan pieces
1 unbaked (9-inch) pie shell

Combine the eggs, sugar, syrup, vanilla and salt in a large mixer bowl and beat until well blended. Sprinkle the pecan pieces in the bottom of the pie shell. Pour the filling over the pecans. Bake at 350 degrees for 30 to 40 minutes or until a knife inserted in the center comes out clean. Yield: 6 to 8 servings.

Dot Johnson, Gadsden Life Member Club

Pecan Tarts

½ cup (1 stick) butter,
  softened
3 ounces cream cheese,
  softened
1 cup sifted flour
1 cup chopped pecans
1½ eggs, beaten (1 egg plus
  2 tablespoons or 2 small
  eggs)

½ cup light corn syrup
½ cup sugar
1 teaspoon flour
½ teaspoon vanilla extract
⅛ teaspoon salt

Beat the butter and cream cheese in a mixer bowl until smooth. Add 1 cup flour and mix well. Chill the dough in the refrigerator. Press the dough over the bottom and sides of ungreased 1¾-inch muffin cups. Place a few pecans on the bottom of each cup. Combine the eggs and corn syrup in a bowl and stir just until blended. Add the sugar, 1 teaspoon flour, vanilla and salt and stir until blended. Do not beat. Pour the filling over the pecans; filling should be about 1/16-inch from the top of the shell. Bake at 325 degrees for 30 minutes. Yield: 6 to 8 servings.

Mrs. Bob H. Henson, Birmingham South Life Member Club

Shoe Peg Corn Dip

1 (12-ounce) can Shoe Peg
  corn, drained
1 cup sour cream
1 cup shredded sharp Cheddar
  cheese
1/4 cup grated Parmesan
  cheese
1/2 cup mayonnaise
1 to 2 tablespoons grated
  onion

Combine the corn, sour cream, Cheddar cheese, Parmesan cheese, mayonnaise and onion in a bowl and mix well. Chill, covered, for several hours. Garnish with fresh parsley sprigs if desired. Serve with tortilla chips or crackers. Yield: 3 1/2 cups.

Narice Sutton, Birmingham Life Member Club

Fruit Dip

8 ounces cream cheese
1 (14-ounce) can sweetened
  condensed milk
16 ounces (or more) whipped
  topping

Beat the cream cheese in a mixer bowl until light and fluffy. Beat in the condensed milk. Add the whipped topping and mix well. Serve with bite-size fresh fruit for dipping. Yield: 3 to 4 cups.

Celia Stephens, Montgomery Council

Jalapeño Dip

16 ounces mild Cheddar
  cheese, shredded
2 medium onions, grated
8 jalapeño chiles, minced
3 garlic cloves, minced
1/2 teaspoon salt
2 cups mayonnaise

Combine the Cheddar cheese, onions, chiles, garlic, salt and mayonnaise in a mixer bowl. Beat at high speed for 4 to 5 minutes or until mixed. Store, covered, in the refrigerator for 1 week before serving. Serve with tortilla chips. Yield: 4 to 5 cups.

Alice Walski, Birmingham Life Member Club

Egg Salad Sandwich Spread

3 hard-cooked eggs, chopped
8 ounces cream cheese,
  softened
1/4 cup grated onion
1/4 cup finely chopped green
  bell pepper
1 (2-ounce) jar chopped
  pimento

2 tablespoons relish
2 tablespoons mayonnaise
1 tablespoon catsup
Salt to taste
3/4 cup chopped pecans

Combine the eggs, cream cheese, onion, green pepper, pimento and relish in a bowl and mix well. Add the mayonnaise, catsup and salt and mix well. Stir in the pecans. Use to make sandwiches or serve as a dip with assorted party crackers. Yield: 1 1/2 to 2 cups.

Mary Ann Sparks Fulmer, Shoals Life Member Club

Italian Cream Cheese Pinwheels

3 ounces cream cheese,
  softened
1 tablespoon grated Parmesan
  cheese

2 teaspoons Italian seasoning
1 teaspoon onion powder
1/4 teaspoon garlic powder
1 (8-count) can crescent rolls

Combine the cream cheese, Parmesan cheese, Italian seasoning, onion and garlic powder in a bowl and mix well. Unroll the dough on a lightly floured surface and press the perforations together to form a rectangle. Spread the cream cheese mixture over the dough to within 1/4 inch of the edges. Roll as for a jelly roll from the short end and seal the edge. Cut into 12 slices. Arrange the slices cut side down on an ungreased baking sheet. Bake at 375 degrees for 12 to 15 minutes or until golden brown. Sprinkle with additional Parmesan cheese if desired. Yield: 12 pinwheels.

Susan Currie, Birmingham South Cahaba Council

Pink Party Pinwheels

1 (8-ounce) can crushed
   pineapple
8 ounces cream cheese,
   softened
1 small jar strawberry
   preserves

Red food coloring (optional)
1 loaf bread
Margarine, softened

Pour the pineapple into a strainer or colander and drain the juice, pressing with a fork. Combine the well drained pineapple, cream cheese and preserves in a bowl and mix well. Add 1 or 2 drops of food coloring to make of the desired tint. Trim the crusts from the bread and roll the slices flat with a rolling pin. Spread lightly with margarine and then a thin layer of the cream cheese mixture. Roll each slice as for a jelly roll. Wrap in plastic wrap and freeze until shortly before serving time. Slice thinly and arrange on a serving plate. Yield: 6 to 7 dozen pinwheels.

Sue (Joe) Small, Selma Life Member Club

Salsa Bites

8 ounces cream cheese,
   softened
1/3 cup thick and chunky salsa
2 eggs, lightly beaten
1/2 cup shredded Cheddar
   cheese

2 tablespoons chopped black
   olives
1 tablespoon chopped green
   onions
1 garlic clove, pressed

Beat the cream cheese in a bowl until smooth. Stir in the salsa, eggs, cheese, olives, green onions and garlic. Spoon into 24 miniature muffin cups sprayed with nonstick cooking spray. Bake at 350 degrees for 15 to 18 minutes or until set in the centers. Cool in the pan for 5 minutes. Remove to a wire rack to cool completely. Arrange on a serving plate and top with additional salsa just before serving. Yield: 24 appetizers.

Brenda Reeves, Birmingham South Cahaba Council

Party Meatballs

1 pound lean ground beef
1 pound sharp Cheddar
  cheese, shredded

2½ cups baking mix
Salt and pepper to taste
Mrs. Dash seasoning to taste

Combine the ground beef, cheese, baking mix, salt, pepper and Mrs. Dash seasoning in a bowl and mix well. Shape into small balls and place in a nonstick shallow baking pan. Bake at 350 degrees for 20 minutes or until cooked through, turning as necessary. Drain on paper towels and serve hot. Yield: 2 to 3 dozen meatballs.

Marcelle Kelley, mother-in-law of Cathy Kelley,
Birmingham South Cahaba Council

Sausage Roll

1 pound bulk hot sausage
1 pound Velveeta cheese,
  chopped

1 pound sharp Cheddar
  cheese, shredded

Cook the sausage in a skillet until brown and almost crispy, stirring until crumbly; drain. Combine the cheeses in a large microwave-safe bowl. Microwave until the cheeses are completely melted, stirring frequently. Add the sausage and mix well. Pour into a bundt pan sprayed with nonstick cooking spray. Chill for 3 hours. Invert onto a serving plate. Cut into slices to serve with crackers. Yield: 12 to 15 servings.

Cathy Holmes, Mobile Council

Nuts and Bolts

2 cups (4 sticks) butter,
  melted
3 tablespoons Worcestershire
  sauce
1 tablespoon garlic powder
1 teaspoon salt
1 (14-ounce) package oat
  Chex cereal

1 (12-ounce) package rice
  Chex cereal
1 (12-ounce) package corn
  Chex cereal
2 packages pretzel sticks
1 can roasted peanuts

Combine the butter, Worcestershire sauce, garlic powder and salt
and mix well. Combine the cereals, pretzels and peanuts in a large
bowl and toss gently. Pour half the cereal mixture into a large
baking pan. Drizzle half the butter mixture over the cereal mixture
and mix gently. Bake at 250 degrees for 2½ hours, stirring every 30
minutes. Spread on paper towels to drain and cool. Repeat with the
remaining ingredients. Store in airtight containers.
Yield: 25 to 30 servings.

Bernice Moore, Birmingham South Cahaba Council

Pitty Pat Citrus Punch

¼ cup citric acid powder
½ cup boiling water
6 cups sugar
5 quarts cold water
1 (46-ounce) can pineapple
  juice

1 (6-ounce) can frozen orange
  concentrate, thawed
1 quart ginger ale, chilled

Dissolve the citric acid in the boiling water and set aside. Dissolve
the sugar in the cold water in a large container. Add the citric acid,
pineapple juice and orange juice concentrate and mix well. Add
the ginger ale just before serving. Serve over ice. Yield: 2 gallons.

Francis M. Tucker, Selma Life Member Club

Cottage Cheese and Fruit Salad

8 ounces whipped topping
1 small container cream-style
   cottage cheese
1 tablespoon mayonnaise
1 (20-ounce) can crushed
   pineapple, drained

3 handfuls miniature
   marshmallows
Pitted cherries to taste
Chopped pecans to taste

Combine the whipped topping, cottage cheese and mayonnaise in a large bowl and mix well. Add the pineapple, marshmallows, cherries and pecans and mix well. Chill, covered, for 8 to 10 hours. Yield: 6 to 8 servings.

Sadie William Bryars, Mobile Council

Spaghetti Fruit Salad

1 cup confectioners' sugar
2 eggs, beaten
1/2 cup lemon juice
1/2 teaspoon salt
8 ounces spaghetti
1 (20-ounce) can pineapple
   tidbits

3 medium tart apples, diced
8 ounces whipped topping
1/4 cup chopped walnuts
Maraschino cherry halves

Combine the confectioners' sugar, eggs, lemon juice and salt in a saucepan. Cook over medium heat for about 4 minutes or to 160 degrees on a candy thermometer until the mixture is thickened, stirring constantly. Remove from heat. Let stand until cool. Break the spaghetti into 2-inch pieces and cook using package directions; drain. Rinse with cold water and drain well. Place the spaghetti in a large bowl. Drain the pineapple, reserving the juice. Pour the reserved juice over the spaghetti. Add the apples and toss gently; drain. Add the pineapple tidbits and the cooked mixture and mix gently. Chill, covered, for 8 to 10 hours. Fold in the whipped topping just before serving. Sprinkle with the walnuts and maraschino cherries. Yield: 12 to 14 servings.

Frankie (A.T.) Vaughn, Selma Life Member Club

Broccoli Salad

1 large bunch broccoli
8 slices crisp-fried bacon,
    crumbled
5 green onions, sliced

½ cup raisins
1 cup mayonnaise
2 tablespoons vinegar
¼ cup sugar

Rinse the broccoli. Discard leaves and tough stems. Cut the florets and tender stems into bite-size pieces and place in a large bowl. Add the bacon, green onions and raisins. Blend the mayonnaise, vinegar and sugar in a small bowl. Add to the broccoli mixture and toss until coated. Chill, covered, for 3 to 4 hours. Yield: 6 servings.

Sue (Joe) Small, Selma Life Member Club

Cabbage Salad

1 large head cabbage,
    shredded
1 cup thinly sliced purple
    onion
1 cup sugar
1 cup vinegar

¾ cup vegetable oil
1 tablespoon sugar
1 teaspoon dry mustard
1 teaspoon salt
1 teaspoon celery seeds

Combine the cabbage and onion in a large bowl. Sprinkle the 1 cup sugar over the vegetables. Combine the vinegar, oil, 1 tablespoon sugar, dry mustard, salt and celery seeds in a small saucepan. Bring to a boil, stirring constantly. Pour over the cabbage mixture. Chill, covered, until serving time. Yield: 6 to 8 servings.

Faye S. King, Huntsville Council

Scandinavian Relish

1 (8-ounce) can tiny peas, drained
1 (8-ounce) can green beans, drained
1 (11-ounce) can Shoe Peg corn, drained
1 (2-ounce) jar chopped pimento, drained
1/2 cup chopped celery
1/2 cup chopped red onion
1/2 cup chopped green bell pepper
1/2 cup white vinegar
1/2 cup vegetable oil
1/2 cup sugar
1 teaspoon salt
1 teaspoon pepper

Drain the peas, green beans, corn and pimento in a bowl and mix well. Add the celery, onion and green pepper. Combine the vinegar, oil, sugar, salt and pepper in a small bowl and mix until the sugar dissolves. Pour over the vegetables and mix well. Chill, covered, for 24 hours, stirring occasionally. Yield: 8 to 12 servings.

Sue (Joe) Small, Selma Life Member Club

String Salad

12 ounces spaghetti
1 (16-ounce) bottle oil and vinegar salad dressing
2 small yellow squash, chopped
2 small zucchini, chopped
1/2 cup sliced black olives
1/2 cup sliced green olives
1/2 cup chopped celery
1/2 cup chopped green bell pepper
2 or 3 scallions, sliced
4 or 5 fresh mushrooms, sliced

Cook the spaghetti using package directions; drain. Rinse with cold water; drain well. Toss with the salad dressing in a large bowl. Add the yellow squash, zucchini, black olives, green olives, celery, green peppers, scallions and mushrooms, tossing to mix. Chill, covered, for several hours. Yield: 20 servings.

Alice Walski, Birmingham Life Member Club

Spicy Beef Salad

8 ounces boneless sirloin steak
1/3 cup lime juice
1 tablespoon brown sugar
1 tablespoon soy sauce
1 teaspoon basil
3/4 teaspoon dried mint
1 jalapeño chile, minced

2 to 3 garlic cloves, minced
1/2 teaspoon ginger
1 large red or green bell
   pepper, julienned
1/2 medium cucumber, chopped
6 cups torn mixed salad greens

Place the steak in the freezer until partially frozen. Cut the steak crossgrain into thin strips and set aside. Combine the lime juice, brown sugar, soy sauce, basil and mint in a small bowl and mix well. Preheat a medium nonstick skillet sprayed with nonstick cooking spray. Add the jalapeño chile, garlic and ginger. Stir-fry for 30 seconds. Add the steak strips. Stir-fry until the beef is of the desired degree of doneness. Toss the steak strips with the green pepper and cucumber in a bowl. Place the greens in a salad bowl. Top with the steak mixture. Pour the lime juice mixture into the skillet and bring to a boil. Drizzle over the salad and serve immediately.
Yield: 4 servings.

Frankie (A.T.) Vaughn, Selma Life Member Club

Amish Sweet-and-Sour Salad Dressing

1 cup sugar
1 cup vegetable oil
1/3 cup vinegar
1 tablespoon mayonnaise-type
   salad dressing

1 tablespoon prepared mustard
1 teaspoon celery salt
1/4 teaspoon pepper
1 medium onion, finely
   chopped

Combine the sugar, oil, vinegar, salad dressing, mustard, celery salt and pepper in a small bowl and beat until well blended. Mix in the onion. Store in a tightly covered container in the refrigerator for up to several weeks. May increase the mayonnaise-type salad dressing to 1 cup, omit the pepper and add 1/2 teaspoon salt. Yield: 2 1/2 cups.

Francis M. Tucker, Selma Life Member Club

Easy Beef Stroganoff

1 small onion, chopped
1 (3-ounce) can chopped
  mushrooms, drained

2 tablespoons margarine
1 (12-ounce) can roast beef
1 cup sour cream

Sauté the onion and mushrooms in the margarine in a large skillet until the onion is tender. Add the roast beef and mix well. Stir in the sour cream. Heat to serving temperature, stirring frequently; do not boil. Serve over hot cooked rice or noodles.
Yield: 2 to 3 servings.

Fran Coleman, Huntsville Council

Mexican Casserole

2 pounds ground beef
1 large onion, chopped
1 (10-ounce) can enchilada
  sauce
2 (10-ounce) cans cream of
  mushroom soup

1 soup can water
2 (4-ounce) cans chopped
  green chiles
12 tortillas
12 ounces longhorn cheese,
  shredded

Brown the ground beef with the onion in a large skillet, stirring until the ground beef is crumbly; drain. Stir in the enchilada sauce. Simmer for several minutes, stirring occasionally. Combine the soup, water and green chiles in a saucepan and heat until well mixed, stirring frequently. Line a greased baking dish with some of the tortillas. Add layers of the ground beef mixture, cheese and soup mixture. Repeat with layers of tortillas and remaining ingredients, ending with a layer of cheese. Bake at 350 degrees for 1 hour. Yield: 8 to 10 servings.

Faye S. King, Huntsville Council

Mommy's Spaghetti Sauce

1 large onion, chopped
1 large green bell pepper,
　chopped
2 pounds ground beef
Finely chopped fresh broccoli
　to taste
Finely chopped carrots to taste

Finely chopped fresh
　cauliflower to taste
5 to 6 (28-to 32-ounce) cans
　tomato sauce or purée
2 teaspoons oregano
1 teaspoon garlic salt
3 bay leaves

Sauté the onion and green pepper in a large skillet until brown. Place in a large stock pot. Brown the ground beef in the skillet, stirring until crumbly; drain. Add to the onion mixture. Add the broccoli, carrots, cauliflower and tomato sauce and mix well. Stir in the oregano, garlic salt and bay leaves. Cook over very low heat all day, stirring occasionally. Divide the sauce into 2 portions. Freeze 1 portion and place the remaining sauce in a slow-cooker. Cook another day in the slow-cooker on Low. The flavor is even better if you have the patience to cook for a third day. Discard the bay leaves. Serve over hot cooked spaghetti. Yield: 10 servings.

Roxann Edsall, Birmingham Metro Council

Plantation Stuffed Peppers

1 pound ground chuck
1 cup chopped onion
1 garlic clove, minced
2 teaspoons chili powder
2 teaspoons salt
1/2 teaspoon pepper

2 (10-ounce) cans tomato
　soup
1/2 cup shredded sharp
　Cheddar cheese
1 1/2 cups cooked rice
8 medium green bell peppers

Brown the ground chuck with the onion and garlic in a large skillet, stirring until the ground chuck is crumbly; drain. Add the chili powder, salt, pepper and soup and mix well. Simmer, covered for 15 minutes, stirring occasionally. Add the cheese and stir until melted. Stir in the rice. Let stand until cool. Cut the peppers into halves lengthwise. Discard the seeds and membranes. Cook the green peppers in rapidly boiling water in a saucepan for about 3 minutes or until tender; drain. Let stand until cool. Arrange the peppers in a shallow baking pan. Fill with the ground beef mixture. Bake at 375 degrees for 45 minutes. Yield: 8 servings.

Bobbie Miller, Anniston Council

Breakfast Casserole

1 pound bulk sausage
6 to 8 slices whole wheat
  bread
8 ounces cooked ham, chopped
1 pound bacon, crisp-fried,
  crumbled
1½ cups shredded peeled
  potatoes
½ cup sliced fresh mushrooms
½ cup chopped onion
  (optional)

Chopped green bell peppers
  (optional)
1 cup shredded Cheddar
  cheese
12 eggs
1½ cups cooked grits
½ cup milk
¼ cup flour

Brown the sausage in a skillet, stirring until crumbly; drain. Trim the crusts from the bread and arrange the slices in a greased 9x13-inch baking pan. Layer the ham, bacon, sausage, potatoes, mushrooms, onion, green pepper and cheese in the prepared pan. Combine the eggs, grits, milk and flour in a blender container. Process until well mixed. Pour over the layers. Bake at 350 degrees for 1 hour or until golden brown and a knife inserted near the center comes out clean. Let stand for several minutes. Cut into squares. Yield: 8 to 10 servings.

Betsy Mickle, Birmingham South Cahaba Council

Western Hash

1 pound ground beef
3½ cups canned tomatoes
1 cup chopped green bell
  pepper
½ cup chopped onion
½ cup uncooked rice

½ teaspoon salt
½ teaspoon basil
⅛ teaspoon pepper
8 ounces Velveeta cheese,
  sliced

Brown the ground beef in a skillet, stirring until crumbly; drain. Add the tomatoes, green pepper, onion, rice, salt, basil and pepper. Simmer, covered, for 25 minutes, stirring occasionally. Spoon into a baking dish. Top with the Velveeta cheese. Bake at 350 degrees until the cheese is melted. Yield: 6 servings.

Narice Sutton, Birmingham Life Member Club

Chicken Casserole

4 to 6 boneless skinless
  chicken breasts, cooked,
  chopped
2 (16-ounce) cans mixed
  vegetables, drained
1 (8-ounce) can sliced water
  chestnuts, drained
1 small onion, chopped
1 cup shredded sharp Cheddar
  cheese

1 (10-ounce) can cream of
  broccoli soup
½ cup reduced-fat mayonnaise
½ cup reduced-fat sour cream
1 sleeve butter crackers,
  crushed
¼ cup (½ stick) margarine,
  melted

Combine the chicken, mixed vegetables, water chestnuts, onion, cheese, soup, mayonnaise and sour cream in a bowl and mix well. Spoon into a baking dish sprayed with nonstick cooking spray. Sprinkle with a mixture of the crackers and margarine. Bake at 350 degrees until hot and bubbly. Yield: 10 servings.

Eulene Miller, Birmingham South Cahaba Council

Southwest Chicken Casserole

2 cups uncooked instant rice
2 cups chicken stock
1 cup chopped cooked chicken
1 medium onion, chopped
1 (10-ounce) can tomatoes
  with green chiles
1 teaspoon chili powder
1 (10-ounce) can cream of
  chicken soup
1 cup sour cream
1 pound Cheddar cheese,
  shredded

Combine the first 8 ingredients in a large bowl and mix well. Spoon into a greased 9x13-inch baking dish. Bake at 350 degrees until hot and bubbly. Top with the cheese. Bake until the cheese melts. Yield: 6 servings.

Mary Gillis, Mobile Council

Asparagus Pasta

4 garlic cloves, minced
1 cup sliced mushrooms
1/2 cup chopped green onions
1/3 cup olive oil
2 cups asparagus tips
1/2 (10-ounce) can tomatoes
  with green chiles
1 (16-ounce) can chopped
  tomatoes
1/2 cup olive quarters
1/2 cup Marsala
1 (14-ounce) can chicken broth
2 tablespoons cornstarch
1 tablespoon Italian seasoning
1 teaspoon pepper
Oregano and rosemary to taste
3/4 package fusilli or rotini
Grated Romano cheese or
  shredded mozzarella cheese
  to taste

Sauté the garlic, mushrooms and green onions in the olive oil in a large deep skillet until tender. Add the asparagus, tomatoes and olives. Bring to a simmer. Stir in the wine. Simmer until the mixture is reduced, stirring occasionally. Combine the broth, cornstarch and seasonings in a bowl. Stir into the asparagus mixture. Cook until the sauce thickens, stirring constantly. Cook the pasta using package directions; drain. Add the pasta to the skillet and mix gently. Sprinkle with cheese. Cook, covered, until the cheese melts. Serve immediately. Yield: 8 servings.

Mike Akridge, Sr., Mobile Life Member Club

Cabbage with Tomatoes

1 (16-ounce) can diced tomatoes	Salt to taste
½ cup vinegar	Chopped cabbage
¾ cup sugar	Chopped onion to taste

Combine the tomatoes, vinegar, sugar and salt in a bowl and mix well. Chill, covered, for 8 to 10 hours. Cook cabbage with onion in a small amount of water in a saucepan just until tender; drain. Place in a serving bowl and spoon the tomato mixture over the cabbage. Serve with hot corn bread. Yield: variable.

Patricia H. Massey, Birmingham Life Member Club

Carrot Soufflé

3 pounds carrots, peeled	6 eggs, beaten
2 cups sugar	1 cup (2 sticks) margarine, melted
1 tablespoon baking powder	
Vanilla extract to taste	1 tablespoon confectioners' sugar
¼ cup flour	

Steam the carrots in a steamer for 45 minutes or until tender. Process the hot carrots in a food processor or blender until puréed. Combine with the sugar, baking powder and vanilla in a bowl. Stir in the flour until smooth. Add the eggs and margarine and mix well. Spoon into a soufflé dish. Bake at 350 degrees for 1½ hours. Sprinkle with the confectioners' sugar just before serving. Yield: 8 to 10 servings.

Narice Sutton, Birmingham Life Member Club

Macaroni and Cheese

12 to 16 ounces macaroni
1 (10-ounce) can cream of
  mushroom soup
¼ cup chopped green bell
  pepper
¼ cup chopped onion
¼ cup chopped pimento

1 cup mayonnaise
1 pound sharp Cheddar
  cheese, shredded
½ cup (1 stick) margarine,
  melted
1 cup butter cracker crumbs

Cook the macaroni using package directions until tender; drain. Combine the soup with the green pepper, onion, pimento, mayonnaise and cheese in a bowl and mix well. Mix in the macaroni. Spoon into a greased baking dish. Toss the margarine and cracker crumbs in a bowl. Sprinkle over the macaroni mixture. Bake at 350 degrees for 20 to 30 minutes or until bubbly and golden brown. Yield: 4 to 6 servings.

Alice Walski, Birmingham Life Member Club

Vegetable Relish

1 peck sand pears
5 red bell peppers
5 green bell peppers
3 hot peppers

5 large onions
5 cups red vinegar
4 cups (or more) sugar
1 teaspoon salt

Peel and core the pears and put through a food grinder. Chop the peppers and onions into uniform pieces or put through the grinder. Combine the pears and vegetables in a large stock pot. Add the vinegar, sugar and salt. Cook for 30 minutes, stirring frequently. Ladle into hot sterilized jars and seal with 2-piece lids. Process in a boiling water bath for 10 minutes. Yield: variable.

Marcelle Kelley, mother-in-law of Cathy Kelley,
Birmingham South Cahaba Council

Broccoli Corn Bread

4 eggs, beaten
1/2 cup (1 stick) butter, melted
1 onion, chopped
1 (10-ounce) package frozen
  chopped broccoli

1 1/2 cups cottage cheese
2 (7-ounce) packages corn
  bread mix

Combine the eggs, butter, onion, broccoli, cottage cheese and corn bread mix in a large bowl and mix well. Spoon into a greased 9x13-inch baking pan. Bake at 400 degrees for 25 to 30 minutes or until golden brown. Yield: 10 to 12 servings.

Louise Wheeler, Selma Life Member Club

Mexican Corn Bread

2 1/2 cups yellow corn bread
  mix
3 tablespoons sugar
1/2 cup vegetable oil
3 eggs, beaten
1 (16-ounce) can cream-style
  corn

1 1/2 cups shredded cheese
1 large onion, grated
2 large jalapeño chiles,
  seeded, chopped

Combine the corn bread mix, sugar, oil and eggs in a large bowl and mix well. Add the corn, cheese, onion and chiles and mix well. Heat a well-greased 9x13-inch baking pan in a 400-degree oven until very hot. Pour the batter into the hot pan. Bake at 450 degrees for 20 minutes or until golden brown. Cut into 2-inch squares. Yield: 24 servings.

Faye S. King, Huntsville Council

Best-Ever Banana Bread

1¾ cups flour
1½ cups sugar
1 teaspoon baking soda
½ teaspoon salt
½ cup vegetable oil
2 eggs

5 tablespoons buttermilk
2 bananas, mashed
1 teaspoon vanilla extract
1 cup chopped walnuts or
 pecans

Combine the flour, sugar, baking soda and salt in a bowl and mix well. Add the oil, eggs, buttermilk, bananas and vanilla and mix until well blended. Stir in the walnuts. Spoon into a greased and floured 5x9-inch loaf pan. Bake at 325 degrees for 1 hour and 20 minutes or until the loaf is golden brown, splits on the top and tests done when a wooden pick inserted in the center comes out clean. Turn onto a wire rack to cool slightly. Slice and serve warm. Yield: 1 loaf.

Della Pearl Dukes, Bon Secour Life Member Club

Blueberry Bread

2 cups flour
3 tablespoons sugar
1 tablespoons baking
 powder
¾ teaspoon salt
½ cup (1 stick) butter

1 cup fresh or frozen
 blueberries
1 egg
¾ cup plus 1 tablespoon milk
Cinnamon to taste
¼ cup sugar

Combine the flour, 3 tablespoons sugar, baking powder and salt in a bowl and mix well. Cut in the butter until crumbly. Add the blueberries to the flour mixture and mix gently. Beat the egg in a small bowl. Beat in the milk. Add the mixture to the flour mixture and stir just until moistened. Spread the mixture on a lightly greased baking sheet to make a 9x12-inch rectangle. Sprinkle with cinnamon and ¼ cup sugar. Bake at 450 degrees for 12 minutes or until brown. Break into pieces and serve hot or cold. Yield: 10 to 12 servings.

Sherry A. Liles, Huntsville Council

Oatmeal Carrot Loaf

1 cup uncooked old-fashioned
  or quick-cooking oats
1/2 cup skim milk
2 1/2 cups flour
1 cup packed brown sugar
1 tablespoon baking powder
1/2 teaspoon baking soda
1/2 teaspoon ground cinnamon
1 1/2 cups shredded carrots

1/2 cup raisins
1 (8-ounce) can crushed
  pineapple
4 egg whites or 2 whole eggs,
  lightly beaten
1/4 cup vegetable oil
1 teaspoon vanilla extract
Cream Cheese Spread

Combine the oats and milk in a small bowl. Let stand for several minutes. Combine the flour, brown sugar, baking powder, baking soda and cinnamon in a large bowl and mix well. Add the carrots and raisins and mix well. Add the undrained pineapple, egg whites, oil and vanilla to the oats mixture and mix well. Stir into the carrot mixture and mix just until moistened. Spray the bottom of a 5x9-inch loaf pan with nonstick cooking spray. Spoon the batter into the prepared loaf pan. Bake at 350 degrees for 60 to 75 minutes or until a wooden pick inserted in the center comes out clean. Cool in the pan for 10 minutes. Remove to a wire rack to cool completely. Serve with Cream Cheese Spread. Yield: 1 loaf

Cream Cheese Spread

4 ounces reduced-fat cream
  cheese, softened

2 teaspoons brown sugar
1/4 teaspoon vanilla extract

Combine the cream cheese, brown sugar and vanilla in a small bowl and beat until smooth and creamy. Store, tightly covered, in the refrigerator for up to 3 days.

Helen W. Shirley, Birmingham Life Member Club

Peanut Butter and Jelly Muffins

2 cups flour
1/2 cup sugar
2 1/2 teaspoons baking powder
1/2 teaspoon salt

3/4 cup peanut butter
2 eggs, lightly beaten
3/4 cup milk
1/4 cup strawberry preserves

Combine the flour, sugar, baking powder and salt in a large bowl. Cut in the peanut butter with a pastry blender until crumbly. Make a well in the center of the mixture. Add a mixture of the eggs and milk. Stir just until moistened. Fill greased muffin cups 1/3 full. Top with 3/4 teaspoon preserves. Spoon the remaining batter over the preserves. Bake at 400 degrees for 15 to 17 minutes or until light brown. Remove the muffins to a wire rack to cool.
Yield: 16 muffins.

Narice Sutton, Birmingham Life Member Club

Yeast Rolls

3 envelopes dry yeast
1 cup sugar
2 cups lukewarm water
1 cup (2 sticks) butter, melted

6 eggs, beaten
1 1/2 teaspoons salt
8 cups flour

Mix the yeast with 2 tablespoons of the sugar in a medium bowl. Add the warm water and stir until the yeast dissolves. Beat the butter and eggs in a large bowl. Add the remaining sugar, salt, yeast mixture and flour and mix well. Shape into a ball. Place in a large greased bowl, turning to coat the surface. Let rise, covered, for 2 hours. Punch the dough down. Let rise, covered, in the refrigerator for 8 to 10 hours. Divide the dough into 3 portions. Roll each into a circle on a lightly floured surface. Brush with additional melted butter and cut into wedges. Roll up the wedges from the wide end and place on a greased baking sheet. Let rise for 2 to 3 hours or until doubled in bulk. Bake at 400 degrees for 10 minutes or until golden brown. Yield: 2 to 3 dozen rolls.

Faye S. King, Huntsville Council

Pecan Cookie Dessert

1 package Pecan Sandies,
  crushed
8 ounces cream cheese,
  softened
1 cup confectioners' sugar

16 ounces whipped topping
2 (4-ounce) packages any
  flavor instant pudding mix
3 cups milk

Sprinkle half the cookie crumbs over the bottom of a 9x13-inch pan. Beat the cream cheese, confectioners' sugar and half the whipped topping in a mixer bowl until blended. Spread over the cookie crumbs. Mix the pudding mix and milk using the package directions. Spread the pudding and the remaining whipped topping in the order listed over the cream cheese mixture. Sprinkle with the remaining cookie crumbs. Chill until serving time. May use reduced-fat Pecan Sandies, reduced-fat cream cheese, reduced-fat whipped topping and skim milk if desired. Yield: 10 servings.

Ben Blasingame, Decatur Council

Twinkie Dessert

8 or 9 Twinkies
3 or 4 bananas, sliced
1 (8-ounce) can crushed
  pineapple, drained
2 (4-ounce) packages vanilla
  instant pudding mix
4 cups milk

8 ounces whipped topping
1 cup flaked coconut
  (optional)
1 cup chopped pecans
  (optional)
Maraschino cherry halves
  (optional)

Cut the Twinkies lengthwise into halves. Arrange cut side up over the bottom of a 9x13-inch pan. Layer with the bananas and pineapple. Mix the pudding mix with the milk using the package directions. Spread over the pineapple. Top with the whipped topping. Sprinkle with the coconut, pecans and/or cherries. Chill until serving time. May use reduced-fat Twinkies, reduced-fat whipped topping and skim milk if desired. Yield: 10 servings.

Ben Blasingame, Decatur Council

Jewish Apple Cake

3 cups flour
2 cups sugar
1 tablespoon baking powder
1/8 teaspoon salt
1 cup vegetable oil
4 eggs

1/3 cup orange or pineapple
   juice
2 1/2 teaspoons vanilla extract
3 tablespoons cinnamon
6 tablespoons sugar
6 apples, sliced

Mix the flour, 2 cups sugar, baking powder and salt in a mixer bowl. Add the oil, eggs, orange juice and vanilla. Beat at medium speed for 10 minutes. Combine the cinnamon and 6 tablespoons sugar. Layer the batter, apples and cinnamon mixture 1/3 at a time in a greased and floured tube pan. Bake at 350 degrees for 1 hour and 15 minutes. Cool in the pan for 10 minutes. Remove to a wire rack to cool completely. Yield: 16 servings.

Mary W. Martin, Birmingham South Life Member Club

Granny's Pound Cake

1 cup (2 sticks) butter,
   softened
3 cups sugar
6 eggs

1 teaspoon vanilla extract
1 cup whipping cream
3 cups cake flour

Cream the butter and sugar in a mixer bowl until light and fluffy. Add the eggs 1 at a time, beating well after each addition. Beat in the vanilla. Add the whipping cream alternately with the cake flour, mixing well after each addition. Pour into a greased and floured bundt pan. Place in a cold oven. Bake at 350 degrees for 1 1/2 hours or until the cake tests done. Cool in the pan on a wire rack for 10 minutes. Invert onto a wire rack to cool completely. Yield: 10 to 12 servings.

Cathy Holmes, Mobile Council

Chocolate Cake

1 cup water
½ cup shortening
½ cup (1 stick) margarine
2 tablespoons baking cocoa
2 cups flour
2 cups sugar
1 teaspoon baking soda
¼ teaspoon salt
¼ teaspoon cinnamon

2 eggs, beaten
1 teaspoon vanilla extract
½ cup (1 stick) margarine
3 tablespoons baking cocoa
6 tablespoons milk
1 (1-pound) package
    confectioners' sugar
1 teaspoon vanilla extract
1 cup chopped pecans

Combine the water, shortening, ½ cup margarine and 2 table-spoons baking cocoa in a saucepan. Bring to a boil, stirring frequently. Combine the flour, sugar, baking soda, salt and cinnamon in a large bowl. Add the eggs and 1 teaspoon vanilla and mix well. Pour the hot mixture into the flour mixture and mix well. Pour into a greased and floured 9x13-inch cake pan. Bake at 350 degrees for 30 minutes or until the cake tests done. Bring ½ cup margarine, 3 tablespoons baking cocoa and milk to a boil in a saucepan. Pour the hot mixture over the confectioners' sugar in a mixer bowl and beat until well blended. Add 1 teaspoon vanilla. Stir in the pecans. Spread over the hot cake. Yield: 15 servings.

Mrs. Bob H. Henson, Birmingham South Life Member Club

Strawberry Cake

1 (2-layer) package yellow
    cake mix
8 ounces cream cheese,
    softened
2 cups (about) confectioner's
    sugar

1 cup sugar
1 cup whipping cream,
    whipped
1½ (21-ounce) cans
    strawberry pie filling

Prepare and bake the cake mix using package directions for a bundt pan. Let the cake cool for about 1 hour after removing from the pan. Slice into 3 layers. Combine the cream cheese, sugar and confectioners' sugar and beat until blended. Fold in the whipped cream. Spread a layer of the cream cheese mixture and a layer of pie filling between each cake layer. Store in the refrigerator. May substitute blueberry pie filling for the strawberry pie filling. Yield: 16 servings.

Diane Douglass, Birmingham Metro Council

Laplander Frosting

2 whole eggs or 4 egg yolks
4½ tablespoons evaporated
   milk
3 tablespoons butter, softened

1½ cups sugar
2 ounces unsweetened
   chocolate, chopped
1 teaspoon vanilla extract

Beat the eggs in a large heavy saucepan until light. Add the evaporated milk, butter, sugar and chocolate. Heat until well blended, stirring constantly. Bring to a full rolling boil, stirring constantly. Boil for 1 minute, stirring constantly. Remove from the heat. Let stand until of a spreading consistency. Add the vanilla and blend well. Yield: 1½ cups.

Sharon Wolfe, Birmingham South Life Member Club

Turtles

78 caramels
2 tablespoons margarine
2 tablespoons evaporated milk

2 cups pecan halves
4 cups milk chocolate chips
¼ block paraffin

Heat the caramels, margarine and evaporated milk in the top of a double boiler, stirring until smooth. Stir in the pecans. Drop by spoonfuls onto a buttered cookie sheet. Chill just until cool. Melt the chocolate chips and paraffin in the top of a double boiler. Dip the coated pecans into the chocolate mixture. Remove to waxed paper to cool. Let stand until set. Yield: 75 to 100 turtles.

Narice Sutton, Birmingham Life Member Club

Caramel Brownies

1 (1-pound) package light
  brown sugar
3/4 cup (1 1/2 sticks) margarine,
  melted
3 eggs

2 teaspoons vanilla extract
1 1/2 cups flour
1 1/2 teaspoons baking powder
1 cup chocolate chips

Blend the brown sugar and margarine in a medium bowl. Add the eggs and vanilla and mix well. Add a mixture of the flour and baking powder and mix well. Stir in the chocolate chips. Spoon into a 9x13-inch baking pan. Bake at 325 degrees for 35 minutes or until the brownies pull from the side of the pan. Cool in the pan on a wire rack. Cut into squares. Yield: 2 to 3 dozen brownies.

Elba Skinner, Selma Life Member Club

Salted Peanut Chews

1 1/2 cups flour
1/2 cup packed brown sugar
1/2 cup (1 stick) margarine,
  softened
3 cups miniature
  marshmallows

2 cups peanut butter chips
2/3 cup corn syrup
2 teaspoons vanilla extract
1/4 cup (1/2 stick) margarine
2 cups crisp rice cereal
2 cups salted peanuts

Combine the flour, brown sugar and 1/2 cup margarine in a bowl and mix until crumbly. Press into an ungreased 9x13-inch baking pan. Bake at 350 degrees for 12 to 15 minutes or until light brown. Sprinkle the marshmallows over the crust. Bake for 3 to 5 minutes longer or until the marshmallows begin to melt. Set aside to cool. Combine the peanut butter chips, corn syrup, vanilla and 1/4 cup margarine in a large saucepan. Cook over low heat until the mixture is well blended, stirring constantly. Remove from the heat and stir in the cereal and peanuts. Spread over the baked layer. Let stand until firm. Cut into bars. Yield: 2 dozen bars.

Wanda Plunkett, Anniston Council

Chewy Fruit and Oatmeal Cookies

¾ cup packed brown sugar
½ cup sugar
1 cup vanilla or plain reduced-
  fat yogurt
2 egg whites, lightly beaten
2 tablespoons vegetable oil
2 tablespoons skim milk
2 teaspoons vanilla extract
1½ cups flour

1 teaspoon baking soda
1 teaspoon cinnamon
½ teaspoon salt (optional)
3 cups quick-cooking or old-
  fashioned oats
1 cup chopped dried mixed
  fruit, raisins or dried
  cranberries

Combine the brown sugar, sugar, yogurt, egg whites, oil, skim milk and vanilla in a large bowl and mix well. Combine the flour, baking soda, cinnamon and salt mix well. Stir into the yogurt mixture. Add the oats and fruit and mix well. Drop by rounded tablespoonfuls onto an ungreased cookie sheet. Bake at 350 degrees for 12 to 14 minutes or until golden brown. Cool on the cookie sheet for 1 minute. Remove to a wire rack to cool completely. Store in a loosely covered container. Yield: 3 dozen cookies.

Helen W. Shirley, Birmingham Life Member Club

Grandma's Spice Cookies

1 (2-layer) package spice
  cake mix
1 cup (2 sticks) butter,
  softened
2 eggs
1 cup flaked coconut

1 cup chopped walnuts
1 cup crushed cornflakes
1 cup rolled oats
1 cup raisins
2 tablespoons (or more) sugar

Combine the cake mix, butter and eggs in a bowl and mix well. Stir in the next 5 ingredients. Drop by rounded teaspoonfuls 2 inches apart onto an ungreased cookie sheet. Flatten with the bottom of a glass dipped into the sugar. Bake at 350 degrees for 8 to 12 minutes or until firm. Cool on the cookie sheets for 1 minute. Remove to a wire rack to cool completely. Yield: 4 to 5 dozen cookies.

Brenda Reeves, Birmingham South Cahaba Council

Fudge Brownie Pie

2 eggs
1 cup sugar
1/2 cup (1 stick) butter, melted
1/2 cup flour
1/2 cup baking cocoa

1/4 teaspoon salt
1 teaspoon vanilla extract
1/2 cup chopped nuts
Vanilla ice cream
Hot Fudge Sauce

Beat the eggs in a large bowl. Blend in the sugar and butter. Mix the flour, baking cocoa and salt together. Add to the egg mixture and mix well. Add the vanilla and nuts and mix well. Spread evenly in a lightly greased 8-inch pie plate. Bake at 350 degrees for 25 to 30 minutes or until almost set. Let stand until cool. Cut into wedges. Serve with ice cream and Hot Fudge Sauce.
Yield: 6 to 8 servings.

Hot Fudge Sauce

3/4 cup sugar
1/2 cup baking cocoa
1 (5-ounce) can evaporated
  milk

1/3 cup light corn syrup
1/3 cup butter
1 teaspoon vanilla extract

Combine the sugar and baking cocoa in a small saucepan. Blend in the evaporated milk and corn syrup. Bring to a boil, stirring constantly. Boil for 1 minute, stirring constantly. Remove from the heat and stir in the butter and vanilla.

Janet T. Streeter, Montgomery Council

CELEBRATIONS

This cookbook is a perfect gift for holidays, weddings, anniversaries, and birthdays.

You may order as many of our cookbooks as you wish for the price of $10.00 each, plus $2.00 postage and handling per book. Mail this form to the address below or save postage and handling charges by picking up your books at the Chapter Pioneer Office:

Alabama Chapter #34
3196 Highway 280 South, Room 301N
Birmingham, Alabama 35243

		Quantity	Total
Calling All Cooks	$10.00 ea.	_____	$_____
Calling All Cooks two	$10.00 ea.	_____	_____
Calling All Cooks three	$10.00 ea.	_____	_____
Celebrations	$10.00 ea.	_____	_____
Postage and Handling	$ 2.00 ea.	_____	_____
Total			$_____ *

_____

Name   (Please Print)

_____

Address

_____

City   State   Zip

*Please make check payable to Alabama Chapter #34
Photocopies will be accepted